Ethics
and Morals

Ethics and Morals

Joseph Gerard Brennan

Harper & Row, Publishers
New York, Evanston, San Francisco, London

170
B838e

Sponsoring Editor: John G. Ryden
Project Editor: Sandra G. Turner
Designer: June Negrycz
Production Supervisor: Stefania J. Taflinska

**Ethics
and Morals**   74-833

Standard Book Number: 06-040945-2
Library of Congress Catalog Card Number: 78-8537

To Nick,
who gave me the idea

Contents

Preface

One day, a year or two ago, I was looking for a book about ethics to give to someone. I wanted something that would be interesting and useful to a general reader, as well as useful and challenging to a student. Such a student might be taking a course in ethics, social philosophy, anthropology, or some general social science or humanities study. I hoped to find a book that would explain what ethics is about, give something solid on classical and modern theories, and set out some opinions of contemporary moral philosophers. Something that might try to show some relation between ethical theory and the problems and practices that interest people generally—war, love, death, social change. I could not find such a book. There were plenty of anthologies and collections of readings in ethics, but I was not hunting for those. I checked through solid old texts and sharp new linguistic essays, but could not find quite the right thing. I forget what I finally gave to the one who wanted the book in the first place.

Then, greatly daring, I thought I might try to do the book I could not find. For inspiration I reread G. E. Moore's *Principia Ethica,* following this up by John Rawls's *A Theory of Justice* and a bit of Pascal. Then I read three popular counterculture books; already their messages seemed a little dated. It occurred to me that it might be fun to use examples and illustrations from imaginative literature, as well as from popular social concerns, to illustrate ethical points. The generously wide concept "morals" (basically, it means the same as "ethics") might be useful in moving from ethical theory to practice, to specific questions about right and wrong, good and bad, and the countless ways people have of loving and killing each other, as well as improving and spoiling Nature.

When my writing was nearly done, I happened to recall what Kant thought of popular ethics books. He did not think much of them: "One need only look at the essays on morality which popular taste favors. One will sometimes meet with . . . perfection and sometimes happiness, here moral feeling, there fear of God, a little of this and a little of that in a marvelous mixture." Except for the fear of God, this was uncomfortably close to my book. But then, some people good enough to read what I had written said encouraging things: there was a good chance it *would* interest the general reader, be useful to students of Left, Right, and Middle; it *did* read as if the author had really enjoyed getting the "marvelous mixture" together. The last is true enough. It was fun to work in Aristotle with Austin, Sartre with Kant, Marcuse with Mill, Nietzsche with Gide, Thoreau with Weil, and to discuss duty and pleasure, "ought" and "is," the way of reason and the life of feeling.

There was some temptation to exploit the Watergate case for ethical examples, but apart from a brief early allusion and a footnote to the last chapter, this was resisted. The widespread reaction to the Watergate scandal, however, did seem to illustrate a public tendency to demand more continuity between personal and political morality, a tendency discussed in Chapter 12.

I would like to thank my colleagues at Barnard and Columbia who helped me. Mary Mothersill and Loren Graham read the entire manuscript; I could not have done without their comments and criticism. Patricia Graham was particularly helpful in criticizing the third part of the book, and gave me much useful periodical literature. Onora Nell advised on Kant's moral philosophy and Beryl Levy (of Hofstra University) on morals and law. Thanks too to David Pinkwas and the staff of the Bethpage Public Library.

J. G. B.

"What is ethics?"

"Ethics?" asked Alyosha, wondering.

"Yes; is it a science?"

"Yes, there is such a science . . . but . . . I confess I can't explain to you what sort of science it is."

Dostoyevsky, *The Brothers Karamazov*

Ethics
and Morals

Introduction

Sparked by war, student revolt, civil disobedience, changes in sexual attitudes and practices, evidence of corruption in high government places, plus various other challenges to accepted standards and values, there is renewed interest today in questions of the kind: what is "moral" or "immoral"? How can we decide what is "right" and what is "wrong"? What ends or goals are good, worthwhile, worthy of human effort to reach for? Such discussions are often carried on in a feverish and excited way, especially when the subject is some burning social issue close to the hearts of those talking about it. Is it right in the name of "national interest" for a country to extend military aid, including bombing planes, to this or that close or distant nation? Is it wrong to beat baby seals to death and traffic in their skins? Is it right for a college girl to sleep with various male classmates? Is it wrong to persuade another to take marijuana? Alcohol? LSD? Heroin? Is it right for a worker to take pay for work he did not do? Is it wrong for a student to cheat on an exam? What about a radical-group leader who proclaims at a public meeting, "Pigs (policemen) are depraved traducers that violate the lives of human beings, and there is nothing wrong with taking the life of a pig"? What about agents of one political party planting espionage devices in the headquarters of another? Given the social and economic system we have, is the good life within the reach of all who are growing up today? Or does that system extend the opportunity of a good life to some and withhold it from others—and does that make the system immoral? What is that so-called good life? Does the concept of it make logical sense? What makes people think that everybody has a right to it? And is there only one good life? What do the words "right" and "wrong," "good" and "bad" mean?

To call for reason and cool heads in such discussions is nearly useless. To ask the participants to consider the principles explained in an ethics book would be almost perverse. Ethics books usually do not answer questions about what the best life is or what are "right" relations between humans. They do not usually enter substantively into questions of love- and war-making, adultery, parent-honoring, revolution, swindling, suicide, and spiritual courage. Those men and women we call *moralists* (they may or may not teach within a religious tradition) often do deal directly with such questions. They will exhort us to act or not to act in this or that particular way, hold up to us an ideal of life to imitate. But writers of books on ethics are usually not moralists; they are usually *ethical theorists.* They like to raise questions about what is meant by "good" or "right" or "ought." They analyze concepts like "pleasure" and "duty." They try to find out from what grounds or axioms moral judgments are derived.

People who are hotly involved in moral discussions are apt to find such inquiries rather abstract and not to the point. For this reason ethical treatises may seem (and often truly are) rather dull. For example, most ethics books try to classify various theories of moral philosophy, and the effect on the reader may range from bewilderment to boredom. Yet if ethics is a science (in the sense that we may call any ordered body of knowledge a science), *some* classification of theories is necessary as is a modicum of technical analysis. People with strong concerns about moral matters grow understandably impatient with what they take to be the unnecessary technicalities of ethical philosophy, or indeed of any philosophy. Who cares what the difference is between deontological and teleological ethics? Between the categorical and the hypothetical imperative? Such distinctions seem no more than hairsplitting and logic chopping. We are convinced, and rightly so, that we do not have to take an ethics course to know what is at stake in the moral situations in which we find ourselves. But this truth has a way of leading to the natural, though false, conclusion that anybody can be an expert on moral philosophy just by saying what comes into his head. Claims that emerge from such free-for-all discussions are apt, at best, to be moralistic clichés:

"I feel it's all right to do what you want so long as it doesn't *hurt* anybody."
"I think everybody acts from selfish motives."
"What's right in our culture is wrong in others. So who is to say what is right and wrong?"
"All war is immoral."
"I believe in being absolutely honest with my children."

Before it is finished, our inquiry will lead us to "morals," that is, to questions about many specific classes of acts that people say are moral or immoral. But a modest grounding in "ethics," including ethical theory, may be helpful if we want to approach such questions with a little more equipment than the usual clichés and biases hastily erected and inadequately defended.

Meaning of Ethics

The word *ethics* comes from an ancient Greek root that meant "habit" or "custom." But even in Aristotle's day *ethiké* already had the meaning of moral virtue or showing moral character.[1] The Greeks thought ethics to be a branch of practical philosophy. Theoretical philosophy (science), they thought, has to do with *knowing,* while practical philosophy is concerned with acting or *doing:* acting or doing, that is, from the point of view of what are the best kinds of actions or deeds and what rules there are, if any, for guiding ourselves with respect to these good actions. Aristotle said there are two kinds of practical philosophy: There is *ethics,* which deals with questions about the good life of the individual, and there is *politics,* which concerns the good of the state. Greek philosophers were well aware of the close connection that holds, or should hold, between ethics and politics. (Today the connection seems almost nonexistent.) Plato's dialogue *The Republic* was written to show that questions about teaching the individual good cannot be answered until they are thrown against a wider screen, the background of the state—which is, or should be, man "writ large."

Most moral philosophers have agreed that ethics has some concern with *rules*—prescribed ways of behaving that, if well formed and carefully observed, may help guide human conduct in a desirable way, although not all of the rules may tell us just what to do in this or that particular situation. We know that rules have a *general* character:

No person shall be deprived of his liberty without due process of law.
Three strikes and the batter is out.
Male guests must wear jackets to dinner.
Promises should be kept.

The practical effect of a rule is that it applies to individual cases. The rules of baseball or cricket are designed (ideally) to cover every situation that might arise in the course of a game. We obey and expect others to obey the rules of sports and games to the letter. (What would we think of a major league baseball player who, after having been struck out at the plate, asks the umpire for a fourth strike because he had not had much sleep the night before?) Whether moral rules are to be applied so strictly is a matter of disagreement among moral philosophers. For example, some say that killing another human is always wrong, while others say that, while the rule "Don't kill" should be generally respected, there may be particular situations in which obeying the rule would bring about a greater evil than breaking it would. In any case, the rules of sports and games apply only to those playing the particular sport or game. But the rules of ethics, such as "Keep promises," extend through the full range of human conduct. Consider Kant's rule: that you should act only so that you can will your act to become universal law. Kant thought that this rule extended throughout human life in every moral situation and that all men of goodwill, not blocked by ignorance, would try to obey it.

Common-Sense Ethics

It is true that one does not have to study moral philosophy to have a practical grasp of the ethical dimensions of things. We are well aware of certain rules of conduct that we assume most people try to follow or at least recommend following. There is considerable rough agreement or consensus about the wrongness of needlessly hurting others, being a selfish beast, doing brutal things to children, stealing or cheating, breaking one's word, plotting a person's injury or death. We aspire toward good things ourselves, but we try to maintain a decent respect for the aspirations of others. Most of us pick up these principles first from our parents, then from teachers, friends, peers, and other people we deal with. Later we may come to see that some rules have a good foundation in reason and experience; others we may come to regard as mere prejudices that lead to stale practices and have no authority of their own. Most of us believe that the growth and development of one's powers is an important good. As parents, we like to see children grow up and flourish. We agree that it is good to be all that one can be, to act and not be acted upon, to choose and not be chosen, to make our small mark on the world so that at least someone—even if that someone is only ourselves—will know that we have lived. We speak sadly of a person when we say that "life has passed him by."

On a particular issue of moral conduct, there is a good deal of agreement that being reasonable about it, using one's head, and not acting stupidly will—if it does not solve the problem—at least help. Most people, too, will agree that in dealing with others we should remember that they are humans like ourselves, that they too have feelings and claims that should be recognized, that a little compassion is in order for those in tough spots, that a helping hand is a good thing. Of course we know that disagreement quickly begins about the way in which these "common-sense" principles should apply to specific situations. Self-fulfillment can become ruthless egoism. Intelligence can lead to taking good care of oneself only. Compassion may interfere with an unfortunate person's self-help efforts. But after all this has been conceded, there remains a surprisingly large residue of practical ethical agreement. Human society seems to require it, if not as right and good in itself, at least for purposes linked to the well-being of that society. Whether society's welfare is the foundation of ethics, the axiom from which all moral rules and aspirations derive, is a question to be looked into in due course.

Professional Ethics

What we call *professional ethics* are sets of rules of conduct of narrower scope than the more general moral rules. Persons in various callings are supposed to follow certain prescribed practices for the good of their particular profession. Physicians have a set of professional rules, many of which go back to Hippocrates—some are moral rules, some not. A medical doctor is bound by a precept against giving his patient a "deadly draft" even if his patient wants it, as well as by a rule barring him from advertising in newspapers. Lawyers are bound not to disclose information received from a client, even if the inquirer is someone interested in the welfare of the client.[2] National and state legislative bodies periodically lay down "ethical" rules for political appointees and elected officials. One of the purposes of "judicial ethics" is to forestall judges from participating in court cases when they may have a conflict of interest. In recent years associations of real estate dealers have formulated codes of ethics, as have undertakers, clothing manufacturers, and beauty parlor operators. Even used car dealers, members of a profession sometimes charged with moral insensitivity, have drawn up rules of "ethical selling." Shortly before the bombing of the German city of Dresden in 1945 (which took the lives of 135,000 people), the RAF Bomber Command chief invited his personal assistant, a tutor in moral philosophy at Magdalen College, Oxford, to lecture to his senior officers on "the ethics of bombing." At the end of the lecture, the RAF unit chaplain innocently asked if the lecture title should not have read, "The Bombing of Ethics."[3]

Ethics, Law, and Religion

One reason why legislative bodies recommend codes of ethics to politicians and judges is that there are many kinds of human and professional conduct that are potentially harmful but that do not break any law. Such conduct, therefore, is often described not as "illegal," but as "unethical." The general distinction between the legal and the moral is similar. Certain acts may be judged both legally and morally wrong—robbery and murder, for instance. Other acts that break no law may be judged morally wrong. Still others may be illegal but not immoral. The diagram below oversimplifies, but it shows areas of overlap as well as areas of distinction:

LEGAL   MORAL

legal only | legal & moral | moral only

Civil law and criminal law need to be formally established by a duly constituted legislative body, written down and promulgated so that the courts can use these rules to decide cases. Moral rules do not have to be formulated in this way. Violation of the law entails *sanctions,* for example, formal punishments like fine or imprisonment. Moral failure does not entail statutory penalties unless it is at the same time a legal breach. There are many moral obligations, such as telling the truth and keeping promises, that are in *some* cases enforced by law (e.g., there are laws concerning perjury and contract violation). But in many, if not most cases, these are left to individual consciences or to the approval or disapproval of society. At the same time, an act that is innocent of moral wrong may be illegal. For example, I may park my car in what appears to be a clear zone in a strange city and be fined for it; I may forget to declare certain currency in a foreign country and be jailed for it. A well-intentioned (though not very bright) tourist recently found himself in violation of the law when he tried to bring past United States customs a quantity of what he had innocently bought on his foreign tour as "Chinese tobacco" but which was actually hashish. In each of these cases, a law was broken, though nothing "immoral" was done.

Most world religions have sets of rules concerning the conduct of men toward God and toward other men. These rules often appear in the form of precepts, exhortations, prohibitions, or commands. The Ten Commandments of the Old Testament is a well-known example, as is the "Golden Rule"—"Therefore all things whatsoever ye would that men should do to you, do ye even so to them."[4] In ages past, in the absence of a separately formulated body of civic rules, religious law often did double duty, guiding moral virtue as well as social behavior. A glance at the Old Testament and related writings in Jewish law will show this close connection. To the Jews of old, "the Law" was at once the Word of God, a guide to the good of the individual person, and a body of rules for the welfare of the community. Many of the Ten Commandments (the prohibitions against killing and false witness, for example) are clearly matters of legal protection as well as moral welfare. But it is hard to see how the Golden Rule could be enforced by law. Because the precept "Love one another" is morally *right,* it does not follow that it can or should be legally *compelled.*

If we have been brought up in one of the great religious traditions, we may be inclined to think of the distinction between right and wrong as having a religious foundation. Western theologians have generally held that all good proceeds from God, who is the source of the right and identical with "the Good." An early meaning of "morally wrong" was *"forbidden by God"* or *"contrary to Divine Law."* It is possible that the solemn power of certain ethical appeals to duty, conscience, moral obligation or insight, had its source in the concept of the Will of God or Divine Law, a notion now fading from human consciousness and leaving behind only the convictions that there are some things that are morally wrong *in themselves* and some things that we are morally obliged to do. We live in a secular age; some call it the first agnostic culture the world has known. We have lost the sense of sin, the idea of wrong as breaking God's law. But the continuity between the ideas of our time and the Ages of Faith (which takes up about sixteen hundred years of Western culture) is still not wholly broken. This historical and cultural linkage frequently produces in us a double attitude toward moral principles. Sometimes we grant them authority in their own right. Sometimes we appeal to their religious foundation. This dual attitude was illustrated by the remarks of a president of the United States in an address made some years ago to a group of law enforcement officers. "We must teach that we should do right because it is right," the president said. Yet he coupled this claim with the further statement that the fundamental basis of "right" as embodied in the nation's law "was given to Moses on the Mount," that it "comes from the teaching we get from Exodus and St. Matthew, from Isaiah and St. Paul."[5]

In any case, whether their backgrounds are religious or not, most moral philosophers have agreed that ethics can be constructed without immediate appeal to a religious framework. Kant, for example, was a good Christian, yet he produced an ethical philosophy that he thought was independent of any particular religious tradition. He believed his moral philosophy to be a practical basis of ethical doctrine to which all reasonable men of goodwill could agree. The fact that they do not believe in the metaphysical assumptions of the Judeo-Christian tradition has not stopped modern philosophers from writing valuable books on ethics. To an important extent it was the study of Aristotle's ethical writings that convinced theologians that the science of ethics was really an independent study. All men, by the light of "natural reason," they agreed, could know the principles of man's natural, if not his supernatural, end or destiny.

The Mixture of Ethical Questions

In the course of its long history, ethics or moral philosophy has become a patchwork of many different questions. A number of separate threads have become matted together and, for this reason, they are very hard to pick apart. The eminent English philosopher G. E. Moore says:

It appears to me that in Ethics as in all other philosophical studies, the difficulties and disagreements, of which its history is full, are mainly due to a very simple cause: namely to the attempt to answer questions, without first discovering precisely *what* question it is which you desire to answer.[6]

Greek ethics provided a miscellany of questions:

1. Is there a highest good, to which all other goods are subordinate?
2. What makes a good life?
3. What makes a man good or bad?
4. What makes an action just or unjust?
5. What sort of rules or guidelines are there for right action?
6. Can that which makes a good man good be taught?
7. For what ends or purposes should we aim?

So important did questions like these seem to ancient philosophers that many of their schools claimed that the aim of the whole of philosophy should be ethical, that love of wisdom must be a practical affair, a guide to life. The Stoics taught that the purpose of philosophy was to teach us how to live, and they took for their model the life of Reason. The Stoic teacher sought the causes of things in order to understand them. He accommodated himself to the will of Nature. He did not let himself be exalted by good fortune or cast down by ill. He noted all things, marveled at nothing. (A Stoic trace is seen in the common phrase "He took it very philosophically.") The Epicureans also took philosophy to be a guide for life. Their ideal good was pleasure, not the satisfaction of bodily desires, but a state untroubled by pain, free of anxiety, a high tranquility like the state of the blessed gods. Through the long Ages of Faith there was little interest in ethics as an isolated discipline. The idea of a science of the Good, constructed by Reason alone, and independent of religious faith, was hard for the medievals to comprehend. But with the growth of the universities in the twelfth and thirteenth centuries, there developed new interest in subjects that could be developed by the "natural light of reason." Thomas Aquinas recommended Aristotle's book on ethics and added that the ideal professor of moral philosophy would be one who could teach Aristotle's text and was at the same time a good man himself!

In modern times, with Kant, we have a shift in the center of gravity of moral philosophy that has had lasting effects on ethical theory. The Greeks tended to think of right actions in terms of the goodness of the *end* or *purpose* of that action. It is right that I eat moderately and abstain from drunkenness because the end or purpose of such temperance is the good of bodily health. It is right that I vote and participate in public affairs because such actions have for their end the good of the state. To the Greek philosophers it was hard, if not impossible, to separate the notion of a right action from the idea of a good man, and the notion of a good man from that of the good life. All of these, they thought, were part of the subject of practical philosophy. Even after the Renaissance, moralists thought the most effective way to teach right conduct was by appeal to ideal examples drawn from classical antiquity. (One reason why we may find it hard to read Montaigne today is his habit of endlessly citing virtuous actions from the lives of heroic Romans.) With Kant the interest shifted from an action being "right" insofar as it tends to a good end to the action as *right in itself.* To Kant the chief factor in the moral situation was not the end or goal to be attained, but the moral judgment itself. Such a judgment, in his view, had to be completely *disinterested* to be moral. As we shall see, Kant's good man does the right, not because it will bring about good ends or achievements, but because it is right, period! He does the right because he is under a moral obligation to do so; he acts rightly because it is his *duty* to do so. Some actions can never be morally justified no matter what their ends or purposes may be. Lying, to Kant, was *always* wrong.

From these shifts in ethical standpoints, there has developed the well-known classification of moral theory with the unattractive names we mentioned earlier. *Teleological* ethics places stress on the goodness of the ends or purposes at which conduct aims. *Deontological* ethics finds the rightness of human action somewhere residing nearer the action itself, in the motive or intent of the agent (the person acting). The first we may call a morality of *aspiration;* it is seen clearly in Greek philosophy, whose ethical ideal is the Good Life, one that aims at excellence and the fullest development of human capacities. The second is a morality of *duty,* concerned with what we are morally *obliged* to do (keep promises, pay our debts, tell the truth, take care of the child) without thinking of the possible good to which fidelity to these obligations may lead. Two examples will illustrate the distinction. In the first we hear the voice of a young man who has just finished college and has made up his mind to break with his family, his country, and his religion:

—I will try to express myself in some mode of life or art as freely as I can and as wholly as I can. . . . Welcome O life! I go forth to encounter for the millionth time the reality of experience and forge in the smithy of my soul the uncreated conscience of my race!

In the second we listen to a woman begged by her lover to leave her husband: "I wish I could, but I can't. I know you don't like the words 'moral obligation.' I don't either. I hate them. But I can't get round it. I feel miserable, but I gave him my word. I promised."[7] In the first example the moral good is seen to lie in the aspiration, or in the end or goal aspired to—to grow, to flourish, to realize oneself. In the second the moral quantum lies closer to the decision itself. A related, though not identical, distinction is often made between an ethic of *motive* and an ethic of *consequences.* In the first (typified by Kant's ethics) an action is judged to be right or wrong without primary reference to its consequences. In the second (Mill, utilitarianism), an action is judged to be right or wrong insofar as it tends to produce a desirable *result*—general happiness, say.

Ethics and Society
An objection to the standard presentation of ethical theories and their classifications is sometimes raised by those committed to social reform. They say that ethics depends for its very existence as an academic discipline on a stable society in which the ultimate values of that society, including the right of that society to exist, are unquestioned. They claim that the usual traditional ethics book mirrors the values of the ruling class on which the order and stability of that society depend. Virtues cited by way of example in the usual ethics book include reasonable conduct, truth-telling, promise-keeping, debt-paying, respect for life and property, and other virtues on which a stable and orderly money economy depends. For such a society these virtues are a social and economic necessity. Traditional ethical theory reveals a yawning gap between private and social morality, between individual ethics and politics. A primary cause of this cutoff is that it simply is not to the interest of the ruling class to have the rules of personal morality applied too closely to the conduct of ruling class, state, or government. This class interest has been reinforced over the centuries by the Christian religion in its teaching that a person's ultimate good is the salvation of his own soul and not his need to work for a just social order.

Consider a society like that of the United States, the objection continues, a society that sharply separates the future open to a white child of affluent suburban culture and a black child in the inner city. When that white child grows to college age, the traditional analyses of moral concepts in terms of the stable virtues of keeping promises, telling the truth, paying debts, respecting property, honoring life, and so on, *make sense* because they are part of the social presuppositions of his class, the class that holds and wields the power in that society. But to the black child, now of college age (he may have long before dropped out of school), the philosophical analysis of such virtues is *meaningless* because, for one thing, the child soon senses that they are part of a class interest that is not his.

This large objection raises too many questions to deal with in these first pages or even—adequately or satisfactorily, at least—in this whole book. The English writer Iris Murdoch noticed how a certain English philosophy book she was reading revealed much of the values of the sheltered and stable life of the older British university class. Contrasting it with Sartre's philosophical writings, she says that the world of *The Concept of Mind* was "the world in which people play cricket, cook cakes, make simple decisions, remember their childhood and go to the circus; not the world in which they commit sins, fall in love, say prayers or join the Communist Party."[8] The usual ethics books read in American colleges and universities draw much from the great British tradition of moral philosophy—Hobbes, Butler, Hume, Mill, Sidgwick, Moore—and from mid-twentieth-century English moral philosophers as well. Many modern English philosophers wrote their books and papers in the context of a society they assumed to be stable. It is also true that the examples they chose to illustrate their theories often do reflect the values of that society. But then all sorts of difficult questions arise, such as what was the extent of wrong and deficiency in those social values, and what available social alternatives would have improved matters substantially, and what would we mean by "improvement" in such a situation?

Certainly in a situation of violent social change the traditional inquiry into ethical concepts may seem a little artificial, but then so do most other academic disciplines. Moreover, in contexts of war, violence, and revolution, moral values are apt to be, for a time at least, transvalued, turned upside down. Lying, murder, deceit, torture, perfidy, assassination, and terror become necessary and, in some cases, praiseworthy instruments of political action. No wonder ethics seems out of place in such contexts. Fortunately, revolution, war, and violence do not seem to be infinitely extensible social phenomena. Peace and relative stability have a way of coming round once more, sometimes in the context of a new social order, sometimes in that of the chastened and revised old.

Divisions of Inquiry

Our inquiry into ethics and morals is divided, like Gaul, into three parts. The first begins with a look into ethical terms such as *right, good,* and *ought* with a view to clarifying their meaning in ethical argument. Then we move on to some substantive questions that people like to raise at the beginning of ethical discussions: the relation of moral values to social use and the associated problem of the relativity of morals. The question of a possible "highest good" comes up, and we examine the claims of pleasure and happiness to that title, with a nod to Mill's utilitarianism, or "greatest happiness" principle. Contrasting with the utilitarian ethic of consequences is the Kantian ethics of duty. Here we will see Kant's idea of moral worth in relation to the question of ethical generalization and the concept of personhood.

The second part of our inquiry centers around the idea of the ethical fulfillment of the individual person or self. The concepts of the good as activity and growth, as seen by Aristotle and Dewey, serve to introduce this part of the discussion with some queries as to the parts played by reason and feeling in moral judgment. Then we move on to the concept of individualism, a complex value that has played a dominant part in our culture for at least the last two centuries and is still present in our value scheme. We illustrate the concept of individualism not from philosophy but from the imaginative literature of the nineteenth and twentieth centuries. The idea of individualism leads to existentialist ethics, with its sharp focus on the personal self as free arbiter of its own acts and destiny. The existentialist morality of freedom leads us to inquiry into the old problem of free will in both its traditional and late-twentieth-century settings.

The third part of our inquiry moves into the area of "morals," into what older philosophers used to call "special ethics." Here we consider certain specific classes of acts, those acts that people tend to call morally right or wrong, to see what ethical principles (if any) apply to particular situations, such as sexual conduct of assorted kinds, as well as to war, capital punishment, and other forms of terminating life, such as abortion, euthanasia, suicide. The last part of our tour looks at today's tendency to extend the limits of personal morality into broader social areas and even to Nature itself. With help from Marcuse and others, we examine some political concepts, including revolution and anarchy, then go on to the relation of science to morals and to the question of moral responsibility to our natural environment. The inquiry draws to a close with questions concerning the relation of personal morality to changes in religious attitudes today.

NOTES: INTRODUCTION

1. The singular form *ethic* is often used to mean a particular set of moral standards and values considered as a unity or whole, as in the expressions "the Christian ethic," "the Kantian ethic," or "the work ethic."
2. American Bar Association, *Code of Professional Responsibility and Canons of Judicial Ethics* (Chicago: 1969), EC 4–1 ff.
3. David Irvin, *The Destruction of Dresden* (New York: Holt, Rinehart & Winston, 1963), p. 52.
4. *Matt.* 7:12.
5. Harry S Truman, reported in *New York Times,* 16 February 1950, p. 2.
6. G. E. Moore, *Principia Ethica* (1903; London: Cambridge University Press, 1951), p. vii.
7. The first passage is from James Joyce's *A Portrait of the Artist as a Young Man* (New York, Modern Library, 1928), pp. 291, 299. The second is by the author in the style of Graham Greene.
8. Iris Murdoch, *Sartre: Romantic Rationalist* (Cambridge, Eng.: Bowes & Bowes, 1953), p. 35. *The Concept of Mind* is a classic of twentieth-century British philosophy of mind by Gilbert Ryle (London: Hutchinson, 1949).

PART ONE

Right and Good

1

Does Ethics Begin with Words?

We might take the basic question of ethics to be "What kind of life is the good life?" Or we might ask:

What ends or goals should we aim at?
What rules or guidelines are there for directing action toward these ends?
What good—or goods—is first and highest?

The Greeks introduced their ethical inquiries with questions like these. But many modern philosophers have preferred to fix their attention on the ethical judgment or the moral act itself, rather than on good or final purposes for humans. They have taken as typical questions of ethics:

What is it that makes an act right or wrong?
What kind of ethical rules shall we form?
What is the nature of ethical judgments in which we apply those rules?
What is the basis or foundation of duty and moral obligation?

Some recent English and American philosophers prefer to limit their inquiries to the *meaning* of ethical *terms.* They take the job of ethics to be the clarification of the meaning of ethical language. From this point of view, the first question of moral philosophy would not read:

What is the nature of the right and the good?

But rather:

What do terms such as "right" and "good," in their moral sense, *mean?*

It goes without saying that we use many words other than "good" and "right" (or "bad" and "wrong") to apply to things people do and to the people that do them:

That was a mean thing you did.
He's a fine man.
That was a low-down dirty trick.
The Vietnam War was immoral.
Sidney Carton performed a splendid deed of self-sacrifice.
He's a real rat.
I find your attitude weak and poor spirited.
There's magnificence in you, Tracy.
Your action was disgraceful.
The Western imperialist bandits are guilty of evil and devilish
    deeds.
You're *sick!*
What an unselfish thing to do!
The assistant librarian is a very vicious woman.

The lexicon of words and phrases that we use to convey moral
judgment is a sizable volume. To keep the matter simple, let us
stick to the words *good, right,* and *ought* to illustrate the points of
explanation.

The Meaning of "Good"
Classical moral philosophers were not ignorant of the importance
of setting out ground rules for the use of ethical *language.* In
fact, since the time of Socrates, moral philosophers have advised their students always to be careful to *define their terms* at
the beginning of their discussions. Aristotle approved of this
procedure, though he warned that we must not expect the
exactness in ethical terminology or the security in ethical conclusions that we look for in mathematical discourse. Now, on the
meaning of "good," there is an old distinction in moral philosophy that sets out three kinds of good or, if we prefer, three different senses of the word "good":

1. The good as useful or instrumental.
2. The good as pleasing or enjoyable in itself.
3. The specifically moral good.

This three-part distinction corresponds pretty well with three
ways in which we use good in everyday language. Usually "a
good watch" means one that keeps time, and "a good pen" is
one that writes clearly and smoothly. That is, a good watch and
a good pen fulfill the purposes for which they were made; their
goodness is *functional,* it lies in their *utility.* "A good tool" is

the one that does the job for which it is intended; "the best saw" is the one we would choose if our job were to cut boards evenly, easily, and smoothly.

Now take the case of a child eating an ice-cream cone. "It's good," he says. The child does not mean that what he is eating fulfills some purpose efficiently. Rather, he finds that eating ice cream is a pleasure, a joy, a good in itself. Lovers find kisses delightful in themselves, although tiresome biologists might insist that these things have a purpose and, in certain cases, disapproving elders might not find them morally good. We do not say that a painting is good simply because it conveniently fills a space on our wall or harmonizes with the color of our sofa. There is something good in the painting itself.

We apply the word "good" in the *moral* sense, not to things, but to *people* and to what they do or leave undone.

So shines a good deed in a naughty world.
Malcolm X was a good man.
She did a great deal of good in her life.
It was good of you to speak kindly to that boy.
Of all the men I have ever known, Socrates was the best.

We see how, in each case, the person making the statement is approving or praising. In the same way, when we use "bad" in the moral sense we almost invariably use it in sentences that express disapproval or blame.

Adolf Hitler was a thoroughly bad man.

Although common usage shows that we can tell the difference between the moral sense of "good" and other senses of the word, it is not easy to mark off just what it is that makes the moral good specifically *moral* and *good*—apart from the fact that usually it has something to do with humans, human acts and human relations. Of course, we sometimes praise animals ("Good dog!"), but do we praise them as moral beings?

Sometimes we use the word "good" in ways that show a blurring or telescoping of the three senses of the term indicated by the ancient distinction. When we speak of "a good husband," for instance, we think of someone who is a useful being (he fixes leaky faucets, brings home money), but he also pleases, or at least tries to, and is, we should hope, worthy of moral approval. Again, sometimes we use good in a way that does not seem clearly connected with utility, delight, or moral excellence. Al is looking at a certain painting, and remarks to his art instructor: "When you look at that shadow there, first it seems black, but when you look at it harder, you can see it's really bottle-green." The instructor says, "That's good, Al!" He is praising, but is it for the utility, the pleasure, or the moral excellence of what Al said or did? Perhaps this use of good belongs to the class of praise we give to instances of skill exercised proficiently—as in the case of a fielder who catches a ball just as it is about to drop into the stands for a home run, or a horse and rider who take a difficult jump with ease. In Al's case, it may be that the instructor is applying good to his developing skill in perception, the clear eye with which an artist or critic must look at a picture. He is certainly praising him, and this leads to the following question: Are there any factors common to *all* senses of the word "good"? First, there always seems to be present an element of praise or approval in the word "good." When we say something is good, says R. M. Hare, we always *commend* it, and he cites *The Oxford English Dictionary* to support him:

Good. . . . The most general adjective of commendation, implying the existence in a high, or at least satisfactory degree of characteristic qualities which are either admirable in themselves, or useful for some purpose. . . .[1]

Second (and the *OED* definition suggests this too), there is present in nearly all senses of good an element of *conformity to some standard,* a matching-up with a set of attributes or specifications. A good watch will keep accurate time, not need frequent repairs, have a neat appearance, and so on. A good golfer will have certain skills and in addition will

. . . love every blade of the grass,
Every inch of the fairway and greens;
And if you don't take care of the course as you pass,
You're not what "a good golfer" means.[2]

A man people call good will have qualities that square with some set of standards or values people have in mind, although missionaries and cannibals might differ as to the particular sets of standards to be applied. (In the next chapter we will look at the question of the real or alleged "relativity" of moral standards.) In this respect, "good" resembles a common use of "true" or "real." There is not much difference, if any, in the meaning of "a good friend," "a true friend," "a real friend." Each implies a matching to a standard or ideal. One Russian historian calls Khmelnitsky "a true Cossack," another calls him "a good Cossack," and in each case the context of description is that Khmelnitsky (1) was an adventurer, (2) was a soldier of fortune, (3) was a tremendous horseman, (4) had tireless energy, (5) had a romantic imagination, and 6) consumed vast quantities of alcohol.

Hare calls the two elements present in the way we use "good" the *evaluative* and the *descriptive* aspects of the term. That is, when I say "X is good," I am doing two things: (1) I am commending or approving X and (2) I am claiming that X squares up to a certain set of characteristics or qualities. In some usages of good the evaluative factor may be weak and the descriptive element strong. When I say "That's a good road map," I mean that the map is easy to read, the roads and distances are clearly marked, and so on. Sometimes the commendatory or praise factor has the upper hand, as in the case of our telling a child he is a good boy. But in some cases it is hard to see either praise or description. Suppose a child is given some chocolate pudding. He takes a spoonful, smiles, and says "That's good!" Is he *commending* the pudding? Or does he mean, "I'm *enjoying* it"? Does his statement imply that the pudding comes up to some standard? We might claim that the pudding at least squares with the characteristics of chocolate pudding he has eaten previously. But suppose we give him a dessert he has neither seen nor tasted before and he says "That's good!" Where is the descriptive or standard-matching element in "That's good!" in this case?

A more important question is, How can we distinguish the *moral* good from the good as useful or pleasing? We have already touched on this: a long line of moral philosophers have claimed that the moral good applies to *persons,* not to things. "A good chronometer" keeps accurate time, "a good aircraft" transports us quickly, comfortably, and safely to our destination. But we do not on that account praise chronometers and aircraft as morally good beings; they are instruments only, not ends in themselves. The good of a glass of wine is not primarily a means to an end; the discriminating diner enjoys the wine for itself, not as a means of getting tipsy. But wines too are things, not people. Questions of moral good seem to have to do with relations between human beings *as* human beings. This is not to say that science and technology are unrelated to morals. If we grant that morality has something to do with human good, science has moral implications. For science can be used to make a bad human situation (disease, famine, poverty) less bad, or to make the good better. But the uses of science and technology are under the control of people. Only people, not things, says Kant, can be truly moral agents. Only the actions of persons can be judged morally right or wrong; the moral "ought" applies to human beings. Now it is easy to agree that we approve of acts aimed at moral good, but it is very hard to say just *what* it is we are approving when we approve of something in the moral realm.

"Right" and "Ought";
Tentative Criteria of the Moral Act

Corresponding to the distinction between the usual senses of "good," there is a difference between the specifically moral and the morally indifferent senses of the terms *right* and *wrong*. The distinction between the two is sometimes blurred, but often clear enough: "For goodness sake, don't *bite* it. That's absolutely the *wrong* way to open a bag of potato chips. The right way is to tear across the top of the bag along the dotted line." If I am watching you trying to mix a can of paint or sew a dress or play chess, I may say, "You are not doing that right," or "That's right—a little more toward the sleeve," or "That was the wrong move." But in so saying I am not claiming that your actions are *morally* right or wrong. There are certain ways to secure certain desired ends, these ends have nothing to do directly with moral rightness or wrongness. *If* you want to open a can of tuna neatly and quickly, there is one or more ways to do·it, and maybe the way you are doing it is not one of those ways. That is why I say, "That's the wrong way to do it." It is the same thing with right roads and wrong answers to arithmetic problems. The "right" or "wrong" in these cases is morally indifferent. But what about the *morally* right act?

Tentatively and provisionally, we may put forward this answer: the morally right act is an act *toward* a human being *as* a human being that conforms to a certain principle or rule. Suppose you return some money you have found that the owner will never miss. I say that your action is right. First, it is a true act, that is, voluntary, one done with intention, freely, carried out without compulsion, an act done in the knowledge of what you are doing and not in ignorance. It is an act in which genuine *choice* exists. It is an act that concerns a human as a human and not as a thing. It conforms to a rule, this rule having a general or universal character.[3] The rule may have been formulated by yourself or implanted in you by others. It may be only dimly present in your consciousness, it may be a sharp nagging prod by your conscience, or it may be clearly written down in a book somewhere with the words, "Always give back to others what belongs to them" or "Thou shalt not steal." Now we must note that this set of criteria for the morally right act is not complete. The set includes nothing, for instance, about the good of the person to whom I do this thing. It *assumes* that the act is for the person's good. It also assumes the rightness of the rule. (Suppose the rule I chose were "Never return what the owner won't miss" or "Finders keepers"?) This set of criteria is, at best, a *partial* identification of what we mean by a right act, the term "right" used here in the specifically moral sense.

A similar distinction between moral and nonmoral usage applies to *"ought"*—a word of great interest to moral philosophers. There appear to be ethical oughts and nonethical oughts. If you are driving me from New York to my house on Long Island, I may say, "You ought to have turned left back there." I do not state this as a moral obligation. As in the case of the morally neutral "right," there is a condition attached. *If* you want to get to my house by the most direct route, or if you want to avoid getting tied up on the Long Island Expressway, you should turn there. But the usage of the specifically *moral* ought will correspond roughly to the usage of the moral right:

You ought to contribute something to your mother's support.

He ought to see that his son does his schoolwork.

Ismay ought not to have left the ship before the other passengers had places in the lifeboats.

You ought not to be seeing that lady.

The senator ought to have reported the accident immediately.

Kant, as we shall see, held that the moral ought is always an ought with no strings attached, no reasons of benefit to self. No reason apart from moral duty can be given for the ethical ought. We ought to be honest, not because it pays or because it lets one sleep at night, but simply because it is the right thing to do. That is, it is one's *duty*.

Hume's Question:
Can an "Ought" be Gotten from an "Is"?

The eighteenth-century Scottish philosopher, David Hume, raised a question about the language of ethics and moral arguments that has been batted back and forth in ethical treatises and textbooks ever since he raised it. Hume claimed that ethical concepts such as obligation or moral "oughtness" do not seem founded in matters of fact:

In every system of morality which I have hitherto met with I have always remarked that the author proceeds for some time in the ordinary way of reasoning, and establishes the being of a God, or makes observations concerning human affairs; when of a sudden I am surprised to find, that instead of the usual copulations of propositions, *is* and *is not,* I meet with no proposition that is not connected with an *ought,* or an *ought not.* This change is imperceptible; but is, however, of the last consequence. For as this *ought* or *ought not* expresses some new relation or affirmation, it is necessary that it should be observed and explained; and at the same time that a reason should be given for what seems altogether inconceivable, how this new relation can be a deduction from others that are entirely different from it.[4]

In other words, Hume claimed that moral statements belong to a type quite different from factual or descriptive statements. For this reason, he believed that we cannot validly derive a moral conclusion from *factual* premises. The "is" bird cannot lay an "ought" egg. Factual statements are *descriptive* (such and such *is* the case), but moral statements are *prescriptive* (such and such *ought* to be the case). So how can we get an "ought" from an "is"? If we look out on the world and notice people doing things, we can describe these doings in many ways. We can say "He knocked the ball over the fence" or "He hit a home run." We can say "He took her money" or "He robbed her." Hume was interested in the difference between "matter-of-fact" and "moral" descriptions of actions. Consider these actions described in matter-of-fact terms:

Paul took fifty dollars out of David's wallet and did not tell David he did it.

Professor Jones stayed overnight in the motel with a male student to whom she is not married.

Saint Francis gave the hungry man his last piece of bread.

Clark drove his army knife deep into Phan Thi Mao's body.

Miss Pysent told the dying woman she would take care of her baby until he had grown, and she did.

Notice that nowhere among the facts described can we see anything like an "ought" or an "ought not," nor a "right" or a "wrong." From what source then, do we get the oughts and the ought nots by which we judge these matters—since the right and wrong do not appear to be part of the factual situation itself? Perhaps there are special kinds of facts, moral facts that, while not observable by the senses, are somehow really there. But if so, by what means of perception do we know that they *are* there? By what special faculty do we apprehend them? On this question, ethical philosophers after Hume have been divided. Some hold that there are such things as moral facts, which we perceive by the faculty of moral *intuition.* Others hold that, while there are no moral facts, there are moral *attitudes toward facts* that ethical language can express. But the second group of moral philosophers agrees with Hume that you cannot derive a value judgment from a description of facts. Unless there is at least one value term in the premises of your argument, they say, you cannot derive one in your conclusion. You cannot get an ought from an is. R. M. Hare says: "No imperative [ought-containing] conclusion can be validly drawn from a set of premises which does not contain at least one imperative [ought]."[5] Karl Popper says: "Perhaps the simplest and most important point about ethics is purely logical. I mean the impossibility to derive . . . ethical rules—imperatives; principles of policy; aims; or however we may describe them—from states of fact."[6]

But there are some cases in which it appears that we *can* derive an ought of sorts from factual statements—in certain contexts of discourse, at least. As we have already seen, we can derive a nonmoral ought from an is if the argument is of the conditional sort, "If you want a reliable circulator, you ought to oil it frequently." Now take another case. Suppose the Long Island Railroad has left part of its right-of-way unfenced near a new school building. I complain to the company representative: "You don't want kids getting killed on the tracks, do you? Then you ought to fence your right-of-way." The statement "You don't want kids getting killed on the tracks" seems to be factual and descriptive. It is a fact that the company does not want children killed or injured by trains. The second statement contains an ought. So it seems that we have derived an ought from an is.

But those who take Hume's side might say that there is already an ought in the first sentence, appearing in the words "You don't want." For the company not to *want* children getting killed by trains is itself a value judgment; the implicit ought in the first statement has simply been made explicit in the second. So an ought has not been derived from an is.

Some recent ethical philosophers (Anscombe, Searle) have called attention to another kind of situation in which an ought conclusion does seem to follow from an is, or factual premise.[7] Take the case of Smith and Jones. Smith borrowed $10 from Jones and promised to repay it. That is a fact. Can we not validly conclude that Smith *owes* Jones the $10 and that Smith *ought* (morally ought, not just legally) to pay it back? Or suppose I order a color television set from a store at which I have a charge account. I find the set satisfactory and use it every day, but I ignore the bills sent to me from the store. Finally a credit representative phones to tell me that I owe the store $400 for the television set and would I pay it please. "Now look here," I say, "I agree that your store delivered me a television set, and that I accepted delivery. I also agree that I have been using the set for three months at home. But these are matters of fact, a case of what *is.* Now you cannot get out of that set of facts any conclusion that I *owe* you anything or that I *ought* to pay you. You can't just slide that way from an is to an ought." What would we say to this argument? Would we not say that it is absurd, and if so the opposite of its conclusion must be true— that there are some cases in which we *can* get an ought from an is?

The cases cited are interesting because they assume the existence of some kind of social or institutional arrangement in which, by doing some special action like borrowing or buying on credit, I thereby take on an obligation. But is the obligation a moral obligation or simply a social one? Perhaps there is no difference. For example, does the *social* fact that I have contracted a marriage *morally* obligate me to cherish and support my wife? You are a father, let us say. Does it follow from that social fact that you have a moral obligation in regard to the welfare and education of your children? Or is the obligation social only? Or are "moral" and "social" simply two different names for the same obligation? This is a hard question to answer unless we take the easy view that "morally right" and "morally wrong" are just names for observing or breaking social conventions and that praiseworthy moral behavior is no more than the practice of following useful social codes. We will discuss this question later.

"Good" as Unique and Indefinable;
G. E. Moore's "Naturalistic" Fallacy

The Cambridge philosopher G. E. Moore was convinced that ethical statements differed from other statements in some crucial way, and in his *Principia Ethica* he tried to isolate that difference. To clarify his arguments, Moore appealed to the way in which people *ordinarily* use words. He criticized other philosophers for securing their points by using words in a peculiar way. Moore believed that all ethical propositions are based on the notion of "good," which is *indefinable.* We can know what good is only by a kind of direct and immediate knowledge. We cannot reach it by reasoning from other knowledge. "Good" refers to a unique quality. There is nothing else like it. It cannot be defined for it is a *simple* notion, that is, it has no parts and cannot be explained in terms of concepts other than itself. It is impossible to set forth the meaning of "good" in statements that do not themselves include the notion of good:

'Good,' then, if we mean by it that quality which we assert to belong to a thing, when we say that the thing is good, is incapable of any definition, in the most important sense of that word. The most important sense of 'definition' is that in which a definition states what are the parts which invariably compose a certain whole; and in this sense 'good' has no definition because it is simple and has no parts. It is one of those innumerable objects of thought which are themselves incapable of definition, because they are the ultimate terms by reference to which whatever *is* capable of definition must be defined.[8]

"Good," added Moore, is unanalyzable in much the same way as the perceived quality "yellow" is unanalyzable. To be sure, yellow may be explained in terms of certain vibrations of light. But it is not light vibrations we perceive when we experience yellow. What we do enjoy when we have the experience of yellow is just the unique, indefinable quality "yellow" and that is all there is to it. In the same way, good, as experienced, is not explainable in terms of anything but itself.

But what about those ethical theorists who *have* explained good in terms of something else? Some moral philosophers have defined good as pleasure; others have defined it in terms of social harmony or the greatest happiness of the greatest number of people; still others have identified it with various kinds of sociological or psychological states. They are wrong, one and all, said Moore: whoever tries to explain "good" in terms of something other than "good" is guilty of the *naturalistic fallacy.* Moore's label is odd and a little misleading, but it has stuck. We commit the naturalistic fallacy whenever we try to analyze good in terms other than itself, whenever we try to make out that ethical statements or beliefs are just a subclass of some kind of psychological or sociological fact. Moore did not object to the claim that pleasure is *a* good or that social harmony is *a* good. What he held is that neither pleasure nor social harmony are what we *mean* by good. Moore denied that ethical statements can best be understood by referring them to something nonethical—pleasure, social utility, reason, sociological welfare, codes, psychological conditions, or whatever. Theories that make pleasure or ego gratification or even happiness *the* good fall flat into the naturalistic fallacy. Good is primitive, as the axioms of mathematics are primitive. It cannot be "proved" or explained in terms other than its unique self. Hence knowledge of the good is *intuitive,* if the meaning of "intuitively known" is taken as "unprovable by other principles." No moral philosopher, Moore contended, however ingenious his arguments, can show that good designates a quality that is "really" something other than good.

Some critics of Moore have said that the Cambridge philosopher's treatment of good as indefinable was like G. K. Chesterton's observation concerning the personal quality "mean." Chesterton said you cannot explain what it is that constitutes meanness in a man; a mean man is just plain *mean,* and that is all. More seriously, critics have accused Moore of having failed to make an important distinction. This distinction holds between two kinds of definition that correspond to two kinds of knowledge that philosophers have labeled "knowledge by acquaintance" and "knowledge by description."[9] You have a famous friend. You know him by acquaintance; I know him only by descriptions of him in books and magazines. You know your home town by direct experience, for you grew up in it. I, a social scientist, know it by having made a careful sociological study of it. Knowledge by acquaintance has a unique quality, but knowledge by description is valuable also *and it too is knowledge.* To state that yellow is light vibrations of such and such a kind does not do justice to the *unique perceptual quality* of yellow.

It is that experienced yellow that cannot be described. Yet we may *understand* what yellow is, we may know *about* yellow, by defining it in terms of its wave length and other properties, and this knowledge will be both sound and useful. Moore may be right, say the critics, in claiming that when we know the quality referred to by the word "good" this peculiar quality is unanalyzable in terms of concepts other than good. But might it not be that we can *know about* good by means of descriptions or instances that do not refer to its unanalyzable quality?

Some critics offer another objection to Moore's comparison of yellow and good with respect to their uniqueness. Yellow is a natural property that can be observed by the senses. Since good is not a natural property, it cannot be observed in the same way that we observe yellow, hot, or soft. How then can good be observed? Are we not forced to postulate the existence of a mysterious and unobservable quality in good situations, an unchanging essence, a quality that we must apprehend by a special moral intuition or ethical sense? Moore would deny that the existence of such a special sense is needed to save his theory. For one thing, he did not sharply divide moral good from good of other kinds. When he talked of the highest goods we can attain, he did not have moral qualities of judgments in mind, nor did he think of "oughts" or "duties." Moore thought of *ends*—what things are good in themselves. In his chapter "The Ideal" (in *Principia Ethica*), Moore says that *personal affections* and *aesthetic enjoyments* are the highest goods we can have and that the good life is one that is rich in these experiences. Whether that position relieves Moore of the charge of needing a special sense to detect the quality named "good" is a question we need not bother with right now.

Moral Statements
as Expressions of Attitudes

Although they were not wholly convinced by his claim of the unique and unanalyzable quality "good," Moore's readers were impressed by his arguments against those who would reduce ethical judgments to socially useful beliefs or scientific facts. The peculiar "ought" character of ethical statements stimulated younger philosophers to try to isolate the elusive quality that makes ethical statements different from those describing matters of fact. They quickly focused on the simple truth that language has many uses other than to *describe things.* Moore's brilliant friend Ludwig Wittgenstein called attention to the variety of ways in which we use language and how hard it is to explain just *what* sorts of things these language utterances point out. Think of the different purposes for which we use words: making up a story and reading it; playacting; singing songs; guessing riddles; telling a joke; solving a problem in arithmetic; translating from one language to another; asking, thanking, cursing, greeting, praying, promising.[10] Think of exclamations alone, with their completely different functions:

Water!
Away!
Ow!
Ugh!
Help!
Fine!
No!

Now suppose that ethical statements such as "You ought to keep your promise" or "It's wrong to steal" are not descriptions of facts, not even of "moral" facts, but rather expressions of our *feelings* or *attitudes* toward facts. A number of moral philosophers, from Hume to Bertrand Russell, have said that ethical statements are essentially expressions of the speaker's *approval* or *disapproval.* That is, when a person says "X is good" or "Y is morally right," he is expressing approval of X and Y and implicitly urging others to feel the same way. The point was sharply presented by A. J. Ayer in his *Language, Truth, and Logic,* a controversial book that appeared more than thirty years ago. Ayer claims that moral judgments are no more than disguised expressions of approval or disapproval:

In saying that a certain type of action is right or wrong, I am not making any factual statement, nor even a statement about my own mind. I am merely expressing certain moral sentiments. And the man who is ostensibly contradicting me is expressing his moral sentiments. So there is plainly no sense in asking which of us is in the right. For neither of us is asserting a genuine proposition.[11]

The dust raised by Ayer's claim has not settled yet. Moral statements do seem to be connected with expressions of approval or disapproval, yet we tend to think that our approval or disapproval rests on grounds outside our psychological attitudes. One can see why a fuss over the question whether young people should stand up when an older guest enters the room might be relegated to no more than a difference in attitudes. But people tend to become bothered about the claim of "no real argument" and "it's only an attitude difference" when it is a question of ethical statements of the sort, "It was OK to do it to those Jews" and "There's nothing wrong in raping a gook girl." It is hard for us to admit that each party to such a dispute is doing *no more* than expressing his feelings. Ayer himself has repeatedly denied that he was counseling moral indifference to murder and rape; he insisted that he was just calling attention to the nondescriptive character of ethical statements.

The American philosopher C. L. Stevenson agreed that statements of the "right–wrong" or "ought–ought not" sort expressed approval and disapproval, and he constructed the following schema:

1. "This is wrong" means I disapprove of this; do so as well.
2. "He ought to do this" means I disapprove of his leaving this undone; do so as well.
3. "This is good" means I approve of this; do so as well.[12]

Some critics want more than this. Ethical statements may indeed be expressions of approval or disapproval, but the approval or disapproval is, in some cases, *justified.* Arguments on moral matters are not always reducible to no more than mutual exhibition of the debaters' psychological states. Stevenson stated that his scheme is only a "working model" suitable for the preliminary stages of analysis of *ethical meaning.* It does not bear on the question which of two given attitudes is substantively the "better."[13] But it was just this question ("Which is 'better'?") that bothered many readers. Granting that in ethical statements we express approval or disapproval of certain actions, granting that in saying "X is right" or "Y is wrong" we are expressing our *attitudes,* is it a matter of indifference as to which attitude we have? Is it not the case that an attitude itself can be right or wrong, well- or ill-founded? If I learn that a certain mother disciplines her child by pressing his fingers on a heated electric stove, I find in myself an immediate and very strong attitude of disapproval. More than this, I believe that my disapproval rests on *objective grounds,* that is, on some basis other than my simple, forceful desire that the mother should not do this. But what *are* these grounds of our ethical attitudes? Where can we locate them so that we may point to them? Bertrand Russell had doubts as to whether ethical feelings were no more than psychological states. He maintained that the moral good must be defined in terms of desire and that a person who judges "X is good" or "X is wrong" is wishing others to feel certain desires. But he asks:

What are "good" desires? Are they anything more than desires that you share? Certainly there *seems* to be something more. Suppose, for example, that some one were to advocate the introduction of bullfighting in this country. In opposing the proposal, I should *feel* not only that I was expressing my desires, but that my desires in the matter are *right,* whatever that may mean. As a matter of argument, I can, I think, show that I am not guilty of any logical inconsistency in holding to the above interpretation of ethics, and at the same time expressing strong ethical preferences. But in feeling, I am not satisfied. I can only say that, while my own opinions as to ethics do not satisfy me, other people's satisfy me less.[14]

Ayer himself, while defending his claim that ethical judgments are basically *emotive* (expressions of our feelings), made it clear that this did not mean that each of two attitudes toward proposed courses of action, "X is right," "X is wrong," is equally preferable. The term *equally preferable* involves a contradiction—how can I *prefer* something *equally* to another? "The moral problem," Ayer says, "is: What am I to do? What attitude am I to take? And moral judgments are directives in this sense."[15]

The question remains, What *are* we, morally speaking, to *do?* Suppose we grant that ethical statements of the form "X is right" and "X is wrong" are expressions of our attitudes toward action, approval or disapproval of doing something or not doing something in a situation where choice exists. But does ethical philosophy provide any guidelines in deciding which attitudes are better and which worse? Can we give *reasons* why one attitude is preferable to another? Let us grant that moral philosophy should begin with a clarification of ethical words. Let us further grant that these ethical words point to expressions of attitudes—approval or disapproval, commending an action or deploring it. But is there any way in which we can distinguish between differing attitudes from the point of view of better and worse? Are there any objective facts to which ethical attitudes can be related, and what is the nature of that relation? Are there specifically human and individual goods the existence of which does not depend on individual or group approval?

The Concept of Ethical Relativism

From a discussion of the meaning of ethical words, we have allowed ourselves to move toward a substantive question of ethics. If ethical words refer to attitudes of approval or disapproval and *only* to such attitudes, this conclusion may suggest *ethical relativism*. There is more than one variety of this popular view on the meaning of ethics and morals. First, there is the *emotive* or psychological variety of ethical relativism, a kind that can be drawn from some of the views in which ethical judgments are seen as no more than feelings of individual approval and disapproval. According to this position, arguments on ethical questions are never genuine arguments since ethical judgments are simply kinds of feelings, and feelings are psychological states. If people really *have* these pro or anti feelings, it is impossible to decide who is right in the case of ethical disputes.

Then there is *egoistic* relativism. This view would have it that the morally good is relative to what is in my interest. Although many people *act* as if egoistic relativism were true, few moral philosophers defend it. The ethical egoist says that *the* good is *my* good. Such egoism cannot be advocated as a general ethical position, for it involves inconsistency or self-contradiction. If I say everybody should seek *his* own good, this is inconsistent with *my* self-interest. The egoist can avoid this self-contradiction by sticking to the position that *the* good is *his* good. He may, in so advocating, be immoral, but he is not inconsistent. But there are many powerful and subtle forms of egoism that transcend this naïve or textbook variety. I might hold, for example, that everyone should strive toward self-realization, to become all he or she can be. This may be taken as a form of egoism but does not involve an inconsistency any more than does the attitude of a tennis player who desires to play only with those who try to win or the industrial capitalist who believes that the general economic good is served if each business enterprise tries to become Number One.

But still another variety of ethical relativism is going to take up our immediate attention—*cultural* relativism. Cultural relativism holds that some degree of objectivity—a social criterion or measurement—exists in the case of ethical judgment and behavior. What is right or wrong is not just an emotive or individualistic matter, but the result of a group or social agreement on the basis of custom or convention. What is morally right is that which is in accord with the customs, mores, socially approved ways of the particular culture to which we belong. What is morally wrong is what is disapproved of by that culture. There is no right or wrong beyond the culture. Ethical rules are derived from the values of the particular group. Therefore, what is morally right in one culture may be morally wrong in another and vice versa. There is no transcendent, absolute, or universal human morality. All morality is relative to the culture in which we humans find ourselves. Such is the argument of cultural relativism. It is an important argument, and we shall examine it in the next stage of our inquiry.

NOTES: CHAPTER 1

1. R. M. Hare, *The Language of Morals* (New York: Oxford University Press, 1952), p. 79.
2. Edgar Guest, "The Proof of a Golfer."
3. The words *general* or *universal* here do not mean "all over the world at all times and places" or "everybody obeys it." They mean, rather, that a rule must have some degree of generality if it is to cover particular cases—"Don't steal," "Keep promises," "Give to those who are hungry."
4. David Hume, *Treatise on Human Nature,* 2 vols. (New York: Dutton, 1911), vol. 2, pp. 177–178.
5. Hare, *Language of Morals,* p. 28.
6. Karl Popper, "What can Logic do for Philosophy" *Proceedings,* The Aristotelian Society, Suppl. Vol., 1948, p. 154.
7. G. E. M. Anscombe, "On Brute Facts," *Analysis* 18 (1958): 69–72; reprinted in *Ethics,* ed. James Thomson and Gerald Dworkin (New York: Harper & Row, 1968). John R. Searle, "How to Derive 'Ought' from 'Is,'" *Philosophical Review* 73 (1964): 43–58; reprinted in *Theories of Ethics,* ed. Philippa Foot (New York: Oxford University Press, 1967), pp. 101–114.
8. G. E. Moore, *Principia Ethica* (London: Cambridge University Press, 1951), pp. 9–10.
9. William James, Henri Bergson, and Bertrand Russell are among those modern philosophers who have made the distinction between knowledge by acquaintance and knowledge by description.
10. Ludwig Wittgenstein, *Philosophical Investigations* (New York: Macmillan, 1953), p. 27.

11. Alfred J. Ayer, *Language, Truth and Logic,* rev. ed. (London: Gollancz, 1948), pp. 107–108.

12. Charles L. Stevenson, *Ethics and Language* (New Haven, Conn.: Yale University Press, 1944), p. 21.

13. Charles L. Stevenson, "Moore's Arguments against Certain Forms of Ethical Naturalism," in *The Philosophy of G. E. Moore,* ed. P. A. Schilpp (Evanston, Ill.: Northwestern University Press, 1942). Reprinted in Foot, ed., *Theories of Ethics,* pp. 16–32.

14. Bertrand Russell, "Reply to Criticism," in *The Philosophy of Bertrand Russell,* ed. Paul A. Schilpp (Evanston, Ill.: Northwestern University Press, 1944), p. 724.

15. Alfred J. Ayer, "On the Analysis of Moral Judgements," *Philosophical Essays* (London: Macmillan, 1954), p. 242.

2

Social Use and Cultural Relativism

In any informal discussion of ethics, people quickly tire of talking about the meaning of ethical words and terms. They want to get down to cases. Analysis of words and sentences is not the burning issue in moral philosophy, they say. Actions, deeds, human behavior are what we call "right" or "wrong," "moral" or "immoral." Now *why* do we call certain actions right and others wrong, they ask. What *makes* them right or wrong? What is the function, the purpose of ethical judgments or rules in human society? And while we are at it, who is to say what actions are right or wrong or what is the criterion of "good" and "bad"— especially since today we know something about societies other than our own? We know there are many cultures, each with its own habits and customs that differ widely from one another. Might not what is called good in our society be bad in another, and the other way around too? Who is to say which is right?

Certainly people do like to ask questions of that sort when the talk turns to what we mean by ethical words and terms and moral behavior. Answers to them are not easy for many reasons. One is that there are several different *kinds* of questions mixed up here. We cannot undo all the tangles, but we may try to loosen one or two.

I

Is "Moral" That Which Is Useful to Society?
If we ask ourselves how morality functions in a society, we can hardly deny that there is a real connection between ethical rules and social utility. It is too simple to say that *all* ethical judgments come from the application of rules society has laid down for its own welfare, security, or smooth functioning. But it seems clear that *many* ethical rules are closely connected with regulations fundamental to the safety, the order, the smooth and dependable

operation of the social organism of which we are a part. Some ethical rules, particularly negative ones ("Don't do that; it is wrong to do that"), have counterparts in prohibitions of *law.* Killing a human being except in self-defense is morally and legally wrong. The danger of murder to social order is obvious. Theft, arson, wanton assault, rape, and enslavement are practices forbidden by law, and we consider them morally wrong as well. The more positive ethical rules ("Do that; it is right or good to do that") are often not compelled by law. But their relation to social usefulness and harmony seems plain. Giving food and clothing to the destitute is morally right; sharing with those who are deprived tends to improve the cohesiveness and stability of a society, whereas withholding such help tends to breed resentment and hostility, thus weakening social bonds. For you to help a student who is having trouble with his algebra is a kindly act; it is not commanded by law but it is certainly conducive to the welfare of the social group, the school class, and to the larger society beyond the classroom. That promises should be kept is an ethical rule. Promise-keeping is sometimes backed by law, sometimes not. To break a promise to a child because it is inconvenient to keep it may be a serious matter, even a destructive act; but the law has nothing to say about it. Yet the kind of promises we call *contracts* are enforced by law. To dissolve them may be no easy matter, and their breach may be subject to penalty. In any case, the relation of promise-keeping to that need of mutual dependability so useful to society is pretty clear.

But many socially useful rules and practices do *not* seem to belong to the moral order. Certainly it is a socially useful practice to have our garbage and other trash picked up three times a week, but would we on this account normally commend the sanitation department for its moral behavior? It is socially useful to have mail delivered to houses, yet we do not consider the mailman's depositing of letters in our box as an ethical act. Of course if he fails to deposit them, or if the trashmen ignore our barrels to get to a card game, we may then raise the ethical question as to whether they may be failing in their obligation to their *duty.* In any event, it seems that all we may safely say at this point is that many ethical rules appear to have a close connection with social utility or welfare. But the converse is not so clearly evident; socially useful acts are not necessarily instances of ethical behavior.

Ethical Rules and the Pressure of Society

All of us feel the pressure of a vague but powerful entity we call by the abstract name *society.* This entity exerts its weight upon us to see that we obey many rules of behavior. When we were little children, this pressure came to us via our parents. Later our teachers enforced it. We soon learn that our parents and teachers are passing on to us the commands and prohibitions of a larger body out there somewhere beyond the home and the school. When we were very young, we usually obeyed our parents and teachers without question. But gradually we realized they were acting for something that went beyond the immediate confines of the family. The philosopher Henri Bergson asks, in his *The Two Sources of Morality and Religion:*

Why did we obey? The question hardly occurred to us. We had formed the habit of deferring to our parents and teachers . . . but behind our parents and our teachers we had an inkling of some enormous or rather some shadowy thing that exerted pressure on us through them. Later we would say it was society.[1]

Why the pressure? It would be fun to do whatever we liked, but in some way—not always clear to us as children—we are made to feel that following our personal inclination at all times will bring us into conflict with the rules of a larger body of which we will one day be members and for which membership our parents and teachers are preparing us. Of course it would be best, we imagine, to be allowed to do what we want. But little by little it is knocked into our heads—sometimes literally, sometimes by gentler indirection—that we are not just little independent sovereign kingdoms, but parts of a whole, members of a great living organism we will learn to call "society." And we will learn that society expects us, under some circumstances, to subordinate our individual personal desires to the values and interests of a comprehensive social whole—even though we may not always be sure what those values and interests are.

   Of course, the society that takes us up into itself—if we think of it as One Thing—is largely an abstract unity. There are *many* societies fitting inside one another like a nest of Chinese boxes. The first social unit we know is that cellular entity, our family, the only social unit completely within the walls of our home. The rest are outside. There are the neighbors whose possessions and privacy we must respect. There is the school, through which we feel for the first time the oppressive and alien weight of higher authority. As we grow up, we find ourselves members of the athletic team, the church, the political club, the labor union, the college, the farmers' cooperative, the business firm, the street gang. Over these, and in some vast way including them, is the nation. When we were small, our parents and teachers spoke of an all-inclusive and wondrous thing—our country. We were told that our country had a glorious though at times troubled history. We were told that we owed respect and loyalty to our country, that we had certain important rights and obligations as citizens.

As children, we were usually respectful when we heard all this. Even in our adult years, however individualistic and even socially rebellious we may have become, we have to admit the truth that Aristotle proclaimed long ago: that to be human is to be a social animal, that it is very hard if not impossible to live outside some form of society. Just to maintain physical life itself we need the help of others, and therefore some kind of association with them is a "must." How miserable it would be without someone to talk to or work with—a husband or wife, a parent, sister or brother, a neighbor, a fellow worker, a comrade-in-arms, a friend. Even on his solitary island Robinson Crusoe lived with the hope and expectation that he would one day be found by rescuers and would return to life among men, his kind of men, who happened to be Englishmen.

One of the first rules many of us were taught by our parents is that we should be "nice to people." Politeness, courtesy, the habit of kindness to others, thoughtfulness—all these have very positive social consequences. If we should ask our parents *why* we should be nice to people, they may reply, "To get along" or "Things will be so much easier and more pleasant for you." Experience quickly confirms the advice of our parents—the habit of courtesy, of attention to and consideration for others, is a wonderfully useful social instrument. When we treat others with kindly and pleasant ways, they tend to smile back at us, praise us for our friendliness, and in their turn do things that make our daily living more easy and agreeable. So it is just as our parents had said. Of course, we would quickly deny that we have adopted these habits of politeness and consideration for others just to benefit ourselves. When people follow the rule of being nice to each other, we say, *"everybody* benefits." By "everybody," we suppose, is meant all those in the particular social groups with which we interact—family, classmates, fellow employees, even (if it is our business to deal with it) the general public. In a word, though an abstract one, *society.*

Can we not conclude then, without further ado, that ethical rules derive their substance from social utility, that the statement "This is a morally right act" means the same as "This is a socially useful act"? Or at least that morally right acts form a subclass of socially useful acts? The answer must be yes and no. That X *derives* from Y does not mean that X *is* Y. Morality may well have *begun* in the need for social harmony and cooperative living. But it does not follow that every ethical rule or act is formulated or performed with the intent or result of supporting the social order. Further, we have already noted that even if ethical behavior is contained in the class of useful social practices, it does not follow that every socially useful deed is an ethical act. Think of cabdrivers, diamond cutters, and short-order cooks. Still, it seems that the ethical realm has something to do with social utility and that the connection, if not a necessary link, is not superfluous. If by "social utility" we mean that ethical acts *directly or indirectly contribute to social welfare,* the connection between morality and social usefulness can hardly be denied. If the term "social welfare" is construed broadly enough, it would be hard to think of a good deed that did not in some way contribute to the commonweal.

But if we concede that one of the qualities of a moral act is that it in some way contributes to social welfare, we should not conclude from this that when we act morally we act with *intent* to promote social harmony or progress. I may stop to help a child in the street, you may refuse to blur the truth in court, she may keep a promise that costs her pride and money—and none of the three of us may have social benefit in mind when we act, even though each act may contribute to the common good.

Let us go back to our parents for a moment, to the time we asked them why we should be nice to people. Their frequent answer "To get along well" or "It will make things easier for you" can be understood in two ways, neither being mutually exclusive: (1) in terms of benefit to *self* (It is to your personal interest to be nice to people) or (2) in terms of the good of the social group (Things are more pleasant for everybody if you are nice to people). But there is a third answer the parent may give to the child's question: "Because it is right to be kind and helpful to others, that's all." In this case, the parents seem to say that we should do what is right, not primarily for the sake of self-benefit or social utility, but for the sake of the right itself. In each of these three cases, the question of *motive* for acting according to the moral rule is pertinent. Later we shall see that Kant (who would agree with the third parent) had something to say on the importance of motive in the moral situation.

We have agreed that moral acts tend to contribute to social welfare, provided "social welfare" is understood broadly enough. If, however, "social good" or "benefit of society" is construed in a narrow institutional sense or identified with the *status quo,* the criterion of social utility may prove to be not so much false as inadequate. From a social utility point of view, all parties might agree that selling heroin on the street (being socially harmful) is properly considered morally bad, while ameliorating the condition of the addict (restoring him to nondestructive life) is morally good. But suppose the case under consideration is that of a man who tells us that he proposes to enter a monastery, there to spend the rest of his life in prayer and fasting, or that of a girl who informs her parents that she intends to dedicate her life to a student revolutionary movement that does not forswear armed action should it be deemed unavoidable. There is a common human tendency to identify social welfare with the good of the established order and not a social life, that could conceivably be an improvement on the present.

These reflections are put forward not in defense of young arsonists or assassins of policemen, but to raise in our minds the question of "utility to *what* social order?" when the criterion of social utility is appealed to in connection with exhortations to moral virtue. Most people agree that Socrates and Jesus were great moral teachers. Yet the teachings of these two men seemed to the official guardians of their respective social orders so *contrary* to social usefulness, so socially destructive, that the moralists in question were hailed before tribunals, convicted of "crimes," and put to death.

Societies tend to *close* themselves, to wall themselves off from other societies, and to consider their welfare and security the highest good. Many families, with a strong "cellular" sense, tend to turn themselves into closed societies, judging the plans and aspirations of their members in terms of whether they will or will not work to the good of "the family." Ethnic and religious groups often do the same. The social groups we refer to as "our country" or "our people" will, in times of crisis, behave like walled citadels whose well-being and safety seem to the inhabitants absolute and beyond appeal. Today people are more ready to recognize the claims of *humanity* above the narrower concepts of tribe, people, or country—Hausa and Ibo, Israeli and Arab, Palestinian and Bedouin, Hindu and Pakistani, Ulster Protestant and Catholic, Hutu and Tutsi, USA and USSR. The Stoics taught the ideal of the brotherhood of man. The Jews—despite a strong sense of their unique and "chosen" quality—defended the right of the stranger within the gates. The Christians strove to internationalize a religion of universal love. In our time, the United Nations was founded on a charter prefaced by a ringing declaration of *human* rights. Yet nations, and peoples and clans within nations, continued to make war, invoking the charter's permission to take up arms in "self-defense." Even Albert Camus, whose poetic humanism inspired a world exhausted by war, fell silent during the Algerian crisis. When the Algerian rebels demanded independence from France and the expulsion of the French colonials, Camus, son of a colon, said "I believe in Justice, but I will defend my mother before Justice."[2] The pressure society exerts on us is constant; but to feel the full weight of that pressure, one must be a member of a closed society in war. In war, truth becomes the truth of the tribe, people, or nation. Lies, deceit, treachery, assassination are turned into heroic virtues. What in peace would be criminal becomes in war a service to the nation. Winston Churchill was not entirely joking when he declared that if cooperation with Satan was necessary in order to defeat the Nazis, he would be willing to make a favorable reference for the Devil in the House of Commons. The rule in war is that *our* people must not perish, not that *humans* must not perish.

Of course, it is easy to take a tone of moral superiority over the question of the dependence of human beings on closed societies, even on measures like war. It may be too early in the long history of social evolution for humans to be able to function in open societies. It may be that only a few prophets and saints have been able to envision a humanity, which in the transcending of the bounds of tribe or nation, discovers the release of great spiritual energies hitherto locked in. Given certain circumstances, it may be that most of us would prefer to take our stand in war with "our people" rather than with "humanity." "Humanity" seems rather abstract, while "our people" seems so familiar and precious as to warrant the sacrifice of blood and lives. We must leave it to the reader to imagine the circumstances in which he would draw his own line. In any event, when peace returns and the knives are put away, the idea of common human interest has a way of emerging cautiously once more. Nations retain their suspicions of other nations, but consent to take part—more or less willingly—in international cooperative efforts.

II

Cultural Relativism

Let us suppose that ethical rules are in some important way derived from or connected to social welfare and that men are not disposed to put the good of humanity as a whole over the good of their particular tribe, people, or nation. It is tempting to conclude—particularly when we read over the mass of ethnological and anthropological material that has been skillfully acquired by investigators in the present century—that there is no moral right or wrong apart from accepted behavior patterns, mores, and folkways of particular countries, peoples, or cultures. The label *cultural relativism* has attached itself to the view represented by this conclusion.

Cultural relativism has been a widely accepted theory of ethics among social scientists, particularly among anthropologists. From them, as teachers, a generation of American undergraduates learned to preface their remarks on social matters with the phrase, "In our culture. . . ." Successive college students, who had been assigned readings in cultural anthropology, quickly took up the claim that widely different standards and values of conduct and life among primitive peoples were equally acceptable. They were convinced that it would be narrowly *ethnocentric* to rate the values of the orderly Pueblo over the unfriendly Dobu, the modest Hopi over the boastful and potlatching Kwakiutl, the individualistic Eskimo over the cooperative Dakota. Although many anthropologists today have veered away from a heavy emphasis on cultural relativism, this popular ideology is found in many current college and high school texts:

The simple fact is that people usually think, feel, and act as they do because they were brought up in cultures in which these ways were accepted, not only as good and right but as natural. . . . Many social patterns, customs, or folkways—whatever we choose to call them—are not inherently right or wrong. . . . When patterns involve basic values important to the society's well being, they get into the category of what people think of as right and wrong.[3]

Some observers, commenting on recent radical changes in the patterns of behavior of youths have listed the academic teaching of cultural relativism as a causal factor. Interviewed in connection with the 1970 annual meeting of the American Anthropological Association in New York, a prominent anthropologist said, "For decades now we have been putting students through classes with the message of cultural relativism, and now the message has gotten through in everything from mind-blowing to the mores of clothing and sex."[4]

Where Did Cultural Relativism Come From?

Cultural relativism is as old as the Greeks. We know that the word *ethics* comes from a word meaning *custom,* although the Greek philosophers used the word in a sense close to our own. The Sophists were known as teachers of relativism. Plato said that they taught one man's truth to be another's falsehood, that man is the measure of all things, that justice is in the interest of the stronger, that the ethical good is no more than personal expediency. Apparently the Sophists did considerable traveling and may have observed how customs and manners differed in various parts of the Hellenic and barbarian world. Many Greek voyagers were struck by the fact that exotic peoples had practices that were offensive to the Hellenes but quite proper for the peoples in question.

The present form of cultural relativism had its origin in the late nineteenth century, when ethnology and cultural anthropology were being developed as special disciplines. In brilliant works such as Frazer's *The Golden Bough* and Westermarck's *The Origin and Development of Moral Ideas* stacks of ethnological data were marshaled to show how closely the notions of right and wrong were bound up with the customs and beliefs of individual cultures. In our own century, continued study of primitive culture has thrown much light on the origin and growth of "moral" behavior and its relation to particular customs and lifestyles. Dealing with highly developed rather than primitive cultures, Oswald Spengler's *The Decline of the West* interprets world history in terms of world cultures, each with its own standards and values, each impenetrably islanded off from one another.

American social scientists were particularly attracted to cultural relativism. Many argued that anthropological evidence demonstrates that moral principles have no objective status. Since moral codes are dependent on the particular culture within which they develop, no one set of moral principles is "better" than any other. Conflicting ethical conclusions are equally valid; to believe otherwise is to be naïvely parochial and ethnocentric. An early champion of cultural relativism, Charles Graham Sumner, made *folkways* a household word in American academe. In his book of that title, Sumner announces:

We shall find proof that "immoral" never means anything but contrary to the mores of the time and place. Therefore the mores and the morality may move together, and there is no permanent or universal standard by which right and truth in these matters can be established and different folkways compared and criticised. Only experience produces judgments of expediency in some usages.[5]

In their enthusiasm, many popular ethnologists early in our century produced verdicts heavily weighted in favor of extreme cultural relativism by choosing isolated concepts such as taboo or sexual initiation and then amassing a huge miscellany of traits drawn at random from various primitive peoples all over the world. Their readers could hardly avoid the conclusion that nowhere on this earth is anything right or wrong but that primitive custom made it so. Later, careful observers like Bronislaw Malinowski insisted on the functional character of primitive traits. It was bad method, he thought, to pile a heap of bits and pieces of the observed habits of widely separated primitive peoples and to think that one had thereby gained much knowledge about universal primitive conceptions. Malinowski's studies of the Trobriand islanders of Melanesia showed how important it is to try to see the traits of a given people as elements in a society that is an organic whole.

The American anthropologist Ruth Benedict developed the *comparative* method analysis of primitive culture. Her well-known book *Patterns of Culture* contrasts the standards and values of the Pueblo Indians, the Dobu of the New Guinea area, and the Kwakiutl, an Indian people of Vancouver.[6] *Patterns of Culture* was influential in spreading the popularity of cultural relativism. Benedict conceded that there are some traits in human behavior that are very widespread. But while she admitted the existence of some near-universal behavior patterns such as exogamous restrictions on marriage, Benedict was suspicious of claims to universality alleged to come from a common human nature: "One may isolate the universal core of the belief and differentiate from it its local forms," she says, "but it is still possible that the trait took its rise in a pronounced local form and not in some original least common denominator of all observed traits."[7] *Patterns of Culture* concludes with a frank defense of cultural relativism and an appeal for the recognition of its importance toward an increase in human understanding and peaceful coexistence of peoples today:

Social thinking at the present time has no more important task before it than that of taking adequate account of cultural relativity. . . . As soon as the new opinion is embraced as customary belief, it will be another trusted bulwark of the good life. We shall arrive then at a more realistic social faith, accepting as grounds of hope and as new bases for tolerance, the coexisting and *equally valid* patterns of life which mankind has created for itself from the raw materials of existence.[8]

Is the "Equally Valid" Claim of Cultural Relativism Valid?

In trying to deal with this question, much depends on the way in which the term *equally valid* is understood with reference to cultural relativism. Let us suppose that the meaning of "valid" is roughly equal to "sound" or "a reasonable conclusion in the light of the evidence." In this case, we must ask: Are we talking about patterns of behavior that have to do with what we understand by "morality" or not? People of different cultures may have patterns of customary behavior that might strike us as strange or odd or even disagreeable but not, morally speaking, right or wrong. An immense number of the ways and customs of primitive people have to do with their contact with supernatural beings or powers in which they believe. Whether we agree with them or not, we could hardly judge these practices right or wrong—unless perhaps we hold that they are superstitions and that all superstitions are morally wrong because they are socially narrowing or destructive. Another vast area of primitive customary practice and attitude concerns their highly complicated arrangements pertaining to kinship. We would not tend to think this touched ethical concerns, except perhaps in the case of a tribal boy forbidden to marry the girl he loves because of a complex kinship disability that seems to us completely irrelevant.

But let us take an instance in which the matter at hand has something more clearly to do with what we understand as morality. An often cited example is the old Eskimo practice—now virtually nonexistent—of abandoning old people of the group, killing them, or helping them to kill themselves. Suppose an Eskimo was getting ready to move camp but was troubled about his father, who was old and blind. The old man says he would like to go seal hunting, something he has not done for years. The son understands, dresses his father in warm clothes, gives him his weapons, takes him out to the seal grounds, and walks him into a hole in the ice. This may seem to us very wrong and sad. No doubt it was sad to the Eskimo son, but not wrong. Until well into the middle of our century the small Eskimo family groups lived entirely by seal hunting and could not survive if they had to take the old and disabled parents with them. These Eskimos had no permanent home; their nomadic life was lived in great privation and constant mortal danger. In this context, the old people often took it as their duty (as we would say) to resign themselves to death, and some of the younger ones believed it *their* duty to abandon or to lead their aged parents to death. In this context, we would not say that it was morally wrong for the Eskimo to arrange the death of his parent. We could not deny the force of objective material conditions in forming the morality of a social group.

But the question remains: is that way of life that has no place for old people to live out their days in peace a good life *in that respect?* This is not to question that the old hunting life of the Eskimo people was not a fine thing, even heroic. Nor is it to claim moral superiority for *our* practice of putting our aged and disabled parents in nursing homes, some of which are very sad places. No, the question is simply this: which of two ways of life is better—one in which aged parents must be abandoned or killed or one in which they may live in comfort, honor, and peace until their natural death?

Similar considerations apply to old practices of wife-lending by Eskimos, Bantu extramarital arrangements, or the various forms of polygamous practices that survive today even in contemporary societies such as Saudi Arabia. The context of these practices is important to know about if we wish to compare them with our ways of doing things.

It is one thing to insist on sensibly seeing such practices in their social contexts before we draw conclusions about the nature and universality of moral judgments. It is another to conclude from these practices that one is equally valid compared to some other. The practices may be equally valid if the differences in contexts are conceded from the start. But would we not think it better if social contexts were improved? Surely we do not hold that the *context* of a black ghetto is equally valid to that of a rat-less neighborhood with decent schools, where heroin is not sold on the streets to young people. By the same token, if we hold that a woman is a person—not a subhuman, a chattel, or a slave—we cannot hold her dignity and worth to be consistent with the low status of women that polygamy inevitably entails. It would be foolish to accuse an individual man who practices polygamy or an Eskimo who lends his wife of moral wrong. But the way of life that forces women to such submission may not be equally valid to one that does not.

Arguments for cultural relativity must be carefully formulated to avoid inconsistencies. When Sumner says, "Medieval punishment of criminals, leaving out of account heretics and witches, bore witness to the grossness, obscenity, inhumanity, and ferocity of the mores," his rhetoric leaves little doubt that he regards the mores of the European Middle Ages as inferior to those of his own time and place.[9] Ruth Benedict argues for the acceptance of the coexisting patterns of life humans have created for themselves as "equally valid." Yet she seems at the same time to suggest that cultural relativity has only a secondary value, instrumental in reaching a higher socio-moral theory. She said, as we noted, that taking adequate account of cultural relativity will prove a "trusted bulwark of the good life" helping us to "arrive then at a more realistic social faith." Such a good life and its more realistic social faith clearly belong to a higher realm of value than the "equally valid" life-styles she has reviewed in order to convince her reader of the importance of cultural relativity.

A defender of Benedict's argument might point out that she was simply urging the importance of taking cultural relativity into account. She believes that codes vary and that it is hard for one culture to understand the culture of another. We should not shape our judgments of what other societies do simply by what *we* do. When an anthropologist rejects *ethnocentrism* (judging another culture exclusively by the standards and values of our own) this does not imply that the anthropologist believes that no moral rules hold.

Recent Changes in the Emphasis on Cultural Relativity

Much of the data on which the older ethnologists and anthropologists relied to support the claims of cultural relativity were based on studies made in the nineteenth or in the earlier part of the twentieth century, before contemporary technology had swept over the world. Today it is hard to find a "pure" primitive culture uninfluenced by contact with the products of the great industrial and commercial economies—the United States, Russia, Japan, Britain, France, and others. The Eskimo no longer has to live as a nomad on the ice; today benevolent governments drop lumber and tools for him to build a permanent dwelling. He still hunts seal and caribou, but often from a snowmobile rather than a dogsled. Detribalization has made its mark on many of the developing nations of Africa. Even the inhabitants of central New Guinea, one of the last refuges of primitive culture, have responded to the call of jobs in Australia. The tribesman works two or three years, then often returns to the life and ways of his people. But he brings back a transistor radio with him. Culturally speaking, he is not the same man; already his children are dancing to hard rock records brought back from Port Moresby. There is another point. Governments of the recently decolonialized countries—many of whose people still live in tribal arrangements—are doing everything in their power *not* to be considered primitive. Today many of these governments refuse to hang out the welcome sign to anthropologists from big industrial countries who wish to treat their people as case studies in fieldwork. Sartre and Lévi-Strauss have pointed out that these new nations do not want their people looked at as objects for scientific study any more than as objects for political and economic domination.[10]

Are there Universal Rules of Conduct Among All Peoples?

Among anthropologists today there is not quite so much emphasis on the importance of cultural relativity as there was in the work of many ethnologists earlier in the century. Many analysts are interested in the possibility of general or universal patterns of behavior that may exist among people all over the world, "primitive" as well as "civilized." A universal source of rules of conduct seems to be *the family,* a social unit that seems to have been found wherever men have lived. According to Claude Lévi-Strauss:

After they had claimed for about fifty years that the family, as modern societies know it, could only be a recent development and the outcome of a slow and long-lasting evolution, anthropologists now lean toward the opposite conviction, i.e. that the family, consisting of a more or less durable union, socially approved, of a man, a woman, and their children, is a universal phenomenon, present in each and every type of society.[11]

The universal existence of the family means the worldwide presence of certain attitudes and practices related to the family. Some of these approach the condition of what we would call "moral" or "ethical" rules. "The structure of the family, always and everywhere," says Lévi-Strauss, "makes certain types of sexual connections impossible or at least wrong."[12]

Richard Brandt made an anthropological study of Hopi ethics in the early 1950s.[13] He found Hopi ethical standards surprisingly similar to the criteria of "right" and "wrong" familiar to us. As a moral philosopher, Brandt believes that standards of ethical behavior are closely related to the parts individual persons are expected to play in social living:

Ethical standards are useful . . . not merely as an efficient means of providing security but also as an efficient system of guides for cooperative living, like laws of the road. Institutions, like the family, marriage, and others, are needed for social living—not necessarily the institutions that we may have, such as monogamy, but at any rate some institutions. And such institutions consist, in part, of ethical standards, of recognized rights and responsibilities. Ethical standards prescribe, for many contexts, the part that given individuals are to play in institutional behavior. Of course, such performance could be prescribed as a matter of law. Ethical standards, however, are more efficient than legal standards.[14]

Earlier in our century, W. C. Willoughby's study of the African Bantu convinced him that the basic conviction of right and wrong that he found among the Bantus is remarkably similar to that of traditional European ethics:

Where moral sanctions of tribal life have not broken down under stress of superficial contact with European civilization, the danger of taking the name of a god in vain is generally acknowledged; reverence for parents and those in authority is commonly inculcated, and disobedience punished; self-control is cultivated; men of probity are respected; brotherliness, courtesy, and hospitality are common virtues; a high respect for property prevails; mercy is highly esteemed and justice praised;

murder, witchcraft, stealing, adultery, bearing false witness against one's neighbor, hatred, and arrogance are all condemned; and there is such a sense of family responsibility that orphans and destitute people are provided for.[15]

Every culture seems to have social and ethical rules concerning the care of human life, family responsibilities, and sexual behavior. Every culture has a concept of murder. In no culture is it right to kill a healthy man who is not an enemy, who has committed no offense. Nearly every culture prohibits incest. In no culture can a man have a woman any time he wants her, just because he wants her. In every culture it is right to respect parents, although some cultures respect them more than others. In every culture there is an obligation to care for and to train one's children; in no culture is it considered right to neglect these responsibilities.

It is easy to prove too much by these cultural similarities in behavioral and moral matters. Uncritical universalism in ethics is as hard to defend as uncritical relativism. The ethical rules of a faraway people may be similar to our own, but the *application* of these rules, depending as it may on local situations and ideas, can be very different. Willoughby's religious background and missionary training inclined him to believe in a "universal moral sense" innate in all men. Yet he admits that the Bantu's application of ethical rules to practical situations varied widely from the standard Western way:

Dread of the magical consequences of uttering a divine name has far more to do with the prohibition than what we should call reverence for the divine; brotherliness is not incompatible with the conviction that there is no such thing as social equality among men. . . . Bearing false witness against one's neighbor is regarded as very wrong; but "neighbor" is defined in terms of political propinquity and members of alien tribes may be traduced, deceived and exploited without compunction so far as is consonant with safety of one's own social group.[16]

The limits placed on universality by local application is not peculiar to the Bantu. Great modern nations under stress—particularly from war or threat of war—will quickly take away the application of rules of benevolence to "alien" peoples. They will "traduce," "deceive," and "exploit," even torture and kill, those peoples beyond their boundaries who they believe threaten their safety. Such changing of rules of ethical behavior when applied to alien peoples is often justified by a nation as part of "the right to self-defense." Would we as individuals hesitate to deceive, traduce, or even kill a person who we believe intends to harm or destroy our lives or those of members of our family? The strength or weakness of the national self-defense argument depends on the validity of the *analogy* between the individual's right to defend himself and the assumed collective right of the nation.

To add it all up, it seems that there is *both* universality and diversity in patterns of moral behavior among various peoples of the world. The question is: Where shall we place the emphasis—on the universality or on the diversity? Are we going to claim that similar moral attitudes among widely scattered social groups are signs of a common "human nature"? Or are we going to say, with Robert Redfield:

Sometimes, when we look at all that ethnography and history have recorded about customs and institutions, it seems as though there had developed varieties of moral judgment so different from one another as to force the conclusion that there is no human nature but only a multitude of natures.[17]

We do find widespread agreement among various peoples on certain matters of behavior concerning the care and nurturing of life. At all times and places we know of mothers have loved and taken care of their children. One could argue, of course, whether this is really an instance of *moral* behavior; a skeptic might point out that the higher animals, like cats or horses, do the same, and we do not consider them moral beings. We could point out that all people wherever we find them consider their children's accomplishments to be good and feel badly at their failure. But that accomplishment may in one culture be the killing of a youth of another tribe; in another, gaining admission to a good medical school. Shall we say the common elements in patterns of moral behavior are essential and the divergent ones nonessential? Or shall we hold that the differences in these cases are more important than the similarities? A contemporary Polish philosopher puts it this way:

Let us assume that everywhere people are capable of love and hatred, joy and sorrow, pride and shame. That is: everywhere people love *some-*

body and hate *somebody;* they are happy about *something,* and unhappy about *something;* they are proud of one thing, and ashamed of another. This is why some authors speak of a basic moral similarity among people, whereas others point to basic differences, considering it important *whom* people love, *what* they are happy about, *what* they are proud of—the number of heads taken or the number of patients successfully operated on.[18]

Where to put the emphasis? For a number of reasons, a case can be made for stressing *similarities* rather than divergences. First, in a century marked by great advances in education, literacy, science, and technology, by the near-universal abolition of slavery and the political liberation of formerly subject peoples; in a century marked as well by shattering wars and atrocities against peoples—it may be useful to search once more for some common agreement on basic humane ideas and attitudes. Second, as we have already noted, the usual cultural relativity arguments tend to assume a *static* condition of world societies—as if headhunting will continue at the same frequency rate as surgical operations. The facts are a little different. Because of the impact of worldwide political and technological influences, the old sealed-off tribal people holding to its cheerful headhunting ways has become an anachronism, hardly more than a textbook fiction. Third, there is a general spiral trend away from shamanism, magic, superstition, torture, and obsessive preoccupation with blood, decay, and physical filth. Of course, there have been terrifying retrogressions, many of them among "educated" peoples. We have seen the photographs of the slain at My Lai, the tortured and executed in Bangladesh, the Belfast shootings, the Hutu massacres. The ultimate example of backsliding among the "civilized" countries is, of course, the Nazi pogram. But the Hitler experiment, though frightful, was relatively short-lived. It was violently rejected by a community of nations, some of which differed sharply in standards and values from others. "Along with the growing disgust with blood and decay and violence toward the human body," says Redfield, "goes a growing concern for the welfare and dignity of others. . . . the moral canon tends to mature."[19] This optimism stands in contrast to Sartre's statement that, after Hitler, he would not trust "the Idea of Man" to any state two hundred years hence, that he could not count on men he did not know.[20] But Sartre was thinking of war and the contemporary technological state, while Redfield has the simpler "developing" peoples in mind—those who now discourage the visits of anthropologists to their countries on the ground that they no longer wish to be studied, or treated, as objects.

III

Ethics and the Social Good

Again we raise the questions: are ethical principles best defined as socially useful rules? Is the essence of moral behavior simply that kind of conduct that promotes social good? A plausible answer seems to be: it depends. It depends on how broadly or how narrowly we construe the terms *social rules* and *social good.* It is hard to deny that in some way all ethical behavior serves the social good, that "right" is what contributes to social welfare, and that "wrong" is what tends to destroy the common good. The very concept of *altruism* implies acting in such a way as to bring about the good of others in contrast to *egoism,* which means concentrating primarily on your own good. Altruism is a social concept, since by behaving altruistically I rate the good of others over my exclusive good. In addition, the very conditions of human life require that if that life is to be good it must be social; and if life is to be social, there must be rules of good behavior on the part of one person to another. Arthur Garnett *defines* "moral rule" as a rule of general applicability that is required for the welfare of the group as a whole:

Human beings cannot live well (and can scarcely live at all) except in social co-operation, and social co-operation cannot exist without rules. It is the characteristic of a rule that it shall apply equally to every person who is a member of a certain class, and a rule the intent of which is to bring about social co-operation must be a rule believed to direct conduct in ways that in general are for the good of the co-operating group. It is no accident, therefore, that these two characteristics, generalizability and contribution to social welfare, have become the defining characteristics for reflective recognition as "right" and approval as "good," of the basic rules whereby men require each other to live.[21]

A question remains: if ethical rules, when acted on, have the characteristic of tending to promote social welfare, must we conclude that this characteristic is a *defining* one? It seems that the quality of tending to promote social good is *one* mark of doing what is right. But is it the only one? Is it the central or defining characteristic? Is acting so as to increase social good the *essence* of morality?

A morally good deed can be done without the slightest intent on the part of the agent to promote social good. Countless good acts are performed every day without the slightest thought of society's good on the part of those who perform them. Further, if morality is defined in terms of the good of society, the question arises: is the society good? Suppose the social order is bad, what then? Marxist philosophers hold a strict social-utility view of ethics. But they argue that the moral good is not simply relative to each society, one of which is as good as another. Only the classless society, they say, will give all men the maximum opportunity for happiness. For this reason, ethics and morals are to be judged insofar as behavior according to their rules helps to build a better socialist society. But there may be a limiting factor in any such view. If the social-utility view of ethics is taken to imply that morality consists in conforming to rules imposed from without, this is morality conceived only as legislative or external. If morality is defined exclusively in terms of social rule, the autonomy of the individual person will be slighted.[22]

Henri Bergson claimed that there are *two sources* of morality. There are the "thou shalts" and "thou shalt nots" of society that are external to the individual person and tend to emphasize the *negative.* But there is as well the positive and internal "I love" of the human heart. According to Bergson, morality has its double origin in (1) necessary conformity to external rule, which society needs if it is to keep its stability, if it is not to be destroyed by the self-seeking drive of the individuals that compose it; (2) the inner impulse to move toward another and to prefer his or her good to our own. The first is the external morality of social command, a morality deriving from pressure without. The second is the internal morality of sympathy or love. A great world religion may contain a table of commandments forbidding certain acts destructive of the social organism *and* a doctrine of universal love. In the same way morality may depend on the necessity to conform to rules that protect and promote the good of the social group as a whole and yet flow from a deeper source too, from the impulse of love that comes not from external law but from somewhere close to the core of our being. Bergson called the first *static*, the second *dynamic* morality. Both are necessary. So long as men live together, morality can be traced to both sources. "The mistake would be," Bergson says, "to think that moral pressure [social rules] and moral aspiration [sympathy, love] find their final explanation in social life considered merely as a fact."[23]

NOTES: CHAPTER 2

1. Henri Bergson, *The Two Sources of Religion and Morality,* trans. R. A. Audra and C. B. Brereton (New York: Holt, Rinehart & Winston, 1935), p. 1.
2. Quoted by Conor Cruise O'Brien, "Camus, Algeria, and 'The Fall,'" *New York Review of Books,* 9 October 1969, p. 8.
3. Ina C. Brown, *Understanding Other Cultures* (Englewood Cliffs, N.J.: Prentice-Hall, 1963), p. 2.
4. Morton H. Fried, as quoted in *New York Times,* 20 November 1970, pp. 43, 83.
5. Charles Graham Sumner, *Folkways* (Boston: Ginn, 1906), p. 418.
6. Benedict's pages on the cult of peyote and jimson weed among the American Indians will interest admirers of Castaneda's Don Juan. According to Benedict, the orderly Pueblo had no use for these "Dionysian" practices. Ruth Benedict, *Patterns of Culture* (Boston: Houghton Mifflin, 1934), pp. 86–90. Carlos Castaneda, *The Teachings of Don Juan: A Yaqui Way of Knowledge* (Berkeley, Calif.: University of California Press, 1968).
7. Benedict, *Patterns of Culture,* p. 19.
8. Ibid.
9. Sumner, *Folkways,* p. 213.
10. The work of cultural anthropology is not limited simply to observing the behavior of primitive people and taking notes on it. Linguistics, kinship structure, and mythology are among the many areas of interest to anthropologists and ethnologists. Lévi-Strauss has analyzed elaborately certain myths of North and South American Indians in order to try to throw light on the unconscious thought structures present in them, structures that may be present in all human thinking. Claude Lévi-Strauss, *From Honey to Ashes. Introduction to a Science of Mythology,* trans. John and Doreen Wightman (New York: Harper & Row, 1973), vol. 2.
11. Lévi-Strauss, "Today's Crisis in Anthropology," in *Anthropology,* ed. Samuel Rapport and Helen Wright (New York: New York University Press, 1967), pp. 143–144.
12. Lévi-Strauss, "The Family," in Rapport and Wright, eds., *Anthropology,* p. 159.

13. Richard B. Brandt, *Hopi Ethics* (Chicago: University of Chicago Press, 1954).
14. Brandt, *Ethical Theory,* pp. 91–92.
15. W. C. Willoughby, *The Soul of the Bantu* (New York: Doubleday, 1928), pp. 382–383.
16. Ibid., p. 383.
17. Robert Redfield, *Human Nature and the Study of Society* (Chicago: University of Chicago Press, 1962), p. 440.
18. Ija Lazari-Pawlowska, "On Cultural Relativism," *Journal of Philosophy* 76 (1970): 581.
19. Robert Redfield, *The Primitive World and its Transformation* (Ithaca, N.Y., Cornell University Press, 1953), p. 164.
20. Jean-Paul Sartre, "Existentialism is a Humanism," in *Existentialism from Dostoyevsky to Sartre,* ed. Walter Kaufmann (Cleveland: World, 1956), p. 299.
21. Arthur Campbell Garnett, "A New Look at the Categorical Imperative," *Ethics* 74 (1964): 299.
22. For more on Soviet ethics, see Chapter 10.
23. Bergson, *Religion and Morality,* p. 91.

3

Happiness, Pleasure, and Utility

One of the best-known attempts of a modern moral philosopher to define morality in terms of social good is John Stuart Mill's *utilitarianism.* But Mill did not interpret the social good to mean the good of this or that particular society. To him, that good was the greatest possible happiness for everybody. The highest human good is happiness, and happiness derives from a favorable balance of pleasure over pain. From these premises Mill concluded that to act *rightly* is to act in such a way as to increase happiness. To act *wrongly* is to act so as to decrease it. In Mill's words:

The creed which accepts as the foundation of morals utility, or the greatest happiness principle, holds that actions are right in proportion as they tend to promote happiness. By happiness is intended pleasure and the absence of pain; unhappiness, pain and the privation of pleasure.[1]

The "greatest happiness" means not just my individual happiness, or yours, but the happiness of all. The standard of utilitarianism, says Mill, is not the maximum happiness of the person who is acting, but "the greatest amount of happiness altogether."

Mill's concept of "utility" is so wide that it passes well beyond what we would ordinarily understand as "social usefulness"—for example, one's saying that monogamy is good because it makes for a cohesive society. We sometimes use the word *utilitarian* to mean the immediately profitable or expedient, as when we say, "The principal took a pretty utilitarian view of the school music program." Mill did not use the word *utilitarian* primarily in these ways. To him an act is right and an end is good if that act or end tends to maximize happiness, not just my happiness or yours, but everybody's.

Mill's doctrine is simple and clear, at least on its surface. But it raises a number of important questions about the ideas basic to that doctrine. To begin with, what do we mean by "happiness" and "pleasure"? What is their place in moral theory and in the good life?

I

Is Happiness the Highest Good?

The notion that happiness is the highest good and that the concept of happiness must therefore be at the center of moral theory is as old as Aristotle.[2] Aristotle noted that there are many goods, or values (as we would say)—health, money, having children, friends, power, fame, and so on. But he asked whether there is a good that is higher or better than all the others and, if so, whether this highest good could be identified. Marks of this highest good *(summum bonum)* would be that (1) all men want it and (2) they want it for itself, for its own sake, and not because it is a means to some other good. According to Aristotle, most men say that this highest good is happiness. Mill agreed with the Greek philosopher. He took for granted that happiness is the highest good. We cannot *prove* that it is, says Mill, for "questions of ultimate ends are not amenable to direct proof. Whatever can be proved to be good must be so by being shown to be a means to something admitted to be good without proof."[3] The way we use the word *happiness* in ordinary conversation lends support to Mill's choice of happiness as the highest good. When we hear that somebody is going to be married, we say "I wish you happiness." When we are trying to dissuade someone from moving to Los Angeles, we say, "I don't think you'll be happy there." Bidding good-bye to a friend embarking on a new career, we say, "I hope you will be happy in your new work." We congratulate a couple who have adopted a child: "I know the baby will make you both very happy." Of a certain man we may observe, "He had fame, power, money, but somehow happiness eluded him"—a tacit admission that these things are goods or values, but *inferior* to happiness. We might have some trouble *defining* happiness, but most of us seem to have *some* idea of what it is when we use the word, and we rank whatever is referred to by the word very high indeed.

But *do* people in fact desire happiness above all other things, or do they just *say* they do? Is it not more likely that happiness pursued for its own sake is never found, that it is a by-product of other things achieved? What people really want seems to be some specific good—the boy wants his motorcycle, the scholar his book published, the sick man his health, the politician his office, the runner his race won. If we asked these people what they wanted those things *for,* would they reply "happiness" or "to be happy"? It may be that happiness *attends* our achieving this or that prized thing or goal, but this does not mean we want the desired object for the sake of happiness rather than for its own sake. People may *say* they marry to "find happiness," but what they really want is each other. What girl would not right-fully resent her lover's telling her that she was desired not for her own sake, but as a *means* to happiness? Mill himself seemed to admit that certain goods, such as health and aesthetic enjoy-ment, are wanted for their own sake and not as means or instru-ments. Nevertheless it is happiness we really want. Mill tries to get around the difficulty by saying that certain values, such as health and musical enjoyment, are *parts* of happiness and that is why we want them for their own sake:

The ingredients of happiness are very various, and each of them is de-sirable in itself, and not merely when considered as swelling and ag-gregate. The principle of utility does not mean that any given pleasure, as music, for instance, or any given exemption from pain, as for example health, is to be looked upon as means to a collective something termed happiness, and to be desired on that account. They are desired and desirable in and for themselves; besides being means, they are part of the end.[4]

Yet a page or two later in the same essay, Mill says that "there is in reality nothing desired except happiness."[5]

II

Happiness and Pleasure; Hedonism
In trying to explain what we mean by "happiness," we may stress its *objective* side; or we may emphasize its *subjective* or psycho-logical aspect. If we explain happiness as an objective state of affairs, we may define it in terms of certain objective conditions—having an interesting job, a fine family, friends, health, being a member of a just social order, and so on. The Greek philosophers tended to emphasize the objective side of happiness, or "well-being." In our day, certain social philosophers have reminded us that happiness has an objective side. For example, Herbert Marcuse: "The notion that happiness is an objective condition which demands more than subjective feelings has been effec-tively obscured; its validity depends on the real solidarity of the species man, which a society divided into antagonistic classes and nations cannot achieve."[6] But the common tendency has

been to lean toward the subjective or psychological dimension of happiness—to talk of it as an enduring kind of good feeling or satisfaction.

A well-known way of defining happiness in terms of subjective or psychological emphasis is to explain it as *pleasure*. Mill formally defined happiness in terms of pleasure. Right conduct is that which tends ultimately to increase pleasure; wrong conduct tends ultimately to decrease it:

The creed which accepts as the foundation of morals utility, or the greatest happiness principle, holds that actions are right in proportion as they tend to promote happiness, wrong as they tend to produce the reverse of happiness. By happiness is intended pleasure and the absence of pain: by unhappiness, pain and the privation of pleasure.[7]

That pleasure is the highest good, and that we should act in such a way as to increase pleasure and diminish pain, is one of the oldest ethical theories of the Western world. It is called *hedonism*. Hedonism, or pleasure theory, was well known to the Greek and Roman philosophers. In modern times, various forms or elements of hedonism have been held by a variety of moral philosophers including Hobbes, Hume, Mill himself, and Sidgwick, although the differences among the ethical theories of these men outweigh their similarities. Hedonism can be a way of life for any one of us, even if we have not been to a university and studied moral philosophy. It can be selfish or selfless, egoistic or altruistic, depending on the variety adopted. But all forms of hedonism agree that pleasure is, or goes to make up, the highest good.

Ancient Hedonism

Hedonism was taught as an ethical doctrine by certain ancient philosophical schools, such as the Cyrenaics and the Epicureans. Tradition has assigned the slogan, "Let us eat, drink, and be merry, for tomorrow we die," to the Epicureans. In modern drama, from Shakespeare and Jonson down through the eighteenth century, various self-indulgent tosspots are called "Epicures," a term that now means no more than a person of discrimination who is interested in the pleasures of the table. There is little evidence that Epicurus himself or any of his immediate disciples identified the good with an earthly paradise of sensual delights —rather, the reverse. Epicurus believed that the pleasures of the table, or getting drunk, were *mixed* pleasures—mixed with pain, that is, for pain is what comes the morning after. To Epicurus, the pleasures of love between the sexes are notoriously mixed. Lucretius, poet of the Epicureans, writes that lovers ". . . press the object of love so closely that it hurts and kiss each other so fiercely that lips are bruised by teeth, and this is because the pleasure is not unmixed and pure."[8] Love, like drunkenness, is fun while it lasts. But it carries with it doubts, bitterness, jealousy, hatred, disgust. So the pleasures of love are fatally "mixed."[9] Epicurus thought the pleasures of the mind were superior to those of the body. The blessed gods, he said, dwell in "the painless state" (*ataraxia*). This ideal condition is approached on earth by the wise man as he discusses philosophy and the classics with friends in his garden. Lucretius makes clear that the pleasure of the philosopher is not money, fame, power, or any of those "goods" aimed at by the majority of men:

. . . nothing is more delightful than having sanctuaries, fortified and serene, built by the wise men's teachings. From them you can look down upon mankind, and see them wandering, straying, and seeking a pathway of life, striving with their wits and fighting for empty honors, struggling night and day with unremitting toil to scale the heights of wealth and power and position.[10]

Now surely there is nothing self-indulgent or sensual in these high-minded sentiments. In fact, Epicurus's moral exhortations seem hardly different from those of any conventional sage of tradition who urges us to spurn the ordinary goods and ambitions of most people and to devote ourselves instead to a life of tranquil enjoyment and benevolent contemplation of noble things. Even G. E. Moore, who pinned the label "naturalistic fallacy" to every form of hedonism, seemed himself not far from Epicurus's ideal when he named personal affections and aesthetic enjoyments as the highest goods.[11]

Hedonism, Vulgar and Refined
There is practical hedonism. Many men and women live in pursuit of pleasure, and their pleasures are by no means exclusively the high-minded sort extolled by Epicurus. If some people define their lives in terms of good food, choice wines, fine clothes, cultivated sexual delights, and related gratifications of the senses, they are "practicing hedonists" in a sense of the term that is not austere. Sometimes such people raise their practical hedonism to the level of self-consciousness. They make a doctrine of their

way of life and defend the pursuit of pleasure as a moral ideal. A. E. Housman, poet and Oxford scholar, repeatedly stated, "In philosophy I am a Cyrenaic or egoistic Hedonist, and regard the pleasure of the moment as the only possible motive of action."[12] A nostalgic whiff of the 1930s accompanies the personal credo of George Jean Nathan, whose hedonism was of the earthly paradise sort:

As it is given to few men to die happy, the best that man can hope and strive and pray for is momentary happiness during life, repeated as frequently as the cards allow. Pleasure, whatever its species, is the drink in the desert. It is the beautiful transient reward to travail and pain. There is no other reward except for those still sufficiently aboriginal to believe in a hereafter.

The ambrosia of the gods, the lovely angels, eternal blue skies and peace, the music of golden harps, are too far off and dubious so far as my own metaphysics goes. I prefer to trust to the more realistic and visible Grand Montrachet, pretty girls, Mediterranean coast and symphony orchestras of the here and now.[13]

Mixed fragrances of the 1960s attend the reflections of Hugh Hefner, whose popular illustrated magazine *Playboy* has afforded a variety of visual and other delights to a generation of young American males of cheerfully indiscriminate tastes. Contrary to what one might expect, there is comparatively little hedonism in Hefner's book *The Playboy Philosophy*. The tone of the volume is earnest, even moralistic. Hefner supports his moralism by citing David Boroff's summarization of American sexual attitudes after World War II: "Sex is one of life's principal goods. The degree of pleasure one derives from it is a measure of one's self-realisation." Paul Goodman is added: "In sex, anything you get pleasure from is good, and that's all there is to it."[14] To the pleasures of sex, *The Playboy Philosophy* adds practical materialism. To acquire attractive material goods has the laudable effect of stimulating the growth of American capitalism:

The acquisition of property—and in the 1960s property may mean a handsome bachelor pad, elaborate hi-fi rig and the latest sports car—is the cornerstone of our American economic system. And a publication that helps motivate a part of our society to work harder, to accomplish more, to earn more, in order to enjoy more of the material benefits described—to that extent, the publication is contributing to the economic growth and strength of the nation.[15]

Certain French writers of the late nineteenth century were fond of constructing ideal models of practical hedonism in which the pleasures of the senses were carefully studied and carried to heights of sensibility, extreme and *raffiné*. Notable among these was Joris-Karl Huysmans, whose famous novel *Against the Grain* became the bible of aspiring hedonists of the artistic sort. The "poisonous book" that corrupted Oscar Wilde's hero Dorian Gray was none other than *Against the Grain,* Huysmans's fictional chronicle of his *alter ego,* the rich and hyper-aesthetic Des Esseintes. Repelled by the vulgarity of Paris humanity, the young French aristocrat retreats to an isolated country house especially constructed so as to wall out the sights and sounds of the everyday world. Wealthy enough to indulge his tastes, Des Esseintes places on his rug a huge tortoise whose shell has been plated with gold and sprayed with jewels. Lovingly he handles rare books bound in cold-pressed leather or wild asses' skin. He plays his "mouth organ," a miniature harmonium that pours out and mixes various liquors into tiny cups when the keys are "played," and eats bonbons, into each of which has been carefully distilled a single drop of "essence of woman." Less innocent pleasures include Des Esseintes achieving delight by having his mistress of the hour, a skilled ventriloquist, imitate the noise of an outraged husband shouting to be let in. When he is tired of that, the ingenious hedonist has the ventriloquist (she is bored to tears with the whole thing) recite the dialogue between Chimera and the Sphinx in Flaubert's novel *The Temptation of Saint Anthony:*

"Here Chimera, stop, I say."
"No, never . . . I seek new perfumes, ampler blossoms, untried pleasures."[16]

Pleasures
and Pains

Though the pleasures aspired to by the heroes of *Against the Grain* and *Playboy* may differ in degree of refinement, they contain common ingredients of sexual gratification and self-indulgence. Pleasure need not be defined that way; in fact, "pleasure" is one of those accordianlike concepts that stretch or compress almost according to the will of those who write about it. In ethical theory "pleasure" can range all the way from gross sensual stimulation to the most lofty and high-minded tranquility. Certainly Mill seemed to think the most preferable pleasures were those of the mind. Hume, as we shall see, took "pleasure" to mean "agreeableness" or "satisfaction." Both philosophers insisted that the highest morality requires a sharing, a social distribution of pleasures.

What is pleasure? Its antonym is "pain." But unlike physical pain, pleasure is hard to localize. We say, "My toe hurts" or "I have a pain in my shoulder." But we do not often speak of having a pleasure in a particular part of ourselves. We do not say, "I have a pleasure in my finger" or "There is an exquisite little pleasure in my foot"—though we may say, when feeling a cold shower on the back of the neck, "That feels good!" More often we use the word "pleasure" in a broader sense, even when referring to states of bodily good feeling. We all know what it means to "please" people—without need to account for the fact that the pleasure cannot be located in a particular place. Neither mental pleasure nor mental pain can be located, and yet we know by experience how intense they can be.

Sometimes we speak of pleasure as if it were a feeling that occurs at a particular time—"He blushed with pleasure when the governor complimented him." By contrast, we sometimes talk of pleasure as continuing enjoyment—"I had a very pleasant talk with Bill after the meeting." Sometimes we mention pleasure as if it were some kind of object or goal—"Those who prefer Grand Montrachet and pretty girls are pleasure-seekers." Plato spoke of pleasure as a replenishment, a making-up of a deficiency; often he dismissed pleasure as no more than the scratch of an itch.[17] But he did admit the existence of certain pleasures that are pure and unmixed, like the smell of a rose.[18] Aristotle spoke of pleasure as something that accompanies unimpeded activity—as we would say that we enjoyed a walk, not for the sake of getting somewhere, but "for the pleasure of walking." The pleasure of skiing, skating, dancing, swimming, surfing, running, and so on, seems inseparable from the free exercise of the faculties involved. Augustine held that pleasure is a passion or emotion and linked it to the *will* and its satisfaction. Aquinas defined pleasure as the *arrest* of desire for a loved object, "the enjoyment of the possession of an object where desire does not fail."[19] Many philosophers distinguish pleasure from happiness by pointing to the fact that pleasures are transient and fade quickly, while happiness may endure. Yet others, like Mill, *define* happiness in terms of pleasure.

Higher and Lower Pleasures:
Does Hedonism Contradict Itself?

Both Mill and Bentham defined happiness, the highest good, in terms of maximum pleasure. But Bentham understood pleasure to be something quantitative and open to measurement. *More* pleasure is simply the heightening of pleasure, and this increase is at least in principle capable of being calculated. Mill modified this Bethamite hedonism in an important respect. Although he defined happiness as pleasure, he insisted that there are qualitatively different *kinds* of pleasure. Some pleasures are "lower" or "grosser," others "higher" or "nobler," the former generally being "bodily" pleasures, the latter "intellectual," or pleasures of the mind. Mill writes: "It is quite compatible with the principle of utility to recognize the fact that some kinds of pleasures are more desirable and more valuable than others."[20] He saw that to maintain hedonism in a simply quantitative form would lead to awkward conclusions. Higher pleasures would just be *more* pleasure. Besides, if all pleasures were alike in quality and differed only in quantity, there would be no reason to suppose that human happiness would be any different from that of a pig. If *knowledge,* said Plato, were no more than *sensation,* then a pig or a dog-faced baboon would know as much, if not more, as Socrates or Protagoras.[21] Similarly, Mill reasoned that if the highest pleasure is no more than maximum quantity of pleasure, then the enjoyment of a styful of swine wallowing in the mud would be no different than a human's enjoyment of personal affections and aesthetic satisfactions. "It is better to be a human being dissatisfied than a pig satisfied," Mill declares. "Better to be Socrates dissatisfied than a fool satisfied."[22]

But if we are to distinguish between "higher" and "lower" pleasures, the former to be pursued rather than the latter, the question arises: how are we to know which pleasure is higher and which lower? Here, for example, is the pleasure of discoursing on women's rights with Harriet Taylor, and there is the pleasure of getting drunk on Saturday night. On the one hand there is the joy of listening to Brahms' First Symphony and on the other, the pleasure of scratching an itch. Which is higher and how do we know? Mill firmly rejects any attempt to settle this question by appeal to *intuition,* by which Mill understood a form of knowledge that could not be publicly confirmed in experience. The test he proposes is to ask those people who have had experience of *both* higher and lower pleasures. Mill claims that by far the greater number of these people have shown by their actions that the higher pleasures are preferred: "Of two pleasures, if there be one to which all or almost all who have experience of both give a decided preference, irrespective of any feeling of moral obligation to prefer it, that is the more desirable pleasure."[23] According to Mill's way of thinking, if you or I were to have experienced *both* the pleasure of getting drunk in the local tavern on Saturday night *and* the pleasure of listening to fine music, we would both unhesitatingly state that the latter was preferable. Mind you, I do not mean Mill would say that, if you take a lout away from his bottle and merely expose him to the playing of a Beethoven quartet, you will thus get a vote for the quartet as the preferable pleasure. No, the man would have had to *experience* both pleasures before rating the latter higher. Nor would Mill hold that you or I, knowing that a pleasure close at hand was lower and a pleasure not nearly as available was higher, would necessarily postpone gratification of the first because we honestly esteem the second more valuable. Men with weak character, says Mill, will often choose the nearer good, though they know it to be less valuable. "This is no less when the choice is between two bodily pleasures," he claims; such men "pursue sensual indulgences to the injury of health, though perfectly aware that health is the greater good."[24]

A second difficulty dogs the hedonist whenever he admits that there are different kinds of pleasures, higher, lower, nobler, grosser, and so on: when we admit, as Mill did, that some pleasures are higher than others, do we not by that very distinction affirm the presence of a factor that *makes* these pleasures lower and higher? Here are two pleasures, one higher, one lower. The first must possess some quality—say, X—by virtue of which it is higher than the second one. But then it must be the X factor that is the good thing about the first pleasure, not the pleasure element alone. The criterion by means of which we distinguish between the *qualities* of pleasures can hardly itself be a pleasure principle, unless "higher" pleasure means merely an increase in the *quantity* of pleasure—which Mill denies.

Any hedonist must answer this challenge: do you distinguish between the pleasures? are some better than others? If the hedonist answers yes, some pleasures are better than others, he must then deal with the question: what is it about the "better" pleasure that makes it "better"? If he holds that pleasures differ in quality, that there are genuine differences in pleasures not merely in degree but in kind, then he cannot escape the conclusion that the pleasures must differ in virtue of some factor that is not pleasure. But this seems to show that hedonism is self-contradictory. The highest good cannot be pleasure, since pleasures are ranked according to some qualitative factor that is not itself pleasure. The hedonist may avoid the difficulty by claiming that "better" pleasures are simply *more* pleasure, or that they *last longer.* He may say, with Jeremy Bentham, "Prejudice apart, the game of pushpin is of equal value with the arts and sciences of music and poetry."[25] But it seems odd to claim that the enjoyment of listening to the last twenty bars of the prelude to *Parsifal* is to be rated higher than the enjoyment of smelling a rose or scratching an itch simply because the musical pleasure lasts longer.

III

Hume on Pleasure and Utility

Nearly a century before Mill, the Scottish philosopher David Hume explained the foundations of morality in terms of pleasure and utility. Like Mill, Hume did not restrict the term *pleasure* to specific enjoyments of the senses like eating, drinking, bodily comfort, sexual gratification. Rather, he used the word pretty generally to mean any kind of "agreeable" state, just as he used "pain" to cover any kind of "disagreeable" state. In fact, Hume admitted that in the end one must stop somewhere in one's explanation, and one might as well stop with pleasure and pain as first principles that need no further explanation. Hume claimed that our actions spring not only from regard of Self, but also from our sympathy with our fellowman. The reason why we have this humane feeling for other people itself goes back to the ultimate principles of pleasure and pain:

It is needless to push our researches so far as to ask, why we have humanity or a fellow-feeling with others. It is sufficient, that this is experienced to be a principle in human nature. We must stop somewhere in our examination of causes; and there are, in every science, some general principles, beyond which we cannot hope to find any principle more general. No man is absolutely indifferent to the happiness and misery of others. The first has a natural tendency to give pleasure; the second pain. This every one may find in himself. . . .[26]

Later, Mill's way of making the same point was to say that whatever can be proved to be a good must be so by being shown to be a means to something admitted to be a good without proof. Action A is good because it tends to produce pleasure; action B is bad because it tends to produce pain. Explanations as to *why* pleasure is a good and pain an evil are superfluous.

Hume's simple moral theory amounts to this in summary: All moral judgments are expressions of *approval* or *disapproval.* Most men agree in approving certain actions (keeping one's word) and disapproving certain others (treachery). The actions most men approve are those that are *useful* in promoting agreeable feelings or happiness. The actions most men disapprove of are those that tend to promote disagreeable feelings or unhappiness. The foundation of *virtues* (those actions or dispositions most men tend morally to approve of) is *utility.* The virtue of justice is useful in protecting life and property. Honesty, fidelity, and truthfulness are virtues in that they tend to promote the interests of society and, as a consequence, are an advantage to the person displaying them. The utility of chastity and fidelity in marriage is plain. Says Hume:

> The long and helpless infancy of man requires the combination of parents for the subsistence of their young; and that combination requires the virtue of chastity or fidelity to the marriage bed. Without such a *utility,* it will readily be owned, that such a virtue would never have been thought of.[27]

In sum, the actions most men approve of are *useful* to society; they tend to increase general happiness. The actions most men disapprove of are *destructive* to society; they tend to increase general unhappiness. The sight or knowledge of a good deed (an act of mercy or humaneness, say) arouses a positive moral sentiment in us—we experience an agreeable feeling as we approve of the action that is its cause. The sight or knowledge of a bad deed (an act of cruelty or treachery, say) wakens a negative moral sentiment in us—a disagreeable feeling attending the disapproval of the act that is its cause:

> The hypothesis which we embrace is plain. It maintains that morality is determined by sentiment. It defines virtue to be whatever mental action or quality gives to the spectator the pleasing sentiment of approbation; and vice the contrary. We then proceed to examine a plain matter of fact, to wit, what actions have this influence.[28]

Hume, it seems, would believe that a factual examination of those actions we approve of would show a positive correlation between approval and social usefulness. But Hume said that we do not refer every virtue directly to its social utility in order to approve of it. Certain virtues come in time to acquire a radiance of their own, and we enjoy the spectacle of these virtues as *agreeable in themselves:*

The utility of courage, both to the public and to the person possessed of it, is an obvious foundation of merit. But to any one who duly considers of the matter, it will appear that this quality has a peculiar lustre which it derives wholly from itself and from the noble elevation inseparable from it.[29]

Hume's moral theory, then, appears to be an earlier version of utilitarianism. Most men approve of certain acts, disapprove of others. This evaluation rests on whether an act tends to promote or to diminish general happiness. What hedonism there is in Hume's theory (he said that happiness is ultimately explainable in terms of increase of pleasure or agreeable feelings and decrease of pain) is not selfish, nor narrowly and exclusively egoistic. Of course, I seek my own happiness, but this I could not find if I had to endure the sight of other people's misery. Because of an inborn and natural sentiment of *sympathy,* the sight of another's pleasure gives me pleasure; the sight of another's pain gives me pain. The comprehensive virtues of *benevolence* and *humanity* are developments of this natural sympathetic sentiment.

Some critics of Hume's ethical theory claim that this moral philosophy is no more than enlightened egoism. According to Hume, I wish and strive for the pleasure of others because that pleasure is agreeable *to me.* I do not want others to be in pain, and I will try to reduce the suffering of my fellows because the spectacle of their misery is disagreeable *to me.* If we put this charge to Hume, he might answer in this way: First, an enlightened egoism is not a self-evidently false moral theory. Acting out of enlightened egoism may lead to consequences just as helpful to the common good as acting in accord with some nonegoist or altruist theory. Second, while concern for others may *spring* from the fact that their pleasure is agreeable and their pain disagreeable to me, that sentiment may, by cultivating and extending it, reach a point of development where it becomes relatively independent of its source and will display a "peculiar lustre" and "noble elevation" of its own. If we now move from Hume's particular moral theory to Mill's ethical teaching once again, we may see some further light on the utilitarian attitude toward egoism and altruism.

IV

Utilitarianism:
the Self and Others; Egoism and Altruism

According to utilitarianism, (1) the highest good is happiness, (2) happiness consists in maximum pleasure and minimum pain, (3) *right* is what tends to increase happiness, and (4) *wrong* is what tends to decrease it. The utilitarian stresses that the highest good is not just *my* happiness. To hold that my individual happiness is the highest good would be *egoism*, and egoism is false. Mill says:

> The utilitarian standard of what is right in conduct is not the agent's own happiness but that of all considered. As between his own happiness and that of others, utilitarianism requires him to be as strictly impartial as a disinterested and benevolent spectator. In the golden rule of Jesus of Nazareth, we read the complete spirit of the ethics of utility. "To do as you would be done by," and "to love your neighbor as yourself," constitute the ideal perfection of utilitarian morality.[30]

But how do I know that egoism is false? How can a man know that his own good, to which he so naturally devotes himself, is not the highest good? Why should I not put my own good first? Why should I subordinate my own happiness to the happiness of others? In short, how does Mill's ethical theory get over the jump from *egoism* to *altruism,* from *my* happiness to the happiness of *all.* There is no jump necessary, Mill would reply. Man is naturally a social being, naturally sympathetic to others as well as self-seeking. The simplest common reasoning tells me that my individual good no more constitutes the *summum bonum* than my individual existence constitutes the whole of society. In man's social origin and social nature, Mill found the foundation of care for "the other." Given the social condition of man, it is evident to any intelligent being that the interests of all should be consulted. Aggrandizing the self, "looking out for Number One," cannot be the highest good, for the self is transient and passes away. The human community endures.

Now an objector might say to the utilitarian: "True enough; I grant that the good of the whole—the general happiness—is more important than the good of my individual self. I know I am not the only pebble on the beach, the only catfish in the sea. But suppose I don't *want* to subordinate my good to that of others? Why *should* I care for others? 'Society' is an abstract word to me, and I am not inclined to prefer society's good to my own.

Suppose I just don't wish to maximize general happiness, what then?" "Well, in the first place," the utilitarian might reply "you don't have to think of the ethical act as working directly for the good of society as a whole. One works for the good of society by working for the good of those close to him rather than those remote from him. There is nothing abstract about that. Second, there is no reason why you must think that the morally right thing to do always requires you to put yourself and your good in second place to somebody else's. The action that tends to promote the greatest happiness may be, and often is, the action that produces happiness for you as well. Helping a poor child, seeing that a man gets a job, arranging for a prisoner to get a fair deal, and a thousand other right acts of this kind need not subordinate your good in the sense it makes you less happy. Such acts tend to promote your happiness together with the happiness of all concerned. Accepting a judgeship, a presidential cabinet appointment, a school superintendency or the post of lead guitar in a rock group would increase your happiness tremendously, let us say. But—assuming that you are competent in that special area—your acceptance promises to increase the general happiness. Indeed, it is for this end rather than the increase of your individual happiness that the post was offered you in the first place."

But we must admit, the utilitarian would remind us, that there *are* times when the greatest happiness is served by suppressing or giving up one's own good. That is why self-sacrifice is one of the highest virtues, if not the highest. As to the questions, Why should I sacrifice my good on these occasions? Why should I sacrifice myself for others? the utilitarian would reply that, first, no one is going to compel you physically. And the day is still a long way off—although it will doubtless come—when the feeling of unity with our fellowman becomes so strong as to have the compulsive force of absolute religious commands. But in the meantime, said Mill, there *are* sanctions, there are compulsions —more or less subtle—that help incline us to act in such a way as to benefit the good of others. There are *external* sanctions— hope of social approval, fear of social disapproval. There is the *internal* sanction of *conscience,* which Mill believed to be an acquired faculty—a feeling of pain when we go against our duty. Our duty is to act in such a way as to promote, not our individual happiness at the expense of others, not even our individual happiness that does not detract from others, but the greatest happiness of the greatest number. And *conscience* is our consciousness, our awareness, of that duty. To Mill, the foundation of *duty* lies in the beneficial results of our actions; in this, the utilitarian must oppose Kant, who believed, as we shall see, that duty is its own foundation.

There is another question. Utilitarianism requires that for my act to be moral I must act in such a way as to promote the greatest happiness of the greatest number. But it seems absurd to suggest that I must weigh every potentially right or wrong act according to the criterion of maximizing happiness. There are many acts that I may perform—such as keeping a promise or refusing to lie—that simply do not seem referrable to the general happiness principle. I refuse to lie, in a given case, not because this leads to general happiness, but because such an action would violate a rule I respect, "Tell the truth." Here is a contract to which I have signed my name. I honor this contract, not because such honoring maximizes happiness, but because I firmly believe in the rule, "People should keep their promises." There are many acts of justice, which are surely moral, but which actually bring about pain—such as depriving a child of a holiday because of his serious misbehavior or sentencing a young criminal to detention. In this light, how can it be said that every moral act must fall under the greatest happiness principle?

Mill would reply that the difficulties here may lie in our confusing the *ultimate ground* of moral rules (the greatest happiness principle) with the moral rules we refer to immediately and directly as guides for action. These rules are secondary to the greatest happiness principle, but they are of primary influence in the direct guidance of what we do or refrain from doing. These rules include the ordinary precepts of moral common sense that spring from the social situation in which every human being finds himself—"Tell the truth," "Keep your promises," "Do not mutilate another human," and so forth. These rules of common morality are based on the shared experience of human beings over untold thousands of years. Thus when I act morally, I need not act *directly* in accord with the greatest happiness principle, but with a particular moral rule in mind; for example, "He who has plenty should share with others" and "Refrain from inflicting needless suffering on animals."[31] What we *do* have to admit, if we are utilitarians, is that these rules of common-sense morality are themselves ultimately founded on the greatest happiness principle. So the utilitarian would say: if you ask me whether you should honor this contract, I would say yes, because it falls under the rule, "Keep your promises." The act is justified according to this rule and needs no further explanation. But suppose this question is asked: what is the *basis* of the moral rule, "Keep your promises"? The utilitarian would reply that *all* rules of common morality ultimately derive their validity from the greatest happiness principle. That principle is their ultimate foundation. Promises should be kept because acting in this way, when made general practice, tends to promote universal happiness. It would be a stupidly *literal* understanding of utilitarianism that would make out that, before I help a child, attend a school-board meeting, or refrain from telling a lie, I must first dither over the question as to whether these proposed actions will or will not lead to universal happiness.

Utilitarianism: An Ethic of Consequences

If we hold, as utilitarians do, that right is what tends to increase happiness and that wrong is what tends to decrease it, then utilitarianism is an ethics of *consequences*. That is, the moral worth of an act lies in the good results that act will tend to produce. Good results, in turn, are defined by the utilitarian as results that tend to maximize happiness. Of course, there is always the question of the part played by *motive* or *intention* in the moral situation. We know that people sometimes do good deeds for unworthy motives or produce bad results out of good intentions. Consider the case of two men, each of whom gives a million dollars to a hospital. The first man acts, let us suppose, from motives of vainglory; he wants to get his name in the papers and on the front of the building. The other man gives anonymously, out of a sense of obligation to help others, and he does it without expecting thanks or reward. Do we not judge the second superior to the first? Yes, the utilitarian replies, if it is clear that we are judging the moral worth of the doer of the deed and not the rightness of the act itself. The two *agents* may differ in moral worth, but the two *acts,* since they have identical good results, come off in Mill's book with the same ethical gold stars:

. . . the motive has nothing to do with the morality of the action, though much with the worth of the agent. He who saves a fellow creature from drowning does what is morally right, whether his motive be duty or the hope of being paid for his trouble; he who betrays the friend that trusts him is guilty of a crime, even if his object be to serve another friend to whom he is under greater obligation.[32]

In so locating the worth of the moral act in its results or consequences, Mill opposed Kant, who (as we shall see) linked the
worth of the moral act with the purity of the doer's motive.

There is a well-known objection to utilitarianism's emphasis on
the part of *consequences* in the moral act, an objection that requires us to make a fantastic hypothesis. Let us admit for the
sake of argument that the utilitarian is right, that the worth of an
act is measured entirely by its results and that these results lead
to the net increase of human happiness as a whole. Now let us
imagine that the happiness of the whole human race were to
be immeasurably increased—poverty eliminated, brotherhood
achieved, disease conquered, adequate food and shelter provided for all, plus every other good thing you can think of. All
of this will be granted to the human race, but on one condition.
The condition is that one man, his life miraculously prolonged,
is to be kept *involuntarily* in a state of continuous and agonizing
torture. According to the utilitarian criterion, which measures the
rightness of an act by its results, it would seem that the bargain
is justified. One man only will be kept in constant torment, but
the rest of mankind will be relieved of evil forever. It would appear that the net balance of the utilitarian's moral scale would
have to point in the direction of maximum happiness and away
from the eternal calvary of that single suffering man. But most
people who consider the proposed bargain feel that there is
something terribly wrong about it. How could we possibly agree
to it? Bergson says:

Well, we should perhaps agree to it on the understanding that some
magic philtre is going to make us forget it, that we shall never hear anything more about it; but if we were bound to know it, to think of it, to
realize that this man's hideous torture was the price of our existence,
that it was even the fundamental condition of existence in general, no!
. . . Better to accept that nothing should exist at all! Better let our
planet be blown to pieces.[33]

Bergson believed that our instinctive protest against this bizarre
arrangement springs from our conviction that it is *unjust.* But this
seems to imply that justice is something more than utility, that
the greatest happiness principle cannot be the foundation, or at
least the only foundation, of moral right. Mill, when talking of
justice, seems to insist to the contrary; he held that all cases of
justice are also cases of expediency (utility), that justice is only
a particular kind or branch of general utility—useful, that is, in
leading to general happiness.[34] But at the same time Mill sup-

ported the rule that everybody has an equal right to be happy. The greatest happiness principle, he says, "is a mere form of words without rational signification unless one person's happiness, supposed equal in degree (with the proper allowance made for kind) is counted exactly the same as another's."[35] It is on this ground that we know Mill would reject the mythical arrangement as unjust. But it seems to the critic of utilitarianism that Mill wants it two ways, holding two principles that are inconsistent with one another: first, that the rightness of an action is measured wholly by its contribution to the general happiness (or to ends that will themselves be means to the general happiness); second, that no single individual, not even one person, should be treated unjustly. Mill firmly claimed that the *equal* happiness principle was a *part* of his general happiness criterion. But critics of utilitarianism have continued to urge this difficulty as an example of a limitation pertaining to any moral theory that locates the *right* entirely in the *results* of an action.

An Alternative to Utilitarianism:
Rawls's Justice as Fairness

The way utilitarianism tends to trip between the greatest happiness principle and the idea of justice becomes clearer when utilitarianism is offered as a social or political theory. This is John Rawls's argument in *A Theory of Justice*.[36] If justice is taken as fairness, then the greatest happiness principle will not produce a good result. For suppose the oppression or even enslavement of a small part of a given society is the condition of such great satisfaction to the large majority that the happiness of that society taken as a whole outweighs the unhappiness of the small oppressed minority. According to utilitarianism's greatest happiness principle, such a society would be justified, but according to the rule of justice as fairness, it would not.

Rawls asks us to imagine ourselves as free, rational and disinterested beings entering into a social contract with one another to form a just society. As we make the agreement, there is a *veil of ignorance* before our eyes concealing our individual places in that society. We do not know what our place or condition will be. We do not know whether we will be man or woman, employer or employee, healthy or ill, well or modestly paid. We do not know what profession or job we are going to have, nor whether we will have positions of great or very limited responsibility. Now what principles of justice shall we have for this society?

Rawls proposes two principles, the first of which has priority over the second. First, each person is to have an equal right to the maximum liberty consistent with a similar liberty for others. Second, social and economic inequalities are to be so arranged that they will be to everybody's advantage, including the worst off. Everyone will have an equal chance to try for and hold any job or profession. The basic liberties will include political liberty, the right to hold personal property, freedom from arbitrary arrest and seizure under a concept of law that will deal impartially with all who come under its rule. The second principle allows inequalities of wealth and income, but only on the condition that such inequalities work to the advantage of all. To illustrate Rawls's second principle, we may imagine an orthopedic surgeon with a very high income as a member of this society. The surgeon will be allowed to enjoy his income, provided that his skills contribute to the welfare of all, including those who have less than himself. The assumption is that such a society *without* the services of the highly paid surgeon would be worse off than a society that can take advantage of his skills.

Such an ideal social arrangement, Rawls believes, is better than the utilitarian model. It preserves the utilitarian value of increasing the general happiness, yet avoids the danger of injustice utilitarianism risks by making the general happiness the highest good, without paying enough attention to the question of fairness to each member of the society. If the maximum amount of general happiness is secured by a social arrangement that requires the oppression and suffering of a minority, then such a social arrangement is unfair, hence unjust. Rawls's second principle permits inequalities—of income, of office, of privilege and power, *only* on the condition that these inequalities contribute to the well-being of each and all. We must remember that the distribution of liberty under the first principle remains prior to that of other primary goods (like income or power) under the second principle. Members of the society cannot swap or trade off liberties in exchange for desired inequalities under the second principle. (Here one might ask what sense it makes to say we shall agree to distribute liberties before we decide on what kind of social and economic arrangements we shall have.)

Mill's greatest happiness principle and Rawls's rule of justice as fairness are norms or ideals, rather than actual facts. Neither moralist claims that societies actually exist which fulfill their conditions or even that there will ever be such societies. Each principle—maximum happiness or justice as fairness—is offered as a model to clarify what we mean when we try to define the highest social good. Each represents an ideal to work toward, even though the best we may ever hope to achieve is a seriously imperfect approximation of that ideal.

Of course, we may reject both models as giving too much weight to the ideal of social equality. If the butter is spread over the entire loaf may it not be too thin everywhere? Critics like Nietzsche would ask how in such circumstances the human race could ever be further ennobled, how it could produce future spiritual or artistic elites, superb life-styles, future Shakespeares or Racines, Michelangelos or Dantes, Goethes, Bachs or Picassos. Would not all these have to be renounced as the price of happiness shared by all equally and justly? Professor Irving Kristol is astonished to find what he takes to be Rawls's argument that a social order is just and legitimate *only* to the degree that it is directed to the redress of inequality. He too is worried about the threat to the ideal of human excellence allegedly posed by so much emphasis on the principle of equality.[37] One answer is that it would be as hard to prove that maximum happiness, equality, and justice as fairness would *not* be the soil of future individual greatness or ennoblement of the human race, as it would be to prove that they *would*.

NOTES: CHAPTER 3

1. John Stuart Mill, *Utilitarianism* (New York: Liberal Arts Press, 1949), p. 7. Mill's essay first appeared in 1863. Its thesis was an extension of a theory he had first learned from his father, James Mill, and from his father's friend Jeremy Bentham. The latter called it "the greatest happiness principle." According to Bentham, "An action is conformable to the principle of utility when the tendency to augment the happiness of the community is greater than any it has to diminish it." *The Principles of Morals and Legislation* (1789; New York: Hafner, 1948), p. 3.
2. An ethical theory that makes happiness the highest good is called *eudaemonism,* from the Greek word for happiness or well-being. Aristotle's ethics are discussed in Chapter 5.
3. Mill, *Utilitarianism,* p. 4.
4. Ibid., p. 39.
5. Ibid., p. 41.

6. Herbert Marcuse, *An Essay on Liberation* (Boston: Beacon, 1969), p. 14.
7. Mill, *Utilitarianism,* p. 7.
8. Titus Lucretius Carus, *On the Nature of Things,* trans. William E. Leonard (New York: Dutton, 1957), 1079–1081.
9. In a famous Chinese novel, a Buddhist priest and a Taoist monk express a similar thought: "Every happiness is spoiled by a certain lack and all good things are poisoned by the envy and covetousness of other men, so that in the end you will find the pleasure outweighed by sorrow and sadness." Tsao Hsueh-chin, *Dream of the Red Chamber,* trans. Chi-chen Wang (Garden City, N.Y.: Doubleday, 1968).
10. Lucretius, *Nature of Things,* 7–13.
11. G. E. Moore, *Principia Ethica,* chap. 6, "The Ideal" (1903; London: Cambridge University Press, 1951).
12. Quoted in a review of *The Letters of A. E. Housman,* ed. Henry Maas Hart-Davis, London *Times Literary Supplement,* 17 December, 1971, p. 1573.
13. Quoted in George Jean Nathan's obituary, *New York Times,* 9 April 1958.
14. Hugh M. Hefner, *The Playboy Philosophy,* 4 pts. (Chicago: HMH Publishing, 1962–1965), 2:53.
15. Ibid., 1:13.
16. Joris-Karl Huysmans, *Against the Grain* (New York: Illustrated Editions, 1931), p. 205. The Sphinx-Chimera dialogue occurs in Gustave Flaubert's novel *The Temptation of St. Anthony,* chap. 7.
17. Plato *Phaedo* 60, in *The Dialogues of Plato,* trans. Benjamin Jowett, 2 vols. (New York: Random House, 1937), vol. 1. In all footnotes, numbers in citations from Plato refer to the Stephens marginal numbers common to all editions of the Platonic dialogues.
18. Plato *Philebus* 32.
19. This is how Aquinas is rendered by Professor G. E. M. Anscombe, to whose analysis of pleasure I am here indebted. J. G. B.
20. Mill, *Utilitarianism,* p. 8.
21. Plato *Theaetetus* p. 161.
22. Mill, *Utilitarianism,* p. 10.
23. Ibid., p. 9.
24. Ibid., pp. 10–11.
25. Bentham, *The Rationale of Reward* (London: 1825), p. 206.
26. David Hume, *An Enquiry Concerning the Principles of Morals* (1777; LaSalle, Ill.: Open Court, 1938), p. 54 n.1.
27. Ibid., p. 41.

28. Ibid., p. 129.

29. Ibid., p. 90.

30. Mill, *Utilitarianism,* p. 18.

31. Ibid., pp. 35–36.

32. Ibid., p. 19.

33. Henri Bergson, *The Two Sources of Religion and Morality,* trans. R. A. Audra and C. Brereton (New York: Holt, Rinehart & Winston, 1935), p. 67.

34. Mill, *Utilitarianism,* pp. 46, 69.

35. Ibid., p. 67.

36. John Rawls, *A Theory of Justice* (Cambridge, Mass.: Harvard University Press, Belknap, 1972), pp. 60–65.

37. Irving Kristol, "About Equality," *Commentary,* November, 1972, pp. 41–47.

4

Duty and Persons

A simple classification of ethical theories divides the ethics of *duty* from the ethics of *happiness.* A morality of duty teaches that every act is to be judged in terms of obedience to a moral rule, principle, or law; the basic moral distinction is between right and wrong. A morality of happiness holds that an act should be judged in terms of the end aimed at; the basic moral distinction is between good and bad. An ethics of happiness stresses the goodness of the end or goal to which we aspire. An ethic of duty emphasizes the rightness of the act itself. An ethics of duty examines the intent and motive of the one who acts. An ethics of happiness tends to look to the results, the consequences of the act. The morality of duty *(deontological* ethics) says that we should do right for its own sake—because it is right. The morality of happiness (*eudaemonist* ethics) says that we should do right because it leads to what is good, ultimately toward the highest good—which is happiness.

I

The Concept of Duty

Happiness has a pleasant sound, but the word *dut*y has a very unappealing ring today. If we asked a group of undergraduates to choose between a morality of duty and one of happiness, probably they would vote unanimously for the morality of happiness and let moral philosophers have the other if they wished. Personal individualism still rates high today, with its stress on the individual self, unique and interesting, with all its feelings, thoughts, and right to judge. But a moment's reflection on the morality of common sense will tell us that even today we take the concept of duty very much into account in the conduct of our own life and in our moral evaluations of other people. Perhaps we call it by some other name—"responsibility" or "moral obligation"—or we may simply say, "It goes with the job." The concept of duty is present all the same. If I marry, I take on certain duties (responsibilities, obligations) toward my partner. If we have children, I am by that fact "stuck" with certain duties or obligations concerning their support and education. If I have aged parents, I consider myself obliged (have the duty, the responsibility) not to allow them to die of malnutrition if I can help it.

Classical Chinese philosophers taught a doctrine called "Rectification of the Names." Confucius said that this was the first principle of governing ourselves as well as provinces and states. If I have the name *father* and I take no thought of my children's upbringing or education, there is something seriously out of line between the name I bear and the neglect of my children—and this should be corrected. If I am a judge and dispense injustice rather than justice, my name, or else my judicial conduct, needs to be corrected.[1]

Common-sense morality agrees with this ancient ethical doctrine. Put in the form of a rule, the formula might read:

If you take on an obligation, you have a duty to discharge it.

If I have a child, it is my duty to support it. If I have signed a contract, it is my obligation to carry it out. If I borrow money, it is my responsibility to pay it back. The words "ought," "must," and "should" can be substituted for "it is my duty to," "it is my obligation to," or "it is my responsibility to." If I have promised to take a child to the zoo, I "ought" to fulfill that promise, unless an important reason (and this does not mean my own convenience) prevents me from fulfilling it. If I have entered into a marriage contract, I "should" act as a husband and not as a bachelor. If I borrow money from you, I "must" pay it back.

When at Trafalgar, Nelson signaled, "England expects every man will do his duty," he was calling for the fulfillment of that obligation he believed every seaman under his command had assumed when he signed on. The captain of the *Titanic* disregarded iceberg warnings; in this he failed in his duty to take every reasonable measure to protect his ship and his passengers, a duty that had priority over his duty to the owners and their interest in a record-breaking crossing of the Atlantic. When American field commanders failed to investigate and report on the civilian killings in the My Lai area of Vietnam, they laid themselves open to the charge of "dereliction of duty"—their neglect was incompatible with the obligation that went with their rank and responsibility.

What complicates even everyday moral situations is the presence of *conflict* of duty, that is, claims being presented to us simultaneously by two or more obligations. I have a duty not to interfere with the destiny of another: that is God's job, or if there is no God, at least it is not my job. Yet as a parent I have the duty to educate my children, to guide them, to try to keep them from harm. What should I do? How should I act? You may conceive it your duty to help destitute people, yet at the same time you may believe it your duty not to promote begging and panhandling. Should you give something to this dirty man who is holding out his hand to you? Or should you pass him by? A Los Angeles man saved his money for five years to take his wife to Hawaii for a vacation. His cousin died in Boston, and the expense of traveling to the funeral means he could not afford to take his wife to Hawaii. Which duty comes first? Many German professors under Hitler were put in the agonizing position of having to decide whether their duty lay in the direction of the safety of their families or in speaking out against barbarous injustice.

War and armed conflict provide textbook examples of conflict of duty, for in such conditions alternatives are so often narrowed to two stark and mutually exclusive choices. According to Navy Regulations, Commander Lloyd Bucher's duty was to do all in his power to prevent forcible boarding of his vessel by foreign agents. But he believed he had the more compelling duty to spare his crew from certain death. He surrendered the *Pueblo* to the North Koreans without firing a shot.[2] Jean-Paul Sartre illustrated his doctrine of existentialist choice by his story of the young Frenchman in wartime torn between his duty to join the Resistance and his obligation to provide for his ailing mother.[3] Sartre cited cases like this to support his teaching that no rule already in existence, no guideline already prepared, can help us decide in these situations. We ourselves must *make* the choice from nothing and without help of rule or reason. Most moral philosophers do not agree with Sartre that no considerations of reason can be brought to bear to resolve conflict-of-duty problems. "It is important to realize that there are moral problems of this kind," says R. M. Hare, "but if *all* moral questions were

treated like this . . . any kind of moral development or learning from experience would be quite impossible."[4]

In any event, though the word *duty* may ring ungratefully on
our ears today, it is hard to get rid of. The best we can do is to
use another term, a synonym or phrase with fewer conservative,
even Victorian associations. "Moral obligation" may do, or "responsibility," or perhaps simply, "that which we ought to do."

II

The Kantian Ethic of Duty

If we want a moral theory that will justify our being easy on ourselves, Kant's ethics is not for us. Kant's theory is based squarely
on the idea of duty. To do what is right because it is our duty
to do so, and for no other reason, is Kant's moral ideal—an ideal
he was frank to admit is rarely, if ever, completely achieved in
ordinary life. Being honest is good business. But that is not why
we should be honest. We should be honest because it is *right,*
because it is our *duty,* because we *ought* to be honest. If profitable results flow from our integrity, fine! But that has nothing to
do with the morality of our conduct. Kant's ideal is a "pure"
ethics, one not mixed up with some other human enterprise,
however praiseworthy. He insists on the *autonomy* of ethics,
just as he insists on the autonomy of the human person; ethics
is a sovereign kingdom, not part of another discipline. The
rightness of an act, the goodness of an end, does not derive
from pleasure or happiness. Ethics is not a subdepartment of
sociology or anthropology; it will not reduce to a subdepartment of applied psychology or the science of civic order.

In Kant's insistence on the unique quality of ethical judgments,
there is some likeness between him and certain English moral
philosophers of our own day. Contemporary ethical theorists
admire Kant's analysis of ethical judgments in terms of commands or imperatives, rather than as descriptive or factual statements. ("You ought not to cheat," may be translated "Don't
cheat!") Moral analysts are very much interested in the concept
of ethical rules as *universalizations*—moral formulas of a general
character that are in some way derivable from particular judgments or acts. Outstanding in Kant's doctrine is the way it calls
attention to the quality of *universalizability* inherent in moral
judgments. This is the principle that any individual act that is
morally right or morally wrong can be extended to yield a gen-

eral rule, "All should do X" or "No one should do Y." ("I ought not to have borrowed the money in those circumstances" may be generalized to "No one should borrow money he knows he cannot pay back.") We will look at some problems concerning universalizability in a moment.

Morality and the Will

Kant's ethical doctrine is often classified as "voluntarism," an ethical theory that stresses the primary role of the *will* in the moral situation. Kant believed that humans are *knowing* beings, and also *willing* and *acting* beings. As knowing beings, we are limited to contact with a world whose orderly nature and character our minds have in large part impressed upon that world. What the world *is,* apart from the way we happen to experience it, is forever hidden from us. The world-in-itself, that is, the world as it *is* apart from our *knowing* it, we can never lay hold of either through science or common sense. What we do know through common understanding and science is an orderly world of appearances, whose unity and order come from the mind that knows it. Innate in the mind are certain concept forms or ordering frames, such as space, time, unity, and causality. When the active knowing mind encounters the world, an ordering process takes place in which the result is that lawlike and regular aggregate of appearances (*phenomena*) we call "the world." This ordering nature of mind makes science possible. But because we know the world only through the ruled lines laid down over it by the mind's concept forms or categories, we never get to the *things-in-themselves* through intellectual activity.

Consider yourself for a moment. When you turn to look at that *self* which is you, you see it under the same ordering frames through which you know the world outside you. Such a self— Kant calls it the "empirical self"—is appearance only. We do not reach our real, our inner, selves by contemplating our empirical selves; the empirical self is but an object known among other objects known. At the root of our being, we are *will,* that is, the "real" self is a moral being, an acting being, a being capable of making moral judgments and performing moral acts. All other things in the world, including our own empirical selves, are conditioned, ordered but at the same time limited by the forms of space, time, and causality. The only *unconditioned* good in existence, Kant said, is a good will. Such a will is not bound by anything. It is moved neither by fear nor desire; it is not attracted by gain nor repelled by threat of disadvantage or danger. If your will leads you to act for my benefit, with no thought of yours, that is a good will in action. The goodness of that will is the only pure goodness there is. "Nothing can possibly be conceived in the world," says Kant, "or even out of it, which can be called good without qualification, except a *good will*."[5] Every will except a good will is a will that deliberately subjects itself to some factual state of affairs, to some empirical condition. By its refusal to be subservient to circumstances, a good will is *unconditioned*.

Morality and Reason

Dostoyevsky's Underground Man says, "You see, gentlemen, reason is an excellent thing, there's no disputing that. But reason is nothing but reason and satisfies only the rational side of man's nature while *will* is a manifestation of the whole life, that is, of the whole human life, including reason and all the impulses."[6] Kant would commend the Russian novelist's perception that reason is only a part, though an important part, of the whole human person—that person being basically a willing, doing, acting being. Kant, however, would be afraid that Dostoyevsky's sharp division between reason and will might be used to support the claims of the pure instinctive or the irrational side of man. To Kant, irrationalism can play no part either in moral theory or in the moral life. Reason and will are not cut off from one another; in the moral situation it is the part of reason to guide the will according to its own rational principles. A truly moral act must be a rational act, for it is the act of a rational being. If a moral act were irrational it would not, properly speaking, be a human act at all. To be morally right an act of the will must be rational. By "rational," however, Kant did not mean something prudent, practical, or self-serving. He would never suggest that a moral act is incomplete unless our own interest is taken care of. To Kant, self-benefit falls under the rule of prudence. Acts that are essentially prudential, acts that look out for "Number One," as we might say, need not be immoral. Under some circumstances, Kant believed, they may be praiseworthy. But they are never truly moral acts. Pure ethical judgments are never simply judgments of prudence. They are rational in the sense that they commit the agent, the doer of the action, to a universal principle.

III

Consequences, Intent, and Motive

Kant held that a truly moral act springs from a pure motive, that is, we must try to do what we ought (our duty) for no end or purpose other than doing what is right. "To duty," he says, "every other motive must give place, because duty is the condition of a will good in itself, whose worth transcends everything."[7] The moral act is a disinterested act—not *un*interested—an act that is separated entirely from the pull of self-benefit or even of social benefit. We have seen that there are ethical theories in which the good is said to lie in consequences, in the *results* of an act. Utilitarianism is such a theory. By contrast, Kant found the kernel of the moral act not in the consequences of the deed, but in the motive of the doer. A "pure" ethic, an autonomous independent morality, cannot measure the good primarily in terms of the results of the act performed. A truly autonomous ethic must give priority to the purity of motive and intent. In this way, the Kantian ethical injunction is a secular version of the scriptural command, "Purify thy heart!"

But what are intent and motive? They are not things or objects. Are they parts of actions? Are they the same? Let us consider intent. Here is a man who has killed a pedestrian with his car. The consequences of the deed are clear enough and bad enough. But did the driver *intend* to kill the pedestrian? In most such cases, the answer is no. Although there may have been an element of carelessness on the driver's part (in which case he is morally and perhaps also legally at fault), the killing of the pedestrian was an *accident.* The result was unwanted. It was not the intention of the driver to kill the pedestrian. Suppose, however, that in this instance the driver *did* intend to kill the victim, and he hit him with his car to make the death *look like* an accident. We might now ask: what was his *motive* in so doing? We know that the killing was intentional, but still we wonder why he did it. Was he jealous? Impelled by a desire to revenge an old wrong? Trying to rid himself of a blackmailer? Perhaps he is a hired killer and did it for money. Or maybe there was a political motive. In any case, we can see that *intent* has to do with an agent's wanting to achieve a certain end, but *motive* is that part of the action leading toward that end: motive concerns reasons for wanting the end. An act that is done freely and with intent may have motives. Motives do not compel or determine an act since they are part of it. Kant would have said that motives are something we *choose* to determine an act.

Most of us would readily admit that intent is an important factor in judging the morality of an act. The law takes account of intent in distinguishing between degrees of culpability. An act done with malicious intent (*mens rea*) is judged much more severely than one in which injury to another is done by accident. This rule is older than the Old Testament. The law distinguishes between negligent homicide and manslaughter, between murder of first or second degrees—and adjusts the severity of the penalties accordingly. But the law does not judge wholly on the basis of intent, for consequences count as well. Conspiracy to murder is one charge, murder is another. In ordinary affairs we hesitate to pronounce a deed morally right or wrong solely on the basis of the intent of the doer. The cry of a child, "I didn't *mean* it," checks the punishing hand. Yet to say of someone, "Poor fellow, he *means* well," is definitely not a tribute of moral esteem. There is a saying that virtue is its own reward, but there is another to the effect that the road to hell is paved with good intentions. If you break my precious china, I am not consoled by the fact that you intended to help me wash the dishes and had no malicious intent.

Sometimes an act or series of acts entails such dire consequences that we may be inclined to refuse to consider the question of intent or say that it has become irrelevant. Consider the following example: A certain nation, X, tries to put down an insurgence hostile to X, its national interests, and its allies. In the fighting that follows, many noncombatants are killed or injured by X's bombing attacks. Critics of nation X say that X's action is *immoral* and as evidence for this point to the large number of innocent civilians killed by X's bombers. But defenders of X reply that this evidence does not support the charge of immorality. X's military commanders do not *intend* to kill or injure innocent civilians; they try to avoid it if they can. What X intends to do is to destroy military objectives and to interdict certain areas to the insurgents. Objectors reply that the killing of so many innocent civilians is a *consequence* or result so bad in itself—as well as being impossible to separate from gaining the desired military results in this case—that the question of X's *intent* fades to the point of irrelevance.

The Double Effect

The situation of nation X illustrates a principle that moral philosophers once called the principle of the "double effect." A surgeon who amputates a patient's leg certainly intends to amputate it. But his primary intent is to save the patient's life. He aims at two effects: one is evil—the loss of the leg; one is good—the saving of the patient's life. The surgeon chooses to effect a lesser evil to prevent a greater. The military example of nation X may not be comparable because one of the effects (the killing of many civilians) may be an evil that outweighs whatever good may be achieved by the primary intent (to destroy military objectives). Moral philosophers trained in the method of *casuistry* used to apply the principle of the double effect to settle disputes over hard cases. In Scott's novel *Ivanhoe,* Rebecca deliberately leaps from a tower to certain death in order to escape her would-be ravisher. Was it suicide, and hence morally deplorable? No, the casuist would say, for Rebecca did not primarily intend her death, though in acting she knew it was inevitable. Her dominant intent was to escape rape, and jumping was the only way open to her at that critical point. The sailor in charge of a lifeboat beats off the clutching hands of persons drowning in the sea. But this sad effect is inseparable from the primary effect he intends: to save his boat, already packed with passengers, from being swamped. Moralists have defended some cases of abortion on the ground that the surgeon performing the abortion does not act primarily for the death of the fetus, but for the life or health of the mother.

While many applications of the principle of the double effect have sound basis in common-sense morality (reasonableness applied to a situation of moral choice), many others belong to the sphere of moral sophistry. Examples can easily be chosen from the numerous cases in which the secondary effect is so bad that it outweighs the good of the primary effect, as in the military example. A trivial instance is a person's defending his smashing of his hostess's lovely glass tray with the plea that he wanted only to swat a fly. Other types of cases to which the application of the double-effect principle is of doubtful merit are those in which the desired effect of greater good may not really be achievable by the means chosen. May we think for a moment of those who once condemned humans to the stake for religious reasons, arguing what matters a little or even a great deal of pain, what matters death itself, if a human soul is saved in the process?

Motives and Acts

The part played by intent and motive in human action is so complex and difficult to study that some philosophers today think it might be a good idea to declare a moratorium on moral philosophy, to withdraw from debates on the meaning of "moral" and "immoral" until certain prior questions about the meaning of intent and the nature of action itself are considered at length. In the past twenty years, some of the best minds in contemporary philosophy have worked hard to analyze the tough notion of what it means to say that someone is *acting,* or *doing* something.

From Aristotle to Sartre, a majority of moral philosophers have agreed that a true act is one in which intent is present, as well as a measure of freedom and choice. Otherwise, we would not have an authentic act, but simply something *happening* to us, like getting pushed down stairs. But to clarify intent, to raise motives to the level of consciousness is a task of great psychological as well as moral difficulty. The law tries to take account of intent, but admits that motives are hard to establish. A medieval jurist once said, "The thought of man shall not be tried, for the devil himself knoweth not the thought of man." Freud called attention to the whole realm of *unconscious* motive. An important part of psychoanalytic therapy consists of trying to get the patient to raise hidden motives and intents from the cellar of the unconscious to the light of consciousness, where they may be recognized and faced. It is the commonest of human failings to misrepresent our motives to ourselves. How often do we justify a course of action on grounds that put us in the right. "I had to be honest with you," we say to someone we have injured, "I may have been cruel, but at least I was honest and sincere." The sad thing about the hypocrite and the pharisee is that they may actually *believe* that their motives in doing something objectively harmful are aimed at securing a higher good. From Pascal and Molière to Sartre and Camus, a favorite theme of French poets and moralists has been the hidden self-serving motive behind the mask of virtue. Kant himself tells us that we can never really know whether our motives are "pure":

It sometimes happens that in the most searching self-examination we can find nothing except the moral ground of duty. . . . But from this we cannot by any means conclude with certainty that a secret impulse of self-love, falsely appearing as the idea of duty, was not actually the true determining cause of the will. For while we like to flatter ourselves with a pretended nobler motive, while in fact even the strictest examination can never lead us entirely behind the secret incentives, for, when moral worth is in question, it is not a matter of actions which one sees but of their inner principles which one does not see. . . . if we look more closely at our thoughts and aspirations, we everywhere come upon the dear self, which is always there, and it is this instead of the stern command of duty (which would often require self-denial) which supports our plans.[8]

True, the "dear self" is always there in human action and it is hard, if not impossible, to know that we are not serving it. To Kant, purity of motive is an ethical ideal toward which we should strive, rather than a simple psychological fact.

Though we cannot with certainty settle questions like "What *really* was his motive?" the ethics of common sense tells us that we do judge the moral quality of an act, at least in part, by its real or supposed motives. Helping those in want, let us say, is right action and worthy of moral approval. Yet suppose a teacher gives money to a destitute man on the street, his motive being a desire to impress some of his students, who are standing about waiting for a bus, with his generosity. The *results* of the act, so far as the destitute man is concerned, are identical with the gift of the same money by a person who offers it simply because he considers it his duty to help the poor. The dollar given by the first person buys as much food as the dollar from the second. Yet the motives of the second person are free (let us concede) from self-interest, while those of the first are dominated by it.

The old Jewish philosopher Maimonides knew how motives tend to be mixed in the best of us. Yet he thought it important to distinguish motives in good deeds as well as consequences. For example, some ways of giving are better than others, since some people give with relatively little thought of their "dear selves" while others are very much concerned with the impression they are making. To illustrate the "Eight Degrees of Charity" (*Tzedakah*), Maimonides constructed the following "ladder":

1. Giving in such a way as to help a person help himself.
2. Giving, with giver and receiver unknown to each other.
3. Giving, with receiver known, giver unknown.
4. Giving, when giver does not know receiver.

5. Giver gives before he is asked.
6. Giver gives after he is asked.
7. Giver gives less than he should, but cheerfully.
8. Giver gives unwillingly, but gives.[9]

By his "ladder of charity" Maimonides showed that consequences do count in assessing the moral worth of a deed, though varying motives may raise or lower the moral quality. The *manner* of doing a good deed also counts for something in the moral scale, since it is part of the deed.

Right Actions and Moral Worth

Kant would consider Maimonides's ranking of deeds a little too easy going, if the Jewish philosopher meant to claim moral worth for all forms of giving regardless of motive. Kant was very strict about this. To give for reasons other than for duty's sake, for motives other than the pure "ought" is not moral at all. Let us not misunderstand. Giving for vainglory need not be *immoral,* said Kant. A rich man contributes the cost of a hospital so that it may bear his name. While this act may be praiseworthy, it is not of moral worth. "If a man paid his debt only for fear of arrest," said Kant, "his action would be in line with duty, but it would not have been done for the sake of duty, hence it would not have moral worth." I should pay my income tax because it is my duty to do so. If I pay to the last dime primarily for fear of what will happen to to me if I get caught cheating, my action may be commendable. It is a right act. It is in accord with duty. But it is not done for the sake of duty. The element of the "dear self" is present in the act. Hence it is not an act of moral worth.

Kant went even further. He denied that an act done out of the natural expression of a loving nature *need* on that account be an act of moral worth. Sympathy and love may impel us to do a right act, a good deed. Yet acts motivated only by natural sympathy and love do not in themselves possess that unique quality we call moral worth, although such acts may help us in achieving the moral life. A person may do the good simply because he is naturally good-hearted and it is easy for him to impulsively do the right thing.[10] But such a person is yielding to a natural impulse, said Kant, and a good will is one that has nothing to do with the mere gratification of one's natural impulses. A good will is one that acts for the sake of duty, out of that law we set ourselves to do the good. We remember that Mill criticized Kant for failing to distinguish between the goodness of the result of an act and the motive of the person performing it, that the motive has nothing to do with the morality of the *action,* though much with the worth of the *agent.*[11] Kant would disagree. In his analysis of the moral situation, we cannot make this sharp separation of deed and doer. Kant would admit that a deed done from motives other than duty—a man rescuing a child, say, in the hope of being paid for his trouble—may be beneficial. The rescuer has performed a right act, one in accord with duty. But to be of moral worth the act must be more than this; not only should it be consistent with duty, it must be willed for the sake of duty.

V

The Imperatives, Hypothetical and Categorical

Kant said that the moral law is made known to us directly in the form of a command or imperative. Such a command takes the form "You ought to do so and so. . . ." But the moral or *categorical* imperative is not the only *ought.* There is also an imperative ("you ought to do X") that has nothing to do with the moral worth of an act, but rather with self-benefit, expediency, or even social welfare. This is the *hypothetical* imperative. We can recognize it by the fact that it always has a reason of prudence or expediency tacked on to its "ought." If I say to Jane, "You ought to get to bed early every night this week so that you will be in good shape for your physics examination," my "ought" has to do with prudence, with desired beneficial results, rather than with duty. "Honesty is the best policy" is a clear example of the hypothetical imperative at work, for it can be paraphrased as "You ought to be honest because it is good for your business." According to Kant, particular hypothetic imperatives take the logical form:

He who wills the end, wills the means.[12]

If you really want to play the guitar well, you will want to practice because practice is a necessary means to that end. It would be strange to say that I wanted a motorcycle but did not want any of the means that would enable me to buy the cycle (e.g., getting a part-time job in the delicatessen). If you really want to do well in school, you must be willing to study. If you want your own fresh flowers, you must be willing to cultivate your garden. If you want to stop the war, you must withdraw your troops—or crush the enemy completely.

The *categorical* imperative is an "ought" with no reasons of welfare or benefit attached. "You ought to do X" commands the categorical imperative, and if we ask "Why?" the answer comes back, "Because you ought, that's why" or "Because it is your duty—that is the primary consideration." Kant believed that an action good in itself is one that every rational being *would* perform if reason had complete control over his instincts and passions. But since we humans are far from completely rational, we are *obliged* to perform such an action—we "ought" to do it. This in no way means that we are compelled to do the good; in fact, humans are naturally inclined *not* to do their duty, said Kant. We are free to fulfill our obligations or not to fulfill them. But in failing them, we fail ourselves. As humans we have the power to act independently; we are autonomous agents. Our moral nature is not directly concerned with obedience to *external* laws. To be human is to make laws *for oneself.*

A Maxim of the Categorical Imperative: Universalizability

Kant did not believe that any ethical rule book could be compiled that would tell us exactly what to do when we have a choice of action or a conflict of duties. It is up to us. Nevertheless, Kant believed that there are certain maxims by which the categorical imperative can yield intermediary rules, general guidelines that we can use for orientation in situations of moral choice. To Kant, a maxim is a description of what I am doing or intend to do. A maxim can always be put in the form of a rule, sometimes as a general rule. If I make it a rule to go to bed by ten o'clock, that is my maxim. But it is not a maxim clearly related to moral choice. The categorical imperative concerns moral choice. It yields this formula:

Act only according to that maxim by which you can at the same time will that it should become a universal law.[13]

In a situation of moral choice, Kant says we should ask ourselves: can I honestly will that what I am now about to do will be done by everybody in like circumstances? Can I declare that what I now choose to do could become general practice? Or am I making an exception in favor of myself? Suppose I am passing a street fruit stand and I am hungry. I am tempted to sneak a banana without paying for it. Can I declare to myself that I can will that *everyone* should do this? Suppose you are inclined to omit acknowledging a kindness by writing a letter. Writing is such a bother. But can you will that what you are now failing to do should be made universal: that no one should acknowledge a kindness by letter?

Suppose an insurance company sends me to an auto body shop to have my dented fender repaired. The shop manager tells me that if I allow him to put in a bill of $600 for repair to the insurance company, he will only charge me $500. Should I accept? What guidance would the categorical imperative give me, if any? If I follow the categorical imperative, I will say no. I refuse the offer from the motive of duty. But a hypothetical imperative might lead me to the same decision, out of *prudence*. I may refuse the offer on the ground that such a practice, if it were to become general, would tend to raise everybody's insurance rates, including my own. In the second instance, my act would be "in accordance with duty," hence a right act; but it would not be "for the sake of duty," hence not an act of specifically moral worth.

At first sight, there appears to be some resemblance between Kant's first maxim of the categorical imperative and the Golden Rule. "Do unto others as you would have others do unto you." The Golden Rule is found both in the Old and New Testaments; in the latter it is phrased, "Therefore all things whatsoever you would that men should do to you, do you even so to them."[14] The Chinese sage Confucius taught the rule of "reciprocity." One day Master Kung was asked by a student whether there is one word that could serve as a rule of practice for all of one's life. The master replied, "Is not RECIPROCITY such a word? What you do not want done to yourself, do not to others." The phrasing here is negative, but later, under the heading of "Golden Mean and Rule," we find that Confucius formulates the principle of reciprocity in positive terms: "To treat my father as I would require my son to treat me; to serve my prince as I would require my minister to serve me—to treat my elder brother as I would have my younger brother treat me—to behave to a friend as I would have him behave to me."[15] The first formulation of the categorical imperative states the principle of universalizability; the Golden Rule and the Rule of Reciprocity imply it. What should I do for others? That which I would want all others to do for me and (presumably) for others in my position. What should I not do? That which I would wish no other to do to me and (presumably) to others in like circumstances.

Universalization rules have their moral uses, but not if applied too literally. Suppose I, an opera fan, desire to treat others as I would have them treat me. So I send you, who detest opera, a ticket to *Tosca.* Where have I failed in applying this rule? In the right use of reason (using your head), as Kant (and nearly everybody else) would say. To act morally does not mean that we should fail to act rationally. Similarly, other formulations of the universalizability principle need to be applied with caution if they are not to be reduced to absurdity. Consider the rule parents often cite to their children to check undesirable behavior: "What if everybody did that?" In the usual context, the rule is appealed to in a sensible utilitarian way to alert a child to the undesirable consequences of certain kinds of behavior—taking things from stores without paying for them, for instance. Yet the same rule could theoretically be used to discourage someone from doing something legitimate, even meritorious. Suppose I want to be a professional bagpiper. You say, "What if everybody did that?" Well of course if *everybody* were a professional bagpiper, the consequences would be disastrous. A universalizability argument of the form,

If the consequences of everybody's doing X would be undesirable, then it would be wrong for anyone to do X

could no more be universally applied as a moral test than its negative variant,

If the consequences of nobody's doing X would be undesirable, then everybody ought to do X.

The consequences of everybody going to medical school would be just as undesirable as those of nobody going to medical school.[16]

There is a crucial difference between Kant's categorical imperative and other universalization formulas such as the Golden Rule, the rule of reciprocity, or "What if everybody did that?" Kant's rule is stern and uncompromising. He said that maxims that violate the categorical imperative are ones that I *cannot* universalize, not simply ones I *would not like to universalize.* The Golden Rule can be construed as a common-sense maxim with a utilitarian purpose: "If everybody does unto others as he would be done by, then the world will be a happier place in which to live." The formula "What if everybody did that?" can be a rule of prudence, a way of calling attention to undesirable consequences if an action were to be made general practice.

But Kant did not care a straw for consequences, desirable or otherwise. He saw morality primarily as a matter of purity of *motives.* For him the sole question is: does the action conform to duty? The strength of Kant's moral theory is the way in which it calls attention to the autonomy of moral judgment—in the moral realm it is I, and no other, who determines the principle of an action. The weakness of Kant's theory is the one-sidedness of any moral doctrine that fails to take sufficient account of consequences. Kant has too little to say about the evil good men may do when acting in accord with duty, with honest intent. Kant's ethic is valuable for its stress on the importance of what guides our action in the moral situation, rather than for its use in helping us pass judgment on others.

V

Second Maxim of the Categorical Imperative: Persons as Ends

Kant's first formula of the categorical imperative, we saw, has to do with universalization as a criterion of the moral rightness of an act—act only so that you can will your act to become universal law. Another formulation of the categorical imperative in maxim form runs:

So act as to treat humanity, whether in thine own person or in that of any other, in every case as an end, never as a means only.[17]

In other words, we should not treat persons as if they were objects to be manipulated or instruments to be used. To Kant, one of the meanest forms of immorality was doing a person a favor in order that he might do something good for you, the person thinking all the while that you had done him the favor *for his sake.* Aristotle had no scruples about acknowledging the value of "business friendships," and Kant himself raised little objection to mutual favors if the parties were aware that each was using the other for convenience. Such a situation is prudential, but not a matter of morality at all. What bothered Kant was the thought that a person might believe that he was being treated as an end in himself while all the time he was being *used.* All of us at one time or another have had the disillusioning experience of thinking that our friendship was being cultivated for the sake of our sweet selves, only to find that all the while we were being manipulated, exploited, *used.* Such treatment is a flagrant violation of the categorical imperative. In Kant's eyes, to treat a person as if he were an object, an instrument, or a tool violates that person's worth and dignity he possesses *as a person.*

By "person" Kant meant a rational being.[18] A *person* is to be contrasted with an *individual,* which is any object, person or not, countable as one. A person is an independent autonomous being; he is capable of moral acts because his nature is rooted in freedom, unlike a stone or any other material object influenced from the *outside.* A person is capable of moral acts, of rational choice, of voluntarily subjecting himself to the rule of law. The persons we know, says Kant, are human beings—though, if there are other rational beings in the universe, they too are persons. If, on a remote galaxy, there exist strange creatures without bodies as we know them, they are *persons* if they are *rational beings.* Unlike a thing or an object, which is incapable of being treated as if it were a free and autonomous being, a person is an end in himself, a potential member of a "kingdom of ends," as Kant says. Things, objects, have *price;* only persons have *worth.*[19] Price is value in exchange; a thing has price if we can put something else in its place as an equivalent. Dignity or worthiness rises above all price and has no equivalent or substitute. Autonomy, says Kant formally, is "the basis of the dignity of both human nature and every rational nature."[20]

But we often do *use* people with no thought of wrongdoing, and in many situations no wrong is done. A manufacturer of paper boxes employs one hundred workers. He pays them neither for their blue eyes nor for their moral autonomy and dignity, but for their ability to produce paper boxes—for private profit if it is a capitalist enterprise, for the state trust if it is a socialist arrangement. By using these workers as means, as instruments, is the employer violating the categorical imperative? According to Kantian principles, the answer is: it depends. If the employer treats his workers *only* as means, if to him they are things to be used and nothing more, he stands deep in moral error. The whole dark history of human slavery is one of degradation of persons to things; so, too, serfdom and the forced child labor of the factories and mines of the Industrial Revolution. Despite protests of their king and their religious leaders, the conquistadores of Mexico and Peru used the Indians solely as means to obtain gold, silver, and other wealth. The original sin in which our American republic was born was African slavery; its dehumanizing consequences have so proliferated that today they constitute the major social problem of the United States. Early in this century, the larger portion of the Congo area was taken over by the King of the Belgians as his own private fief, and his overseers used every means, including torture and mutilation, to get more rubber out of the enslaved blacks. At the same time a similar situation existed in the Putumayo country of the upper Amazon, where the exploitation of the Indians by the whites was, if possible, worse than the Congo slavery. Even today, in certain regions of this hemisphere, Indians are considered animals to be hunted down on occasion for sport.[21]

But let us suppose that our factory owner is a decent man who has nothing in common with those who enslave others for profit. He remembers that his workers are persons, not things, treats them as such in the matter of decent wages, protection in case of injury, sickness, or old age, as well as in other less tangible but no less important ways related to their human worth and dignity. Such a man is not violating the categorical imperative, even though he hires and pays his workers as means of producing paper boxes. Kant would say that there are many ways of treating people as means that are *morally indifferent* so long as the manner of treatment does not violate their autonomy or end-in-itselfness as persons. Today, of course, we tend not to trust workers' welfare entirely to the goodwill of the individual employer. Trade union regulations and government laws exact considerable respect for the worker's welfare and security.

Concept of a Person: Religious and Secular

Just as Kant's rule of universalizability shows a link to the religious teachings we associate with the Golden Rule, so his principle of the autonomy of persons is itself a philosophical variant of a religious concept close to the heart of the Jewish and Christian traditions as well as the Western political theory of "natural rights" and the secular humanism nourished by it. The notion that man is an ethical being and, as such, requires that unique kind of treatment we call *justice* is one of the oldest precepts of Jewish law. The idea that all men, regardless of wealth, power, and gifts, are equally dear in the sight of their Creator is fundamental to traditional Christian as well as to Jewish teaching. A president of the United States summed up the teaching this way: "We believe that men are equal because they are all created by God. . . . Because of that relation between God and man, we believe that each man in himself has dignity and individual worth."[22] The tradition of secular humanism affirms the same concept of human equality and dignity but denies that the value of the human person must be based on a religious foundation. John Dewey, for example, declares that "the assertion that the rights and freedom which constitute democracy have no validity save as they are referred to some center and authority outside nature" reflects an "intrinsically skeptical, cynical and pessimistic view of human nature."[23] But if the belief in the autonomy, dignity, and value of the individual person is not to be derived from a divine source, what does it mean to say that it derives from human nature itself? Kant believed that human autonomy follows from the fact that man is a rational being who can integrate his reason with his will in such a way as freely to bring himself under the moral law. Kant's formalistic humanism may not be so far away as it may seem from the simple reasoning of common-sense morality that says, in effect, that we should respect others and do them no injury because "other people are human beings too."

Whatever its foundation, sacred or secular, the idea of the independence and absolute worth (Kant would say "unconditioned" worth) of the human person is at least a verbal and legal presupposition of a humane and cultivated society, wherever it is found. The notion of individual inviolability is at the source of law and justice as well as at the heart of compassion and charity. The belief that each human being is a *person*—an autonomous being capable of free acts and moral decisions, fundamentally different from a stone or can opener and therefore not to be used simply as an object or tool—is a basic ethical assumption concerning relations between people; one does not have to study ethical theory in order to be aware of it. We praise people for their recognition of the rights and worth of others, and we blame them when they fail to treat others as ends. Even in a competitive society like ours, which encourages such treatment, we condemn the "manipulation" of human beings, that is, treating them as means only, not as ends in themselves. We censure the "exploitative" treatment of others in all types of human relations from business to sexual. Civil rights activists have called forcible attention to the exploitative tendency inherent in racism as well as to the pious hypocrisy inherent in those who pay lip service to the concept of "human dignity" while implicitly denying it by their actions and attitudes. In recent years, the demeaning treatment of women as sexual ob-

jects—a treatment disguised in the postwar years by a shallow
rhetoric of "femininity" and "fulfillment"—has been the subject
of analysis and polemic in the books of a number of women
writers, from Simone de Beauvoir in France to Kate Millett in
the United States. Even the nonhuman environment of man is
now being regarded as more than raw material for exploitative
treatment. In our country a line of environmentalist writers from
Rachel Carson to Barry Commoner have insisted on the claims of
our natural environment—animal, plant, mineral, the earth itself
—to a certain autonomy and in-itselfness that render immoral
any indiscriminate ransacking of the nonhuman world for purely
human benefit.

A Religious Interpretation of the
Categorical Imperative: Martin Buber

The doctrine of the autonomy of persons is at the heart of Martin
Buber's *I and Thou.* First published in 1923, but attaining international popularity only after World War II, this eloquent book
by a Hasidic Jew unites the philosophical tradition of the autonomy of person (Kant) with the doctrine of personal sovereignty
implicit in the Jewish and Christian traditions. Buber distinguishes between two "primary words"—the combination *I-Thou*
and the combination *I-It.* These primary words do not signify
things, but relations. The primary word *I-Thou* can only be
spoken with my whole being, while *I-It* (or *I-He* or *I-She*) can never
be spoken with my whole being. When I see "Thou" I do not
have a *thing* for my object. When "Thou" is spoken, there is
no thing. "If I face a human being as my Thou," Buber writes,
"and say the primary word 'Thou' to him, he is not a thing among
things, and does not consist of things."[24]

To think of another human as "It," says Buber, is to think of
him as a possible object of use. When a self-willed man says
"Thou" he means "O my ability to use."[25] Like Kant, Buber believed that the I-Thou relation pierces the empirical surfaces of
people and reaches to the "unconditioned" side of human nature, the human core beyond appearances. The I-Thou is subject
neither to the laws of space or time nor to those of causality.
With the I-Thou we penetrate beyond thinghood, beyond phenomena, to unconditioned reality, to the realm of that "goodwill"
that Kant says is the only absolutely good thing in this world
or out of it. It is hard to achieve the I-Thou relationship and,
having achieved it, harder to sustain it. The sad necessity of the

human condition, Buber admits, is that every "Thou" in the world must once more become an "It." By a law of moral inertia, every Thou tends to slip back into the condition of mere object in our eyes. Only by continual moral effort of concentrated order can we keep the "Other" (the being to whom we stand in the I-Thou relation) from diminishing in our thoughts and prospective actions to the old status of "thing." That is why Simone Weil says that true morality lies not in judgment but in *attention*.[26] To the religious man, Buber says, sustaining power may come from the "Eternal Thou," which is God. The *dialogue*, that true conversation with another person that has nothing in it of the vanity of the competitive monologues that pass for conversation in our daily lives, can be extended along lines of relation that meet in the Eternal Thou. "Every particular Thou," Buber says, "is a glimpse through to the eternal Thou."[27]

In morals, the more noble a doctrine the greater the danger of sentimentalizing and exploiting. Just as in dialogue between human and human the personal Thou tends to slip back to the objectlike It, so any ethical doctrine, however exalted, tends to fall into catchwords and lip service once it becomes public property. Buber's phrases quickly became taken up and used for propaganda purposes by public establishments. His concept of "I-Thou" became sentimentalized, his ideal of "dialogue" was turned to use by advertising offices and public relation firms of state, religion, and education. Buber's is not the only form of *personalism* that has become sentimentalized and exploited. Official education manuals and corporation personnel folders today sprinkle their pages abundantly with easy phrases like "respect their dignity as persons," "refuse to violate their dignity," and "deep commitment to human values." But as Buber and Kant before him pointed out, true dialogue requires not only truisms and good feeling alone, but the pledging of the whole being. This is not easy to do, although the idiom of "commit-ment" facilely adapts to catchwords and slogans, even to hypoc-risy and phariseeism. In 1878, the year of Martin Buber's birth, Friedrich Nietzsche, a sworn foe of hypocrisy and unmasker of hidden motives, published his *Human All Too Human*. In this book we see Nietzsche gathering his forces for an assault on what he considered the fake doctrine of the sacredness of the individual human person, a presupposition of a Judeo-Christian tradition Nietzsche thought was worse than sentimentality. In his opinion it was the greatest moral swindle ever perpetrated.

NOTES: CHAPTER 4

1. Confucius, *Analects,* bk. 13 (Tsze-Lu) "Rectification of the Names," in *Confucius: Confucian Analects, The Great Learning, and The Doctrine of the Means,* trans. James Legge (1893; New York: Dover, 1971), p. 263.
2. Lloyd M. Bucher, *Bucher: My Story* (Garden City, N.Y.: Doubleday, 1970).
3. Jean-Paul Sartre, "Existentialism is a Humanism," *Existentialism from Dostoyevsky to Sartre,* ed. Walter Kaufmann (New Pork: Meridian, 1956), pp. 295–296.
4. Richard M. Hare, *Freedom and Reason* (Oxford: Clarendon, 1963), p. 41.
5. Immanuel Kant, *Foundations of the Metaphysics of Morals,* trans. L. W. Beck (1785; New York: Liberal Arts Press, 1959), p. 9.
6. Fyodor Dostoyevsky, *Notes from the Underground,* in *The Short Novels of Dostoyevsky,* trans. Constance Garnett (New York: Dial, 1951), p. 147.
7. Kant, *Metaphysics of Morals,* p. 20.
8. Ibid., p. 23.
9. Maimonides, *The Ladder of Tzedakah* (New York: Ktav Publishing, 1964).
10. Kant, *Metaphysics of Morals,* p. 14.
11. John Stuart Mill, *Utilitarianism* (New York: Liberal Arts Press, 1949), p. 19.
12. Kant, *Metaphysics of Morals,* p. 34.
13. Ibid., p. 39.
14. *Matt.* 7:12.
15. Confucius, *Doctrine of the Mean,* chap. 13, in *Confucius,* p. 394.
16. Hare, Singer, Lyons, and other contemporary ethical theorists have examined various formulas of universalizability or moral generalization; their writings are listed in the Suggested Readings for this chapter.
17. Kant, *Metaphysics of Morals,* p. 47.
18. Kant defined a "person" as a "rational substance," but like many moral philosophers he held that the property of *being free* is essential to the concept of a person. Some contemporary philosophers (Ayer, Strawson) follow a different tradition. They define a person as a being that has both a body and a mind. See Suggested Readings for this chapter.
19. Kant, *Metaphysics of Morals,* p. 53.
20. Ibid., p. 54.

21. At the trial of six cowhands charged with the 1967 mass murder of Indians on the Colombian *llanos* ("prairies"), the range boss who planned the massacre said, "For me, Indians are animals like deer or iguanas, except that deer don't damage our crops or kill our pigs. Since way back, Indian-hunting has been common practice in these parts." Reported in *New York Times,* 9 July 1972, p. 9.

22. Harry S Truman, reported in *New York Times,* 15 May 1950.

23. John Dewey, "Anti-Naturalism in Extremis," in *Naturalism and the Human Spirit,* ed. Y. Krikorian (New York: Columbia University Press, 1944), pp. 98–99.

24. Martin Buber, *I and Thou,* trans. R. G. Smith (1923; New York: Scribner, 1958), p. 8.

25. Ibid., p. 60.

26. " 'You do not interest me.' No man can say these words to another without committing a cruelty and offending against justice." Simone Weil denies that true personhood is anything other than the whole being, including feet and hands. "There is something sacred in every man, but it is not his person. Nor yet is it the human personality. It is this man; no more and no less. . . . At the bottom of the heart of every human being, there is something that goes on indomitably expecting in the teeth of all experience of crimes committed, suffered, and witnessed, that good and not evil will be done to him. It is this above all that is sacred in every human being." Simone Weil, "Human Personality," in *Selected Essays,* trans. Richard Rees (New York: Oxford University Press, 1962), pp. 10–11.

27. Buber, *I and Thou,* p. 75.

PART TWO

Growth, Reason, and Individual Choice

5

Activity, Growth, and Intelligence

A morality of duty, as we have seen, considers the ethical act in terms of obedience to a moral rule, principle, or law. By contrast, a morality of happiness tends to judge the rightness of an act in terms of the good to which it leads. In our earlier look at Mill's utilitarian theory, Aristotle's doctrine came up in the discussion of happiness as a moral end. Aristotle identified the highest good with happiness. He took for granted that there are many goods or values; that we know what some of them are; that we rightly prize health, wisdom, having children, friendships, a modicum of money and leisure, and so on. But Aristotle asked whether there is a good that is better than all others and, if so, whether we can know what this highest good is. Aristotle concluded that the answer was happiness or "well-being" (*eudaemonia*). He was led to this answer by his belief that happiness is the only thing that we desire as an end in itself and not as a means to some higher good.

Our earlier discussion of Mill's theory brought out that it is possible to hold that things other than happiness—health, wisdom, love—may be desired "for their own sake," that indeed happiness itself may be a by-product of the attainment of other goods. But Aristotle held that happiness takes first place in the hierarchy of goods because it is never wanted for the sake of anything else. He noticed that people generally *agree* that happiness is the highest good. He observed, however, that people do not agree on what happiness *is;* one person identifies it with pleasure, another with wealth, a third with fame, and so on. But these things cannot all be what happiness *is,* though one or more may be *conditions* of happiness.

The Greeks tended to put more emphasis than we do on the *objective* conditions of happiness. To them, a happy man is not just someone who enjoys an extended sort of good feeling, but a man who is related to people and things in certain objective ways. A man who has children is, other things being equal, happier than a man who has no children. A man who stands in a relation of justice to his fellowmen is happier than one who stands in a relation of unjust dealing, even if the latter is "enjoying himself" more than the first. This notion of happiness as an objective state of right relations may seem a little strange to us, for we moderns like to stress the subjective or psychological side of things when we think of happiness. But we do not entirely lack a notion of objective happiness. Take the case of someone who is blissfully making a fool of himself—an elderly gentleman, say, doting on the ambitious young woman who leads him around by the nose. We say of such a person that "he is living in a fool's paradise." The observation shows that we really do see a difference between happiness conceived purely as a subjective or psychological state of enjoyment and happiness including this subjective element but transcending it to comprise certain objective elements. Contemporary ideologists, such as Marcuse and Fanon, criticize as social folly our habit of dwelling exclusively on the subjective side of happiness. For most people on the surface of the earth today, they claim, there can be no good life until certain objective ingredients and conditions of happiness, such as right social and economic relations, are achieved.[1]

I

Aristotle's definition of happiness is *"activity in accordance with virtue or excellence."*[2] Such a definition of happiness may seem odd, but a look at Aristotle's explanation of his terms may help us to see what he is getting at. By placing happiness in the class or genus of *activity,* Aristotle wants to make clear that happiness is not just a passive state or something to be *found.* ("Can Samantha find happiness with her director and new husband Rodney?") To the Greek philosopher, the good of any living thing is always to be equated with the activity or fulfillment (actuality) of that living thing's capacities or powers. The highest good of any being is to become all that it can be: the sapling to be a flourishing oak; the foal to be a fleet and healthy horse; the child to be a mature adult, with all the human powers brought to fulfillment in harmony "guided by what is reasonable."

Virtues or Excellences
Happiness is activity, but not just any kind of activity. It is activity according to virtue or excellence. According to Aristotle, the virtues or excellences are states of *character.* We are not

born good persons, but we are naturally adaptable to the good. This is accomplished by cultivation of good *habits,* for which training by parents and teachers is necessary at first, but which we must continue on our own when we have left our parents' home and have finished our education. To Aristotle, the good person does the good from habit. It is true that good acts are *voluntary,* that they are done in situations where genuine *choice* exists, but the good man does not go into a dither every time he is confronted by a moral choice. He does the good by habit and needs to deliberate only rarely. He not only exercises his body, but he has the habit of exercising; he not only studies, he has the habit of studying. Aristotle's good man is not like the house-keeper who is an "impulse cleaner," one who seizes the broom to raise great clouds of dust only when the house is in danger of being buried under the weight of dirt and disorder. Just as the good housekeeper maintains the house by regular cleaning, so does the good man or woman do the good by habit or prac-tice. "Neither by nature nor contrary to nature do the virtues arise in us," Aristotle says, "rather we are adapted by nature to receive them, and are made perfect by habit."[3]

Just what are these virtues or excellences that mark the activity of a good person? Aristotle says there are two kinds, *intellectual* and *moral.* The intellectual virtues pertain to mind, or intelligence, and its use. The pursuit of knowledge is an intellectual virtue and at its highest point of development may be called *wisdom.* The moral virtues pertain to the proper exercise of those human pow-ers that are not specifically rational. Of virtue or excellence in general, Aristotle says that it aims at a *mean* or equilibrium be-tween two extremes:

Virtue, then, is a state of character concerned with choice, lying in a mean, that is, the mean relative to us, this being determined by a ra-tional principle, and by that principle by which the man of practical wisdom would determine it. Now it is a mean between two vices, that which depends on excess and that which depends on defect.[4]

That virtue or excellence "finds and chooses" that which is intermediate is clear in the case of moral virtues, taken sepa-rately. For example, courage is a mean between an excess of rashness and the defect of cowardice. Liberality or generosity is a balance between the defect of miserliness and the excess of prodigality. Pride or self-respect is an equilibrium between con-ceit or vanity on the one hand and self-deprecation or excessive modesty on the other. We can add to Aristotle's list of moral virtues as we like. Honesty in speech is a mean between tactlessness and falsehood. Modesty in sexual matters steers a midcourse between prudishness and shamelessness. Proper parental guidance of children is a mean between excess (too repressive) and a defect (too permissive), and so on.

But are there not some moral virtues that cannot have an excess? Or a defect? Can we be too honest in money matters? Too careful with another's reputation? Aristotle himself warns that not every act admits of a mean. With a rare twinkle in his cool Macedonian eye, he says that the goodness or badness of adultery does *not* "depend on committing adultery with the right woman, at the right time, and in the right way, but simply to do any of them is to go wrong."[5]

A key moral virtue in Greek philosophy is *sophrosuné.* It is usually translated "temperance." Just as the word *virtue* has a rather old-fashioned fragrance and many prefer to use "excellence," so "temperance" is a weakish equivalent of a strong Greek word that might better be rendered "self-control" or "self-mastery." Nietzsche thought of *sophrosuné* as that state of mind called "spiritual calm."[6] Aristotle was well aware of the powerful instincts and drives that exist in humans along with "reason." He was not an enemy of these dynamic drives, but he believed they must be guided and controlled by the rational part of ourselves; otherwise they may run away with us like horses out of control and plunge us to destruction. Greek tragedy, which was Aristotle's favorite art, provided many examples of the damage that may be done when a man throws self-control to the winds. The *sophron* ("self-controlled man") may drive as fast as lightning in his chariot, so long as he holds the reins firmly in his hands.[7] Although *sophrosuné* is a moral rather than an intellectual virtue, it is nevertheless a characteristic excellence of a rational being.

Morals and Moderation
Aristotle's definition of moral excellence in terms of a *mean* begins an ethical tradition that holds up *moderation* as an ideal of conduct. This includes the later Stoic school, from which we derive the tags *Nihil nimis* ("nothing too much") and *In medio virtus stat* ("the good stands in the middle"). Classical Chinese ethics also taught a doctrine of moderation and exalted the ideal of the "mean." Confucius's "superior man," we are told,

took hold of extremes of doctrine, determined the mean, and used it in dealing with others. The mean of classical Chinese philosophy was a balance or equilibrium that, in turn, produced harmony and order:

While there are no stirrings of pleasure, anger, sorrow, or joy, the mind is in a state of *equilibrium*. When those feelings have been stirred, and act in their due degree, what follows is *harmony*. This equilibrium is the great root from which grow all the human actings, and this harmony is the universal path all should follow.[8]

Some commentators say that an ethic of moderation is a characteristic ideal of *secular* or naturalistic ethical doctrines, in contrast to the ideal of complete commitment and self-abandonment found in the ethics of many *religious* teachings. It is as hard to imagine Aristotle urging his students to get rid of their possessions and give all their money to the poor as it is to imagine Jesus of Nazareth defining virtue as a mean between an excess and a defect. ("Sell *all* that you have and follow me!")[9] For these reasons, the Aristotelian ethic is sometimes criticized as cautious and bourgeois, the classical source of the careful virtues of prudence and counting the cost. But in fairness to Aristotle, he did not see moral excellence as a mere compromise. The metaphor he uses to describe the good person is not fence-sitting, but shooting the arrow straight and true to the center of the target. That is where the mean is, and to hit the gold disk is not easy. "It is hard to be good," Aristotle says.[10]

The Good Life: Political and Social

Aristotle laid down certain conditions that pertain to the good life. The good life cannot be solitary, but must be lived in some kind of community—familial, religious, cultural, political. Human capacities cannot be realized or fulfilled in isolation. Our potential comes to fruition only within the larger frame of relations between ourselves and our social or political community. The *state* is natural and essential to man. He who tries to live entirely apart from society is not living as a human, but either as a subhuman or as a superhuman:

Man is by nature a political animal. . . . The individual, when isolated, is not self-sufficient; and therefore he is like a part in relation to the whole. He who is unable to live in society or who has no need because he is sufficient for himself, must be either a beast or a god.[11]

In Aristotle's political philosophy, there is no myth of social contract; he did not teach, as did Thomas Hobbes, of a time when
men existed as isolated marauders, preying upon one another
in a lawless state in which life was nasty, brutish, and short, and
then joining in a contract in which a Leviathan comes into being
—the state, created artificially to protect humans against their
own greed and brutality. To Aristotle some kind of community,
some sort of social arrangement, must have existed so long as
humans existed. For humans are *by nature* political.

The class system of Aristotle's state was woven in with his
conception of the good life. The Greek city-state was small and
constricted in comparison to the modern Western nation-state.
Its social and economic arrangements are now nearly, though
not quite, obsolete. Aristotle's *polis* ("city-state") depended for
basic labor on a large slave population. Most merchants were
foreigners and not citizens, though even in Aristotle's time a
small but influential money-economy, profit-making class had
developed. The voting citizen depended on slave and noncitizen
classes; he had property and funds enough so that he did not
have to work and could devote part of his leisure to taking his
turn at public office. The rest of the time he could, if he wished,
devote himself to study and to those other pursuits which be-
fitted a free man. (Here we see the beginning of the historic
distinction between the free or *liberal* arts from the "servile"
arts, that is, skills and learning connected with profit or making
a livelihood.) Those pursuits included some devoted to a rather
elaborate social life in which women took little part, though they
had (at least theoretically) supreme authority in matters pertaining to running the household. (A Greek citizen's house included
numerous servants; even the poorest citizen could manage a
slave or two.) In ancient Hellas, men tried to make social life a
thing of beauty, and that is one reason why Aristotle puts *friends*
at the top of his list of "external goods" that supplement the internal excellences of the good man.[12] *Money* is another of the
external goods that help us attain the good life. Aristotle found
it hard to conceive of a poor man being a good man; the poor
man simply does not have enough leisure to develop his human
capacities, to "fulfill himself," as we would say, as a human. A
man who has to toil every minute of the day just to keep alive
is only potentially a man; he is not actually so.[13] To put it in our
idiom, poverty and destitution dehumanize a man. Aristotle would
not be surprised at the high crime rate in the poverty areas of our

cities. What do you expect, he would ask? To be *good,* a man must develop his truly human capacities in an orderly and harmonious way. How can he do that if he is deprived of those external goods without which a human cannot flourish? Nevertheless, it is a mark of Aristotle's time and class that he showed little interest in social measures to better such a man's lot, though he considered the most practicable form of the state to be one in which there were few very rich or very poor—one that had a heavy majority of "middle class."[14]

The Life of Reason; Contemplative Wisdom

Social and political participation is important to the good life. But the fullest personal activity can be reached only by our cultivating a higher excellence—Aristotle calls it *contemplative reason.* We know Aristotle believed that human good requires bringing into harmonious fulfillment all the capacities a human possesses. Such a fulfillment, if successful, would be guided by the highest and most specifically human power we have—reason or intelligence: "For man, the life according to reason is the best and pleasantest, since reason more than anything else *is* man. This life therefore is also the happiest."[15] But the very highest kind of intelligence activity is *contemplation.* We know that Aristotle classified various levels of wisdom or "dispositions to act intelligently" in a lower-to-higher order. Practical wisdom tells us how to look after ourselves and our affairs and to see that others get their just due. Moral and political (social) wisdom is a species of practical wisdom. Scientific intelligence in action draws demonstrable conclusions from basic scientific evidence, principles, or axioms. Philosophical wisdom includes the scientific but adds as well an intuitive understanding of the ground or basis ("first principles") of science. Highest of all is contemplative wisdom, which Aristotle describes as that activity of reason that aims at no end beyond itself, that has its "own pleasure, self-sufficiency, leisureliness, and unweariedness." This "active intellect," as Aristotle calls it elsewhere, seems to be connected with what he believed to be a *divine* element in the human mind or soul. This highest element in us, which belongs more to God than it does to us, seems to be a kind of exalted *knowing,* which has for its ultimate object unchanging and timeless being, the kind of being God is:

If happiness is activity in accordance with virtue or excellence, it is reasonable that it should be in accordance with the highest virtue or excellence; and this will be that of the best thing in us. Whether it be reason or something else that is this element which is thought to be our natural ruler and guide and to take thought of things noble and divine, whether it be itself also divine or only the most divine thing in us, the activity of this in accordance with its proper virtue or excellence will be perfect happiness. That this activity is contemplative we have already said.[16]

Knowledge pursued for its own sake, science as the highest satisfaction of the unquenchable human desire to know, search for that kind of being that is unchanging and deathless, and the incandescent pleasure of the mind as it merges for a critical moment with that eternal Being as a spark joins the flame that is its source—all this may be included in what Aristotle means by "contemplation." If it is hard for us today, in the vastly expanded social and scientific fabric of the twentieth century, to understand Aristotle's theory of contemplative reason as the highest good of life, it is harder still to follow the practice he recommends as the means to attain it.

Although today we may not be able to sympathize with Aristotle's identification of highest happiness with contemplative reason, there are many elements of his moral philosophy that are relevant to any inquiry we may make into ethics and morals today. Among them are the beliefs that:

Intelligence is at the root of moral judgment and action.

The good of human beings is inseparable from their proper growth, development, "flourishing."

Actualization and growth must take place within a social environment.

A test of Aristotle's way of looking at moral theory and the human good may lie in the fact that certain modern philosophers have arrived at similar conclusions. A striking instance is the American philosopher John Dewey, who made the concepts of growth and intelligence central to his own theory of human nature and social conduct.

II

The Moral Good as Growth: Dewey

John Dewey, whose long life extended from mid-nineteenth to mid-twentieth-century United States, was one of the few major philosophers to take a deep interest in education. A progressive of the era that saw the transformation of rural America into an industrial and urbanized superstate, Dewey had abiding faith in the ability of the native democratic process to pass on the best qualities of American life to young people by bringing together school and society. He taught at the University of Chicago, where his "laboratory school" for children was an important part of his work in education. Then he moved to Columbia University, where his disciples quickly dominated Teachers College. Dewey's work in educational theory at Chicago and Columbia was all part of his notion of the job of philosophy. In the broadest sense of the word, he said, morals *is* education. Both are inseparable from the *growth* of the child. The end or purpose of the educational process is not something outside it: "Growth itself," said Dewey, "is the only moral end."[17]

Dewey's ethical doctrine stresses the *social* nature of moral acts. He praises Aristotle's "profound insight into the relation of man to society and the dependence of the individual upon the social body." To Dewey, moral behavior is not reducible to subjective and relative preference. Although every moral situation is, in its way, unique, morality itself is objective because it concerns the human response to objective natural and social conditions. Dewey saw moral acts deriving their meaning from a modern social structure, far more complex than the democracy of the small city-state within which Greek life was so tightly contracted. Dewey believed modern democracy to be the widest and most inclusive category of social adaptation. The value of a democratic society must be judged by its success in serving the interests of each of its individual members. Democracy has emerged historically, "as a kind of net consequence of a vast multitude of situations no two of which were alike, but which tended to converge to a common outcome." Dewey believed that persons are best able to realize their individual capacities within a democratic society, for:

All social institutions have a meaning, a purpose. That purpose is to set free and develop the capacities of human individuals without respect to race, sex, class or economic status. And this is all one with saying that the test of their value is the extent to which they educate every individual into the full stature of his possibility. Democracy has many meanings, but if it has a moral meaning, it is found in resolving that the supreme test of all political institutions and industrial arrangements shall be the contribution they make to the all-around growth of every member of society.[18]

The significant word here is *growth.* The metaphor is biological. Growth is a biological process. Aristotle was a marine biologist, and Dewey was deeply impressed by the Darwinian theory of biological evolution. Aristotle defined the good of anything as its highest development, the fullness of its growth. What an organism strives toward is maturity, flourishing. The good of a tree is not something *outside* the tree at which it aims; the good of a tree is to be all a tree can be. So in the case of humans, Dewey sees our good, not in fixed results to be attained, but in continuing improvement and progress. Of society as a whole, he says:

Only by being true to the full growth of all individuals who make it up, can society by any chance be true to itself.[19]

Of parental and school guidance, he says:

Guidance is not external imposition. It is freeing the life-process for its own most adequate fulfillment.[20]

And the individual child's good is not the outcome of some future potential he may develop, but:

The case is of [the] Child. It is his present powers which are to assert themselves; his present capacities which are to be exercised; his present attitudes which are to be realized.[21]

Morals are part of the social process. In Dewey's view, morals concern, or should concern, intelligent behavior guided to the end or purpose of liberating the self and other selves so that the talents and capacities of all may have freedom to flourish and to attain fulfillment, thus leading the way to maximum enjoyment of the goods of life.

Habit and Intelligence
in Moral Activity: Dewey

Like Aristotle, Dewey held that a right act must include the factor of *choice.* "Only deliberate action," Dewey says, only "conduct into which reflective choice enters is distinctly moral, for only then does there enter the question of better and worse."[22] But he adds that *all* of our acts represent potentially moral conduct for, whenever the consideration of worse and better is involved, that is a moral situation. An ally of good choice is good habit. Like Aristotle again, Dewey stressed the importance of *habit,* the acquired dispositions we use in dealing with problems posed to us a hundred times a day by our contact with people and things. To deal with school tasks, the habit of study is needed. A hunter must have the habit of alertness. To deal with problems of human communication, the habit of attention and listening is required. At the root of scientific method is a set of habits, and so it is with every skill and art. Reason itself is a set of habits that enable us to discriminate among possible alternatives of action. Thus intelligence is an essential factor in moral judgment and action. (Dewey added the qualities of sympathy and sensitivity.) Reason in morality is intelligent choice in a practical situation. It concerns the ability to foresee, to project the consequences of an act we propose to ourselves. It is the capacity to compare and to evaluate those alternative consequences in the light of the ends we wish to achieve. It is competence in assessing the claims of other people who may be affected by those consequences. "Moral insight, and therefore moral theory," Dewey says, "consists in the every-day working of the same ordinary intelligence that measures dry-goods, drives nails, sells wheat, and invents the telephone."[23]

Dewey's conception of reason or intelligence is rather different from Aristotle's. To Dewey, intelligence is a practical faculty, a set of habits developed in experience. It is not a semidivine element with which man is endowed, nor is its highest activity contemplative. The social and economic arrangements of ancient Greece explain its philosophers' inclination to look down on practical knowledge and to exalt contemplation, to exalt "knowing that" far above "knowing how." Greek citizens lived in and depended on a slave economy, wherein most work was regarded as servile and theoretical knowledge was considered an activity only those with leisure could cultivate. But, to Dewey, a human's proper business is practical action. Aristotle was wrong in fixing on contemplation as the fulfillment of the highest human capacity. Esteem of contemplative activity arises from a "leisure class" social bias, from a false "spectator" view of the relation of man to Nature. Since contemplation affects nothing, makes no difference, it is worth little. "While saints are engaged in introspection," says Dewey, "burly sinners run the world."[24]

So reason is a practical affair. Intelligence has developed in man in the course of the long evolutionary struggle as a means of dealing with forces pressed in upon him, first by the weight of the natural environment—cold, hunger, danger from wild beasts, then by the pressure of the social environment in which man, in order to survive, must live and move. "Knowledge" is the name we give to the *results* of thinking. Thinking is an activity; it begins with a problem—there is something blocking action, an obstacle to be removed if we are to go on. Dealing with a stalled car, a fallen tree, a family quarrel, begins with facing the fact of stopped action, the troubled and uncertain situation. Intelligent handling of the situation means hypotheses constructed, reflected upon, some rejected, others acted on in such a way that whatever is inhibiting or oppressing is removed, thus freeing movement and life to resume. So often for Dewey intelligent behavior in the moral realm was a question of removing the stones so that the grass could grow.[25]

Ideas are instruments of action. Moral judgments are tools of moral behavior. Intelligence at work to control and exploit the pressures exerted upon us by our *material* environment Dewey calls *science.* When that same intelligence is applied to problems arising from our *social* environment, from our relations with other people, that is *morality.* Dewey was not one of those people who say that human progress in science has far outstripped progress in morals. Such a claim, Dewey thought, assumes falsely that science and morals come from two different faculties in human nature, two sources with a wide gulf between them. Dewey denied this radical dualism between science and morals. The scientific discovery of penicillin, diphtheria antitoxin, and poliomyelitis vaccine, had immense moral significance. Scientific method is concerned with the understanding of natural processes. This leads to human ability to control natural forces and to turn them to human benefit. Methods in morals help us to meet those problems that arise from our relations to other humans. Yet the two methods are not cut off from one another. Rather, they interpenetrate. Science has towering moral potentialities, for it has massive power to better the human condition. Moral problems can yield to the application of scientific method. For a moral problem, too, is a situation of blocked action that stimulates reflection, hypothesis, intelligent choice, renewed action, and confirmation in experience. Like other ends at which we aim, moral ends are instruments that remove obstacles to action and growth: they are *ends* that are, at the same time, *means.*

Various objections have been offered to attempts, such as Dewey's, to define moral judgment in terms of reason or intelligence. Some critics say that in making morals a function of intelligence we will be forced to construe "moral" so broadly as to make it cover situations better taken as morally indifferent—

such as taking the right or wrong road, using a heavy or light chisel. Others say moral conduct is still too closely tied to non-rational cultural and societal patterns to try to clarify it in terms of reason. Still others complain that an ethic defined in terms of intelligence yields at best a *prudential* set of moral principles; these will work to secure the interest of the self, perhaps, but will leave the good of our neighbor distinctly in second place. "Intuitionists" may say the definition or moral insight and conduct in terms of reason or intelligence will leave too little room for ethical intuition and conscience. Those who suspect the whole idea of rationality as a criterion now outworn may argue that any theory that allows reason to dominate morality will give too little place to feeling, sympathy, emotion—the whole affective, noncognitive side of the human being, a side that cannot successfully be defined in rational terms.

The question of the part played by reason or intelligence in moral judgment is not an easy one. We have been led to the problem by noting that both Aristotle and Dewey thought of human good in terms of a development or growth that must in some way be guided by reason or intelligence. In the first part of our next discussion, we will try to clarify the question of the relation of reason to moral judgment by means of examples or cases. Then we will consider the claims of *feeling* versus reason in the moral situation. Is that puzzling faculty having to do with right and wrong we call *conscience* basically reason or feeling? The concepts of feeling and impulse in turn will lead us to consider a set of ethical values connected with the idea of self-realization or self-actualization, a concept of personal and unique selfhood that has in our day dominated our sense of what matters most.

NOTES: CHAPTER 5

1. For more on Marcuse, see Chapter 12.
2. The late President John F. Kennedy liked to quote Aristotle's full definition of happiness: "The good of man is in the active exercise of his soul's faculties in conformity with excellence or virtue, or, if there be several excellences or virtues, in conformity with the best and most perfect of them." Aristotle *Nichomachean Ethics* 1098a17, in *The Basic Works of Aristotle,* ed. Richard McKeon (New York: Random House, 1941). (The marginal numbers are common to all standard editions and translations of Aristotle.)
3. Aristotle *Nichomachean Ethics* 1103a24–26.

4. Aristotle *Nichomachean Ethics* 1106b36, 1107a4.

5. Aristotle *Nichomachean Ethics* 1107a14.

6. Friedrich Nietzsche, *The Birth of Tragedy*, 15, trans. William A. Haussman (New York: Macmillan, 1924) p. 118. Aristotle tends to restrict the idea of *sophrosuné* to the human control of "the kind of pleasures the other animals share in," contrasting the *sophron*, or self-controlled man, with the self-indulgent man.

7. Plato uses the image of a driver controlling a dark horse and a white horse in his allegory of human nature in *Phaedrus* 246.

8. Confucius, *The Doctrine of the Mean,* chap. 1, in *Confucius: Confucian Analects, The Great Learning, and The Doctrine of the Mean,* 1893, trans. James Legge (New York: Dover, 1971), p. 384.

9. *Matt.* 19:21.

10. Aristotle *Nichomachean Ethics* 1109a24. Aristotle is quoting a well-known saying of Simonides.

11. Aristotle *Politics* 1253a2, 1253a27.

12. Friendship is the topic of books 8 and 9 of Aristotle's *Nichomachean Ethics.*

13. In Aristotelian language, "potential" refers to having what it takes to be something, while "actual" refers to the fulfillment or realization of those powers. A mature oak tree is actual in relation to the sapling, which is potentially the mature oak. The sapling in turn is actual in relation to the acorn. The distinction persists in modern usage, such as "potential energy" in physics, "living up to one's potential," or "self-actualization" in psychology and educational theory.

14. Aristotle *Politics* 1295b35.

15. Aristotle *Nichomachean Ethics,* 1178a6.

16. Aristotle *Nichomachean Ethics* 1177a12.

17. John Dewey, *Reconstruction in Philosophy* (1920, New York: New American Library, 1950), p. 141.

18. Dewey, *Reconstruction in Philosophy,* p. 147.

19. John Dewey, "The School and Society," in *Dewey on Education,* ed. Martin S. Dworkin (New York: Teachers College, 1959), p. 34.

20. Dewey, "The Child and the Curriculum," in *Dewey on Education,* ed. Dworkin, p. 101.

21. Ibid., p. 111.

22. Dewey, *Human Nature and Conduct* (New York: Modern Library, 1930), p. 279.

23. John Dewey, *The Philosophy of John Dewey,* ed. Joseph Ratner (New York: Holt, Rinehart & Winston, 1928), p. 310.

24. Dewey, *Reconstruction in Philosophy,* p. 154.

25. For further discussion of morality of growth, see pp. 164–165.

6

Reason and Feeling

Because they give high priority to the part of reason or intelligence in moral conduct, ethical theories like Aristotle's and Dewey's are often classified under the dry heading of *ethical rationalism.* The common element in this kind of ethical theory is the belief that any truly moral judgment or act must be *reasonable,* that moral behavior is intelligent behavior. In moral virtue, Aristotle says, both desire and reasoning are present and "both the reasoning must be true and the desire right." Most classical philosophers have in some sense been ethical rationalists— though Hume said pretty flatly that the rules of morality are not conclusions of our reason. The Greek moralists did not make the sharp distinction between "intellect" and "will," later stressed in the Christian tradition. They tended to think of ethical goodness as a kind of wisdom. Socrates taught that knowledge is virtue, that for a person to *know* the good is to *do* it. Though he was aware that "weakness of will" may prevent a person from doing what he knows to be right, Aristotle believed that the controlling principle of the human good was reason—moral virtue is found in a mean to be determined by a "rational principle." The Stoic philosophers believed that everything in Nature occurs according to laws of universal reason; so they considered rationality as a defining mark of a good act. The Scholastics taught that we know what is morally good "by right reason," although the good need not be identical with reason. Kant believed that right acts have their foundation in a good will, rather than in reason; yet the truly good will is a rational will. Though reason of itself does not determine the will, Kant says, "all moral concepts have their seat and origin entirely *a priori* in reason."[1] The French have always been admirers of *la raison.* One of their older poet-moralists, Marie-Joseph Chenier, finds reason at the heart of every good thing we humans do, including moral virtue:

Good sense, reason makes everything:
Virtue, genius, spirit, talent, and taste.

What is virtue? Reason put into practice:
Talent? Reason brought forth with *éclat:*
Spirit? Reason expressing itself with *finesse;*
Taste is no more than delicate good sense,
And genius is reason sublime.[2]

John Dewey, we have seen, believed that reason plays the leading role in moral judgment, if by "reason" is meant intelligent insight into the consequences of desire. Many contemporary moral theorists insist that moral argument must be reasonable argument. R. M. Hare points to the universalizability criterion as a rational test of moral argument. "The answering of moral questions," he says, "is, or ought to be, a rational activity."[3] Oliver Johnson says there is one self-justifying moral axiom from which all other moral obligations can be derived. This is the obligation to be rational. "Broadly speaking," he says, "a rational person is one whose beliefs are determined by the weight of evidence and arguments that can be given in their support. . . . The irrational person, on the other hand, clings to his beliefs regardless of the weight of either evidence or arguments."[4]

In practical life, we are all to some degree ethical rationalists. Society presupposes that "using one's head" not only tells us when to come in out of the rain, but guides us in matters of moral right and wrong. In law, the actions of a defendant are often tested in the light of what a "reasonable man" would or would not do under the circumstances. In most courts, a legally responsible person is assumed to have at least the degree of intelligence by which he can discriminate between right and wrong.[5] Commenting as a member of the military jury that found Lt. William Calley guilty of deliberately killing defenseless Vietnamese civilians, Major Walter Kinard said, "There are some things that a man of common understanding and common sense would *know* are wrong."[6] A German who rescued some Jews from certain death at Auschwitz explained his action "reasonably" by an informal application of the universalization principle, "I only did what any decent man would know was right to do."[7]

I

Let us consider the claim that ethical acts are simply *reasonable* acts of a certain kind, that moral conduct is a certain type of rational behavior. Is not moral judgment just *intelligence* applied to a problem concerning relations between ourselves and other people, so long as we do not confine the meaning of the word to the narrow sense of "intelligence quotient" (IQ)?[8] So many acts we call "immoral" seem no more than selfishness. And is not the selfish man really just a stupid man? He is stupid because he does not seem to understand that others, as well as he, have claims. He is stupid because he acts as if he were the only pebble on the beach, unaware that there are others in the world, as human as himself, with rights and feelings comparable to his own. In Henry James's novel *The Golden Bowl,* Mrs. Assingham says to her husband, "Stupidity pushed to a certain point *is,* you know, immorality. Just so what is morality but high intelligence?"[9]

We know so many moral situations that intelligent insight brought to bear would help resolve. Let us look at two instances, the case of Mr. Brown and that of Mrs. Green.

Brown is a man of thirty-five, married, with three young children. After many years at his engineering job, he has become dissatisfied. He now wishes to change his vocation and to become a schoolteacher. This problematic situation, like so many others, has begun with an unsettled troubled state of affairs in which the routine of daily living is seriously disturbed by doubts and uncertainty. It is a moral situation, since Brown is faced with a choice that involves not only his good, but that of others—the welfare of his wife and children will be affected by his decision. Moral decision, in this case, will resolve doubt, restore equilibrium, and clear the way for action.

The terms in which Brown's case has been set out are clearly Deweyan. A person in these circumstances, Dewey would say, can make a moral decision only by intelligent reflection. This means that he will formulate his desires, examine his feelings critically and reflectively. He will consider the alternative consequences of the choices open to him, insofar as it is possible to project them. He will take into consideration the claims of others, particularly those of his family. Will they suffer because of his diminished income, their uprooting and move to a new part of the country? He has discussed the matter with his wife, who has spoken encouragingly to him. But he wonders if it may not be too much to ask of her to pick up and follow him simply because he is dissatisfied with his present job. No all-binding moral law, written or unwritten, will help him here. Even the universalizability principle seems abstract. ("Can I honestly will that all men in my position . . .?") Every moral situation is unique, though rules drawn from moral experience can often be brought to bear on them. Like many moral situations, Mr. Brown's case simply cannot be abstracted from its particular circumstances with a view to solving the problem. A successful solution will be specific and will depend on the quality of intelligent insight the man can apply to the probable net results of each of the alternatives among which he must choose and their relevance to the ends he desires to reach.

Mrs. Green is of the same age as Mr. Brown and of similar family circumstances. Her husband is a good-natured, hard-working man, who has done well in a material way. He is rather dependent on his wife and feels lonely when she is not with him. (Mrs. Green also works.) A year ago Mrs. Green met another man at her office and they fell deeply in love. For a year they tried not seeing each other, but their attachment is now stronger than ever. For some time now, Mrs. Green has been seriously considering asking her husband for a divorce. But she has been reluctant to do so. Though her husband bores her, he has always (as she says) "been good" to her. But what few interests they had in common now seem eroded, and she no longer feels any tenderness toward her husband. Her lover, on the other hand, shares many of her interests. She tells him she "comes alive" when they are together. The children are fond of both their parents. The lover has no children and is separated from his wife. The Green children know the lover, who is a frequent visitor, and they like him too. He is considerably less well-off than Mr. Green, though he holds a job with a decent salary.

While most observers would agree that Mrs. Green has an important moral problem here, some might think that the role of intelligence in any solution of it is not as clear as in Mr. Brown's case. His case may seem to warrant little more than considerations of ordinary prudence. But in the case of Mrs. Green we have a troubled and uncertain situation in which the person concerned finds it very hard to carry on with ordinary life. (Frequently people in these circumstances are heard to say, "I can't go on!") In Mrs. Green's case, as in all moral situations, we have the question of *choice.* If she had no choice, there would be no moral decision to make. Where there is choice, we may have what is very common in moral situations—conflicting claims and desires, each of which is "good" in its way. We have the claims of husband, the children, the lover, Mrs. Green's own. She is sure that a life with the man she now loves so deeply will make her "come alive," bringing to fruitfulness things within her now lying dormant. She is convinced that with him she will blossom, flourish, be all that a woman, all that a human, can be. Yet she is strongly aware of the claims of her husband; she feels it her duty to stay with him, and Mrs. Green is a woman who takes seriously what she believes to be her duty. She feels bound by an obligation that seems to have nothing to do with blossoming, flourishing, or fulfillment, but everything to do with a commitment she once made. Mrs. Green wants to marry her lover and go off to a new life with him, yet she wants to stay with her husband and not get a divorce. She is faced with a choice, not between a "good" and a "bad," but between two "goods." But it is obvious that choosing one of these goods means the exclusion of the other. There is no more to be said; one cannot have it both ways. The nature of evil, Whitehead says, is that the characters of things are mutually obstructive—the realization of one set of values so often entails the smothering of others.[10] But Whitehead's sage observation is no more than a metaphysical version of an aphorism of common-sense morality: "You can't eat your cake and have it too."

Can the universalizability principle help here? The categorical imperative? Well, Mrs. Green can ask herself, "If I couldn't want every woman in my position to do what I so desperately want to do, doesn't that mean that it's wrong for me?" But unfortunately the universalizability principle is no moral can opener, the categorical imperative no handy guarantee of the resolution of any moral problem. Mrs. Green might honestly answer her own question, "Yes, I *could* want every woman in my position to do what I so desperately want to do!"

Moral Decision Under Stress

The Brown and Green cases may provide some basis for a Deweyan analysis of moral judgment in terms of intelligent choice. Mr. Brown and Mrs. Green have time in which to deliberate, time in which to reflect, analyze, hypothesize, weigh the claims of others against their own. But a person in a stress situation does not have time to project in imagination the consequences of alternate choices—or does he?

Situations of peril and conflict provide countless examples of forced choices that are cut off from time to weigh and reflect. Two wounded prisoners are slowing up a squad of Wingate's men in Burma. Shall they be disposed of? A Dutch girl is trussed up by the Gestapo and asked about the whereabouts of her friend. A Bolivian revolutionary is captured, and his wife is pressed to disclose certain membership lists. A Jew crawls into the house of a Catholic family in Poland and begs shelter—the special execution squad is three streets away. An Algerian rebel is ordered to assassinate a French official who has befriended him. An American platoon leader conducts a sweep through a village in Indochina with what he believes to be an order to "kill everything that moves." In none of these cases do we have the long watches of the night in which Mr. Brown can think and think again about the consequences of leaving his job, or in which Mrs. Green can think about leaving her husband. Here decisions must be made at once—and under stress.

War provides a simple, stark stage for moral decisions; human choice and action in armed conflict provides sharp contrasts in black and white. But moral choice with immediate decision required is by no means confined to settings of war and revolution. A patient has died suddenly, and the doctor must choose at once between reporting a death that will discredit him and forgetting he ever saw the patient. A congressman must decide whether to inform the police of an accident that may compromise his political future. A news correspondent is pressed by his wire service to make up his mind at once whether to file a newsworthy story he knows will ruin an innocent man. Called to the telephone, a professor must decide then and there whether to accept a desirable position he knows will displace a friend and colleague who cannot get another job. A college student is wondering whether to inform the authorities about a friend who has just gone off with a boy who may get her to experiment with a dangerous drug. Not all examples of instant ethical decision are so drastic. Tomorrow, as you go to school or work, a wretched-looking man may come up to you on the street saying "I'm hungry" and holding out his hand. Either you will stop or you will pass him by.

These examples show an obvious truth: that we do not always have time for carefully projecting the possible consequences of the alternatives before us in moral situations before reaching a decision. Some moralists (Aristotle, Dewey) say that in such circumstances the act in question springs from the whole person, from the set of *habits* and dispositions built up out of a lifetime of doing and experiencing. The good man does good from habit, said Aristotle; he does not need to deliberate at length in all situations.

Sartre, on the other hand, claimed in his early writings that there is no antecedent nature of "me," no self *already there* that responds to such situations with an appropriate and characteristic act. Sartre's wartime ethic stressed the uniqueness of each moral situation. There is no prior "I" to furnish me the clue to what to do, how to act in an individual case of moral decision. A man is the sum of his acts. The decision made, the act done, form just one more element in the buildup of *what I am*. Sartre's critics have pointed out that our prior experience is very much a part of our "self," and if we can bring this experience reasonably to bear, as we do on the hundred obstacles life puts daily in our path, it is hard to see why we cannot apply that experience in a reasonable way to moral issues that confront us. Later, in our chapter on existentialist choice, we will look more closely at Sartre's evaluation of the human predicament.

Intelligence and Sympathy: Bergson

The French philosopher Henri Bergson did not accept intelligence as the sole, or even the dominant, ingredient in moral choice. "Because we have established the rational character of moral conduct," Bergson says, "it does not follow that morality had its origin or even its foundation in pure reason."[11] From arguments drawn from evolutionary biology, Bergson held that intelligence is by its very nature self-seeking and ego-centered. Intelligence looks out for Number One, and the most we can get out of intelligence alone by way of an ethic, is a prudential one—that is, a morality of enlightened self-interest.

Society itself is a self-centered organism, Bergson says, and the self-seeking character of intelligence pulls against it. Humans share with bees, wasps, and ants a strongly developed social instinct. With the insects this built-in social order is so powerful that the individual member of an insect community never acts for itself, only for the good of the community of which it is a part. It never occurs to the toiling ant to pause in its task to ask, "Why am I working so hard for this society? Why should I labor for others until I'm exhausted and dying, never thinking of myself for an instant?" Bergson says that if a ray of intelligence were to pierce the consciousness of the ant, it might say to itself, "I have had enough of sacrifice for the commonweal; now is the time to look after myself a little." But there can be no such self-seeking gleam in the ant, whose individual behavior is linked so completely by instinct to the good of its complex social and economic order. The ant's society protects itself against the dissolvent effects of intelligence by not having any.

With man, says Bergson, the road of evolution was a different one. In the course of evolution, intelligence appeared in one of the higher primates as a function of his tool-making, tool-using skill. With sharpened stones man (or protoman) learned to cut material objects such as branches, hides, and other stones into smaller, shaped pieces. From these he made tools, weapons, clothing, and shelter for himself. This was the beginning of *analysis* (literally, "breaking up"), the powerful and characteristic way in which human intelligence grasps and deals with the material world. Faced with a problem, intellect "cuts up" the relevant matter, the object of thought, into smaller, handlable pieces, then arranges these pieces in a pattern or model it can manipulate and apply to fresh problems. Thus, Bergson believes, from the cutting of stones or hides some million years ago there developed intellectual analysis—the process of intelligence that one day would break down gross matter into elementary electrical particles to form the atomic theory.

Intelligence, according to Bergson, is always a *practical* affair. It does not understand altruism or self-sacrifice. To the individual it counsels egoism, self-seeking. No wonder, then, that intelligence has a potentially individualistic and dissolvent character. What holds human groups together is not intelligence. Man is an intelligent being, but he is not just that. He is a living being, a social being. He is bound to his social group by strong ties that have nothing directly to do with intelligence. Hence the need for social rules. Our willingness to sacrifice our individual freedom for the sake of family and social group does not spring from intelligence, but from the need of *life* to preserve itself, flourish, and to pass itself on. Life can dispense with individuals. But in its most highly evolved forms, life cannot do without social community.

But if intelligence is by nature self-seeking, why is it that philosophers like Mill and Dewey believe that intelligence is what makes the human a moral being? For Socrates (though not for St. Paul), to *know* the good was to *do* it. But how can these moral philosophers find the key to unlock the barrier of individualism and self-seeking in intelligence alone? In what way do they break down, with rational arguments, the wall of the "dear self" to reach altruism and the doing of good for others. Bergson said the answer lies in the fact that these moralists are exceptional, highly integrated persons. Only a rare intelligence is powerful enough to find *in intelligence itself* the luminous awareness that the good of others has claims equal if not greater than our own individual good.

Can we ask Bergson to explain the existence of unselfishness and self-sacrifice on the part of those who are not built on the scale of Socrates, Mill, or Dewey? We know so many people who ask for little for themselves and give much to others. Often they are simple persons, not intellectually complicated at all. What leads them to subordinate their own good to the good of others? Bergson would answer that it is not intelligence that impels these people to self-sacrifice, altruism, charity—but another source quite other than reason. Distinct from though not wholly independent of intelligence, this source lies deep in us at the core of our being, at the point where we touch the source of all life. It shows itself in feeling, sympathy, concern and care for others, and, in its highest manifestations, disinterested love. Thus we see that there are *two* moralities, Bergson says: there is the morality of external law, exerting pressure on us from without. This pressure is a social necessity to keep the self-seeking individual in line so that his individualism, born of intelligence, does not threaten the harmonious functioning of that great organism of which we are all a part and which we call "society." Contrasting with this morality of pressure from without, this *legislative* morality, there is the morality of impulsion from within. This morality springs from that core of ourselves popularly called the "heart." Illumined by intelligence, the ideal fulfillment of this morality would be that universal *love,* of which religious teachers have so tirelessly preached.

Bergson is not the only moral philosopher to advance the idea that humans have a natural capacity for sympathy or concern for others, as well as a self-seeking drive, and that this capacity is at the base of human ethical concern. In *Emile,* Jean-Jacques Rousseau lays down as basic to his educational creed that, though self-love is the child's first instinct, it is soon supplemented by a natural sympathy for others. Upon this impulse of our nature, social and moral behavior are dependent.[12] Psychologists have made many observations of sympathetic behavior on the part of very young children. While it is true that much of the toddler's concern for others is *learned* rather than instinctive, conditions that favor this learning do seem to exist naturally in the child. All of us have noticed how unhappy a very small child can become when he senses the distress of another little one. Children not yet able to talk will go to a crying child, make small soothing noises, try to give comforting pats and hugs. Such behavior confirmed Rousseau in his conviction that, while our first love is, *and should be,* ourselves, we are also by nature disposed to sympathy and concern for others. From this sympathy love one day will rise.

To some extent Mill himself shared this view. He believed that the roots of altruism were not separate from the natural capacity of humans for sympathy. In his *Utilitarianism,* Mill tried to show how this sympathy can be extended to human concern for universal happiness. Through rational perception of the general happiness principle, the individual is led "to identify his *feelings,*" once directed only toward his own concerns, "with the welfare of others." Bergson remains sceptical of Mill's attempt to find motivation for the general good in the intelligent extrapolation of individual sympathetic dispositions. Such individual sympathy may be enough for rare persons like Socrates and Mill, so highly integrated that for them to know the good was to do it; they, perhaps, were capable of extending individual sympathy to universal care by the light of intelligence alone. But for humans in general the source of the commonweal lies not in intelligence but in the group-survival drive of the human organism we call society, a cohesive force the biological origin of which lies back on the evolutionary road to present human life. On that road, Bergson says, a few rare beings—saints, mystics, religious teachers, and even a moral philosopher or two—have been able to follow this cohesive force to its source in the principle of life itself, for which "God" may be another name. They have purified and extended this force until it transcends the limits of particular societies and reaches toward humanity in an impulse of universal love.

II

Feelings and Self

Someone may say, "It is foolish to talk of reason and intelligence in moral situations. People do what they feel like doing, then rationalize their feelings. Look at Mrs. Green's case. Shall she leave her husband or not? It's all a matter of feeling. Mrs. Green will decide according to which of her feelings are stronger. Where she has a choice between two lives, it's a question of whom she loves. Intelligence has little to do with it. What matters in relations between people is not what you *know,* but how you *feel.*"

No one will deny that people often *do* act according to their feelings, and not reasonably. But is that quite the point at issue here? The question may be, rather, how *ought* they to act? To act according to one's feelings may, in some circumstances, be morally admirable, but in others sheer criminality. One may "feel like" giving food and shelter to a destitute man; one may also "feel like" slapping a child across the face. It is easy to assume that our acts proceed from our feelings. But maybe it is the other way around; perhaps we have feelings because of our acts. "Feeling is formed by the deeds one does," says Sartre, "therefore I cannot consult it as a guide to action."[13] Freud noticed how often his patients' behavior was motivated not by the rational side of their personalities, but by deep-seated drives that were instinctive and irrational. Yet for all his emphasis on the power and influence of these hidden dynamic drives, Freud did not advocate that his patients should live according to such pressures. Rather, the aim of his therapy was to uncover these drives, to raise them by analysis to the level of consciousness and in this way help to free the patient at least in part from his bondage to them. "Where id was, there ego shall be!" Freud said, "This is the work of civilization, like the draining of the Zuydersee."[14]

To say that people always do what they feel like doing is hardly more than a truism or *tautology*—something true by definition, like "A bachelor is an unmarried man." I can only "prove" that people always do what they "feel like" doing by assuming that every human act performed could only have been done by a person who "felt like" doing it. This is an instance of the fallacy in argument known as "begging the question"—assuming as true what is to be proved. The statement that people only do what they feel like doing closely resembles the claim "All persons are selfish." If there is no such thing as an unselfish act, the claim that everyone is selfish is an empty claim; it really does not say anything factually at all, and we are reduced to the bother of classifying an act of greed as "Selfishness: Type A," an act of martyrdom as "Selfishness: Type B," and so on. There are many misunderstandings about the part of the self in human acts. A person who acts in his own interest is not necessarily selfish, according to the ordinary usage of that term; he is selfish only if he refuses to put up with the interests of others. It is true that whatever I do I always act *with* a self (myself), but it does not follow from this truth that I always act *for* myself.

Immediate and Postponed Gratification

We do not always do what we feel like doing, at the moment anyway. If we understand "feel like" to mean "desire" or "want," we must admit that we gratify some wants immediately, if we can—drinking a glass of water or lying down for a rest. In the case of other wants, we postpone gratification. Whether the situation is morally significant or not, people do not always choose the path of their immediate desire, and intelligence (which foresees consequences) plays an important part here. A child saving up for a bicycle may resist buying the frozen custard he wants very much when he hears the bell of the ice-cream truck. A boy may feverishly desire to take advantage of a sexual opportunity, yet pass it up out of consideration for the girl. A sick man, knowing that drinking water is bad for him, may desire a cold drink to the point of craving. Yet he declines to take it.

But is every case of "moral obligation" a case of postponing gratification of desire? It does not seem so. Suppose Mrs. Green in the end resists yielding to her desire to leave her husband and marry her lover. She believes she has a moral obligation to remain with her husband. At the time she was married she promised to stay with him, and she believes herself still bound by that promise. So she remains with her husband and breaks off with her lover. What gratification has she postponed here? It seems that she has *renounced* a gratification, rather than put it off. The moral obligation she regards as determining her decision seems to have little to do with desire postponed; her case is unlike that of the child and the sick man, each of whom postponed an immediate good for a more remote one. Mrs. Green refuses to act on her desire because of something that binds her *now* (the moral obligation) rather than a future desired good. It may be simpler to think of Mrs. Green's case in the familiar terms of conflict of desire and the choosing of one of two goods, the realization of each of which excludes the other. The renunciation, rather than the postponement, of her love affair could be explained in terms of Mrs. Green's choice of what she deems the better, though not the more pleasant, of two mutually incompatible goods.

The Morality of Impulse and Spontaneity

There is a common kind of "feeling" familiar to us from experience. We often call it *impulse.* Impulse may be described as a want or desire, suddenly present, that presses us to gratify it immediately. Traditionally, "impulsive" conduct has been scolded and contrasted unfavorably with reflective or "rational" behavior. Moralists have written that we should "control" impulses, resist the pressure of impulsive desires. Instant gratification of desire, immediate yielding to impulse can produce destructive results. This is only common sense. If we carried into act every impulse we have, the state of the world would be even worse than it is now. So in the name of common sense we postpone or cancel fulfillment of our impulses, we check the urge to gratify every desire, however strong.

But because in the name of intelligence or reason we often postpone or cancel gratification of impulse in favor of some future or "better" good, it does not follow that immediate gratification of impulse is necessarily less "moral" than its postponement. True, there is a heavy load of traditional argument in favor of putting off or renouncing immediate satisfaction of impulse. Platonists, Puritans, Jansenists, and others have regarded the very presence of desire as cause for alarm. Spinoza believed mankind to be in bondage to the passions and in his *Ethics* recommends mastery of the passions by means of rational analysis. Locke advises parents to teach their children that "the Principle of all Virtue and Excellency lies in the power of denying ourselves the satisfaction of our own Desires where Reason does not authorize them."[15] An essential element of reason, says Dewey, is circumspection, to look about at the context of the direction in which impulse would hurry us: "The clue of impulse is, as we say, to start something. It is in a hurry. It rushes us off our feet. It leaves no time for examination, memory, and foresight. But the clue of reason is, as the phrase goes, to stop and think."[16]

In our own day, the contrast between reason and impulse sometimes takes a sociological or "urban affairs" turn. Edward C. Banfield, professor of government at Harvard, labels as "lower class" a certain type of people who make up between 5 and 15 percent of the population of large central cities. According to Banfield, these people are chronically unable to stay out of trouble with the law, to maintain a stable family life, to get and hold a job. They are not to be confused with the working class, or believed to be identical with those who are simply poor or deprived. The defining feature of "lower class," says Banfield, "is its inability or at any rate failure to take account of the future and to control impulses. The lower (as opposed to the working) class person never sacrifices any present satisfaction for the sake of a larger future one. He lives from moment to moment."[17]

The term "lower class" has unpleasant connotations; it is the term traditionally used by snobs to apply to their supposed inferiors. Some social analysts believe that we should recognize that people who prefer to gratify their desires without postponement may have values that are not *inferior* to the values of the Western-industrial middle class, but only *different.* Others, upholding the soundness of our traditional work ethic, say that postponement of immediate gratification for a deferred but higher good is a mark of cultivated human intelligence wherever it is found. Those who disagree say no, that deferred gratification, like the work ethic, is *culturally* motivated and has little to do with native intelligence. The other side replies: the "instant gratification" value you are defending is no more than the extension of infantile behavior into adult and social life. The consequences of such behavior cannot be confined to the society that prefers it, but must spill over to other societies and to their detriment. Take conservation, for example. It takes much time and patience to get through to a man that he should not place his immediate want of cutting down trees ahead of the future and greater good of uneroded land. It is an essential quality of human intelligence to be able to foresee consequences and to act in the light of them even if this means postponing gratification. To this, the answer is sometimes made that no sensible person would argue that *all* desires should be gratified immediately. One must distinguish between which sorts of gratification it is better to postpone and which it is not necessary to postpone—before waving the righteous flag of gratification-postponement and work ethic. And the debate continues.

There is a certain kind of act we admire, one of a class of acts performed on impulse, without forethought, spontaneously. A sudden gesture of generosity, say, or an act of courage when there is not time to think are cases in point; they seem to manifest freedom and spontaneity, and they strike us as a characteristic and vital act of the person performing them. Such acts appear to spring on an instant from the core of the doer's real self.

They are neither superficial nor capricious, but authentic acts, genuine and full of life, done without a moment in which to calculate the consequences, count the costs. Such acts, we may think, would be *spoiled* by deliberation; their value lies largely in their lack of any constraint. Calculation would ruin the spontaneity of the act in which so much of its virtue resides. To have thought over the probable consequences before performing such an act, we might say, would have "taken all the good out of it," reduced it to a prudential and careful performance, put it into the routine chain of cause and effect that marks the turning wheel of our everyday life. In its spontaneity, such an act seems to us a free act, the mark of a free person—appears to flash out from the authentic nature of the person doing it.[18] Although the idea of moral spontaneity is not something we tend to associate with Aristotelian ethics, Aristotle himself would not find our admiration for this kind of spontaneous act inconsistent with his own moral theory. The good man does the good by habit, he would remind us, and that is why his deeds often appear both spontaneous and admirable.

Sincerity: Virtue or Vice?

Is there a connection between spontaneity and sincerity? Both suggest honesty and absence of hypocrisy. Sincerity is a virtue rated very high by the morality of common-sense. Classical moralists, East and West, approve "the man without doubleness." But what *is* "sincerity"? The word comes from the Latin *sincerus* which means clean or pure. It appears in medieval French and comes into English in the sixteenth century. Lionel Trilling says that we cannot sensibly ask whether Abraham or Achilles or Beowulf was sincere; the concept dates from the time when the individual person begins to set himself over against society.[19] An older use of "sincerity" stressed honesty and absence of deception of others. A newer use emphasizes being true to oneself. A classical description of sincerity is: consistency between what we *say* and what we *do,* between what we seem to be and what we are, between what we seem to want and what we really want. A sincere person does not flatter. He is honest in speech and does not mislead us by his attitude. He deceives neither us nor himself. He fakes neither facts nor his own emotions. Meursault, hero of Albert Camus's novel *The Stranger,* refuses to display emotions he does not feel, even though at his trial for murder he is condemned for his alleged callousness at his mother's funeral.[20] The sincere person is not a pharisee. He is not one who is virtuous in externals, conforming to law on the outside, but who in his heart really wants to do what he condemns others for doing. Shakespeare's Lear knows the type:

Thou rascal beadle, hold thy bloody hand!
Why dost thou lash that whore? Strip thine own back;
Thou hotly lust'st to use her in that kind
For which thou whip'st her.[21]

People today talk a great deal about their own honesty and sincerity. They admit their errors, but will insist that they are, at least, sincere. Casual sleeping arrangements are often justified on the ground that they lead to more "open and honest relationships." Politicians publicly compliment themselves on their honesty and sincerity. Celebrities on television "talk shows" may admit all kinds of irregularities in their private lives, but insist that they are absolutely honest with themselves, and—they often add—with their children. The young are drawn to the ideal of sincerity, often extending it to their determination to cultivate and reveal their real selves, their true identity. A popular maxim of sincerity is "Be yourself!" It is interesting that the tiresome burgher Polonius says it as eloquently as any—and so long ago:

This above all: to thine own self be true,
And it must follow, as the night the day
Thou canst not then be false to any man.[22]

But sincerity is a tricky concept. As a virtue, sincerity is not as difficult to achieve as commonly supposed. In many instances in which it shows itself, sincerity is not a virtue at all, but a mark of weak or destructive persons. The sexual exhibitionist is sincere. So are the assassin and the terrorist. Hitler was sincere. Do we on that account judge his sincerity to be virtue? If sincerity means being true to one's self, it can mean being true to an egotistical or a criminal self. In Thomas Mann's novel *Joseph in Egypt* Potiphar's wife, trying to stifle her growing passion for Joseph, answers her husband, who has argued that we must live in sincerity:

Sincerity . . . is easy, and therefore it is not lofty. What would become of men if each would live only in the sincerity of his own desires, claiming for them the dignity of truth and unwilling to be strict with himself to his own improvement? The thief too is sincere, and the drunkard in the gutter and likewise the adulterer. But shall we by reason of its sincerity pass over their conduct?[23]

The worst instincts of human beings often appear their sincerest. Where then do we draw the line between sincerity as virtue and as vice?

III

Feeling and Reason

Feeling is a category of human awareness that enjoys high priority today. In part, the popularity of feeling as a value is related to the bad press that words like *reason* and *rational* have had in recent years. In the minds of many progressives, reason is associated with conservatism, and controlling radical student activism on college and university campuses. Students denounced the Vietnam War and the alleged neglect of the poor and minority groups by various levels of government as "immoral." Many parents and teachers tried to convince the students that violent tactics were not the proper means to use to bring about social reforms, however desirable and overdue. Students were told that educated men and women settle their differences by "rational" means, by the standard democratic procedures of fair discussion, debate, and vote. But the rebellious students scornfully cried their elders down. They associated these counsels of "reason" with an older generation brought up in the liberal tradition of Dewey and the old-line progressives who had idealized democracy as a kind of "social reason." The elders had thought that morality and social justice would continue to evolve from the very system of democracy itself. Student activists, on the other hand, believed that democracy had been taken over by the military-industrial complex, by an amoral corporate state. "Reason" and "rational" had come to mean little more than pale essences emanating from the tranquility of a professor's study, isolated from the rough realities of campus and street.

Along with impatience with arguments appealing to reason and the rational, there developed a parallel tendency to exalt *feeling* as a superior criterion of what is true and good.

An illustration may be found in the report of a discussion held by Peace Corps staff and volunteers at the University of California in Berkeley. One student said he felt that the Peace

Corps was a bureaucracy like all the rest. When asked for evidence to support this feeling he replied, "I don't need to supply evidence. The facts are not important, it is my feeling that counts." A comment on the report adds:

. . . the students feel that personal feelings are more important in relationships than Platonic truths. In discussions and negotiations, students want to be considered according to their feelings rather than according to the quality of their information. They think it is each person's task to find out what the other feels, then discover ways to deal with those feelings.[24]

Many middle-class couples join radical youths in preferring feeling to reason as a guide in personal relations. In New York, a member of the Marriage Encounter Group describes their method: "Each morning we decide on a question. Today it was 'What are my feelings about the party we had yesterday?' Not what you think about it, but how you feel about it."[25]

Exaltation of Feeling

Contemporary reaction against reason has roots that go back far into the cultural past and much deeper than new politics or social injustice. Antirational rebellion is endemic in modern Western thought. Rousseau says, "I felt before I thought." Romanticism exalted feeling and the instinctive over reason and analysis. Early anthropologists and ethnologists showed how little reason has to do with the complex taboos according to which primitive societies ordered themselves. Composers like Wagner, the expressionist painters and dramatists, novelists like Joyce, Mann, and D. H. Lawrence portrayed in their works the power of the instinctive and irrational over individual souls and bodies. Philosophers lent their support to the primacy of the infrarational. Behind the phenomenal world, Schopenhauer found a blind amoral "cosmic will." Nietzsche blamed Socrates for having superimposed a rationalist moralistic direction on Western culture. Bergson's "first cause" is a unified life-force that exists prior to intelligence, the *élan vital.* Whitehead insists, as opposed to Descartes, that feeling comes before thought:

It is never bare thought or bare existence that we are aware of. I find myself rather essentially a unity of emotions, of enjoyment, of hopes, of fears, of regrets, valuations of alternatives, decisions—all of these are my subjective reactions to my environment as I am active in my nature. My unity which is Descartes' "I am" is my process of shaping this welter of material into a consistent *pattern of feelings.*[26]

Freud's concept of the unconscious, of instinctive, irrational, sometimes savage drives too lightly chained by reason to render them powerless seemed to many to be confirmed by twentieth-century wars and revolutions. The grim spectacle of "educated" governments engaged in the mass slaughter of World War I; the Russian Revolution; the rise of fascism in Italy and Germany; the Stalinist terror; the new confrontation of nations in World War II; the extermination camps; the atomic bomb; the confrontation between superstates; the cold war started when the ink on the surrender documents was not yet dry; Vietnam; Arab-Israeli; Nigeria-Biafra; Ireland; Pakistani-Bengali; Hutu-Tutsi. All these and other bloody displays of the irrational seemed to deprive the traditional "appeal to reason" of its cogency and relevance. The end of World War II saw the rise of existentialism, which some interpret as a moral theory based on the concept of an irrational freedom. "The impulse to transcend rational mind," Lionel Trilling says, "would seem to be very deeply rooted in human nature."[27]

In their more peaceful ways, the developing sciences of psychology and psychiatry underlined the power of feeling and the instinctive as against the claims to supremacy of logic and reason. "The development of psychoanalysis," says Rollo May, "has led to a resurgence of the primacy of feeling."[28] From psychology and psychiatry the general public learned of the importance of the affective and noncognitive side of human nature. The media played it up. Progressive educational theorists made "feelings" respectable in the schoolroom. Charles Silberman's *Crisis in the Classroom* cites student reaction in a contemporary experimental public school program:

The students learned to handle feelings, too, and to view feelings as an aspect of thought. "Feelings are important at Murray Road," one student remarked, in explaining how the school differed from the regular high school. "Even in a subject like math it becomes harder and harder to separate feelings from thinking." "Yeah," another student chimed in, "I remember hearing myself say in class, 'Now I know what I'm about to say is emotional, so don't take it too seriously'—and suddenly I thought, 'Who says we shouldn't take emotion seriously? Who says that a reaction to a situation is only valid if it is cerebral?' *Sure,* feelings are important and there's no reason to delegate them to some sort of second place."[29]

The recent popularity of personal retraining in sensory experience is characteristic of the current high value put on "feeling."

Numerous courses and programs are available that have for their object a new awareness of feelings and sensations. "Social and formal education stress the cognitive and motor functions of the organism," says a manual developed at the Esalen Institute at Big Sur, California, "without regard for sensory development." The Esalen activities are described as having "the no-goal of feeling, allowing, being your body."[30]

Unity of Mind and Feeling

Much current playing off of reason against feeling—a dualism that results in a tendency to belittle the part of intelligence in moral judgment—is based on the common simplistic belief that reason and feeling are by nature absolutely opposed to one another. From the time of Plato on, philosophers and the public alike have represented human nature by a model human having reason or intelligence (symbolically located in his head) elevated above feeling or emotion (located in the heart or gut). But this sharp cutoff of intelligence from feeling is the kind of presupposition that needs to be questioned seriously. The popular dualism between reason and emotion fails to take account of the way our intelligence and feelings are *unified.* Intelligence may well have emotional content, and feelings may well have their rational aspect. When the painter Matisse died (his circle had been named *fauves,* or "wild beasts"), the French minister of education praised his art for its *rational* perception. Consider the emotion of fear (an *emotion* is a kind of feeling)—fear of a tiger, perhaps. The somatic or bodily side of fear has a static, even a paralyzing effect. But the rational or cognitive aspect of the emotion of fear is a conscious awareness that does not result in paralysis, but in practical action. That is, the emotion of fear working with *intelligence* leads us to take account of the tiger in such a way that a meeting with him is successfully avoided. Similarly, people often talk as if love and intelligence were separated by a gulf; but, just as our admiration for a work of art may be a function of our clear and rational perception, so it is possible for intelligence to be on the side of love, the one reinforcing the other. A man in love with an intelligent woman may believe (and rightly so) that he loves her because she is so beautiful. Yet the beauty that draws him to her may subtly be nourished by the intelligence that illumines it.

More generally, what we call *mind*—intelligence and reason are aspects of it—arises from and imperceptibly blends into the far more inclusive activity we call "feeling." The ability to feel, *sentience,* is the characteristic property of all animals, including man. "Feeling" is a name we give to the most comprehensive of all awareness. There are many degrees of it—emotion is only one. In her *Mind: an Essay on Human Feeling,* Susanne Langer says, "Feeling includes the sensibility of very low animals and the whole realm of human awareness and thought, the sense of absurdity, the sense of justice, the perception of meaning, as well as emotion and sensation."[31] To Langer, *mind* is a heightened, concentrated kind of feeling. Such a concept of the relation between mind and feeling has an advantage of simplicity. It tends to break down the hard dualism of reason versus emotion. It dispenses with the model human, his reason locked in his head, well segregated from the feelings in his heart or gut. Langer's model of the unified relation between mind and feeling might help to show how ethical judgment may be continuous with intelligence, yet not cut off from the whole affective side of the human person. If we think of mind as a heightened kind of awareness, a clarified focus of feeling, there is no need to segregate the moral realm from either cognition or emotion. Such a unifying concept may help to reconcile *some* of the differences between Mill, who finds the promise of universal altruism in utilitarian reason, and Bergson, who discovered the source of universal love in natural sympathy and instinct.

But a critic unsympathetic to Langer's extension of the concept of feeling to include cognition might call attention to the danger of the metaphysician's fallacy of redefining terms in such a way as to fit the metaphysical theory. Such a critic would say that Langer can define "feeling" in any way she likes, but to group, even loosely, highly intentional attitudes of the human mind with "the sensibility of very low animals," of which we know little or nothing, is a dubious procedure.

IV

Moral Sensibility: a Note on Conscience

Part of common-sense morality is the belief that we all have an internal moral perception called *conscience.* Often this is described as a faculty of moral *feeling,* though sometimes it is thought of as a kind of inner *knowing.* Conscience is frequently described in popular language as a "still small voice" that tells us that what we have done or are about to do is wrong. If we do something wrong—hurt someone, say—we may "feel bad" afterward. This feeling, in which sorrow, regret, and shame may be mixed, is sometimes called *remorse.* Psychologists and psychiatrists often use the concept of "guilt-feeling" to cover the many ways in which we judge ourselves adversely in moral matters. Guilt feelings may have an objective basis. A person may actually have murdered, injured, or cheated. But in many cases, the guilt feelings may be all out of proportion to the act we regret, and sometimes they have no basis in fact at all. Such guilt feelings are often part of the complex we call neurosis or even psychosis.

Religious teachers have traditionally considered the authority of conscience superior to external law, should there be a conflict between the two. Aquinas said that a man should perish in excommunication from his church rather than violate his conscience.[32] A modern Catholic theologian testifies to the absolute authority of conscience versus civic and ecclesiastical law:

In this realm of personal freedom there are no longer any determining influences from outside. Here even the Catholic has to make the judgments of conscience entirely by himself, and in this respect his position is in no way different from that of the Protestant or true humanist, unbeliever though he may be. The Catholic has to follow the judgment of conscience even if, objectively speaking, it is erroneous, and even if it should separate him from his church. The judgment of conscience is absolutely binding: it commits man to himself and to God. No excuses and no appeals to the commands of military or ecclesiastical authorities are of avail here. There is no replacement or substitute for personal conscience. Authority is valid only to the extent that it can justify itself as competent and binding before the bar of a mature and serene conscience.[33]

Martin Luther did much to dramatize the concept of the absolute character of conscience by his flat refusal to recant his religious teachings before the Imperial Diet at Worms in 1521. Against the assembled representatives of authority of church and state, Luther appealed to his own personal conviction of what was right, a conviction he believed to be supported by the Bible. "My conscience is bound by the Word of God," Luther said, "I cannot and will not recant anything. . . . Here I stand; I can do no other."[34] Cranmer, Archbishop of Canterbury, said, when ordered to say Mass in Queen Mary's presence, "The Queen could not command him to do anything against his conscience."

Many psychologists hold that the origin of conscience lies in the authority of parents or other early teachers and that conscience is this authority internalized. Our parents and other authorities approved of certain actions, disapproved of others. Gradually these precepts became taken into ourselves so that they became a part of us. "Father is displeased with me" begins as a wholly parental voice, but extends itself to society, even to God, who Freud identified with a father image. But the voice of authority becomes a wholly personal one. In *Civilization and its Discontents,* Freud maintains that humans are naturally aggressive, even violently so. Unless these aggressive drives are checked by some powerful agency, human civilization would be impossible. External taboo, parental or social authority, is not enough. The check to aggressiveness must be administered by the aggressive being himself. This is accomplished by an internalization of aggression in the following way:

There is taken over by a portion of the ego, which sets itself over against the rest of the ego as super-ego, and which now, in the form of 'conscience,' is ready to put into action against the ego the same harsh aggressiveness that the ego would have liked to satisfy upon other, extraneous individuals.[35]

In Freud's lexicon, *id* means that part of ourselves that is instinctive, unconscious, irrational. The *ego,* aggressive and self-seeking, is the conscious self. But under the influence of the internalized commands of parental and other authority, part of the ego separates itself as a distinct entity that criticizes, judges, checks, and controls the id. This is the *superego,* which we may identify with conscience or our "better self."

Difficulties concerning the *reliability* of conscience as a guide to action are similar to those raised in theory of knowledge about the reliability of the way of knowing called *intuition;* in fact, conscience is often said to be a form of intuition. Intuitive knowledge is usually made out to be private, internal, immediate, direct, and above all certain. But the certainty is no more than *subjective* if the intuition cannot be tested in some way independent of the intuition itself. How can intuition be shown to be reliable? The usual tests of beliefs that claim to be authentic knowledge involve verification from the outside, proof procedures including evidence open to public inspection. If I have an internal conviction that wheat germ can cure skin cancer or that there are the makings of an oil well under my backyard, these intuitions are worth very little, epistemologically speaking, unless I can verify them by some process independent of the intuition itself. Such verification processes involve public tests open to the inspection of observers other than myself. Can a dictate of conscience be "verified" at all? Some critics—those of the school of early Ayer, for example—say that moral convictions cannot be verified because they are neither statements about matters of fact, such as claims about curative agents for cancer or the presence of petroleum, nor statements about purely formal matters, such as algebraic equations or definitions like "A bachelor is an unmarried man." According to this way of thinking, statements about one's conscience and its dictates are statements about psychological states that people genuinely do *have* (e.g., some students' conviction that a certain war is immoral), but there is no way of showing that these moral intuitions or feelings are true or false. The defendant in a military draft evasion case had appealed to his conscience in refusing induction, and the judge sentencing him cites *his* conscience in applying the strict letter of the law to him. Each party's conscience is supreme to himself. But according to what procedures open to public inspection can such a dispute between consciences be settled, other than by measures available to the stronger party in the dispute—in this case the weight of the law? Joan of Arc defended her position according to her conscience.[36] But the Bishop of Beauvais who turned her over to the secular arm to be burned at the stake went to bed that night presumably with *his* conscience clear. Within the context of this discussion on conscience we are thus brought back to the dialectical opposition between ethical relativism, psychological style, and the Kantian doctrine of the absolute autonomy of the human person, that rational being who chooses to be guided by a law he has set himself.

With a certain tendency of our day to stretch the concepts of personal morality to cover problems of war, civil rights, and even our natural environment, the authority of conscience as ultimate arbiter of morality has come in for considerable publicity. The stage, motion pictures, television and other media have exhibited the drama of conscience, spotlighting individual appeals to personal moral convictions over against the authority of civil law. Like Luther at Worms, the Berrigans and "the Catonsville Nine" defended their illegal activities, which included the burning of military draft records, by an appeal to conscience.

The *conscientious objector* has been on the scene since before World War I, deriving his name from his refusal of military service on the grounds of conscience. In the past, the usual treatment of the conscientious objector was for the courts and boards to honor his scruples only if they were based on religious grounds and involved opposition to all wars. In 1971 the Supreme Court of the United States decided to allow "purely ethical" grounds as valid for conscientious objection, but did not set aside the traditional requirement that the objector must oppose all wars, not just a particular war. These decisions disappointed many young men eligible for military draft who believed intensely that the Vietnam War was "immoral" though they could not conscientiously claim to oppose all wars.[37]

Suppose Robert refuses military service on the ground of conscience. Would we support him? Why? Suppose Philip sets fire to military records at the induction center, defending his action by an appeal to conscience. Would we support him? Why? Suppose Peter attempts to blow up a truck convoy loaded with troops of his own country, claiming justification for his action on the ground of conscience. Would we support him? Why? Such questions quickly widen to the larger issues of obedience to law and to the morality of war itself. In Chapter 11, we shall encounter them again.

NOTES: CHAPTER 6

1. Immanuel Kant, *Foundations of the Metaphysics of Morals,* trans. L. W. Beck (New York: Liberal Arts Press, 1959), pp. 28–29.
2. Marie-Joseph Chenier, "La raison," *Poésies* (Bruxelles, 1842).
3. Richard M. Hare, *Freedom and Reason* (Oxford: Clarendon, 1963), p. 2.
4. Oliver A. Johnson, *The Moral Life* (London: Allen and Unwin, 1970), p. 37.
5. This assumption is often called the M'Naghten rule. See Chapter 9, note 31.
6. Cited by Francis B. Sayre, Jr., "The Cry of America," *New York Times,* 3 April 1971, p. 33.
7. *New York Times,* 9 January 1972, p. 24.
8. Note that the sense of the term *moral judgment* shifts when it moves from meaning "my judging the rightness of my own proposed act" to "my judging the rightness of another person's act or moral worth." Kant understood moral judgment only in the first sense.

9. Henry James, *The Golden Bowl,* 2 vols. (New York: Scribner, 1909), Vol. 1, p. 88.

10. Alfred North Whitehead, *Process and Reality* (New York: Macmillan, 1929), p. 517.

11. Henri Bergson, *The Two Sources of Religion and Morality* (New York: Holt, Rinehart & Winston, 1935), p. 76.

12. Jean-Jacques Rousseau, *Emile,* trans. Barbara Foxley (New York: Dutton, 1957), p. 182.

13. Jean-Paul Sartre, "Existentialism is a Humanism," in *Existentialism from Dostoyevsky to Sartre,* ed. Walter Kaufmann (New York: Meridian Books, World, 1956), p. 297.

14. Sigmund Freud, *The Complete Introductory Lectures on Psychoanalysis,* trans. James Strachey (New York: Norton, 1966), p. 544.

15. John Locke, "Some Thoughts on Education," in *John Locke on Education,* ed. William Boyd (New York: Columbia University Teachers College, 1964), p. 28.

16. John Dewey, in *The Philosophy of John Dewey*, ed. Joseph Ratner (New York: Holt, Rinehart & Winston, 1928), pp. 292–293.

17. Edward C. Banfield, "The Cities: the 'Lower Class,' " *New York Times,* 12 October 1970, p. 37.

18. In his novel *Lafcadio's Adventures,* André Gide makes a comic drama out of a type of impulse-yielding he christened "the gratuitous act"—a simple, unmotivated act that springs, not from the series of mechanical causes and effects that may determine the run of our daily lives, but from the whole self, the natural and spontaneous expression of our inner being. While the gratuitous act might be ethical, it could just as well be nonethical, even what society might call a crime. The gratuitous act that gets Lafcadio in trouble is his impulsively pushing a fellow passenger unknown to him from the door of a moving train. André Gide, *Lafcadio's Adventures,* trans. Dorothy Bussy, bk. 5 (New York: Random House, 1953).

19. Lionel Trilling, *Sincerity and Authenticity* (Cambridge, Mass.: Harvard University Press, 1972), pp. 2, 12.

20. Albert Camus, *The Stranger* (New York: Knopf, 1946).

21. *King Lear,* act 4, sc. 6, lines 159–162.

22. *Hamlet,* act 1, sc. 3, lines 78–80.

23. Thomas Mann, *Joseph in Egypt,* trans. H. T. Lowe-Porter (New York: Knopf, 1939), p. 417.

24. Reported in the *Peace Corps Volunteer,* Washington, D.C. (July–August 1968).

25. *New York Times,* 9 January 1972, p. 19.

26. Alfred N. Whitehead, in *Alfred North Whitehead, His Reflections on Man and Nature,* ed. Ruth Nanda Anshen (New York: Harper & Row, 1961), p. 28.
27. Lionel Trilling, *Mind in the Modern World* (New York: Viking, 1973), p. 35.
28. Rollo May, *Love and Will* (New York: Norton, 1969), p. 305.
29. Charles Silberman, *Crisis in the Classroom* (New York: Random House, 1970), p. 359.
30. B. Gunther and Paul Fusco, *Sense Relaxation* (New York: Macmillan, 1968), pp. 20, 24.
31. Susanne K. Langer, *Mind: An Essay on Human Feeling,* 2 vols. (Baltimore, Md.: Johns Hopkins Press, 1967), 1:55.
32. Thomas Aquinas, *Commentary on the Sentences of Peter Lombard,* 4. 38, article 4.
33. Josef Rudin, "A Catholic View of Conscience," *Conscience,* Curatorium of C. G. Jung Institute (Evanston, Ill.: Northwestern University Press, 1970), p. 149.
34. Roland H. Bainten. *Here I Stand: A Life of Martin Luther* (New York: Abingdon Press, 1960), p. 185.
35. Sigmund Freud, *Civilization and its Discontents,* trans. James Strachey (New York: Norton, 1962), p. 70.
36. Joan of Arc had an inner sign or voice she claimed was "from God to help me govern my conduct." Joan's voice gave her explicit directions, including instructions to raise the siege of Orléans. Jean Lemaître, representative of the Inquisition at Joan's trial, expressed his reluctance to interfere in the proceedings because of his "scruple of conscience." Regine Pernoud, *Joan of Arc* (New York: Stein, 1966), pp. 35, 165.
37. The two relevant U.S. Supreme Court decisions are reported in *New York Times,* 9 March 1971, respectively.

7

Individualism and Identity

To classical moralists, the good of a human tended to be the good of a *type*—a noble and beautiful model, to be sure, but nonetheless a type, something like an essence or changeless form. Greek philosophy had only a shadowy notion of the unique and individual excellence that may pertain to a human because of his uniqueness, his specific difference, his never-to-be-repeated qualities. Moralists of ancient Hellas placed little stress on the importance of whatever qualities Agathon or Apollodorus might possess, qualities not sharable with others. If Phaedrus were beautiful and good, he was fortunate enough to possess attributes that, in principle, all young men might have, had Fate or the blessed gods so endowed them. To the Greeks, it was sufficient if Simmias or Cebes had characteristically *human* virtues; whether they had qualities unique and peculiar to themselves was a matter of less interest.[1] The modern poet Rainer Maria Rilke's cry, "No—there is no one like me. There has never been anyone like me," would have sounded odd to the Greeks.

Contrasting with this classical tendency to focus, for moral purposes, on those excellences *common* to human nature, we find in modern thought a pervasive tendency to place high value in the process of *individual* self-discovery. Modern literature is packed with heroes whose trials are the search for Self and whose triumphs lie in finding it. The concepts of identity and self-realization play dramatic parts in recent psychology and psychotherapy. This notion of the value and importance of the unique qualities of an individual person came very late in human history, and in a practical way it has emerged only very close to our own time.

I

Sources of the Idea of Individualism

Where did the notion of individual personal value come from?
Where first do we find the idea that, for all the excellences we
share as humans, there are qualities that belong to ourselves
individually alone and that these confer on the individual person
a unique value, a worth, a dignity that may not lightly be in-
fringed. Some scholars find it in the writings of the ancient Jews,
in which for the first time the specifically *ethical* notion of a
person emerges. Others find this ethical notion of Judaism fulfilled in the Christian ethic, with its basic belief that all souls—
not only those of the rich, the clever, the powerful, but also those
of the poor, the wretched, even the criminal—are equally dear to
God. With Protestantism, individualism becomes heroic. Kierkegaard declares: "One cannot know what it is to be a Christian
until he knows what it is to exist . . . the Christian heroism is to
venture wholly to be oneself as an individual, this definite man,
alone before the face of God, alone in this tremendous exertion
and this tremendous responsibility."[2] Kant was a good Protestant
Christian, and his insistence on the absolute ethical autonomy
of the human person did much to strengthen the basis of the
emerging value of personal individualism as the West moved
through the Industrial Revolution.

Secular-minded reformers of the eighteenth and nineteenth
centuries dropped the religious element from the concept of individualism, but they kept the notion of the inviolable value of
the individual human person and his rights before the bar of
law, reason, and justice. The writings of Locke and Rousseau,
of Comte, Mill, and others carried the message of political individualism to Europe and America. But when national security or
national aggrandizement became an issue, questions about the
dignity and value of the individual person were given a low grade
of priority. John Dewey's insistence that the liberation of individual capacities is the sole end of human institutions made little
impression compared to the forces that brought about the great
wars of the twentieth century. Arnold Zweig wrote a novel on
the strength of a line imputed to General Erich Ludendorff—"The
State creates justice. The individual is a louse." Zweig's *The
Case of Sergeant Grischa* is the story of one lousy Russian prisoner of war, innocent and known to be so, put to death as a
deserter and spy so that the wheels of governmental and military

bureaucracy might continue to turn smoothly. Aleksandr Solzhenitsyn carries on the tradition, staging in his novels the drama of the individual life versus the official political apparatus. Oleg, hero of *The Cancer Ward,* recalls the old Stalinist days to his comrade: "Do you remember how the newspapers used to say, 'The whole Soviet people rose as one man in indignation when they learned of the unprecedented villainies. . . .' Do you know what that 'as one man' meant? We are each, each of us, different, and suddenly 'as one man' . . . ?"[3]

Types of Individualism

Like most words that end in "ism," the term *individualism* has a wide range of meanings that often blur into one another. *Economic individualism* refers to placing high value on single competitive effort in an open market. Its ideal is "each for himself according to his particular talents," unhampered by government regulation or social restriction for the common good. Early industrial capitalism exalted economic individualism; the careers of Andrew Carnegie, John D. Rockefeller, Henry Ford, and other heroes of America before the welfare state were considered triumphs of "rugged individualism." *Political individualism* springs from the conviction that arrangements of politics and law should always guard the inviolability of the individual person, however pressing the needs of state and society may be. The writings of Zweig and Solzhenitsyn are in the classic tradition of political individualism. But in a common nonpolitical usage, the word *individualist* refers to a person who does not go with the crowd, who stubbornly insists on his own way of doing things. This usage approaches the meaning of *personal individualism* in the context of the discussion that follows, but it may suggest no more than mere quirkiness or personal eccentricity.

Personal Individualism as a Moral Value

Suppose we take the term *personal individualism* to refer to the belief that the good life for any person means that he lives according to those qualities that are his alone, that he or she does not share with anybody else. Let us assume that the reader of this book is a young person, a student perhaps. Make this experiment: Think for a moment of the qualities you share with others. Not so much the common biological characteristics, but the shared social qualities, economic aspirations, and moral assumptions. There are the obvious common qualities—race, social and economic position, educational level, type of parents and their expectations. Then there are the presuppositions you share with your peers, perhaps: that education is to be valued; that hard work and professional employment are necessary; that certain kinds of careers are desirable; that marriage and a family are to be aspired to; that certain beliefs and attitudes in social matters are desirable; that one should dress in such and such a fashion, find value and enjoyment in this kind of music or that kind of sport; that there are certain qualities one looks for in friends and associates.

But now ask yourself: what are the qualities that belong to you alone, qualities that you possess in virtue of your own self rather than those you have as a student with a set of values and attitudes you share with your group, friends, or peers? Are there any important qualities that belong to you alone? Can you identify them, raise them to the level of consciousness, know what they are? Ask yourself how you propose to live your life. Perhaps you can live according to those qualities that you share with others. Or perhaps you can live your life according to those qualities that belong to you alone. Will you do those things that others could do as well as you? Or will you live a life that is open only to you? Will "right" be just what is right for others, or will it be what is right for you?

II

Individualism American Style: Emerson and Thoreau

One of the first impressions visitors had of the new American republic was the individualism of its citizens. Like others who were to follow him, Alexis de Tocqueville saw American individualism closely related to the new democracy, so different from the stable European social and political arrangements. " 'Individualism' is a word recently coined to express a new idea," said Tocqueville. "Our fathers only knew about egoism." He added a warning about the possible dangers to American democracy from the dissolvent and isolating tendencies within individualism.[4] Many American historians have observed that a dependence on the immediate community for survival did not blur the fierce individualism of the American pioneer, farm settler, mountain man, rancher, Indian fighter. A man who had to carve his home out of the wilderness and to wrest life from nature tended to develop striking powers of self-reliance. What counted on the frontier was not what a man's class, family, type, or social status was, but what he himself could do. Today historians disagree about how much of this familiar account of American individualism is myth, how much justified conclusion from facts. In any case, the first *philosophical* defense of individualism came not from a frontier philosopher but from a cultured and privileged New Englander—Ralph Waldo Emerson.

Emerson was a Unitarian minister who applied individual judgment to the question of the Eucharist and found that he could no longer in good conscience administer that sacrament.[5] On leaving the ministry, he supported himself by giving public lectures that later appeared in book form as his *Essays.* Emerson exalted the power and value of the individual self to provide guidance for life and warned against the common human tendency to think and live according to the beliefs of some group—family, friends, peers, colleagues, church, government, nation. Characteristically, his best-known essay on this theme is titled "Self-Reliance." The ordinary man depends on others to tell him the truth, says Emerson, but:

To believe your own thought, to believe that what is true for you in your private heart is true for all men—that is genius.[6]

Not only truth, but moral goodness must square with my own selfhood:

No law can be sacred to me but that of my nature. Good and bad are but names very readily transferable to that or this: the only right is what is after my constitution; the only wrong is what is against it.[7]

Charity itself should be rejected if it is not *my* charity:

Do not tell me, as a good man did to-day, of my obligation to put all poor men in good situations. Are they *my* poor? I tell thee, thou foolish philanthropist, that I grudge the dollar, the dime, the cent I give to such men as do not belong to me and to whom I do not belong. There is a class of persons to whom by all spiritual affinity I am bought and sold; for them I will go to prison if need be; but your miscellaneous popular charities; the education at college of fools; the building of meeting-houses to the vain end to which many now stand; alms to sots, and the thousand-fold Relief Societies; though I confess with shame I sometimes succumb and give the dollar, it is a wicked dollar, which by and by I shall have the manhood to withhold.[8]

Whatever its native origins, Emerson's conviction in the absolute moral reality of the individual self was backed up by his idealist philosophical belief. This doctrine, derived in part from Kant, in part from Indian thought, asserts that the world itself is determined by my perception of it. The world is my idea. "I," Emerson says, "this world which is called I—is the mold in which the world is poured like wax."[9] The visible world is but a sign of a spiritual one. Every natural fact is just one pole of a unity whose other end is moral. This metaphysical belief led Emerson from individualism to community. All individual selves, he thought, are connected in a transcendent Self, a universal consciousness, a moral reality that is the ground of community of all men and things. Each one of us is part of that Oversoul, "that unity within which every man's being is contained and made one with all other."[10] Emerson called this doctrine *transcendentalism*. The supreme moral reality that transcends the physical world unites individual selves into a moral community. Autonomous though my individual self may be, I cannot take license from its independence to draw scornfully away from others I deem inferior to myself. For, through the Oversoul that contains us both, as well as all men and things, I *am* that other. In Indian thought, *Brahma* is the one reality of which all things are parts, the supreme flame of which the individual *Atman*, or soul, is a spark. So Emerson takes "Brahma" as the title of a poem:

They reckon ill who leave me out;
  When me they fly, I am the wings;
I am the doubter and the doubt,
  And I the hymn the Brahmin sings.[11]

Emerson's Concord friend Henry Thoreau was not so interested in the metaphysical side of transcendentalism. But he carried individualism into radical political action. His essay "Civil Disobedience" urges passive resistance as the individual's response to unjust government. Any law that requires us to be agents of injustice to others should be broken at once. He opposed the Mexican War on the grounds that it was an expansionist aggression that would spread slavery. Thoreau set up his individual conscience as a judge of law and went to jail rather than pay his poll tax. As in Emerson's case, no law could be sacred to the author of *Walden* but that of his own nature. "The greater part of what my neighbors call good," he said, "I believe in my soul to be bad."[12] (He was thinking of their sheeplike docility in paying taxes to support what Thoreau believed to be social injustice.) Both Emerson and Thoreau were champions of democracy, yet both feared loss of the individual man in the democratic mass. Democracy liberates the individual person, yet threatens to suppress his individuality.

Whitman's "Myself"

When he read *Leaves of Grass* on its publication in 1855, Emerson instantly responded to the bold note of individualism in the rough Long Island poet Walt Whitman—an individualism that linked itself to American democracy, yet transcended political arrangements to universal community:

I swear nothing is good to me now that ignores individuals.
The American compact is altogether with individuals,
The only government is that which makes minute of individuals,
The whole theory of the universe is directed unerringly to one single individual—namely to you.[13]

Early in *Leaves of Grass* comes "Song of Myself," a rhapsodic hymn to the "I" by a man who has experienced self-discovery. Like the Psalmist who cried, "I will praise thee, O God, for I am fearfully and wonderfully made," Whitman sings of the wonder of himself, his body, his feelings, his senses. Like Emerson and Thoreau, Whitman proclaims the self to be its own law:

I know I am august
I do not trouble my spirit to vindicate itself or to be understood. . . .
I exist as I am, that is enough.[14]

But the communal "transcendental" element is there too. Whitman's "I" cannot remain isolated, but must bridge the gap to the "Thou" and to all things:

I celebrate myself and sing myself
And what I assume you shall assume
For every atom belonging to me as good belongs to you.[15]

Individualism, affirming sovereignty of self, led Whitman, as it did Emerson, to the opposite concept—community. The Indian sages intoned the formula *Tat twam asi* ("This thou art") in counseling their disciples not to draw back for anyone or anything, not from the lowly, the outcast, the despised—to have compassion on the thief and degraded one, to say of all they encountered, good or ill, *"I am that!"*[16] Whitman insisted that,

Whoever degrades another degrades me.[17]

And in the song of himself *all* selves are interconnected in the whole of creation:

In all people I see myself, none more and not one a barley-corn less
And the good or bad I say of myself I say of them.[18]

He, Walt Whitman, is at one with the Yankee mill girl, the butcher's boy, the young mother, the prostitute, the suicide, the man on the cross. And for every human being tortured, mutilated, murdered, led out to the place of execution and greeted with howls of execration, Whitman had a word:

I am the man, I suffered, I was there.[19]

To Whitman, the self mirrors the world and unites itself with the world and all it contains. That metaphysical fact implies moral community and brotherhood.

III

Individualism in European Thought and Expression
The tradition of individualism in the Occident is a long one. André Malraux says, in his book *Anti-Memoirs* "The basis of the West was individualism, an individualism which was at the same time the crucifix and the atomic reactor." But self-conscious personal individualism in European culture is only one late chapter in the great swing to the self, or "I," that marks modern Western thought as it emerges from the Renaissance and moves toward our own day. In art, as late as the fourteenth century, painters did not sign their names—their work was "anonymous and communal." In contrast, Albrecht Dürer, Luther's contemporary, wanted to become not only a great but a *unique* artist; he signed his pictures with his initials, conspicuous and stylized. By the seventeenth century, Descartes had reconstructed intellectual method by making the conscious thinking "I" the basis of a method of inquiry and the beginning of all philosophy. Kant found in the moral self that part of our nature that alone touches the reality of things beneath the phenomenal world. Kant had been much impressed by the writings of Rousseau, and it was this writer who gave modern subjectivism a definite turn in the direction of personal individualism. On the opening page of Rousseau's *Confessions,* we pick up the full flavor of modern personal individualism: "Myself alone! I know the feelings of my

heart, and I know men. I am not like any of those I have seen. I venture to believe that I am not made like any of those who are in existence. If I am not better, at least I am different."[20] Exaltation of the self and dedication to personal individualism was an integral part of the program of that cultural movement we call "romanticism." Goethe stood at the head of that tradition in Germany. His young bourgeois hero Wilhelm Meister declares, "The cultivation of my individual self, here as I am, has from my youth upward constantly though dimly been my wish and purpose."[21]

John Stuart Mill's classic essay "On Liberty" includes a formal defense of personal individualism in a setting of liberal political philosophy. The great utilitarian prefaces his defense of liberty by identifying the human good, not with external ends or goals, but with the internal good of growth and development. In this respect, Mill resembles Aristotle and Dewey. To Mill, human nature is not a machine built after a model, but a tree that needs to grow and develop itself in every aspect, according to the tendency of the inward forces which make it a living thing. While Mill concedes much value to the Christian ideal of *self-denial,* he asks his readers not to forget the pagan ideal of *self-assertion.* Mill places the good of individual and personal fulfillment well above that conformity that the pressure of social convention would enforce:

It is not by wearing down into uniformity all that is individual in themselves, but by cultivating it and calling it forth, within the limits imposed by the right and interest of others, that human beings become a noble and beautiful object of contemplation. . . . In proportion to the development of his individuality, each person becomes more valuable to himself and is therefore capable of being more valuable to others.[22]

Mill identifies individuality with development, claiming that in order to produce well-developed human beings, the cultivation of individuality is necessary. He warns against the tendency of most of us to take our cue from what others expect of us rather than from our individual preferences. It does not occur to most men to have any inclination except for what is customary.

Nietzsche's Individualism
Nietzsche's individualism quickly rose to a pitch of fervor that the sober Mill did not have at his command. Nietzsche believed that most people are afraid to be themselves and there-

fore live according to rules and patterns laid down by others. The individual self is unique and will be on this earth only once; no play of chance will twice fabricate this unity out of such wonderful diversity. The young soul hears his conscience call, "Be yourself! Be all that you can be!" But the exhortations of his parents, his teachers, his friends and peers all too easily drown out that call that he should hear day and night and tremble at the sound of. Some day, in middle or old age, each of us shall have to account to ourselves for what we have done with our youth. Only a few of us will have had the courage of fidelity to our individual nature and existence. Out of fear of society's censure, most people run away from their true selves; they look to others to tell them how to live. They look before they leap, they hesitate and count the cost. That is bondage. Only in the self, and in life according to the deepest inclinations of that self, is there freedom.

Such are the thoughts of young Nietzsche in an essay of 1874 dedicated to Schopenhauer, his master, of whom he is now taking leave so as to go his own way, think his own thoughts, follow his own genius (*daimon*). Here Nietzsche is addressing a young person, a student such as he had just been. He tells him that home, parents, education, class, nation, religion, even the opinions and values of friends his own age—all conspire to cover over each individual "I" with an artificial conventional self that is mistaken for the true "I." Family, education, expectations of parents, teachers, friends:

All that is not really you. No one but yourself can build a bridge on which you must cross the river of life, no one but you alone. It is true that there are numerous paths, bridges and demigods that wish to carry you across the river, but only at the cost of your self; you would pledge yourself and therefore lose yourself. In the world there is a unique way along which no one but you may pass: where does it lead? Do not ask, follow it. Who was it that said: "A man never rises to greater heights than when he does not know where his way may lead him"?[23]

While still a young man, Nietzsche became a professor of classical philology at the University of Basel, and a life of academic honor and dignity lay before him. But he gave it all up; he resigned his chair and salary out of a strange mixture of illness and passionate desire to be free to write those unique books whose brilliance and "dangerous thoughts" shocked the world of European letters at first, then gradually won its admiration.

But how do we recognize ourselves? How can a man know himself? He is a dark and hidden thing; the hare is said to have seven skins, but a man can take off seven times seventy skins and still not be able to say: "That is you as you really are, that is no longer mere external appearance."[24]

Nietzsche asks the youth he is addressing to stop and think for a moment. Suppose this life is the only one there is, what then?

One must be bold and ready to take risks with his existence especially as he will inevitably lose it in any event. Why stick to this piece of earth, to this trade, why strain the ears to hear what the neighbor is saying?[25]

But to live according to one's difference is not easy. Not many can do it. For those who can, the way of the unique self may be perilous. There is a good chance of breaking one's neck, or even one's mind, for such a life can—Nietzsche saw—lead in some cases to the border of mental illness:

It is a painful and dangerous undertaking to dig down into oneself in this way and to descend violently and directly into the shaft of one's being. How easily a man could injure himself doing this, so that no doctor can cure him.[26]

But given the authenticity of youth, Nietzsche says, it is worth the risk. If you still have not yet thrust your roots firmly down into life, he recommends that you take inventory of those qualities that belong to you alone, then take the cue to your life's direction from them:

Let the young soul ask itself, looking back on life, "What have you really loved up to now, what has drawn on your soul, what has dominated it and made it joyful at the same time?" Consider these sacred objects in order, and perhaps they will show you, through their being and sequence, a law, the fundamental law of your true Self. . . . See how they form a stepladder on which you have climbed up to yourself so far; for your true being does not lie hidden deep inside you but immeasurably high above you, or at least above what you usually consider to be your ego.[27]

A true teacher helps us to free our true self from our former self. True education consists in liberating the self from all those hopes and aspirations of *others* we have foolishly mistaken for our own:

Your true educators and molders disclose the true original meaning and the basic material of your being, which is something quite incapable of being educated or molded, and to which access is in any case difficult since it is fettered and chained as it is. Your educators can be nothing more than your liberators. And that is the secret of all education: it doesn't provide artificial limbs, false noses or eyeglasses—on the contrary, what could provide these gifts is merely pseudo-education. Education is rather liberation, a rooting out of all weeds, rubbish and vermin from around the buds of plants, a radiation of light and warmth. . . .[28]

"Immoralism" and Egoism

Personal individualism has many corollaries. One is the "great man" theory of history. Emerson defined an institution as "the lengthened shadow of a man." Nietzsche believed, "A nation is Nature's excuse to produce five or six great men—and then to get around them." Another frequent corollary of personal individualism is what is sometimes referred to disapprovingly or ironically as *immoralism.* An immoralist need not be a person who simply tears down established moral doctrine or practice. He may want to substitute values of his own that he believes to be "higher." But since these values run counter to those of most men of his time and place, he may seem like a man who wants to turn moral values upside down, to transform "bad" into "good" and the other way around. We have seen that the American transcendentalists believed that the self should obey the laws of its own nature, even if these laws should run counter to those of convention and society. Emerson said that the only right was what accorded with *his* constitution, the only wrong that which went against it. Thoreau would have it that what most of his neighbors called good, he would call bad. Nietzsche proudly declared himself "the first immoralist"—not because he was a wicked man (he was personally polite and gentle), but because he believed that the values he deemed superior would one day replace those he believed inferior, although at the time few others besides himself could see this. Nietzsche called this transposition of right and wrong "transvaluation of values" and thought it the key to many of his writings, especially *Zarathustra,* his book which hails the Superman.

André Gide's novel *The Immoralist* has been interpreted as a parable of Nietzschean individualism, a tale that plays off "pagan self-assertion" against "Christian renunciation." Michel, a young archeologist-historian, just married, reveres his bride but feels no desire for her. On his honeymoon to North Africa he falls ill and is tenderly nursed by his self-sacrificing wife.

Convalescing in the desert under the influence of sun, sand, and the unabashed advances of some Arab boys, Michel feels that he is being reborn, that his real self is emerging from the broken casing of his "surface" self, a self he now believes to be no more than the artificial product of family expectations, tradition, and education. A historian, he now develops the typical radical individualist's distaste for history. What can the past teach him? All his scholarly interests now mean no more to him than "books and ruins." Intoxicated with delight by his emerging "I," which feeds on immediate sensuous response, Michel ruthlessly pushes aside everything that he feels may get in the way of its development.

A friend of Michel, a fabulous creature called Menalque, is fashioned somewhat after the model of the poet Oscar Wilde. (The outlawed poet was actually labeled an "immoralist," not only because of his scandalous behavior, but because his epigrams seemed to say that "the worse was better and the better worse.") In *The Immoralist* Menalque counsels Michel, who, for all his feverish awareness of his new self, hesitates to carry out its promptings to their logical conclusion. Is Michel afraid of isolation from society if he finds his real self at variance with it? Most people are afraid of their real selves and will resort to any social cowardice to suppress them. People like to conform to patterns, to live as types rather than as individual selves. Menalque says:

Most of them believe it is only by constraint they can get any good out of themselves, and so they live in a state of psychological distortion. It is his own self that each of them is most afraid of resembling. Each of them sets up a pattern and imitates it; he doesn't even choose the pattern he imitates; he accepts a pattern that has been chosen for him. . . . The fear of finding oneself alone—that is what they suffer from—and so they don't find themselves at all. I detest such moral agoraphobia—the most odious cowardice I call it. Why, one has always to be alone to invent anything. The part in each of us that we feel is different from other people is just the part that is rare, the part that makes our special value—and that is the very thing people try to suppress. They go on imitating. And yet they think they love life.[29]

Gide's fable spins to its close with Michel abandoning everything that might give him stability—his apartment, his farm, his university lectureship, his wife. After the death of his wife, Michel confesses to his friends that now that he is free he does not know what to do with his objectless liberty. Self-discovery does not necessarily bring self-direction. The conclusion of *The Immoralist* has less optimism than that of *Fruits of the Earth,* an earlier work in which Gide celebrated the joys of self-discovery, the years in which the authentic "I" is found and brought to light breathing the fragrance of desire and fulfillment. Such personal individualism is absolute; its prescription cannot be filled for another. In *Fruits of the Earth,* Gide writes

Nathanael, throw away my book; there is nothing there to satisfy you. Don't believe *your* truth could be found by someone else. . . . If I made your bed, you would not be sleepy. . . . Throw away my book; tell yourself that it is only one of a thousand postures possible in face of life. Look at your own. Whatever another could do as well as you, don't do it; whatever another could write as well as you, don't write it. Attach yourself only to that which you feel has no part of anything besides yourself, and make yourself, impatiently or patiently, ah! the most irreplaceable of beings.[30]

Immoralism of the sort preached by Nietzsche and poeticized by Gide can be taken as a variety of *egoism,* and some critics would recommend shifting the discussion at this point to the limitations of egoism as ethical theory and practice. A conventional way of dealing with egoism as an abstract ethical theory is to construe egoism as advocating that *everyone* should maximize his or her own self-interest. But such a position cannot consistently be advocated. If others follow it, that is not to my interest because, presumably, others will act in *their* interest and not in mine. If I change my brand of egoism to advocating that everyone should maximize *my* self-interest and mine alone, I may get rid of the self-contradiction but will find few people who will adopt my ethical theory. One trouble lies in the *abstract* character of the egoism debated. What Nietzche and Gide had in mind was the good of a particular lived life, not the self-consistency of some theoretical egoism in a textbook of moral philosophy. Understood as placing the highest good in self-fulfillment—as Goethe's "Become what you are!"—egoism need be neither self-contradiction nor moral solipsism.

Hermann Hesse: Self and Mystic Community

Another from the school of Nietzschean individualism is the German poet and novelist Hermann Hesse. People often wonder why the young have been so drawn to this eccentric expatriate German who died in Switzerland in 1962. The attractive props of his novels are well known—the psychedelic effects, the mind-expanding experiences, the tincture of orientalism, the techniques that seem to musically combine the psychoanalytic and the mystical. But a deeper answer lies in the fact that Hesse's art has the magic of the poetry of the inner self. As Ralph Freedman says, Hesse's writing reflects, on the level of art, the young person's need to reveal himself and seek justification. Bringing to light what is buried deep within, finding a language both personal and symbolic to correspond to a young person's need to clarify himself or herself—these are the elements of the poetry of personal individualism.[31] Novels like *Demian, Siddhartha,* and *Goldmund* tell of the search of a self, unique and alienated, for a community or creative society in which the loneliness of the self can be transcended. They are pedagogical novels, celebrating a youth's search for an ideal teacher who will guide him partway along the difficult road to self-fulfillment, then let him go his way alone. In *Demian* we learn how a youth from a bourgeois family is taught by an older, wiser schoolmate the secrets of living in accord with the laws of one's own self:

There was only one true vocation for everybody—to find the way to himself. He might end as poet, lunatic, prophet or criminal—that was not his affair; ultimately it was of no account. *His* affair was to discover his own destiny, not something of his own choosing, and live it out wholly and resolutely within himself. Anything else was merely a half life, an attempt at evasion, an escape into the ideas of the masses, complacency and fear of his inner soul.[32]

In *Steppenwolf* the reader is introduced to Harry Haller, an older man whose life (as Nietzsche's was) is a lonely, suffering round of boarding houses.[33] Harry is now so alienated from life and society that he is on the verge of suicide. But at this point he is taken in hand by a nightclub girl who teaches him how to analyze himself through the medium of a magic theater. From this metaphysical shock treatment, Harry learns that his precious self, which he had scornfully withdrawn from those less intellectual than he, is linked to those other selves much more closely than he suspects. He is exposed to the ancient Hindu doctrine that our belief in the reality of our individual selves is *maya*, illusion. In the magic theater he is allowed to shoot people in cars, and in one victim's pocket he finds a slip of paper with the Upanishad formula *Tat twam asi* ("This thou art") written on it. In the end he realizes that each person's self is unique but also multiple by virtue of its participation in the community of humanity and of nature itself.[34] Harry is permitted to act out a symbolic suicide by killing the nightclub girl Hermine, who has grown so strangely to resemble him. A jury of immortals then condemns him to eternal life and laughs him out of court.

To Hesse's individualist hero, the process of self-discovery is twofold. You raise to the level of self-consciousness your own uniqueness and at the same time you discover that this unique self of yours is not estranged, isolated, alienated, islanded off. By clarifying your difference from others, paradoxically, you discover your relation to all:

What that is, a real living man, one certainly knows less today than ever. For men are shot down in heaps—men of whom each one is a precious unique experiment of Nature. If we were nothing more than individuals, we could actually be put out of the world entirely with a bullet, and in that case there would be no sense in telling stories. But each man is not only himself, he is also the unique, quite special, and in every case the important and remarkable point where the world's phenomena converge, in a certain manner, never again to be repeated. For that reason the history of everyone is important, eternal, divine. For that reason, every man, so long as he lives at all and carries out the will of Nature, is wonderful and worthy of every attention. In everyone has the spirit taken shape, in everyone creation suffers, in everyone is a redeemer crucified.[35]

To Hesse's individualist heroes, as to Whitman and Emerson, the supreme ethical law is the law of one's own nature. Yet the self is in some way a member of a transcendent community. Sinking the shaft of discovery deep into oneself should lead one from individualism to a sense of that community. But the way is not easy. A sign posted in Steppenwolf's magic theater says *Nicht für Jedermann* ("Not for Everybody"). To Hesse, as to Nietzsche, the highest and hardest form of self-discovery is finding out what unique future lies in yourself, learning your destiny, then *wanting* that destiny, loving one's fate (*amor fati*), desiring nothing beyond it. To the ancient Stoics, accommodating oneself to one's destiny was an ethical commonplace. But that accommodation was a submission of one's shared humanity to Nature, of which humanity is a part. For Hesse, as it was for Nietzsche, one's destiny is never general, never shared, but personal, "existential," and unique. "The man who really wants nothing beyond his destiny," Demian's music teacher tells his young pupil, "no longer has his neighbors beside him; he stands quite alone and has nothing but the cold world around him. . . . Jesus in the garden of Gethsemane. . . . It is beyond imagining."

IV

Self-Realization: Ego and Identity

In ethics, the term "self-realization" refers to a desirable kind of growth we associate with fulfillment of our capacities or talents. Moral theories of the Aristotelian or Deweyan kind are often classified as ethics of self-realization. Aristotle held that the good of anything is its actuality, the fulfillment of its potential. The aim of any living thing is its maturity, its flourishing. For Aristotle, the good of a man is the development of his capacities toward harmonious acts, the process guided by the highest of human powers—reason.[36] Dewey believed that our highest aims should be viewed not in terms of external goals, but as actualizations of our powers and talents illuminated by intelligence. For Dewey, growth is *the* moral end.[37] Twentieth-century psychology has added its weight to the ethical claim that self-realization is the aim of the good life, with special emphasis on the psychological need to liberate the real and authentic self from all that holds back its development. In growth and self-realization, psychiatrist Karen Horney found concepts in which ethics and psychology interpenetrate:

You need not, and in fact cannot, teach an acorn to grow into an oak tree, but when given a chance, its intrinsic potentialities will develop. Similarly the human individual, given a chance, tends to develop his particular human potentialities. He will develop then the unique alive forces of his real self: the clarity and depth of his own feelings, thoughts, wishes, interests; the ability to tap his own resources, the strength of his will power, the special capacities or gifts he may have, the faculty to express himself, and to relate himself to others with his spontaneous feelings. All this will in time enable him to find his set of values and his aims in life. In short, he will grow, substantially undiverted, toward *self-realization*. And that is why I speak . . . of the *real self* as the central inner force, common to all human beings and yet unique in each, which is the deep source of growth.[38]

According to Horney, the neurotic personality is unable to accept his or her real self, and hence develops self-hatred. This negative feeling tends to block development or growth of the real self.

Problems of self and identity began to concern therapists before World War II. Defenses of self-love and self-esteem by a series of analysts from Jung to Fromm brought reassurance to many people who could no longer find security in traditional religion. As early as 1933, Jung had stated self-love to be an ethical norm as well as a therapeutic need:

> The acceptance of oneself is the essence of the moral problem and the epitome of a whole outlook upon life. That I feed the hungry, that I forgive an insult, that I love my enemy in the name of Christ—all these are undoubtedly great virtues. What I do unto the least of my brethren, that I do unto Christ. But what if I should discover that the least among them all, the poorest of all the beggars, the very enemy himself—that these are within me, and that I myself stand in need of my own kindness —that I myself am the enemy who must be loved—what then?[39]

The concept of identity attracted particular attention during the late 1940s and early 1950s, deriving from psychological studies by Erik Erikson, Rollo May, Wheelright, and other interpreters in psychotherapy and psychoanalysis.[40] *Identity* quickly became a key word in clinical psychology, and *identity crisis* became a label for a large and miscellaneous number of nervous and emotional difficulties. In the 1960s Abraham Maslow introduced his concept of "self-actualization"—the growth process by which an individual satisfies psychological and ethical needs. On a popular level, self-fulfillment books and articles by psychologists and counselors writing for family magazines, newspaper columns, and television shows continued to appeal to readers through the 1960s into the 1970s.

Psychology and Ethics of Identity: James and Erikson

In the eighteenth century, Hume had denied the existence of any self at all besides the bundle of impressions received in experience and the persistence of these impressions as "faint images" or memories. A hundred years after Hume, William James changed the metaphor in his *Principles of Psychology*. Not a bundle, said James, but a stream of impressions is all we can lay hold of when we look into the self. The "I" seems to be a "stream of consciousness."[41] James left accounts of certain personal experiences that read today like case histories of "identity crises." He had, besides, a deep sense of a "real self," a self that in some way unifies the multitudinous wavelets of the stream of consciousness:

A man's character is discernible in the mental or moral attitude in which, when it came upon him, he felt himself most deeply and intensely active and alive. At such moments there is a voice inside which speaks and says, *"This* is the real me."[42]

With the rise of psychoanalysis in our own century, the concepts of self and identity underwent a heightened scrutiny. Freud divided the self into three elements—ego-id-superego. The id, as we know, is the instinctive part of ourselves, the invisible bulk of the iceberg, the seat of will, eros, libido, power, and dynamic drive. The ego is the conscious element, the "Self" par excellence, whose aggressive behavior is controlled by the superego, the internalized teachings of parents and other authorities embodying the standards and values of the culture to which they belong. To Horney, Freud's ego is too much like an employe who functions but has no initiative and no executive powers. "For me," she says, "the real self is the spring of emotional forces, of constructive energies, of directive and judiciary powers."[43] Erikson defines the ego as "a concept denoting man's capacity to unify his experience and his actions in an adaptive manner." The "Identity-psychology" of Erikson, May, and Wheelright assumes familiarity with Freudian concepts and builds beyond them. As early as 1950, Erikson saw psychoanalysis "shifting its emphasis from the concentrated study of conditions which blunt and distort the individual ego to the study of the ego's roots in social organization."[44]

Erikson noted that the term *identity crisis* was first used for certain psychoneurotic casualties of World War II. Because of war pressures, some ailing servicemen had lost that sense of personal sameness most of us take for granted—the immediate and unquestioned awareness of the continuity of our present state with our past. Erikson called this malaise a loss of "ego identity." Later, therapists extended the concept to cover the disorders of badly conflicted young people whose sense of ego identity is damaged or lost because of conflicting pressures, not of external battle, but of war within themselves. Erikson did not restrict the concept of identity to that sense of unique "me-ness" that is at the core of what we have called "personal individualism," although he included it as one of the many facets of identity. One's sense of identity can be supported by one's feeling of *belonging to a group*—ethnic, occupational, social class, family.

Personal identity may include an ingredient of self-esteem that begins in childhood, first constructed, perhaps, when the child for the first time *walks* in an upright position. There is the sense of identity that comes from one's own awareness that one is a self, that one's existence is continuous in time and space, that one's existence is recognized by others. In addition to this awareness of the *fact* of my existence is my awareness of its *individual quality.* It is this second dimension of awareness that includes my sense of the unique reality of my individual self.

What kind of identity experience is the source of Emerson's and Whitman's affirmation of the sovereign self? How can we classify experiences of the emerging self cited by Nietzsche, Gide, and Hesse? These seem to be a particular type of the second mode of awareness indicated: awareness, not of the fact of my existence nor of its continuity over changes in space and time, but a special kind of awareness of the individual quality of my existence, a consciousness of the reality and value of my individual self, both in my own eyes and in the eyes of those about me. Of course, persons like Emerson and Nietzsche are rare; the identity crises they experienced are probably rather special. Yet, if we still follow Erikson's analysis, the genius is the most human of men; in the unique nature of genius, all humanity is mirrored: "Trained minds of genius . . . have a special identity and special identity problems often leading to a protracted crisis at the onset of their careers. Yet we must rely on them for formulating initially what we can then proceed to observe as universally human."[45] A strong sense of identity is the foundation of an ethical sense that Erikson distinguishes from morality, if we mean by morality *mores* or customary modes of behavior. Moralities wear themselves out, says Erikson, but the ethical sense persists:

Moralities sooner or later outlive themselves, ethics never: this is what the need for identity and for fidelity, reborn with each generation, seems to point to. Morality in the moralistic sense can be shown to be predicated on superstitions and irrational inner mechanisms which, in fact, ever again undermine the ethical fiber of generations; but the old morality is expendable only where new and more universal ethics prevail. This is the wisdom that the words of many religions have tried to convey to man.[46]

Jung makes a similar distinction. Moralities prescribe duties. The ethical sense discriminates and decides between two conflicting duties. When obligations collide, moral codes will not help. A third standpoint is created, drawing on the deepest foundations of personality. This is the ethical aspect of conscience.[47]

Growth and Self: Education and the Limits of Individualism

Although a morality of growth and development does not necessarily entail a morality of personal individualism, it can create favorable conditions for individualistic theory. Personal individualism has always had a strong appeal to youth who are attracted by educational theories that stress "creativity" and "growth" as the end of education. In passing, we might note that we have become so accustomed to "growth" as a *good* word in the rhetoric of educational and psychological theory that we often talk as if growth by its very nature must be good.[48] But there are good growths and bad ones. It often depends on the point of view. Flourishing plants are called weeds if they interfere with the growth of vegetables and flowers we want. A tumor is often referred to as a growth; it is malignant if its increase invades and destroys healthy cells. Some kinds of growth inhibit or stifle the powers of the organism whose good concerns us. Others release these powers so that the development of the whole is helped. But growth *per se,* unqualified by any rule of better and worse, cannot be the only moral end any more than "evolution" can. Some principle of distinction between good and bad has to be added to the concept of growth before it can serve ethical theory or moral practice. Feverish industrial growth can crowd out qualities necessary for a humane existence. Unchecked armament growth leads to war. Population growth without control may call human survival into question. So we can understand why George Battaille says that we must not try to grow all the time or look on growth as a supreme principle, that we must also admit the virtues of *decrease.*[49]

The doctrine that the highest good consists in personal growth, in bringing to fulfillment the unique qualities of the individual person, is especially appealing to young men and women who have been repelled by what appears to be the standardized values represented by the socio-economic class in power. The morality of personal individualism thus may show a *class character.* In embracing personal individualism, young people may be reacting against the standards and values of a money economy in which a man is judged by what he can get. But such a reaction against "bourgeois materialism" in favor of personal individualism is often itself a bourgeois phenomenon. It is a commonplace of applied sociology that middle-class youngsters tend to have far greater self-awareness than children from deprived backgrounds. Lower-class children from impoverished milieus, says one commentator, "are likely to have developed no self-image. It is as if they do not know who they are and do not care."[50]

Educators of the progressive tradition—whether in the 1920s or the 1970s—agree in stressing the importance of "individual differences" and "unrealized potential." Such stress is always needed against the insensitive and unimaginative formal schooling most youngsters are forced to endure. Few who have read the eloquent books by John Holt, Herbert Kohl, George Dennison, Jonathan Kozol, and other advocates of radical school reform can doubt this need. "Each individual is different," says Elizabeth Monroe Drew in her description of the school Fernwood, a radical experiment in American public education:

Only a fraction of the potential of each is developed and used. Each is unique as to rate, style, tempo, and pattern of learning. Each chooses his own values and interests and develops personal tastes. By honoring these directions of growth and allowing them to flourish naturally, we found that students could master what had been difficult topics and material and do this easily.[51]

In such statements—they are commonplaces of enlightened educational ideology—we can see the perennial attractiveness of the moral ideal of growth with its linked concept, the value of individual differences. No one who has worked closely in the classroom with children can fail to be moved by the way certain youngsters, put down as dull or even hopeless, can come alive when their interests are aroused and their sympathies engaged by teaching methods that take individual differences into account skillfully and compassionately.

Trouble may come, however, when the moral ideal of personal individualism is applied *uncritically* in educational theory and practice. If such a view of personal individualism tries to persuade the young person that he has a precious unrealized self or "identity" that suitable experiences or teaching can surely discover and bring shiningly forth, certain expectations may be raised that may not, in the nature of things, be capable of being fulfilled. Pessimistic critics have noted that schools and colleges harbor many sons and daughters of the affluent middle classes who are waiting around for "relevant" education and "meaningful" experiences that will reveal to them their own hidden identity and enable them to live according to the rules of this precious and newly realized self. A large number of these young people may become seriously disillusioned, these critics say, for they may no more have hidden wonderful selves than the emperor of the story had new clothes. Complaining about the meaninglessness of the demands of education conceived in the traditional sense, such students may reject outside rules and external discipline for an inner direction and authority they rarely, if ever, find.

The concept of a precious latent self, a marvelous identity waiting to be uncovered, a real ME, is often linked to the belief in the gap between what a young person does and that sometimes mysterious state called "his potential." "Lynda is not living up to her potential," may be a shrewd observation of common sense, capable of being acted on with practical results. But it may also be used as a teacher's crutch, picked up from the uncritical belief in the existence in a kind of double or hidden self, a child or youth who *is* something fundamentally other than what he or she *does.* Educators who in this way overdepend on the concept of a hidden potential self versus an observable actual one have probably forgotten Sartre's saying, in his early existentialist writings, that a man is the sum of his acts, a human is what he does and no more. (Later Sartre would say that the truth of a man is his work and his wages.) Certainly a person may be tempted to use the idea of his potential as a comforting device to excuse failure to act. Some may be guilty of this bad faith when they wax nostalgic over "what I *could* have done." And surely powers, capacities, and dispositions are not thinglike entities like marbles in a box waiting to be uncovered or even seeds waiting to germinate. But a child *is* a growing thing, a developing unity that has not yet reached maturity. A boy or girl, young man or woman who has not yet thrust roots firmly down into life may really possess powers that have not yet been actualized. He or she may never achieve self-actualization, and the capacities themselves may (to speak only metaphorically) starve and die from want of exercise. But it might have been otherwise.

The question "Who am I?" has dominated much of the literature and psychology of the twentieth century. People have turned to novelists and psychiatrists to find an answer to the question of who "I" am, what is the "real self" beneath the daily duties, roles, and activities of a competitive middle-class world. This puts the emphasis on the human being as an individual apart from his context in social reality. The young Danish novelist Svend Aage Madson has said that the question *"Who am I?"* is the wrong one. The right question is *"What can I do?"*[52] This question leads back to those social and material realities that have played such a heavy part in making this "I" what it is. How long can this "I" usefully abstract itself from these social and material realities, separate itself from that active encounter with "them" that Sartre calls "praxis"?—any meaningful or purposeful human activity.

The writers we think of as "existentialists," including Sartre, have insisted on the reality of the individual self against the ever present tendency to dissolve that self in the social group; they have insisted on the reality of an individual life versus the threat of political abstraction. Whether existentialism's day is over, as Sartre himself now seems to say, whether that cultural movement is now no more than a rearguard action of "bourgeois individualism" is a question we must postpone at least until we have had a chance to consider existentialism's ethical implications.

NOTES: CHAPTER 7

1. Socrates is the great exception. Plato portrays his teacher as the first great Western individualist, describing Socrates' magnetic personality, informal manner, and humor, as well as eccentricities such as the philosopher's unconventional attire (bare feet) and his way of standing rapt while listening to his *daimon,* or inner voice. Aristophanes caricatures some oddities of Socrates in his comedy *The Clouds,* in which the philosopher appears as a kind of mad scientist. Plato testifies to Socrates' uniqueness by his words on his teacher's death: "Of all the men of his time whom I have known, he was the wisest, justest and best" (*Phaedo* 118). But it is arguable whether Plato is emphasizing Socrates' personal individualism or his possession of the general human virtues of goodness, justice, and wisdom—but in the highest degree.

2. Sören Kierkegaard, *The Sickness Unto Death,* trans. Walter Lowrie (1849; Princeton, N.J.: Princeton University Press, 1941), p. 142.

3. Aleksandr I. Solzhenitsyn, *The Cancer Ward,* trans. Rebecca Frank (New York: Dial, 1968), p. 501.

4. Alexis de Tocqueville, *Democracy in America,* trans. George Lawrence (1848; Garden City, N.Y.: Doubleday, 1969), pp. 506–507.

5. William Ellery Channing (1780–1842), an older Unitarian spokesman for personal individualism, declared characteristically, "No empire is so valuable as the empire of oneself."

6. Ralph Waldo Emerson, "Self-Reliance," in *The Writings of Ralph Waldo Emerson* ed. Brooks Atkinson (New York: Modern Library, 1940), p. 145.

7. Ibid., p. 145.

8. Ibid., p. 148.

9. Ibid., p. 149.

10. Ibid., p. 262.

11. Ralph Waldo Emerson, "Brahma," *Poems* (Boston: Houghton Mifflin, 1895), pp. 170–171.

12. Henry David Thoreau, *Walden and Civil Disobedience,* ed. Owen Thomas (New York: Norton, 1966), p. 231.

13. Walt Whitman "By Blue Ontario's Shores," from *Leaves of Grass,* in *Complete Poetry and Selected Prose and Letters,* ed. Emory Holloway (London: The Nonesuch Press, 1967).

14. Walt Whitman, "Song of Myself," from *Leaves of Grass*, p. 45.

15. Ibid., p. 26.

16. *Tat twam asi* is a closing for many of the parts of the *Upanishads,* which form part of the canon of ancient Hindu scripture. See The Thirteen Princial Upanishads, trans. R. E. Hume (London: Oxford University Press, 1921).

17. Whitman, "Song of Myself," p. 49.

18. Ibid., p. 44.

19. Ibid., p. 63.

20. Jean-Jacques Rousseau, *Confessions* (1770; New York: Dutton, 1931), p. 1.

21. Goethe, *Wilhelm Meister's Apprenticeship* (New York: Dutton, 1912), p. 250.

22. John Stuart Mill, "On Liberty," in *On Liberty, Representative Government, The Subjection of Women* (1859; London: Oxford University Press, 1960), pp. 78–79.

23. Friedrich Nietzsche, *Schopenhauer as Educator,* chap. 1, trans. J. W. Hillesheim and Malcolm R. Simpson (Chicago: Regnery, 1965), p. 4.

24. Ibid., pp. 4–5.

25. Ibid., p. 4.

26. Ibid., p. 5.

27. Ibid.

28. Ibid., pp. 5–6.

29. André Gide, *The Immoralist,* trans. Dorothy Bussy (1902; New York: Knopf, 1951), pp. 126–127.

30. André Gide, *Fruits of the Earth* [*Nourritures terrestres*], trans. Dorothy Bussy (1897; London: Secker & Warburg, 1949), p. 163.

31. Ralph Freedman expresses thoughts like this in his review of Hesse's *The Glass Bead Game, New York Times Book Review,* 4 January 1970, pp. 4, 20.

32. Hesse, *Demian,* trans. N. H. Priday (New York: Holt, Rinehart & Winston, 1948), p. 108.

33. Hesse, *Steppenwolf,* trans. Basil Creighton (New York: Holt, Rinehart & Winston, 1929).

34. In his old age at Princeton, the physicist Albert Einstein received a letter from a rabbi saying that he had sought in vain to comfort his daughter over the death of her younger sister, "a sinless, beautiful, sixteen year old child." In his reply, Einstein wrote, "A human being is a part of the whole, called by us 'Universe,' a part limited in time and space. He experiences himself, his thoughts and feelings as something separated from the rest—a kind of optical delusion of his consciousness. This delusion is a kind of prison for us, restricting us to our personal desires and to affection for a few persons nearest to us. Our task must be to free ourselves from this prison by widening our circle of compassion to embrace all living creatures and the whole of Nature in its beauty. Nobody is able to achieve this completely, but the striving for such achievement is in itself a part of the liberation and a foundation for inner security." From *The Einstein Papers* excerpted in *New York Times,* 29 March 1972, p. 20.

35. Hesse, *Demian,* prologue.

36. See Chapter 5, pp. 113–114.

37. See Chapter 5, pp. 114–116.

38. Karen Horney, *Neurosis and Human Growth: The Struggle Toward Self-Realization* (New York: Norton, 1950).

39. Carl G. Jung, *Modern Man in Search of a Soul* (New York: Harcourt, 1933), p. 235.

40. Rollo May, *Love and Will* (New York: Norton, 1969), p. 26.

41. William James, *Psychology: the Briefer Course,* ed. Gordon Allport (1892; New York: Harper & Row, 1961), Chap. 11.

42. William James, *Letters of William James,* 2 vols., edited by his son, Henry (Boston: Atlantic Monthly, 1920), 1:99.

43. Horney, *Neurosis and Human Growth*, pp. 173–174.
44. Erik Erikson, *Childhood and Society*, 2d ed. (New York: Norton, 1963), pp. 15–16.
45. Erik Erikson, *Identity: Youth and Crisis* (New York: Norton, 1968), p. 21.
46. *Ibid.*, pp. 259–260.
47. Carl G. Jung, *Conscience* (Zurich: Curatorium of the C. G. Jung Institute), pp. 200–201.
48. See Dewey on growth, Chapter 5, p. 115.
49. Review of George Bataille, *Oeuvres complètes,* 5 vols. (Paris: Gallimard, 1971) *Times Literary Supplement* (London), 3 March 1972, p. 234.
50. Lindley S. Stiles, *Introduction to College Education* (New York: Putnum, 1969), pp. 131–132).
51. Elizabeth Monroe Drew, quoted by R. Cross and B. Cross, eds., *Radical School Reform* (New York: Simon & Schuster, 1969), p. 265.
52. Cited by Hans-Jörgen Nielsen, "The Breakdown of an Institution," *Times Literary Supplement* (London), 9 October 1971, p. 1089.

8

The Existentialist Choice

"Existentialism" may be described as a particular kind of philosophical individualism. We can label just about any theory of human nature "existentialist" so long as it stresses the importance of the individual person over system, theory, group, or abstraction. Any doctrine that measures things by a particular lived life has some claim to being labeled existentialist. In Jean-Paul Sartre's early writings, two elements are emphasized: *subjectivity,* the inward sense of each human existence, and *freedom,* the responsibility of each person for choosing his or her own destiny. Both entail the corollary of *solitude,* an anxious isolation following from the very fact of human existence. The word *existentialism* itself became closely associated with the work of certain writers who achieved international reputation after World War II, particularly Sartre, whose book *Being and Nothingness* (*L'Etre et le neant*) became the bible of the movement. Other names were associated with this current of thought—Simone de Beauvoir, Marcel, Camus, as well as prophets and fellow travelers like Kierkegaard, Nietzsche, Dostoyevsky, and Kafka. Not all these people were professional philosophers; the postwar vogue of existentialism was advanced as much by literature as well as by philosophy. Sartre wrote plays and novels as well as philosophical treatises. So did Marcel. Camus and Beauvoir had been graduate students in philosophy, but both preferred imaginative literature to formal metaphysics or ethical theory.

I

We know that one of the characteristics of modern thought is its emphasis on the subjective, the progressive discovery of the importance of the self, the "I," in affairs of knowledge or being. Descartes announced that philosophy itself must begin with our knowledge of our own existence because it is of that existence that we are most sure. Kant saw the world order, not as an objective fact "out there," but as a product of the action of Mind, of subjective forms shaping an unknown material according to the categories of the Understanding. Human knowledge, including science, is conditioned by its inner forms of space, time, and causality. The world we apprehend by sense is one altered to our purposes by the act of knowing. Only in the moral self, Kant said, only in the good Will, do we break through to the transcendent realm of the Unconditioned.

But for all their emphasis on self as the beginning and standpoint of all knowledge and moral action, we find in Kant and Descartes no sense of the "feel" of each unique human existence. For that we have to turn to certain unusual religious thinkers such as Pascal or Kierkegaard. The young geometrician Pascal was Descartes's contemporary. He took Christianity seriously: if there is no God, then human existence is an absurdity without explanation. Neither in himself as an individual nor in the nature of man in general could Pascal find any reason—save for the goodness of God—why he should exist, why anyone or anything should exist at all. Why should he, Blaise Pascal, exist at this time, in this place? Logically, the atheist *could* be right; in any case, whether there is a God or not, an eternity begins after death:

When I consider my brief span of life, merged in eternity before and after, the little room I fill and even see, engulfed in the infinite immensity of spaces which I know not and which know not me, I am afraid and I wonder why I am here rather than there, for there is no reason why here rather than there, why now rather than then. Who has set me here? By whose order and direction have this place and this time been assigned to me? . . . The eternal silence of these infinite spaces frightens me.[1]

The Danish eccentric Sören Kierkegaard seems to have been the first to use the word *existential* in its now familiar sense of the inexplicable fact of a lived life, here and now, specific, individual, the unique "felt" quality of *my* life and *yours*. Like Pascal, Kierkegaard thought that each man had the lonely task of choosing his own fate, standing with God or against him in the soul's solitary rendezvous with eternity. We recall him saying that the Christian heroism is to venture wholly to be oneself as an individual, this one definite man, alone before the face of God, that one "cannot know what it is to be a Christian until he knows what it is to exist." Like Pascal, Kierkegaard observes that the universe does not explain itself; it returns no answer to our demand for a reasonable account of this tremendous enterprise and our place in it:

How did I obtain an interest in this big enterprise they call Reality? Why should I have an interest in it? Is it not a voluntary concern? And if I am to be compelled to take part in it, where is the director? I should like to make a remark to him. Is there no director? In what direction shall I turn with my complaint? Existence is surely a debate—may I beg that my view be taken into consideration.[2]

To talk of "human nature" is idle—"man" is only an abstraction. There is only this man or woman, myself, living, enjoying, suffering, dying. Do not talk to me, Kierkegaard says, of knowledge or truth, or of ethics either. These remain abstractions only unless I personally, subjectively assimilate them. Truth, for Kierkegaard, *is* "subjectivity," the highest degree of personal self-realization. For "systems"—religious, philosophical, scientific, or social—he had no use at all. The crucial fact of an individual person's existence is incommensurable with *any* system, however efficient. The individual is lost in universal laws, even in ethical laws. Everything in Kierkegaard's teaching points toward the individual person standing in freedom and solitude before God. Out of that freedom he must decide whether he will direct his life to God. It is a question of either/or.

Early in our century, Franz Kafka wrote stories about employes summoned to work by hidden officials who ignore their workers' existences, about defendants tried by courts that meet only in abandoned lofts and at irregular intervals, about land surveyors vainly trying to locate the officials of an unreachable castle. Perhaps court or castle contain the key to the enigma of human existence, but no way reaches there. When you try to telephone the officials, you find that there is no central switchboard— only a sound like "the humming of countless children's voices."[3] Existence is all important, but it has no meaning, if we take "meaning" to signify "capable of rational explanation." One of Dostoyevsky's characters suggests that if God does not exist, some embarrassing questions will have to be faced, such as, "Why then isn't everything permitted?" Nietzsche claimed that God was dead.[4] Yet while God "lived" he gave the universe a meaning, however obscure. Nietzsche has been called an existentialist, and it is easy to see why this elastic classification can be made to fit him. A fervent defender of personal individualism,

Nietzsche never worked out a systematic ethics, although he became a powerful moral critic.

Nietzsche preached that God was dead, Pascal and Kierkegaard proclaimed that he lived—yet the three moralists are said to be important in the history of existentialist thought. What do believing and nonbelieving existentialists have in common? How can some (like Karl Jaspers) be Christians while others (like Sartre) are atheists? One answer usually given is that all of them share a belief in man's ability to freely choose his life. Despite periodic pendulum swings toward theological determinism (the belief that man can do nothing of himself, not even choose his own salvation), the dominant Christian tradition assumed the freedom of the human to achieve his being, to choose or reject his own salvation, the freedom to "make himself" as the existentialists say. Time and again, Christian teaching rebounded from the rigors of theological fatalism to insist that the acceptance or rejection of the good was up to each individual person, that directing one's life to God was a matter of free and individual choice. Many twentieth-century religious thinkers have criticized systematic theology as "essentialist." Such thinking tends to concern itself with nature, kinds, essences, types, abstractions. They reject a theology that seems concerned with principles and with deductions from them rather than with the unique presence of God, the reality of the individual lived life, the reality of the faith and despair of the individual man of flesh and bone. With this in mind, it is not hard to see why Gabriel Marcel, Jean Wahl, Karl Jaspers, Paul Tillich, Martin Buber, and other philosophers or theologians with ties to Western religious traditions have been labeled existentialists as well as self-avowed atheists and nonbelievers like Sartre, Beauvoir, and Camus.

II

Above all others, existentialism is associated with the name of Jean-Paul Sartre, the French philosopher and man of letters whose book *Being and Nothingness* became the movement's definitive testament almost as soon as it was published in 1943. Gabriel Marcel named Sartre's philosophy "existentialism." Sartre accepted the label and included Marcel, Jaspers and Heidegger in the existentialist category as well as himself. The postwar popularity of existentialism—for which Sartre was directly responsible—related in part to the hunger of an exhausted world for some kind of explanation or at least acknowledgement of the irrationalities of the human condition. Existentialism became a world intellectual mode. Sartre, however, moved on; his thinking became strongly Marxist-oriented, and he all but repudiated existentialism as a theory of man—valid enough for wartime with its simplified conditions of choice, but inadequate to the social complexities of the century's second half. But Sartre's early existentialism left a lasting mark on our time's way of thinking and feeling about the world, and no book on ethics and morals can ignore Sartre's existentialist writings, nor dismiss them as being part of an intellectual fad.

One trouble with trying to say something about existentialist ethics is that existentialism does not have a great deal of explicit ethical theory. It does have what might be called a philosophical anthropology, that is, a theory of man and human nature, from which some ethical consequences seem to follow. This is particularly the case where existentialism's characteristic doctrine of human freedom is concerned. But *Being and Nothingness* is not a book like Mill's *Utilitarianism,* in which an ethical theory is presented, its basic principles clearly explained, its implications arranged in logical order and defended, one after another, by reasonable arguments. Like so much of existentialist thought generally, the ethical implications of Sartre's book relate to a kind of tone, an attitude or manner of looking at the world, rather than to the explicit statements and conclusions of traditional moral philosophy.

Sartre's existentialism draws heavily on technical philosophical concepts and vocabulary borrowed from two influential German philosophers, Edmund Husserl and Martin Heidegger. Sartre subtitled his *Being and Nothingness* "An Essay in Phenomenological Ontology." Phenomenology is a philosophical method associated with the name of Husserl and his followers.[5] Husserl's sometime pupil, Heidegger, took *ontology* as the locus of the most important problems of philosophy. Ontology is the study of Being and its kinds. Analysis of Being and its kinds is the starting point of Sartre's work in *Being and Nothingness*. Whatever ethics this early book of Sartre may contain stands there as part of a general metaphysical or ontological scheme. We begin with our being-in-the-world. Like Heidegger, Sartre claims that philosophy must start from analysis of human reality, the kind of Being we know better than any other because it is our own.

Sartre distinguishes between human reality (*l'être pour soi*— being-for-itself) and that kind of Being that things or objects have (*l'être en soi*—being-in-itself). Human reality is incomplete, filled with a consciousness of a *lack* at its base. We yearn for the wholeness, the four-square completeness that physical objects, even nonhuman animals, have. Unlike other kinds of Being, human reality *projects itself,* pushes itself forward in the direction of its desired completion. Future-oriented man is never at one with his body. He is always projecting himself out from it toward the future, toward that which is not yet. From my body there stands out an invisible radiation of purpose, an intentional arc. Failure to take this intentional arc into account limits the usual simple psychological explanations of human behavior in terms of conditioned reflexes. Such mechanistic accounts tend to tear our living bodies from their purposeful projected contexts and to turn them into simple objects, *mere* bodies. But I am not just a body. I discover my existing self to be incomplete. I try to complete it by attempting to transcend myself.

Value is connected with this urge to transcend; it is the totality of being that I strive for but never reach. Hence value does not preexist; I *confer* it on things. Sartre draws an ethical corollary that is characteristically individualistic. If it is I that confers value on things, then each one of us creates his own morality; I must make my own choices without the aid of ethical rules, codes, or principles. A man may want to join his comrades in the Resistance; yet he may have an ailing mother at home who needs his help. In deciding, the man creates the value; it is in no sense a value existing a priori—it exists after the fact. A man makes a moral decision out of Nothing, a little like God creating the world *ex nihilo.*

Existence and Nausea

Sartre's individualism permeates the ontological foundations of his early existentialism as well as the ethical conclusions so sketchily implied in that philosophy. In ordinary experience, most of the time we see objects in terms of types, classes, essences. When we encounter the bedrock of reality, bare existence, we hastily throw over it the canvas of classes and kinds. Sartre's early novel *Nausea* tells of the experiences of a certain writer called Roquentin who encounters objects that he experiences as single and unique occurrences, basic raw things that only *exist* and have no general character. Result: ontological hallucinations.

At our core *we* exist, and our existence is a fact for which no reason can be offered. But very few of us *experience* raw existence because we continually cover up our reasonless existing, as well as that of other things and people, with veils of justifications and bogus explanations. Though surrounded by other existences, including human ones, we automatically turn them into essences or types. We do this to protect ourselves so that existences will not touch us. *Nobody* loves human existences, says Roquentin to his café companion, the Self-Taught Man, who claims to feel brotherly warmth toward the other human presences in the restaurant: " 'You wouldn't recognize them in the street. They're only symbols in your eyes. You aren't touched by them at all; you're touched by the Youth of the Man, the Love of the Man and Woman, the Human Voice.' "[6] In a word, we turn things into types. Or into things that exist merely *for us,* like pots and tools. Roquentin, however, is that rare human who has experienced the terrible feel of bare existence. That experience causes his nausea, a metaphysical disgust that shakes him to the gut, makes him bid farewell to an old love, abandon his writing project, leave Bouville—the port city where all this happens—forever.

On a certain Monday, Roquentin has an attack of nausea. He had put down his manuscript for a moment, looked at the solid objects surrounding him—furniture, table, bed, in all their four-square self-sufficiency. Then he experiences *himself* as an object. He senses his existence as absurd because there is no reason for it; he, like the existence of which he is a part, is contingent, unnecessary, *de trop:* "I am the Thing. Existence, liberated, detached, floods over me." Tuesday, the next day, he does nothing—just exists, as he notes in his diary. Wednesday he eats his dinner at the restaurant, listens to the Self-Taught Man expound his naïve brotherhood-of-man humanism until he can stand it no longer. He runs to the street, boards a trolley, and rides it—panic stricken. Finally he flings himself off the tram, throws himself breathless on a bench in a public park. He is looking down at something. The desolate thing is part of a chestnut-tree root. Roquentin, horrified, sees it as bare existence:

A tree scrapes at the earth under my feet with a black nail. I would like to let myself go, forget myself, sleep. But I can't, I'm suffocating: existence penetrates me everywhere, through the eyes, the nose, the mouth. . . . And suddenly, suddenly the veil is torn away, I have understood, I have *seen*. . . . Existence had suddenly unveiled itself. It had lost the harmless look of an abstract category: it was the very paste of things, this root was kneaded into existence.[7]

Like many heroes of classical twentieth-century novels, Roquentin has experienced a moment of illumination, an epiphany in which the deep meaning of things becomes manifest, doubts and uncertainties fall away in a moment of luminous certitude. But the viscous light of Roquentin's illumination is by no means a bright radiance. The time is 6:00 P.M. Roquentin's dark epiphany has at last come to its exhausting end. He writes in his diary what he had seen in the park, how he now understands the meaning of "existence."

Freedom and Nothingness
The title *Being and Nothingness* names the two principle compounds of which, according to Sartre, man is composed. Man is the "nothing-making" animal. An earthquake, a flood, any natural disaster simply redistributes matter; only man can actually destroy. Auschwitz and the Katyn Forest were human devices. Yet the *nothingness* at the heart of our human reality is all one with our *freedom*. How can this be? In answer, Sartre adapts an old metaphysical distinction to his purpose—the distinction between *essence* and *existence*.[8] Essence refers to *what* a thing is—its kind, its qualities, its characteristics, its definition. Existence means *that* a thing is. Long ago Aristotle said, "What man is, and that man exists are two different questions." In things, in objects, says Sartre, essence precedes existence. The nature, the whatness, the character of a table I am designing is prior to its actual manufacture. We can have a pretty good idea of that table before it comes into existence. But, apart from being a vertebrate that talks and walks erect, uses tools, has certain social contexts, man's nature does not exist before he begins to act, to *make himself* out of the choices that spring from his freedom. What Sartre has in mind here is not what we might call the universal or general essence a human has, but the qualities he possesses as an individual, unique, incapable of being substituted for. Each human person constructs his own *individual* essence; his existence is a prior given fact.

Freedom to make ourselves, to create what we are, is insep- arable from the nothingness that is one of the two primal ingredients in human reality. Alone among things, man is able to erase the moment just past, to *cancel out,* and to start making himself again. Alone among things, he has the power to modify Being, to throw the past out of court, to create himself anew on the site of the erasure. True, a man cannot erase the past in the sense that he can wipe out what he did. It is impossible to disown, to get rid of one's acts. They are done, fixed, as ineradi- cable as a fresco painting. But what a man can do is to break with his past and start completely from scratch. You who are read- ing this book are free to put it down, throw off your duties and responsibilities, leave friends, family, church, college, nation, work, loves—and make yourself over again. The fact that most people do not elect to do this does not argue to the incapacity of human reality to "nothing-make" the past in the sense of throwing it out of court as far as our immediate lived life is concerned. Human freedom precedes essence in human reality; out of our freedom, we become what we are. All our lives long, we are painting a self-portrait—in fresco. This picture—our indi- vidual essence, *what we are*—will not be finished until we lay down the brush at the moment of death. Only then, when ex- istence comes to an end, do we become wholly essence. As Hegel says, *Wesen ist was gewesen ist,* essence is *what has been.* Speaking of the death of Camus, Sartre says, "Every life that is cut off—even the life of so young a man—is at one and the same time a phonograph record that is broken and a com- plete life."[9]

Freedom and Bad Faith

For a human to *be,* then, is to *act.* A man is the sum of his ac- tions. There is no such thing as a "mute inglorious Milton," for if a man is "mute" he is not a Milton. Useless to talk about the music Schubert might have written had he not died so young. He did not write it. A man is what he has done. And what he has done, *he has chosen to do.* A man is not simply the product of the people and things in his environment—his family, his church, his government, his education—although in their name he may deny his freedom and thus stand in what Sartre calls "bad faith." How often do we hear people say things like this: "I tried to do an honest job on the paper, but I was tired because I didn't have any sleep the night before and my mind went blank."

Or: "I know I insulted him, but I was drunk and didn't know what I was doing." Or: "I can't do that—my family wouldn't let me." Or: "I'd *like* to help you, but my hands are tied." Unhappy childhood, glands, religion, a traumatic experience—all these can be used by people so that they can *escape from freedom.* Freedom is hard to bear. Knowing that I am *responsible* for my acts is the source of anguish, so I tend to deny responsibility for my acts. I parade reasons for acting or not acting that really have nothing to do with it. This is bad faith (*mauvaise foi*).

Heidegger said that there are two possible modes of existence, the authentic and the inauthentic. In the first, one lives facing the truth; in the second one evades the truth, pretends it isn't there. Sartre's bad faith is a particular case of the latter, but it is also continuous with the tradition of French moralism. From Pascal to Camus, the search is for *sincerity.* Hypocrisy and phariseeism have been eternal targets of France's spiritual directors as well as its writers of farce and directors of comic films. Summing up Sartre's ethical teaching, Mary Warnock says, "Moral man is sincere man; immorality is phoniness."[10] But Sartre's subtle analysis of bad faith would include even cases of actual sincerity —not only obvious examples of the person who *proclaims* his sincerity ("I may have had difficulties with her, but at least I was *honest!*"), but also the person who *is* sincere, like a waiter who so wants to appear a good waiter that he exaggerates his skill to a ritual degree, turning himself into an object, into the Platonic idea of "waiter." By perpetually striving to be sincere a man may turn himself into an object that he is not; he may succeed in separating himself from himself. Thus, "the goal of sincerity and the goal of bad faith are not so different."[11]

One of Sartre's amusing illustrations of bad faith may be found in *Being and Nothingness.* A woman is with a man who has taken her out for the first time. She is well aware that the man has intentions of some warmth toward her, and she knows that at some time during the evening she must make a decision. The man is talking to her in a sincere and respectful manner. Is he addressing himself to her as the full and complete personality she is? Or is he regarding her only as a body, as a sexual object? For the moment she treats his regard as if it were admiration and respect:

But then suppose he takes her hand. This act of her companion risks changing the situation by calling for an immediate decision. To leave the hand there is to consent in herself to flirt, to engage herself. To withdraw it is to break the troubled and unstable harmony which gives the hour its charm. The aim is to postpone the moment of decision as long as possible. We know what happens next; the young woman leaves her hand there, but she *does not notice* that she is leaving it. She does not notice because it happens by chance that she is at this moment all intellect. She draws her companion up to the most lofty regions of sentimental speculation; she speaks of life, of her life, she shows herself in her essential aspect—a personality, a consciousness. And during this time the divorce of the body from the soul is accomplished; the hand rests inert between the warm hands of her companion—neither consenting nor resisting—a thing.[12]

Sartre says this woman is in bad faith. She is aware of her own body, but behaves as if it were not in any way connected to herself as a conscious being. She rises above her body, looks down on it as a passive object to which things can happen—but things that she did nothing to provoke.

The ethical reasons people give to justify their acts, the moral rules they invoke as guiding precepts—these too are often in bad faith. The moral act is irrational in the sense that there is no set of reasons inclining us to act one way and outweighing a set of reasons for another course. Indeed, says Sartre, when I make a show of deliberating, I have already chosen; the chips are down. Moreover, it is I alone who act. I cannot put my act off on anyone else; I cannot ask someone to share responsibility for what *I* do. Freedom is a lonely business, and it is its solitude that is central to the human condition. The choice to "engage myself" is mine and mine alone. I may try to escape the burden of freedom by denying that I am free, by resting my actions on this or that kind of determinism. But whatever course I choose, whatever side of the barricades I find myself on—even if I decide not to act at all—it is *my* choice. In the world of *Being and Nothingness,* there are no innocent victims.

Intention and Action

Speaking in conformity with the classical tradition of ethics, Sartre says that a true act is a free act. If I am pushed down the subway steps by someone behind me, this is not, on my part, a true act. It may or may not be a true act on the part of the pusher. But in my situation as the one pushed down the stairs, I am not free; there is no choice, I have no intention, it is not an *act* at all. To Sartre, freedom is the first condition of action:

We should observe first that an action is on principle intentional. The careless smoker who has through negligence caused the explosion of a powder magazine has not *acted*. On the other hand the worker who is charged with dynamiting a quarry and who obeys the given orders has acted when he has produced the expected explosion; he knew what he was doing or, if you prefer, he intentionally realised a conscious project.[13]

Sartre is aware of the need of action, in any philosophy, to analyze the part played by motive and intent. Intention and motivation are not thinglike objects inside us, mental dominoes that push us into action. Rather, they are parts of a complex of attitudes and dispositions related to our possible action upon our surroundings. According to Sartre, no factual state, no physical or social situation, is *by itself* capable of motivating an act at all. (A physical push may knock you down, but remember that even that is not, on your side, a true act at all.) To effect action, human consciousness must perceive a *lack*, a negativity, and must be disposed to perceive that it is *capable* of changing that lack, filling that negativity, with a positive alternative situation. It is an ethical axiom that in order to be held morally responsible for an action, I must be capable of performing that action. I do not expect to be held morally accountable for my failure to swim to the rescue of a child if I cannot swim. Sartre's version of this axiom is that in order to act, truly to act, I must perceive that I am capable of changing the shape of even a little corner of my world. Glasgow factory workers in 1845 did not revolt against their deplorable conditions of work because they were so stupefied as to be incapable of imagining their hardships as anything but part of the natural order of things. That there was an alternative, an "otherwise" that could be effected, did not occur to them. Autocracy and lack of bread did not "cause" either the French or the Russian revolution; the revolutionaries had to perceive that there was a lack of a social order that would be better for them, that there was a genuine alternative to their miserable condition, and that they really could do something about it—that they could do something to fill the lack, the gap, the emptiness, with a positive alternative.

Do actions have causes? Of course they do, though no physical or social fact is by itself a sufficient condition of action. A causeless act is, for Sartre, a contradiction in terms, because he defines an act as intentional. "Each action," says Sartre, "must, in fact, have an end and the end in turn is referred to a cause. . . . To speak of an act without a cause is to speak of an act which would lack the intentional structure of every act."[14] No act is free if by "free" is meant "causeless." But "cause" is bound up with that intentionality that is part of the act itself. The existence of ends and motives is indispensable to true acts, yet this does not mean that they are not free. It is naïve to posit causes as entities *outside* the intentional situation, to think of them as external (physical) billiard balls that knock internal (mental) billiard balls into configurations that could have been predicted. To Sartre, causes and motives related to action have meaning only within a situation in which consciousness projects itself toward a future that does not yet exist.

Are Individual Acts Universalizable?

In his well-known essay "Existentialism is a Humanism," Sartre states flatly that every person is responsible for what he does with his existence. The moral decision is essentially a solitary affair—it cannot be referred for approval to a code, a guidebook, the criterion of reasonableness, the expectations of society. The decision is completely up to me; there is no preexisting set of reasons to which I can appeal in making my choice. If there are, other reasons could be found that would enable me to justify my acting otherwise. What set of ethical rules would tell the young Frenchman in wartime whether he should join the Resistance or stay at home to take care of his ailing mother? All he can do is to decide—one way or another.

So far, clear enough, but Sartre goes further. Not only does each person choose himself by his act (that is, choose what he wants to be), but every choice is an implicit *universalization.* When I choose for myself, I choose for all. When I commit myself, I implicitly commit everybody. Socrates once said that no man knowingly chooses evil; if it is evil he has chosen, he sees it under the guise of good—we always choose what we believe to be our good. Sartre agrees with this Socratic principle, but extends it. When I choose my good, I thereby affirm that it is good, not just for me, but for all. *"L'acte individuel engage toute l'humanité."* Sartre says:

When we say that man chooses himself, we do mean that every one of us must choose himself; but by that we also mean that in choosing for himself he chooses for all men. For in effect, of all the actions a man may take in order to create himself as he wills to be, there is not one which is not creative, at the same time, of an image of man such as he believes he ought to be. To choose between this or that is at the same time to affirm the value of that which is chosen; for we are unable ever to choose the worse. What we choose is always the better; and nothing can be better for us unless it is better for all. . . . Our responsibility is thus much greater than we had supposed, for it concerns mankind as a whole.[15]

Here Sartre has performed a remarkable feat. In the very *individualism* of the ethical decision he finds the *universalizing* principle that ethical theorists proclaim to be essential to the moral judgment. We remember the maxim of Kant's categorical imperative: "Act so that you can will your act to become universal law." Sartre seems to be claiming that when I act in a moral situation, I implicitly create a law, for when I decide, I am in some way deciding for all men: "What we choose is always the better; and nothing can be better for us unless it is better for all." There is no difficulty in our accepting the first part of the statement, if we hold with Socrates that a person always chooses what he believes to be his own good and that no one knowingly chooses evil. It is the second part of Sartre's generalization principle that raises the question of consistency. How is this universal ingredient logically to be found in Sartre's ethical individualism—or, for that matter, in our own moral decisions? If I am a college student, I may choose to run for the University Senate rather than join the Left Collective. By joining the senate, I choose to signify that working for political change within the ordinary processes of university government is the best attitude. But it is more than this. According to Sartre's principle of universalization, by my action I signify that it is not only best for me, but best for all. In this example, the principle seems to fit. But suppose I am thinking of getting married. Sartre is ready for this:

Or if, to take a more personal case, I decide to marry and to have children, even though this decision proceeds simply from my situation, from my passion or my desire, I am thereby committing not only myself but humanity as a whole, to the practice of monogamy. I am thus responsible for myself and for all men, and I am creating a certain image of man as I would have him to be. In fashioning myself, I fashion man.[16]

But there is a problem here. Does my decision to marry imply that it is a good for everybody? That for someone else, in circumstances different from mine, remaining a bachelor would *not* be good? That I oppose a Saudi Arabian taking a fourth wife? It does not seem so. When I marry, I signify that monogamy is a good and a good for me—I do not claim to legislate for others. But that is just what Sartre seems to claim we *do* when we act in a situation of moral choice. I implicitly declare that this action is more than a decision for me alone; it is a *rule* and not just a rule for me, but for all. Sartre does *not* mean that when I marry, I commit myself to superimposing monogamy on others, or that I deny others the right to differ with me as to what they shall do with their lives. But still he seems to imply that when I act, I implicitly legislate: I make a law or rule for all. This seems contradictory.[17]

Critics of Sartre point out that a radically individualistic ethic, a moral philosophy announcing that the decision of the agent has no reason apart from the decision and that no reason can be given for ethical choice, should not be able to create a universalizability principle so easily. The use of such a principle *is* moral reasoning. The rational character of the ethical judgment shows itself in its universalizability. Sartre's rule, "Nothing can be better for me unless it is better for all," cannot be a *description* of how people do in fact act, for they do not generally act as if they were choosing for everybody—at least, they do not think they do. Perhaps Sartre intends his maxim to be a moral exhortation rather than a description of how people do in fact act—a Kantian rule like "In a moral situation, act only *as if* you were committing mankind by what you do."[18] At the very least it seems as if Sartre believes that we should treat others as if, like ourselves, they were centers of freedom—neither objects nor instruments, but ends in themselves. But this leads us back to Kant again: "Now I say man and generally every rational being exists as an end and must never be treated as a means alone."[19]

If there is one concept that links Kant's moral philosophy and Sartre's existentialist ethic, it is the concept of *autonomy.* Perhaps Sartre did not mean to say more than this: each must decide for himself or herself, and not take it from some authority. But this claim that agents ought to be autonomous does not commit Sartre to regarding a person's decision as beyond reason and therefore a denial of universalizability.[20]

Sartre as Marxist
Sartre's outlook changed fundamentally after World War II. He sharply modified his doctrine of the essential freedom of the individual person in a situation of choice. After the war, per-

suaded by his studies in Marxism as well as by world events, he came to admit to the power of circumstances (*les forces des choses*) to bend or break the life of a man. *Being and Nothingness* was a wartime book, and the situation of that war was exceptional; its ethic was one of extreme situations. In the Resistance, he says, there was only one virtue—courage; there was one choice, yes or no, and that choice was always possible: "A Frenchman was either for the Germans or against them, there was no other option. The real political problems of being 'for, but' or 'against, but' were not posed by this experience. The result was that I concluded that in any circumstances, there is always a possible choice. Which is false."[21] The war over, the choices open to a man in regard to what to do with his life were not so simple. Radical emphasis on absolute personal freedom may be little more than a class product—*bourgeois individualism,* decking itself out in high moral colors. The question now is to see if there is *anything* to a man beyond his social and economic milieu, anything besides his work and his wages.

The rapid postwar development of Sartre's thought can be seen in his *Critique of Dialectical Reason* (1960), together with its prefatory essay "Search for a Method." The premise of Sartre's *Critique* is that Marxism is the philosophy of our time, the only philosophy that takes man in his totality—historical, social, economic, philosophical. We cannot go beyond Marxism because we have not gone beyond the circumstances that had brought it about. On the intellectual stage of the cold war that followed the initial confrontation of Russia with the Western powers, the West was forced to reach back into its past—to Kierkegaard, Nietzsche, Kafka—in order to construct anything like an ideology with which to confront the Soviet ideological apparatus. The traditional Western appeal to reason and democracy had lost its dynamic. To Sartre, Marxism does not mean Soviet Marxism or the Marxism of Stalin or Brezhnev or of the French Communist party. Sartre defends what he calls "Marx's own Marxism," by which he understands a theory of history and of nature in which facts are never taken as isolated appearances. When facts come into being together, it is always within the higher unity of a whole. As Hegel pointed out, man is part of a historical process that has its reasons and its laws: these reasons and laws can be known and used by men to better their conditions. Under capitalism, Marx said, men become alienated from the fruits of their labor. A factory combine or big business corporation means to them something threatening and hostile. Under capitalism, it is impossible to understand a man by abstracting him from his social and economic situation. The truth of a man is his work and his wages.

Now the obvious question is: how can one be an existentialist and a Marxist at the same time? For the one claims a radical freedom of the individual person; the other implies a historical determinism in which the individual lived life seems to be no more than a product of social forces. Engels taught that if Napoleon had not existed, another man would have filled his place and the replacement would have made little historical difference. Sartre denied that Marxism need mean the denial of human freedom. He finds Engels's statement on Napoleon arbitrary; it gives up the reality of an individual human life and career too easily. Sartre prefers to cite another passage of Engels, one from a letter to Marx: "Men themselves make their history, but in a given environment which conditions them."[22] Sartre reconciles Marxist theory with his own earlier views by saying that existentialism

. . . intends, without being unfaithful to Marxist principles, to find mediations which allow the individual concrete—the particular life, the real and dated conflict, the person—to emerge from the background of the *general* contradictions of productive forces and the relations of production.[23]

Sartre has expressed the hope that future Marxism will develop to a point where its abstract and theoretical character will be filled out by a specifically *human* dimension. He looks to the day when Marxist theory will take up into itself the existentialist truth of the reality of the individual concrete life and act. From that day existentialism will fade out as a separate doctrine, for it will have been absorbed in Marxism, the totalizing "philosophy of our time"—the only one that takes man in "the materiality of his condition."

Despite his postwar awareness of the massive effects of social conditioning—poverty, family, race, money, power, work—Sartre never wholly gives up the concept of personal autonomy that is at the core of existentialist philosophy whatever its setting. He never surrenders entirely the notion of personal freedom, of personal responsibility for one's individual fate:

For the idea which I have never ceased to develop is that in the end one is always responsible for what is made of one. Even if one can do nothing else besides assume this responsibility. For I believe that a man can always make something out of what is made of him.[24]

I may *respond* to the conditioning forces of society and circumstances by not giving back everything that their conditioning has given to me, or by giving back some degree of response *beyond* what has been pressed into me. Flaubert was conditioned by his nineteenth-century French provincial bourgeois society, and his work is indelibly colored by that influence. But there is something more than this in Flaubert's work, and it is that "something more" that he gave back in response to his social conditioning, which makes him a great artist. Sartre says:

This is the limit I would today accord to freedom: the small movement which makes of a totally conditioned social being someone who does not render back completely what his conditioning has given him. Which makes of Genet a poet when he had been rigorously conditioned to be a thief.[25]

As for his early novels and plays, Sartre became so anxious to make the point that he has moved beyond them that he occasionally slips, if not into bad faith, at least into the error Gilbert Ryle has christened a "category mistake"—an error one makes by comparing two completely different *types* of being. Speaking of his early writings, Sartre told an interviewer, "I have changed since. I have seen children die of hunger. In the face of a child who is dying, *Nausea* has no weight."[26] But are the two comparable? Can a string quartet be weighed on the same scale as an act of injustice? Sartre's remark is like Camus's statement in *The Myth of Sisyphus* that he regards technical philosophy as a game—he has never seen anyone die for the ontological argument.

As we read over Sartre's work, early and late, it sometimes seems that no ethical rule, no categorical imperative emerges other than the simple, forceful injunction of more than one character in Sartre's stories:

Don't be a bastard.

In its way, this seems to be a rough equivalent of what English philosophers of a more genteel tradition meant when they referred hard decisions to "the fundamental sense of human decency."

III

Camus and the Morality of the Absurd

Albert Camus was not a philosopher but a poet. And like many French poets he was also a moralist. This does not mean that the author of *The Rebel* (*L'Homme revolté*) was an ethical theorist. Camus was not interested in discussions of the meanings of ethical terms nor in analyses of the conditions of moral judgments. He had a certain idea of what humans are and what humans should be. He recognized the presence of evil and the promise of good, called attention to them in his essays, made poetry out of them in his novels and tales.

Camus's death in an automobile accident in 1960 caused nearly every obituary writer to find in that fatal crash a striking example of the Absurd. For the Absurd (a notion dramatized earlier in the work of Sartre and Malraux) was linked in the public mind with the author of *The Stranger* and *The Myth of Sisyphus.* Camus did not call himself an existentialist. Though he shared common points of view with Sartre and worked with him in the Resistance, Camus quarreled with his friend over political questions, particularly the issue of communism. Briefly a party member at the University of Algiers, Camus broke with communism entirely after the war, calling it a lie that tried to pass off a police state as a proletarian revolution. Camus applied the word *existentials* to Kierkegaard and Jaspers—Christian believers who clearly see the unreason and arbitrariness of human existence and because of that fact make "the leap" to God. Camus made no such leap. It is essential to his view that there exists no supernatural order, no transcendent meaning that justifies the fate the universe deals out sooner or later to all of us—death and annihilation.

The basic meaning of *absurd* contains two notions: the idea of contradiction or inconsistency and the element of the ridiculous or laughable. Camus described the human condition as absurd. Why? Because there is an inconsistency between the longing of every human heart for that which transcends us, for something that goes beyond time and death, and our actual fate, which is annihilation. Every human mind seeks some rationality in the universe that would explain, even a little, what we are doing as an infinitely small, though conscious, part of that universe. Camus was convinced that the entire enterprise is lacking in meaning and rationality. "The world in itself is not reasonable," he says in *Sisyphus,* "that is all that can be said. But what is absurd is the confrontation of this irrational and the wild longing for clarity whose call echoes in the human heart."[27] Like his predecessor Pascal, Camus was struck by the discrepancy between our feverish quest for happiness and the vanity of our actions.

There have been times in the history of the West when people believed that there was indeed an explanation and a reward for the human heart's longing for immortality. Throughout that span of centuries we call the Ages of Faith, people believed that the grace of God would save them from the annihilation toward which every created thing spins down. Such a faith persisted in Camus's older colleague in French letters, François Mauriac, who accepted his death, confident that "a key to the enigma exists, that each tear counts, each drop of blood." As the Ages of Faith disintegrated, as science and enlightenment turned men's minds to *this* world, men transferred their faith in God to the Idea of Man. The individual will die, but the Idea of Man will live on, nourished by reason, progress, and political enlightenment. This was the humanist tradition, an echo of which is found in William Faulkner's Nobel Prize speech—"I believe that man will not merely endure: he will prevail."[28] But disillusion with humanism set in even before the great world wars of the twentieth century. By the time the death camps sprang into existence, it was a struggle to defend humanism in the traditional sense. Sartre thought that Hitler came too close to winning for him to put his trust in "Man" two hundred years from now. To many of those who rejected the bourgeois humanism of the nineteenth and twentieth century, the Bolshevik Revolution brought fresh promise of transcending of the limits of the individual human condition. I, as an individual, may die, but my death can achieve significance as I participate in the great struggle for Socialist brotherhood. Camus recorded his disillusionment with that ideal, indeed with *any* political ideal that promises transcendence. In his book *The Rebel* there is a suggestion of the old quietist doctrine that all action (Camus would say all *political* action) contains the seeds of its own corruption within it. Camus's generation watched the Moscow trials and read Koestler's *Darkness at Noon.* The revolution was like Saturn devouring his own children.

To Camus, as to his fellow North African Saint Augustine, *death* is the enemy. The world is, in its simplest, sensuous aspect, a lovely place. There are simple incomparable pleasures—the feel of sun, sand, saltwater, a cup of coffee, a street light caught for a moment by a bangle in the ear of a pretty girl. The simplest lucid reason tells us that this short life is the only life there is; we are subject to time and death. Yet men kill each other for *ideas*—religious or political. A man must find in his heart, Camus says, the point at which he will say "no." Camus's categorical imperative takes the form of the maxim: *"I will not act so as to mutilate another human being."* Camus's novel *The Plague* tells of an epidemic in the Algerian city of Oran. A few of those caught in the quarantine—among them, Doctor Rieux, the physician-narrator—do what they can to fight the gruesome disease. But they can do very little. The plague withdraws when it spends itself, not before. And it is still there, lying in wait for a future sortie against guilty and innocent alike. Camus's journalist Tarrou underlines the allegory in words that recall Simone Weil's saying that morality lies not in judgment but in attention:

Each of us has the plague within him; no one, no one on earth is free from it. And I know too that we must keep endless watch on ourselves lest in a careless moment we breathe in somebody's face and fasten the infection on him. The good man, the man who infects hardly anyone, is the man who has the fewest lapses of attention.[29]

Now if there is no transcendent meaning to life, if there is nothing after death but annihilation, according to what rule can we live? Camus finds a rule in the exhortation of the Greek poet Pindar:

Oh my soul, do not aspire to immortal life,
but exhaust the limits of the possible.[30]

Camus names certain kinds of men—men aware, consciously or unconsciously, but all the same aware of the absurd—who try to snatch every moment of their existence from their future death. These men are the actor, the seducer, the conqueror, the artist. The actor, playing his multiple roles, tries to crowd a hundred lives into one. The Don Juan seeks to drain the earth, which is his limit—to concentrate intense living, to live as in a flame. The conqueror chooses the anguish of action over contemplation; he turns his back on the Cross to take the Sword and strives to change the shape of the earth. The artist is a metaphysical rather than a political rebel: he constructs out of his work *a rival to this world*. In such a way a man can know what his fate is—annihilation—and refuse to be reconciled to it. He can learn to live a life "without appeal":

The absurd man thus catches sight of a burning and frigid, transparent and limited universe in which nothing is possible but everything is given, and beyond which all is a collapse and nothingness. He can then decide to accept such a universe and draw from it his strength, his refusal to hope, and the unyielding evidence of a life without consolation.[31]

With Camus, the word *absurd,* applied ethically, is always a compliment. For he means by "the absurd man" one who knows he is beaten and fights back anyway. The absurd man recalls Pascal's definition of man as a "thinking reed" who is superior to the mindless universe about to annihilate him because he *knows* he will be crushed by it, and the universe knows nothing of this. A man's clear knowledge of his inevitable fate and his refusal to reconcile himself to it constitutes what Camus calls *revolt.* The lucidity that accompanies such revolt is greater than hope, since hope is founded on self-deception:

One of the only coherent philosophical positions is thus revolt. It is a constant confrontation between man and his own obscurity. . . . It is that constant presence of man in his own eyes. It is not aspiration, for it is devoid of hope. That revolt is the certainty of a crushing fate, without the resignation that ought to accompany it. . . . That revolt gives life its value. Spread out over the whole length of a life, it restores its majesty to that life. To a man devoid of blinkers, there is no finer sight than that of the intelligence at grips with a reality that transcends it.[32]

From Individualism to Commitment

"All writers of this generation," wrote Simone de Beauvoir, having herself, Sartre, and Camus in mind, "moved from individualism to commitment."[33] Camus's *The Stranger* is a parable of individualism, the story of an outwardly ordinary young man whose "differentness" brought down the hostility of society upon him. It is also a story of *sincerity,* a characteristic virtue of the individualist. Meursault is a man who refuses to fake emotions he does not feel. *The Stranger* and *The Myth of Sisyphus* appeared in the war year of 1942—the year preceding the publication of Sartre's *Being and Nothingness.* In his postwar novel *The Plague,* Camus moved away from individualism toward the ideal of fraternal community. He had become suspicious of the individualism that comes so naturally to bourgeois poet and novelist. Following *Sisyphus* he had denied worth to the narcissism of the bourgeois individualist poet who sees in the artist the highest type of himself, proud, alienated, "interesting," different: "One of the temptations of the artist is to believe himself solitary and in truth he hears this shouted at him with a certain base delight. But this is not true. He stands in the midst of all, in the same rank neither higher nor lower, with all those who are working and struggling."[34] Then later in his Nobel Prize speech, Camus dealt both with the "difference" of the artist and the humanity he shares with all men:

To me art is not a solitary delight. It is a means of stirring the greatest number of men by providing them with a privileged image of our common joys and woes. Hence it forces the artist not to isolate himself; it subjects him to the humblest and the most universal truth. And the man who, as often happens, chose the path of art because he was aware of his difference soon learns that he can nourish his art *and* his difference, solely by admitting his resemblance to all.[35]

The Myth of Sisyphus and *The Stranger* were wartime books. *The Plague* appeared while the world was in the first shock at the revelation of the extermination camps. The last works of Camus's short life were written during the struggle for Algerian independence. Camus was himself the son of a poor French Algerian, and he loved the land whose bright sun, sand, and sea he had so often celebrated in his creative work. Which side to take: Algerian independence or French colonial rule? Sartre had pointed out that war and revolution sharpen the moral choice to an either/or. The ifs, ands, and buts come later. In war involving one's native land one takes one side or the other; there is no third. But Camus kept silent. That silence shocked the French liberal and leftist intellectuals who supported the Algerian drive for independence. In existentialist ethics, silence itself represents a side taken, a choice made. We remember Camus's defense of that silence when he said that he believed in justice but would defend his mother (his homeland) before justice.[36]

Existentialist Ethics: Conclusion
It is hard to draw sharp conclusions as to the relation of existentialism to moral theory and practice. Existentialists rarely put forward explicit ethical theories, and the term "existentialism" has been used to label a miscellany of thought and writing in the past twenty years. Sometimes the phrase "existentialist ethics" means no more than any general view that emphasizes the primacy of feeling over the rational. In educational ideology or psy-

chiatric theory, "existentialism" has been used to label any outlook that focuses on the feeling of alienation that seems to so
many to go with life in contemporary urbanized and technological
society, as well as the need for the individual person so alienated
to make up his own mind to act decisively and to take upon himself the responsibility for his own acts, his own future, his own
being. Many ethical injunctions associated with existentialism
were moral commonplaces in other cultural periods. Victorian
poets experienced what we call "alienation," a feeling of shock
and estrangement in the wake of the agnosticism that accompanied scientific and technological advances of the nineteenth
century's second half. In "Dover Beach," Matthew Arnold's metaphor for the "absurd" in human existence is a "darkling plain
where ignorant armies strive by night." W. E. Henley agreed, yet
insisted that a man is free to determine his own direction, though
he knows not what lay at the end of the path he has chosen:

It matters not how strait the gate,
How charged with punishment the scroll,
I am the master of my fate;
I am the captain of my soul.[37]

Centuries before, in a world still not quite modern, Shakespeare
cast his vote for individual freedom over cosmic compulsion, in
Julius Caesar:

The fault, dear Brutus, lies not in our stars
But in ourselves that we are underlings.[38]

In *King Lear* even the rascally Edmund knows evasion and bad
faith when he sees it:

. . . when we are sick in fortune . . . we make guilty of our disasters
the sun, the moon, and stars: as if we were villains by necessity,
fools by heavenly compulsion, knaves, thieves, and treachers by spheri-
cal predominance; drunkards, liars, and adulterers, by an enforced
obedience of planetary influence; and all that we are evil in, by a divine thrusting on: an admirable evasion of whoremaster man, to lay
his goatish disposition on the charge of a star![39]

Historically, the radical individualism of the existentialist philosophy—its stress on the freedom and autonomy of the individual person, its sense of the priority of the individual lived life—
can be interpreted as a powerful cultural response to the totali-
tarianism that led to World War II, with its suppression of the

individual person, its exaltation of the selfless community under the will of Leader or Party. With some change, the same is true of the period of the cold war that succeeded the armed conflict, when, for a time, expanding Soviet Marxism seemed to threaten the West with outright conquest. But when war and postwar tensions receded—as Sartre himself pointed out—existentialism's stress on individual freedom, stark, solitary and anguished, had to be modified in view of the pressing need to reassess the part of social conditioning in making people's lives what in fact they are. A man's work and wages may not be the whole truth about him, but they constitute a basic part of it. The child of a middle-class Paris or New York family has choice; the child of Johannesburg blacks or homeless Bengalis has little or none. Mindful of conditions of poverty in southern Italy, an observer says: "The basic condition of the poor is the impossibility of choice. There is no alternative to the life to which they are born. Because they have no choice, the poor provide an ideal field for economic and cultural imposition of the class in power."[40] Sartre himself was always sensitive to the charge by Soviet and French Marxists that existentialism was no more than a metaphysical defense of bourgeois individualism. The eagerness with which Western middle-class intellectuals adapted existentialism to their postwar theories of society, education, religion, and psychiatry seemed an uncomfortable confirmation of this charge.

We can raise the question in our own time and in our own way. What is there to the existentialist ethic that bears upon the situation of masses of deprived people living in urban or rural ghettoes? The existentialist moralist's emphasis on the ultimate importance of the individual person, his particular and specific flesh and bone, is a perennially needed corrective to bureaucratic habits of thinking, the abstract systematizing applied to people inevitably generated by the need to deal with social and educational problems involving large numbers of anonymous and invisible poor. But existentialism is by no means the only moral or social philosophy that stresses the ultimate value of the individual person. The ethics of the Jewish and Christian traditions were founded on that concept. Old-line liberal democracy, dated and suspect as it may be, focused on the sovereignty of the individual person for over a century, without attaching the existentialist claim of the irrelevance of reason in guiding the moral life. It may be stimulating to persuade a boy or girl of the affluent middle classes that he is essentially free to make what he likes

out of life, at the same time assuring him that he must assume
responsibility for his destiny. But does this pedagogy of personal
individualism have the same relevance to a boy or girl from a
jobless, drug-ridden slum? Can such a young person throw his
social conditioning out of court, construct himself, "make" himself, as he likes? Unless he or she is truly exceptional, a Malcolm
X, perhaps, or a Genet, it is doubtful in what sense he or she is
free to choose his fate. Is that fate not already cut out for the
boy or girl by the iron shears of economic and social stratifica-
tion? Such hard questions may throw some light on the limitations of the existentialist ethic as well as the application of its
central concepts to problems of practical education and social
theory. Whether they help to clarify the old problem of freedom
of the will versus determinism is a question to which we must
now give some thought.

NOTES: CHAPTER 8

1. Blaise Pascal, *Pensées,* trans. H. F. Stewart (New York: Pantheon,
   1950), pp. 312, 313.
2. Sören Kierkegaard, *Diary,* trans. G. M. Andersen (New York: Philosophical Library, 1960), p. 22.
3. Franz Kafka, *The Castle,* trans. Edwin and Miller Muir (1924; New
   York: Knopf, 1946), pp. 26–27.
4. Friedrich Nietzsche, "The Joyful Wisdom," in *The Complete Works
   of Friedrich Nietzsche,* 18 vols., trans. T. Common and ed. Oscar Levy
   (1881; New York: Russell & Russell, 1964), vol. 10, p. 125.
5. Phenomenology is a method of philosophical investigation that
   takes for its subject matter the actual content of conscious experience, not asking what may lie in back of the experience or what
   causes it. For certain practical purposes of both science and common sense, causal explanations are useful. But the phenomenological method of philosophy takes for its material the actual content
   of consciousness, events as they come, things as they show themselves. Merleau-Ponty says that phenomenology "tries to give a
   direct description of our experience as it is, without taking account
   of its psychological origins and the causal explanations which the
   scientist, the historian, or the sociologist may be able to provide."
   Maurice Merleau-Ponty, *Phenomenology of Perception,* trans. Colin
   Smith (New York: Humanities, 1962), p. vii.
6. Jean-Paul Sartre, *Nausea,* trans. Lloyd Alexander (New York: New
   Directions, 1964), p. 162.

7. Ibid., pp. 170–182. According to Simone de Beauvoir, Sartre was suffering from the aftereffects of a single mescaline injection while writing this novel.

8. The simplest account of the priority of existence over essence in human reality appears in Sartre's "Existentialism is a Humanism" (1946), but the argument appears earlier in the first chapter of *Being and Nothingness*. (See Sartre listings in the Suggested Readings for this chapter.) Heidegger has said of *dasein,* or human reality, that in this kind of being, "existence precedes and commands essence."

9. Jean-Paul Sartre, *Situations*, trans. Benita Eisler (New York: Braziller, 1965), p. 111.

10. Mary Warnock, *Existentialist Ethics* (New York: St. Martin, 1967), p. 49.

11. Jean-Paul Sartre, *Being and Nothingness,* trans. Hazel Barnes (1943; New York: Philosophical Library, 1956), p. 65.

12. Ibid., pp. 55–56.

13. Ibid., p. 433.

14. Sartre, *Being and Nothingness,* pp. 436–437.

15. Jean-Paul Sartre, "Existentialism is a Humanism," in *Existentialism from Dostoyevsky to Sartre,* trans. Philip Mairet and ed. Walter Kaufmann (1946; Cleveland: World Publishing, 1956), pp. 291–292.

16. Ibid., p. 291.

17. Sartre's rule, "The act of the individual person commits all humanity," resembles Kant's variation of the first formulation of the categorical imperative, "Act only on that maxim which is also worthy to become a universal law of nature."

18. See Pepita Haezrahi, "The Concept of Man as End-in-Himself," in Robert Paul Wolff, ed., *Kant* (London: Macmillan, 1968), p. 305.

19. Immanuel Kant, *Foundation of the Metaphysics of Morals,* trans. Lewis White Beck (New York: Liberal Arts Press, 1959), p. 46.

20. Sartre's universalizability argument appears in his lecture "Existentialism is a Humanism" and in no other place. This lecture has been widely reprinted and is often taken as a definitive statement of existentialism. But Sartre later asked that his views be disassociated with this lecture, stating that it should not be taken as a formal statement on either existentialism or his own later views.

21. Jean-Paul Sartre, "Itinerary of a Thought," *New Left Review* (London), November–December, 1969, p. 44.

22. Jean-Paul Sartre, *Search for a Method,* trans. Hazel Barnes (New York: Knopf, 1963), p. 85. Sartre appears to be paraphrasing a statement made by Engels in a letter not to Marx but to Joseph Bloch

(21–22 September 1890) and a similar statement made by Engels in a letter to Heinz Starkenburg (25 January 1894). The latter also contains the statement about Napoleon. See Karl Marx and Frederick Engels, *Selected Correspondence,* 2nd ed., trans. I. Lasker (Moscow: Progress Publishers, 1965), pp. 417, 467.

23. Ibid., p. 57.

24. Sartre, *New Left Review,* p. 45.

25. Ibid.

26. From "Jean-Paul Sartre s'explique sur 'Les Mots,'" *Le Monde* (Paris), 18 April 1964, p. 13.

27. Albert Camus, *The Myth of Sisyphus and Other Essays,* trans. Justin O'Brien (New York: Knopf, 1955), p. 21. The title essay was first published in 1942.

28. William Faulkner, "Man Will Prevail," in Leo Hamalian and Edmond L. Volpe, eds., *Great Essays by Nobel Prize Winners* (New York: Noonday Press, 1960), p. 85.

29. Albert Camus, *The Plague,* trans. Stuart Gilbert (New York: Knopf, 1954), p. 229.

30. Pindar, *Pythian Ode.* III, 61–62.

31. Camus, *Myth of Sisyphus,* p. 60.

32. Ibid., pp. 54–55.

33. Simone de Beauvoir, *The Prime of Life,* trans. Peter Green (Cleveland: World, 1962), p. 444.

34. Albert Camus, "The Artist and his Time" (1953), in *The Myth of Sisyphus and Other Essays,* p. 212.

35. Albert Camus, *Discourse de Suede,* Nobel Prize Speech, Stockholm, 10 December, 1957 (Paris: Gallimard, 1958), p. 13.

36. See Chapter 2, p. 42. Camus's "silence" on the Algerian question refers only to his refusal to support either the revolutionaries or the status quo. The third series of his *Actuelles* (Paris: Gallimard, 1958) consists of articles on the Algerian problem. Some of these may be found in Camus's *Resistance, Rebellion, and Death,* trans. Justin O'Brien (New York: Knopf, 1961), pp. 111–153.

37. William Ernest Henley, "Invictus," in *Poems* (New York: Scribners, 1901), p. 119.

38. *Julius Caesar,* act 1, sc. 2, lines 140–141.

39. *King Lear,* act 1, sc. 3, lines 117–127.

40. Review of Annabella Rossi's *Le feste dei poveri, Times Literary Supplement* (London), 25 September 1970, p. 1113.

9

Freedom and Responsibility

In the last chapter we saw how Sartre shifted from an individualistic doctrine of nearly absolute personal freedom to a social philosophy stressing the determining part played by the material conditions of human life. The existentialist Sartre said that the truth of a man is his freedom to make himself. The newer Marxist Sartre declared the truth of a man to be his work and his wages. What freedom is left to a human being after his material circumstances have done with him is that little (though sometimes crucial) bit he can give back to his environment other than what the environment has pressed in upon him. By this shift in emphasis from individualistic responsibility to social determinism, Sartre added to the endless argument among philosophers and social scientists as to just what kind and degree of freedom an individual person possesses in regard to the choices he makes. The classical philosophical version of this question is often called the problem of *free will*—though some moralists prefer to name it the problem of personal *responsibility*. Freedom, John Locke said long ago, is a property of the whole person rather than of a faculty called the will.

I

The question is often put this way: is a person ever free to do what he wants to? Or are his actions determined by causes over which he has no real control? Evidence for affirming the first alternative seems to lie in our immediate personal experience. It seems to be a matter of direct awareness that I am free to go out for coffee or to remain at my typewriter, to stay in school or to quit it, to include this item of income on my tax return or to leave it out, to apologize to someone I have spoken sharply to or to ignore him. On the other hand, we tend to believe that whatever happens has a cause or causes. If the lights suddenly go out, there is a cause for it. If you faint, I should assume that there are some causal factors that brought this about. My decision to go for coffee should not, it seems, be an exception to this general causal law. But if my decision is caused by some factor, A, that factor in turn (assuming events are causes) must be caused by B, and so on until the causal series leads outside my personal self and into the world at large. If so, it would appear that my decision is *not* free, but *determined* by causes (childhood, ancestors, genetics, glands, parental upbringing, last year's conditioning, yesterday's conditioning) that have their source outside myself. And if this is so, why should I be held *responsible* for what I do? I should not be held to account for my actions, nor should I be praised or blamed for them.

But this conclusion that I have no freedom of choice, that I am not responsible at least for some of my acts, seems absurd. It appears contradictory not only to immediate experience and basic personal belief but inconsistent with social and legal practice as well. True, we sometimes *modify* such personal beliefs as well as legal practice. We make excuses for our behavior with a view to showing that our responsibility is diminished or absent altogether. Sometimes we hold that a person is *not* responsible for his acts by reason of causes we know to have been operating upon him at the time of his "bad" action. But because we frequently ask and accept modification of the rule of responsibility does not mean that we do not believe that it holds. Assume for the moment that there is no such thing as *uncaused* behavior, that everything people do is *caused* by something. How do we square this with the assumption that people sometimes freely choose and that it is right, at least in some circumstances, to hold them responsible for what they have done? If a person's action can be shown to be caused by something beyond his control, his behavior cannot properly be condemned as "immoral," nor can he justly be held legally responsible. But if strict determinism is true, then all our actions are ultimately so caused. If so, how can anything one does be properly called "wrong"? Would it not seem then that whatever one does is "all right"? But if this is true, the concepts of "right" and "wrong" lose their meaning. If everything is all right, nothing is all right. Logically, nobody can be called to account for his actions.

It is obvious that the sense of "freedom" we talk about in connection with the problem of free will and responsibility is not quite the same as the meaning of political freedom enjoyed, say, by citizens of a Scandinavian democracy as opposed to a military dictatorship. Nor is the freedom that concerns us here identical in meaning with the personal liberty of a man who goes about his lawful business in contrast to another who is confined to jail for a crime. The freedom discussed in the present context is my freedom, and yours, to choose between alternative courses of action and to act upon that choice. What does it mean to say that you or I have freedom of choice and action? That we can freely decide? That it is sometimes "up to us"?

II

The Free Will Problem in Historical Perspective

Tradition says that the question of free will first arose in the fourth century with Saint Augustine. Greek philosophy was not overly concerned with it. In his ethical writings, Aristotle deals with the matter briefly and apparently sensibly—his common-sense distinctions on the matter are quoted with approval by moral philosophers even today. Aristotle says that the necessary condition of an act to which praise or blame may rightly be given is that the act be done knowingly and without constraint.[1] We cannot justly hold a person responsible for his deed if he acted from ignorance. You should not blame me if I failed to greet your father, not knowing that the man is your father. Nor should we expect someone to do something that is beyond his power to do. A man should not be blamed for refusing to jump twenty feet across a chasm to rescue an injured person. You may blame him for not seeking help—assuming that it was in his power to do so. Greek poets sang much about Fate, and some philosophers talked darkly of the influence of Necessity in the cosmos. But Aristotle did not usually apply such brooding notions to ordinary human affairs when it was simply a question whether a man acted generously, chastely, or justly. If the act in question is within our capacity, he said, and if we are not constrained, then we can choose to do it or not do it. Aristotle noted the difference between acting voluntarily and acting under constraint and between giving where choice is present and giving under compulsion, on threat of torture or death. But he pointed out that even in a situation of constraint, I retain a measure of freedom of choice; I *could* choose not to yield under threat of death and die for my refusal.

Augustine was bothered by a number of problems concerning

free will. He conceded that we have the power to deliberate and to choose among alternatives. But, when we are confronted by a choice between good and evil, he asked, why do we so often find ourselves lacking in power to *act* on our choice? Socrates said that no one knowingly chooses his own evil. But Saint Paul seemed to contradict this, saying, "For the good that I would, I do not: but the evil I would not, that I do." Augustine was troubled by the contrast between an abstract freedom of choice and the apparent lack of *efficacy* that marks our will in choosing that which is known to be good and acting on that choice. To give up self-indulgence is good—admitted. Now at this moment I have the opportunity to give up self-indulgence of some sort. But I find myself strangely lacking in what it takes to make me carry the conclusion of that practical syllogism into action. Greek philosophers tended to think the root of this trouble was lack of self-mastery; Aristotle noted how weakness of will (*akrasia*) can inhibit our doing good. Augustine believed the ultimate cause of weakness of will, a weakness common to human nature, to be Original Sin. Before the Fall, man was truly free, chose freely, but on one fatal occasion chose wrongly, thus alienating himself from God. After this primordial catastrophe, human freedom remained almost irreparably damaged, with human nature dragged down by its own inertia toward nonbeing in the moral realm (sin) and in the physical (death). God becoming man in Christ (the Incarnation) and the sacrificial death of Jesus on the cross released the flow of divine grace without which all men would be doomed to annihilation. According to Augustine, grace *restores* freedom to man; but he was aware of the difficulties raised by any attempt to make individual freedom and responsibility coexist with the irresistible power of divine grace.

A related problem concerned Augustine's belief that only *some* humans would be saved and that God, being omniscient, has foreknowledge of those who are to be saved. But how can men be free if their ultimate fate is foreknown?[2] How can you escape the conclusion that what is foreknown by God is foreordained by him? Augustine was reluctant to admit certain implications of the doctrine of predestination, according to which humans are no more than puppets in God's hands. Throughout the long history of Christian philosophy and theology, the fathers and doctors of the church tried to ameliorate the harsh conclusions concerning human freedom implied by Augustine. By the thirteenth century, Thomas Aquinas was teaching that human nature was not *corrupted* by the Fall, only *weakened;* freedom of the will, though impaired by the Fall, is not lost. With the Reformation the pendulum swung back to Augustine's pessimism (Luther was an Augustinian monk), to renewed emphasis on the alleged total depravity of human nature. John Calvin taught a theological determinism that filtered through to the Puritans of our early colonial days in the form of the doctrine of predestination. As François Mauriac's Abbé Calou puts it: "For by ourselves we can do nothing; we can do nothing but walk in front of Grace, as a dog precedes the invisible hunter, with more or less efficacy, according as we are more or less attentive, docile, or pliable in accepting the will of the master and indifferent to our own."[3] But if by ourselves we can do nothing, if we must accept what "the master" has in store for us, it would seem that the only tenable doctrine is *fatalism.*

III

Fatalism and its Limitations

Whether it appears in theological or secular form, fatalism is a common human belief. Tragedians of ancient Greece declared that what happens to humans is in the hands of *Moira*—Fate. The Greek atomists believed that Necessity (or Chance) ruled the flow of atoms that constitute the cosmos. A burning fatalism gave Moslem warriors an extra measure of courage, already high. For ages, some people have believed that their destinies are determined by the stars. Astrology is enjoying a new wave of popularity in this country, though most devotees today would hold that the stars incline us but do not compel.

Che sera sera is folkish wisdom; "what will be, will be," is part of the metaphysics of simple souls. A soldier under fire may tell himself that only one particular bullet "has my number on it" and until this comes along, why worry? We may think we are more sophisticated, but can we altogether repress a feeling of discomfort when we realize that a certain date already set down on some future calendar is the day of our death? Knowing that we are going to die on a date—the day, month, and year will be recorded—may put the idea in our mind that the day of our death has already been marked down in advance, and there is nothing we can do about it. Dickens's talkative midwife Sairey Gamp was inclined to think that days of our deaths and births are predetermined, but she sensibly advised her friends not to inquire too closely into the matter;

. . . what a little way you've travelled into this wale of life, my dear young creetur! As a good friend of mine has frequent made remark to me, which her name, my love, is Harris, Mrs Harris through the square and up the steps a-turnin' round by the tobacker shop, "Oh, Sairey, Sairey, little do we know wot lays afore us!" "Mrs Harris, ma'am," I says, "respectin' wot the number of a family will be, comes most times within one, and oftener than you would suppoge, exact," "Sairey," says Mrs Harris, in a awful way, "Tell me wot is my indiwidgle number." "No, Mrs Harris," I says to her, "ex-cuge me, if you please. My own," I says, "has fallen out of three-pair backs, and had damp doorsteps settled on their lungs, and one was turned up smilin' in a bedstead, unbeknown. Therefore, ma'am," I says, "seek not to proticipate, but take 'em as they come and as they go." 'Mine,' said Mrs Gamp, 'mine is all gone, my dear young chick. And as to husbands, there's a wooden leg gone likeways home to its account, which in its constancy of walkin' into wine vaults, and never comin' out again 'till fetched by force, was quite as weak as flesh, if not weaker.'[4]

All forms of fatalism have this limitation: they belong to a metaphysical model of reality in which the future is not a real future, but one that has already in some sense happened or taken place. It is as if reality were a continuously unrolling carpet of which we see only the part already unrolled. That portion of the carpet not yet rolled out we do not see; but it is there, every part of it complete with its pattern and figures. Our future is already fixed, a *fait accompli;* we just do not happen to know about it yet. Such belief in a future already accomplished, a future that stands in the wings waiting for its entrance cue, is very attractive—the human mind likes simple and clear explanations of why things happen the way they do. The belief is especially attractive to certain poets, mystics, and writers of science fiction. But there are serious reasons to consider it to be false. Such a view, as Bergson points out, denies the reality of time. It demotes that basic trait of being, the transcience inherent in the nature of things, to secondary status, as did the old theologians who held that in God's world there is no time—no past or future, only one eternal present. Fatalism implies that we cannot do anything about future events, that the strings controlling these events are not held by human hands. Many social critics claim that, historically, beliefs of this type have proved all too compatible with a resigned acceptance of hunger, disease, poverty, and human degradation. In contrast, the belief that something can be done about human ills, that the future is to some degree *open,* has led *some* peoples and cultures to *some* measure of success in shaping the future in such a way that, for them at least, the worse was made better. True, they usually had a little something to start with by way of advantageous material conditions. The Western powers possessed the abundant natural resources needed for heavy industry. But it is possible for a people schooled in resignation for thousands of years to rise up under dynamic leadership to create for themselves an entirely new future. China is an example.

IV

Determinism

Fatalism is a simple, naïve form of a more general view known as *determinism.* Determinism comes in many varieties, including the theological type we have already noted. Here we shall be concerned with what we may call "causal" or "scientific" determinism. This type of determinism holds that all events, including human decisions and actions, are the result of causes—that no human act, however "free," is spontaneous in the sense of being independent of causal laws. An extreme, or "hard," form of this determinism teaches that ultimately everything we do is a product of causes beyond our personal control, that free will is an illusion. Modified, or "soft," determinism holds that the deterministic model of the universe as a causally interrelated system is a correct model, but that it is *compatible* with personal responsibility and free choice, if those terms are properly understood. Historically, determinism followed as a corollary from the new emphasis on material causality that accompanied the rise of the natural sciences in the West. Mechanist and causal models of the universe were popular from the seventeenth century on. The popularity was deserved because many of these physical models enabled scientists to predict natural events, the causes of which had, prior to this time, not been understood.

The older Aristotelian interpretation stressed *internal* causality: bodies act the way they do because of certain inner characteristics or tendencies. Causal explanations were heavily weighted in terms of *purpose;* natural happenings were accounted for by positing a *telos,* an end or goal toward which the process in question moved. But the new scientists (Galileo, Newton) emphasized *external* causality. They held that bodies behave in a certain way because they are influenced by other bodies or forces outside them. The seventeenth-century English philosopher Thomas Hobbes proclaimed the true doctrine of Nature to be *materialism,* the view that reality is matter in motion. Nature is a vast aggregate of moving physical bodies and forces, acting and interacting. The material bodies that constitute Nature are related to each other according to certain causal laws that, when known, lead us progressively to the understanding and control of Nature. Hobbes applied these principles to *human* nature, which he believed was itself wholly subject to material causality. Hobbes denied any meaning to arguments about free will—a person is free if he is not constrained, and that is the only sense in which we can talk sensibly about freedom.[5]

The philosopher Spinoza, an admirer of Hobbes and Descartes, made a spectacular attempt to combine the old theological determinism with the new scientific determinism. In his greatest work, *Ethics,* Spinoza says that God is reality itself. God manifests himself in visible Nature through the two infinite attributes of extension (matter) and thought (mind). The universe is an infinite *mode* of God, following from God's nature by divine necessity. The world proceeds from God like the property of 180 degrees following from the concept of triangle. God has no design or plan for the world; the cosmos simply follows from God's essence, as part of that essence. The behavior of ordinary things and events ("finite modes") follows by necessity the laws of matter and mind, which have their ultimate source in that supreme reality we may call God or Nature (*Deus sive Natura*). Just as there is no design in God (he does not create from a divine plan), so there is no free will in man. Nature is a vast system of causes and effects, the uniformity of which permits of no break. The proper sense in which a human person can be said to be free (apart from absence of constraint) is that he understands the causes of things; he comprehends how he and everything else in the world are subject to the laws of Nature that science has perceived and formulated. "A thing which has been determined by God to any action" says Spinoza cannot render "itself indeterminate."[6]

Determinism and Natural Science

The popularity of mechanistic causal models of the universe reflected the brilliant successes of physics and astronomy in the early centuries of modern scientific discovery. Accepting these models as true, if simplified, pictures of reality, scientists and philosophers found it easy to extrapolate from these models, to bring all events in the world, including human action, under the rules of external material causality. "In whatever manner man is considered," said Baron d'Holbach, "he is connected to universal nature, and submitted to the necessary and immutable laws that she imposes on all the beings she contains."[7]

The mechanical-causal model of the universe was well established in the eighteenth century. The patron sciences were astronomy and physics. Soon biology added reinforcement. In the nineteenth century, interest in the biological sciences rose to fever pitch, the flame fanned by controversies over theories of biological evolution and the origin of life. If a uniform system of causality holds throughout Nature, the biologists taught, then purposive or teleological causality should be abandoned as a category of scientific explanation. The fact that a sunflower orients itself toward the sun is not to be accounted for on the ground that the sunflower *intends* to do so or because it unconsciously fulfills some purpose thereby. The behavior of the sunflower is *determined* by physical factors present in the external situation. To interpret physical, chemical, and biological processes in terms of external and nonpurposive causality was proclaimed to be basic to scientific method. Darwin's theory of evolution called attention to the crucial role of accidental variations and adaptations of organisms to environmental conditions. The author of *The Origin of Species* placed causal weight on factors external to the organism, a circumstance that later proved favorable to determinist explanations of human behavior. In our own century, the importance of *genetic* factors in the development and character of living forms was grasped. How much did these genetic elements influence human conduct? It was obvious that an individual person could not be held responsible for his genes. Did this fact not constitute an argument favorable to the concept of determinism? In the nineteenth century, theories of material causality developed that drew heavily upon the character of the social, economic, and political contexts in which human beings are rooted. Marx pointed out how the affairs of men and nations are shaped by powerful material forces that shape the economic and class conditions of their historical time. A problem for Marxists presented itself: if an individual person is the product of the class conditions of his society, if he or she is shaped by the material forces of history, where does this leave that individual freedom for which so many revolutionary heroes fought tyrants and despots to achieve? Engels gave the double-edged answer, "Men themselves make their history, but in a given environment which conditions them." At the opposite end of the political spectrum, Bismarck gave his version: "Man cannot create the current of events, he can only float with it and steer."[8]

Though the determinist stresses the importance of *external* causality where human action is concerned, he would not deny that some causes acting upon persons are *internal* to that person. The contemporary determinist's conclusion is that all human actions are necessitated by material causal factors. Some of these factors operate upon us from the outside. Others come from within the person. These include the internal material mechanisms of a person, among them the physicochemical constituents of his brain, which record his personal experience and knowledge, as well as his evolutionary history.

Determinism and Psychology
In our century, determinism has drawn strength from new psychological theories. Behaviorism and Freudian psychoanalytic doctrine are prominent among them. There is a good deal of determinism in Freud's theories. His concept of the unconscious implies that many of my acts, which I think are freely done, are really the products of unconscious motivation. Now if my decisions, which I consciously believe freely chosen, are actually the results of unconscious motivation on my part, how can they be free? In what sense, if any, am I responsible for them? In a 1961 defense of psychological determinism, John Hospers says:

The mother blames her daughter for choosing the wrong men as candidates for husbands; but though the daughter thinks she is choosing freely and spends a considerable amount of time "deciding" among them, the identification with her sick father, resulting from Oedipal fantasies in early childhood, prevents her from caring for any but sick men, twenty or thirty years older than herself. Blaming her is beside the point; she cannot help it, and she cannot change it. Countless criminal acts are thought out in great detail; yet the participants are (without their own knowledge) acting out fantasies, fears, and defenses from early childhood, over whose coming and going they have no conscious control.[9]

Should we hold these criminals responsible for their acts? No, Hospers says, for they have no control over them. Since Aristotle, moral and legal philosophers have agreed that we cannot hold a person responsible for what he does if the act is done under compulsion. But if the psychoanalytic theory is correct, many forms of unconsciously motivated behavior are exactly that—compulsive. The agent cannot help what he does. Should we put such criminals in jail, then? Hospers's answer agrees with a long line of social-determinist reformers: there is no inconsistency in holding a criminal not responsible for his act and shutting him away from society. Putting criminals in jail is not inconsistent with the truth of determinism; we may simply wish to preserve ourselves from their destructive behavior. We can put a murderer behind bars without holding him responsible for what he did.

In the celebrated case of Nathan Leopold and Richard Loeb, their defense attorney, Clarence Darrow, appealed to a more general form of psychological determinism with strong social-environmental overtones. Loeb and Leopold were two young men from wealthy families who, in Chicago in 1924, slaughtered a ten-year-old boy to satisfy (it was said) Leopold's fascination with Nietzsche's "superman" doctrine and Loeb's desire to commit a "master crime." Darrow blamed factors in the defendants' childhood, social environment, and education. He claimed that these environmental factors damaged, if they did not entirely destroy, personal responsibility in the case of the two young men. Darrow's eloquent plea that their lives be spared enabled the murderers to escape the death penalty.

Behaviorism: Watson and Skinner

Behaviorism is the psychological theory that most, if not all, human behavior can be understood in terms of external or environmental influences and that behavior can be controlled by applying the proper "conditioning" factors to the animal or human in question. According to John Watson, an early American behaviorist psychologist, human behavior is (with the exception of a very few basic unlearned drives) simply the product of conditioned reflexes. Pavlov's dog drooled at the sight of meat accompanied by the sound of a bell; after some time the bell's ring alone produced the salivary response. Watson claimed that human behavior can be explained in terms of conditioning, making allowance, of course, for the complexity of many human behavior situations. If society could only make up its mind what it wants, Watson said, psychologists armed with data and technical equipment sufficient to allow application of the necessary conditioning could turn out any kind of human being desired:

Give me a dozen healthy infants, well-formed, and my own specified world to bring them up in and I'll guarantee to take any one at random and train him to become any type of specialist I might select—doctor, lawyer, artist, merchant-chief, and, yes, even beggar-man and thief, regardless of his talents, penchants, tendencies, abilities, vocations, and race of his ancestors.[10]

Today Watson's behaviorism is considered oversimple; but behaviorism remains at the conceptual center of much, if not all, of American experimental psychology.

The most influential American psychologist of our day is B. F. Skinner, whose brilliant work on learning problems testifies to the continuing importance of behaviorism as a psychological method as well as its relevance to future solutions to social questions. Skinner's early book *Science and Human Behavior* considered problems related to a behaviorist society of the future, and he wrote about a utopia of his own, *Walden Two.* In his latest book, *Beyond Freedom and Dignity,* Skinner argues that the concepts of autonomous man and free will were for their times progressive and good; they helped overthrow political despots and reactionaries. But these ideas served their purpose and have become outworn and positively dangerous to human welfare of the future. The behavior of men and women must be controlled in a scientific manner if the enormous problems related to the increase of human population, including pollution and the stripping of natural resources from the planet, are to be solved. Skinner proposes that sophisticated techniques of control be applied to humans, conditioning them to modes of behavior desirable from the point of view of human welfare as a whole. The concept at the base of conditioning is simple: reinforcement of desired behavior by rewards, negative reinforcement of undesired behavior by punishments. The rewards and punishments need not be crude and compulsive; they can be subtle and persuasive. The concept of an autonomous human being, a citadel of moral dignity and independence, Skinner says, belongs to an age that has passed. Only by dispossessing autonomous man, he argues, can we turn to the real causes of human behavior:

Freedom and dignity . . . are the possessions of the autonomous man of traditional theory, and they are essential to practices in which a person is held responsible for his conduct and given credit for his achievements. A scientific analysis shifts both the responsibility and the achievement to the environment.[11]

Skinner freely grants that his behaviorist view of society is inconsistent with any doctrine of free will or inner causal independence. He holds that men and women are *incapable* of controlling their behavior through free choice. The old concepts of individual free will and responsibility should be dropped. This does not mean the abandonment of rewards and punishments as techniques of social controls. Like many enlightened determinists, Skinner argues that the whole question of the efficacy of reward and punishment is independent of the supposed moral responsibility of the animal or person whose behavior is being reinforced. People can be led to behave in desirable ways and to stop behaving in undesirable ways by means of reinforcing techniques that do not require the concept of personal responsibility.

Skinner's book called down upon itself the expected denunciations and comparisons by critics to the behavior-conditioned "Big Brother" societies described in Aldous Huxley's *Brave New World* and George Orwell's *1984*. Skinner's defenders reply that the conditioning described in these books was bad and the ends to which it was directed worse. There is no reason, they argue, why a behaviorist-conditioned society, using means of persuasion rather than coercion, cannot be directed to good ends, including the welfare of humanity itself—increasingly hungry, truculent, and crowded on the surface of our planet. But before this set of social ends can even be approached, Skinner's argument goes, the old concept of personal individualism must be discarded, together with its implicit claim that the inner autonomous man is the free chooser and final arbiter of good.

The nonbehaviorist public, of course, is not convinced. Who *decides* what is "desirable" and "undesirable" behavior? Who *decides* what conduct should receive positive or negative reinforcement? And by what authority do they decide and implement their decisions? The behaviorist may reply that *already* society decides such matters and implements its decisions through government and law, often by force, and that we give our consent to it. But the present system is haphazard and inefficient. Why not put it on a scientific basis? But the word "science" frightens people, Skinner admits; all the same they may realize before the century ends that they have no choice but to submit to a more adequate system of conditioning than present society affords. It is a question of survival.

Determinism and Predictability

In classical mechanics, there is an important property of any system of events connected one to another by external causal relations. This property is *predictability*. Given a body in a certain system—a planet in the solar system or a billiard table will do—and given also certain data about the mass, direction, and speed of that body, we can predict with close accuracy just what the body will do under the circumstances of a certain force applied to it. Good pool players know that, given the position of the ball and the force and direction of the stroke, they can get the ball in the pocket. We can tell in advance much of what will happen should we run our automobile into a parked car at a speed of thirty miles an hour. With greater precision, space technicians can predict and control the speed and direction of a space vehicle under their guidance by applying the laws of motion first formulated by Galileo and Newton. The enormous success of the investigations of natural science led nineteenth-century philosophers and scientists to affirm that *any* and *every* event is predictable, at least in principle. The astronomer Laplace, Napoleon's contemporary, said that an intellect that knew the situations of all the bodies in nature and the forces operating upon them could calculate with certainty, not only the past states of the universe, but every future state as well. Thomas Huxley announced that, if our intellects had sufficient knowledge of the properties of the molecules of the vapor that constituted the primal nebulosity of gases that was our universe in its infancy, the state of the fauna of Great Britain in 1869 could have been predicted with as much certainty as we can say what will happen to the vapor of our breath on a cold winter's day.[12] Bertrand Russell's way of putting it shows the interdependence of the ideal of universal causality and that of predictability:

The law of universal causation . . . may be enunciated as follows: There are such invariable relations between different events at the same or different times that, given the state of the whole universe throughout any finite time, however short, every previous and subsequent event can theoretically be determined as a function of the given events of that time.[13]

Contemporary scientists have modified the rule of universal predictability to take into account certain findings in twentieth-century physics. Heisenberg's "principle of indeterminacy" was formulated on the basis of experiments that indicate that certain aspects of the behavior of subatomic particles, taken individually, are not predictable. Heisenberg's conclusion is related to the so-called complementarity principle of quantum mechanics, according to which the more exactly the position of a microparticle is known, the less exactly is its momentum known, and vice versa. The complementarity principle is tied to the concept of measurement. According to the principle, velocity and position of a subatomic particle have no value before a measurement of that velocity and position has been made. Indeterminacy arises from the fact that *simultaneous* measurement is in principle impossible. The quantum theory itself allowed more accurate mathematical predictions of atomic states (though in terms of probabilities rather than exact values) than previous theories about the inner structure of the atom. Scientists are now inclined to grant that some micro-events in nature may be *random*. But if this is so, it does not help us one way or the other with the problem of free will.

Common-sense observation and reflection tell us that we can predict human behavior quite well in many areas of practical life. Think of the beach store managers who lay in extra supplies of frankfurters and hamburgers; they are predicting the behavior of thousands of people on a hot summer weekend. Fashion designers and toy manufacturers put millions of dollars on the line as they forecast fall or Christmas buying behavior. If I tell my neighbor that her precious Siamese cat is up a tree, I am confident that she will run out to coax her pet down. The old technique of reward and punishment that parents, teachers, and governments still apply is tied to a concept of predictability of human behavior, a concept warranted by past experience and refined and extrapolated by contemporary behaviorist psychologists. If Andrew knows that he will not be allowed out tonight unless he cleans the windows this afternoon, his parents can expect him to perform that chore. If the federal government knows that I am aware of the penalties for falsification of tax returns, that government can make a reasonable prediction that I will pay most, at least, of what I owe. If an urban ghetto is jammed with 200,000 people in conditions of poverty and unemployment, it takes no genius to predict a high incidence of crime and violence. True, some of these examples of predicting human behavior have, at best, a statistical validity; they do not guarantee what an individual person will do. It is also true that we do not know all the causes of human behavior, and much of it we simply cannot predict—particularly in individual cases. For all their elaborate techniques, social scientists did not predict the university disorders of the 1960s and the generalized youth revolt of which they were a part. But, the determinist says, that we do not *now* know does not mean that we *will not* know. Is it not reasonable to suppose that if we knew *all* the factors and could control *all* the variables, we could then predict *all* human behavior? But this is what predictability in principle *means*.

This universal predictability in principle is just one aspect of the comprehensive fact that we humans are part of Nature and that we are subject to the same causal laws that govern all natural events. Why not conclude that all human behavior, including acts of so-called free choice, is governed by causal factors grounded outside the individual, hence beyond his control? Such is one argument for strict determinism.

Now there are many tricky points in the case for determinism—some are important, some not. We shall look at a few of these in a moment, but let us make two brief notes before moving on. First, predictability does not *prove* determinism, though it is compatible with it. I may successfully predict an individual person's action—but this does not necessarily mean that the action belongs to a context of determinism and not freedom. For example, your father is a kind and generous man. When you see a deserving person approach to ask him for help that he is in a position to give, you may successfully predict that your father will offer his aid. But the success of your prediction does not mean that your father's act was determined and not free. Or does it? Second, the fact that causal lines lead back from human actions ultimately to a point *outside* the person performing the act does not necessarily imply that the act in question is determined and not free. The catch lies in the term *ultimately*. If an individual pushes his causal ancestry back far enough, he will find that he *is* "ultimately" grounded outside himself—in his biological parents (and they in theirs). But does the fact that we depend on our parents as causal factors in bringing us into the world mean that all our actions must be determined, and none free?

Determinism, Hard and Soft

In discussions of free will versus determinism, we often find a distinction made between "hard" and "soft" determinism. William James introduced the distinction in a lecture to Harvard divinity students in 1884. According to James, hard determinism is part of a tight metaphysical doctrine of a rigorous mechanical kind, a sort of causal fatalism encouraged by certain scientific world-pictures in which, given the state of the universe at its beginning (if it had a beginning), every following state is necessarily contained: "It professes that those parts of the universe already laid down absolutely appoint and decree what the other parts shall be. The future has no ambiguous possibilities hidden in its womb: the part we call the present is compatible with only one totality."[14] According to James, such a universe leaves no room for *chance,* a notion the Harvard psychologist-philosopher took to signify possible alternative happenings. If an event happened by chance, it could have been otherwise. But hard determinism, in James's sense, excludes alternative possibilities—chance, that is. Presumably a hard determinist would say (though James did not make this point explicit) that "chance" is simply a concept we apply to events the causes of which we do not know. If we *did* know the causes of that event, we would not call it chance. James says that in the hard determinist universe there is no room for freedom—of the will or of any other kind—save, perhaps, that accommodation to necessity that the Stoics and Spinoza praised as the posture of the truly rational man. In James's lexicon, chance means alternative possibilities that really exist; freedom of will *requires* a situation of genuine alternatives.

What is soft determinism? James remarks that there is more than one kind, perhaps, but they all boil down to little more than substituting gentler words for necessity. One soft determinist might stress the real distinction between human action constrained and unconstrained (giving money to a robber at the point of a knife or giving to a destitute man begging). Another soft determinist might reassure us that there *is* true freedom, the freedom of the person who, knowing that science is true, understands that all events are part of a necessary causal pattern.

Freedom is only necessity understood. A third might say that it is possible to combine belief in personal free will with universal determinism—a doctrine known today as *compatibilism.*

Today it is really difficult to say just what constitutes a hard or soft determinist—in fact, there are certain problems that stand in the way of even *defining* determinism. (J. L. Austin says he thinks that "determinism itself is still a name for nothing clear.")[15] At the risk of repetition, we may say that the hard determinist generalizes or extrapolates from a model of the universe in which all events are causally connected with one another in such a way as to include human acts. The hard determinist believes that all our actions are governed by causal laws, that our decisions are traceable to causal factors that lie outside the individual human situation, and that over these factors we, as individuals, have no real control. The hard determinist model of society would show that the behavior of every person is clearly determined, necessitated, or conditioned by external influences. I am a hard determinist if I claim that what I am and what I do today is to be tracked down, causally speaking, to genetic and environmental factors in my childhood and that therefore I should not be held morally responsible for what I am or what I do. I accept hard determinism if I believe that all human behavior, praiseworthy and criminal alike, is the inescapable effect of deep underlying compulsions over which people have no control. In sum, hard determinism implies that not only is all human behavior *caused,* but that it is *unavoidable.* When a person has done something, praiseworthy or blameworthy, he simply could *not* have done other than he did.

But what then does the soft determinist say? He agrees to the hard determinist's premise that all events in Nature are causally connected. He agrees that "free" human acts are not exceptions to this rule, that there is no such thing as a purely spontaneous or noncaused act. But he denies the hard determinist's conclusion to the effect that in all cases the individual human act is beyond the control of the agent. Instead, he would hold that there really are situations in which the agent could have done something other than he did. He would defend the position that we are sometimes justified, morally or legally, in holding a person responsible for what he did—since, knowing the circumstances, a reasonable person would believe that he *could have done otherwise.*[16] But here soft determinism may blur over into compatibilism, that is, the doctrine that the concepts of determinism and free will are not contradictory and may be true simultaneously. Compatibilism in turn tends to shade over into "libertarianism."

Instead of trying further to distinguish among variations and combinations of these views, it may be easier at this point to go directly to arguments in favor of the *libertarian* position which defends the importance and reality of the dimension of freedom in human action. While some libertarian arguments make positive appeal to immediate experience in support of free will, some are negative and critical, based as they are on the alleged inadequacy of the determinist model of human action.

V

Free Will

Let us look over once more some of the elements traditionally ascribed to a "free" act. It is an act that is *not compelled,* not performed under constraint. It is an act that is *voluntary* and one that we are *able* to do. *Choice of alternatives* is present and we can deliberate, if need be, over these alternatives. It is a true act, done with *intention,* not just something that *happens to us.* Strictly speaking, "free" is not a quality that pertains to the act isolated as such. Freedom belongs to the context of the act or, if you prefer, to the way in which the act is done. ("She pushed me on purpose"; "He intentionally stepped on the cat"; "Meursault deliberately fired four times.") On this understanding, we may continue to refer to the act itself as "free."

Now *are* there such acts? Do we ever perform them? It seems that we do, and the evidence is both internal and external to our personal selves. First we seem to know from the direct and immediate data of consciousness that we have the power to choose between alternative courses of action. I am sitting here typing, but I could have chosen otherwise. It is a warm summer day, and I would very much enjoy a swim. I could have it by jumping into the car and driving for fifteen minutes to the beach. Instead, I have chosen to type two or three pages before supper. I'll go swimming tomorrow morning. So here I am typing, though I am completely convinced that I could have gone swimming had I elected to do so. You, in your turn, are reading this book. You know, as directly as you can know anything, that you could have chosen to do something else. You could be having a nap, visiting a friend, practicing your oboe, saying a prayer, drinking beer, attending a Maoist study group.

You may say that you are reading this page reluctantly, that you really would rather be doing something else. No matter. You have elected to do this although you would prefer to be doing something else. And you know that you *could* be doing something else, if you had so chosen. You say that there are reasons why you are reading this page: you want to find out about the problem of free will, or it has been assigned to you, or you must obey a maxim you have adopted that you would read a chapter of moral philosophy before making any hard decision. All that may be true—indeed it usually *is* true that we do what we do for reasons (reasons call attention to causes), whether the reasons we give be pressure exerted on us by others or only "I just felt like it."

But the fact that we have reasons or motives for doing what we do—even motives that may be unconscious—does not mean that we have not chosen freely, that we were ineluctably compelled, that we could not have done otherwise. A person "obliged" to do something could have done something else. A student "made" by his teacher to read a book could toss it aside. A sailor who is obliged by a storm to make for the nearest port nevertheless *decides* to make for that port. In this respect, his case is different from that of a sailor whose ship is driven off course by the wind.[17] A person "compelled" to hand over his money to an armed bandit *could* choose to grapple with him or to try to run away. A captured pilot, under duress, *could* refuse to sign a confession that he is a spy and that his country is planning bacteriological warfare. Or could he? Maybe this man could, but that one could not.

Who Has the Burden of Proof?

The determinist might say: you *believe* that you can choose freely between certain alternatives, but this consciousness of freedom is only an illusion. Your belief is false, it has no basis in fact. You are really *compelled* to do whatever you do. Your actions are unavoidable. To this the libertarian (defender of free will) may reply: that may be, but it is *your* job to prove it. I am aware that I choose freely, just as I am aware that I exist or that I feel warm. You can try to demonstrate that I do not exist or that I do not feel warm, but the burden of the proof rests on you. Similarly, the immediate data of my consciousness—and that of countless numbers of other people—tell me that we are sometimes able to choose freely. There is a *prima facie* case for free will. You must overturn that case, and your arguments must rest on such good reasons that my conviction and the conviction of others that we sometimes choose freely will be clearly refuted. A deductive argument is not enough. Logically, my acts may be determined; practically, I know sometimes they are not. You may insist that psychoanalysis tells us that our conscious actions are "really" motivated by unconscious wishes, that this man's Oedipal desire is so powerful that he simply cannot help destroying the rival who threatens to take his dead father's place. To which I (as libertarian) reply: you must show me reasonable evidence not only that Freud's rather special theory of unconscious motivation is true but also that, even if it *is* true, these motivations compel my actions and make them unavoidable. You may argue that every event has a cause, that my actions, being events, are no exceptions to this rule, and that moreover the bases of the causes of my actions lie outside me in the total causal system and hence beyond my control. To this I may answer that this must be shown, that any causal model you may produce to support this claim will be, at best, an abstract argument when weighed against the concrete and direct intuition of my own ability to deliberate and to choose among alternative courses of action. On the screen of a model world dominated by causal explanations, my actions will appear to be determined. But by direct evidence of immediate experience—phenomenologically, if you like—I know that sometimes at least it is "up to me." And I believe that you have similar experiences.

The Sense of Responsibility

To uphold the libertarian argument, the fact that people *hold themselves responsible* for at least some of their acts may be offered as evidence. Could they be justified in so doing if their acts were always necessitated and unavoidable? Remorse, bad conscience, self-blame for what we have done or left undone is a basic part of human experience. Since the days of ancient Egypt, a mass of art, poetry, religion, literature, and moral teaching has sprung from this universal theme of regret. In the face of this universal human testimony, is it reasonable to believe that personal responsibility is no more than illusion? Which of us now, at this moment, taking thought of our own past, examining our consciences, can say yes, we have hurt, deprived, swindled another human being and do not now wish it otherwise—knowing that we *could* have done otherwise? True, modern psychology has suggested that many of our feelings of guilt and self-blame are largely subjective, self-punishment for what has no real or deserved basis in matter of fact. But if *some* of our guilt feeling is unwarranted, exaggerated, illusory, it does not follow that *none* of these feelings have relations to objective fact. It may be moral evasion or bad faith to wave aside remorse as "morbid guilt feelings" or "masochism."

Besides, it is not only I who hold myself responsible for those acts of mine done with intent and purpose. Society itself holds me accountable for my deeds. Personal responsibility seems to be a universal and indispensable presupposition of any social arrangement we know—even in societies of gangsters. If we hold a person responsible, legally and morally, for what he does, at least what he does under some circumstances, can we deny the premise required for this conclusion—that a person can sometimes deliberate among alternatives and choose freely? Systems of justice, East and West, are based on the assumption that humans are in some sense responsible for some of their acts. The language of morals, as well as the concepts of law, are based on a syntax of personal accountability. Even the most radical cultural relativist would be hard put to find an instance of a people, of any time or place, who did not hold its constituent adult members accountable for some of their acts, underlining this conviction with a system of rewards and punishments.

What Do the Russians Say?

In the Soviet Union, the official philosophy is *dialectical materialism,* a doctrine that states that all reality is a material process developing according to dialectical laws, that societies change according to the laws of historical necessity.[18] Yet the great weight given by Soviet theorists to the power of material forces in history does not lead Soviet society to diminish the reality and importance of individual responsibility. On the contrary, Soviet society holds the individual strictly to account for what he or she does or leaves undone. Soviet moral philosophers base individual responsibility on the ability of a person to foresee the consequences of his actions and to choose among actions that have different consequences. This is the simplest ethical rationalism—moral choices are made by persons presumed to have the capacity to decide reasonably. If the individual lacked the power to choose among alternatives, V. P. Tugarinov says, he could not be held morally accountable any more than a wolf for eating a lamb or a snowslide for destroying a house.[19] A person should hold himself responsible for his actions, but if he does not society can and must do so.

An important supplement to the doctrine of *individual* responsibility in Soviet ethics is the concept of *collective* responsibility.[20] The individual is morally responsible for the welfare of the group to which he belongs, and this collective in turn must be held accountable for each of its members. If a member of a farm collective were to sabotage a machine, the individual would be held responsible for his antisocial deed. But the collective would also be responsible for the bad conduct of its member. Perhaps the group failed in educating this person or was neglectful in guiding him or her. The idea of Soviet ethics, so far as responsibility is concerned, is an equilibrium between the individual and the collective. The same principle holds, with at least as great an emphasis on collective responsibility, in Maoist China. A rule of collective responsibility still pervades modern industrial Japan; it is not Marxist-Leninist, but is of ancient cultural origin.[21]

Excuses and Mitigating Circumstances
Even though in practical life we operate on the assumption of personal responsibility, in ordinary affairs we constantly amend those acts of ours that have undesirable consequences by our claims of diminished or absent responsibility. We urge misunderstanding ("I didn't *know* it was your wife!"). We claim lack of intent ("I didn't *mean* to offend him"). We call attention to circumstances ("It was so foggy I couldn't *see* him"). The rich variety of excuses we offer for acts for which we are held accountable called the attention of J. L. Austin, the English philosopher, to the important role of *adverbs* in the language of moral accountability:[22] did X produce the injury knowingly, voluntarily, intentionally, carelessly, inadvertently, maliciously, hastily, deliberately, honestly, and so on. When it is a question of responsibility, Austin calls attention not so much to the act itself, but to *how* the act is done. He stepped on the cat. Well, yes, but did he do it on purpose? She took the money. Yes, but didn't she think it was hers? He shot the boy. Yes, but didn't he think it was a deer?

Under *law,* we focus on a limited but dramatically highlighted area of excuses. Small children are not held legally responsible for what they have done because it is not clear that they have the power to control their actions by reasonable choice. Nor do we hold mentally incompetent persons responsible for their acts;

they are not permitted to stand trial. In the case of persons we *do* hold responsible for their acts, there must be criminal intent (*mens rea*) before we judge them fully culpable. Of course, there is such a thing as criminal carelessness, and we punish that according to its due. In the case of some persons we *do* hold responsible for their acts, we allow that the blame for them should be softened and the punishment reduced because of the presence of certain mitigating circumstances. In the Loeb-Leopold case, the defense attorney argued that, although his clients were not insane, they were *mentally impaired* because of certain environmental conditions. The judge in the case did not award the death penalty, but he made it clear that it was the *youth* of the defendants that had moved him to sentence them to life imprisonment instead.

The ethics of common sense tells us that it is unreasonable to hold to full responsibility a young criminal who had never known his parents, who had lived in vacant lots and doorways from the time he was twelve years old, who had known nothing but rejection and persecution from those representatives of officialdom with whom he had come in contact. Nevertheless, without *some* concept of freedom to choose—however impaired or absent that freedom may be under certain conditions—there could be no defensible concept of personal responsibility. And without that the usual systems of law and justice, imperfect as they may be, could not operate at all. Perhaps in the scientifically regulated behaviorist society of the future there will be satisfactory alternative methods of social control that will dispense with the concept of responsibility.

The Determinist Model: Are Human Actions Caused?

Many antideterminist critics argue that the notion of "cause" in a statement like "All human actions have causes" is quite different from the sense of cause so usefully employed in scientific models of material systems. Yet it is this physical model kind of causality that determinists superimpose upon human actions. Some critics deny that the concept of cause should be applied to human actions at all, if by "cause" is meant some kind of entity that must be present in domino fashion before an action can happen. Austin says that "causing" was probably a notion taken from our experience of doing simple actions like pushing, pulling, dropping, and throwing. The causal model constructed out of these simple experiences is then applied to all kinds of actions with a view to explaining them.

Do we know what "cause" *means?* Certainly we do, roughly at least, for if we did not, we could not use the notion as widely as we do. ("I wonder what caused his stomach upset." "There were three principle causes of World War I.") But it is very hard to find a satisfactory *definition* of cause. There are a few abstract formulas useful within limitations. For example:

A is a cause of B, if, when A occurs, B occurs; and when A does not occur, B does not occur.

Maud's cat is at least one causal factor in her allergy—when he is present she breaks out in splotches and when he is absent she does not. The formula may not be satisfactory for all causal situations, and we do tend to focus narrowly on the domino ("this pushed that") type of causality to the neglect of certain other kinds of causal concepts.

The rule that every event has a cause holds in this sense at least: when certain things happen, we suppose that an account or explanation of them can be given in terms of causes. If you find your window broken or your motorcycle gone, you assume that *something* caused it. ("It didn't just break itself!" "It didn't go off by itself!") If your friend walks past you without speaking, you assume there is some cause for his unusual behavior. ("He didn't see me," "He is angry with me," and so on.) If somebody loses a lot of weight we assume there is a cause or causes. (Dieting? A tumor? Hunger strike?) Of course, there are many events for which the causal question may be inappropriate. It would be odd for a person who has just finished listening to a Beethoven symphony or looking at a rhinoceros to ask, "What caused that?"

Causal Models and Human Actions

At the core of the antideterminist line of argument we are now considering is the conviction that the determinist is *using the wrong model* for drawing conclusions about human action, including choosing, deciding, intending, acting. Early versions of this model, inspired by scientific world-pictures of the Newtonian type represented the universe as an enormous mechanism. All things in this world-machine were said to be connected by causal relations, the whole being subject to a uniform set of causal laws. Causes were taken to be primarily external and material, rather than internal and purposive. That scientists could predict events by appeal to uniform causal laws was taken as verification of the accuracy and adequacy of the model.

According to the antideterminist, such mechanical universe-models were adequate for certain important practical purposes. The history of science leaves us in no doubt as to their successful application to astronomy or mechanics. Trouble comes when this model, either in its relatively simple eighteenth-century format or in its sophisticated twentieth-century version, is extrapolated to cover human actions of many kinds. The actions of human beings, the antideterminist says, are not to be understood as "immune from" or "untouched by" causality, but causal explanations of certain human actions may not always be the best way of clarifying them. The determinist's mistake lies in applying a model *with built-in determinism* to cover and account for all human behavior. Naturally, after being molded upon or processed through such a model, human actions cannot be seen as *anything but* determined.

Plato's Socrates used this antideterminist type of counter-argument: the determinist confuses two really distinct modes of causality, mechanist and intentional. In *Phaedo,* Socrates raises the question as to what causes brought him to prison, where he now awaits death. A scientific philosopher like his predecessor Anaxagoras, he says, would claim that the muscles attached to his bones brought him to prison. But Socrates tells his students:

It may be said, indeed, that without bones and muscles and other parts of the body, I cannot execute my purposes. But to say that I do as I do because of them, and that this is the best way in which mind acts and not from choice of the best, is a very careless and idle mode of speaking.[23]

That is, what brought Socrates to prison and execution was his own intentional acts, the purposes of a lived life, not the mechanical efficiency of his body.

In modern times, Kant would make the distinction another way. To make sense of the external world, we must interpret it in terms of cause and effect. To make scientific and common-sense explanations possible, we must superimpose on the flux of experience a causal pattern. To supply a Kantian illustration: it is as if we put down ruled graph paper over an unruled sheet in order to work out a geometrical problem. The ruled squares provide ordering patterns and guidelines. When we superimpose this causal pattern on the flux of experience, all events are seen as determined by the universal and necessary relations that include causality. But we may err in trying to understand the grounds of human action in this way. In trying to understand, we confuse two orders of causality—scientific and moral—if indeed we can speak of the moral ground of our being in causal terms at all. Natural events, Kant says, are determined by causes from the outside, while human actions in the moral realm are *self*-determined.[24]

Acting and Happening

The notion that human action is not something caused from the outside, like a push or a shove, but is initiated by the agent himself is as traditional as Aristotle or Aquinas. But contemporary ethical theorists have refined the distinction, pointing out that failure to take account of it leads to a characteristic weakness in the determinist explanation of human action. The determinist model is one of *making other things happen,* not a model of a man *doing* something. There is an important difference between my picking up a garden rake, and the rake pressing down the blades of grass. According to Roderick Chisholm:

If we consider only inanimate natural objects, we may say that causation, if it occurs, is a relation between *events* or *states of affairs.* The dam's breaking was an event that was caused by a set of other events—the dam being weak, the flood being strong, and so on. But if a man is responsible for a particular deed, then . . . there is some event, or set of events, that is caused, *not* by other events or states of affairs, but by the man himself, by the agent, whatever he may be.[25]

The causal model before the determinist's eyes is, as we have noted, one that depends heavily on the concept of external causality. External causality is a very helpful notion if we wish to understand how things are *made to happen.* But the explanations of human behavior we normally give, particularly of moral action, do not use this form of causal account. Most explanations assume that human action is in some sense self-initiating and purposive. I might allow that every single one of my acts may be determined by a cause. But these causes are not wholly outside me. I am not a passive block pushed by them. I have something to say about the disposition of these causes. In some fundamental way, it is up to me as to what is done about them.

This argument does not mean that we cannot speak correctly of causing another's action from the outside. For example, suppose you tell your friend that there is a particular film at the local cinema that you know he would like to see. Your friend is delighted to hear the news and that evening he goes to the film. Your telling him about the film was certainly a cause of his going to the cinema, and it was an external cause. But it does not act like an external force pressing on a passive surface, as a fall of a domino or the closing of a door. Your friend *could* have regretfully decided that he had important duties to perform and not have gone to the movies that evening at all. The decision was grounded somewhere in his own psychic processes; in some sense it was internal to him.

Descriptive and Prescriptive Laws

Strict determinists often speak of events being "subject to laws of causation," drawing from this some questioning conclusions about the status of free will. But phrases such as "governed by physical laws" and "subject to laws of causation" are tricky; in this context especially the use of the word "law" is highly metaphorical. The basic meaning of "law" is *prescriptive,* as Morris Schlick pointed out: a law is a rule laid down by someone stating how people should behave or not behave. But the use of the word "law" in science is *descriptive:* it means a pattern of regularity or uniformity in Nature. "A body in motion tends to remain in motion in a straight line" is not a law in the sense that it is a statute passed by a parliament of Newtonian physicists. It is simply a description of an important uniformity of behavior of bodies in Nature, an inductive generalization very useful in predicting what billiard balls and spaceships will do. Schlick thought that by pointing out the distinction, the old-line "hard" determinism, with its implicit denial of human responsibility, was shown to be false. Human action can be admitted to be caused, yet human freedom and accountability saved. Most contemporary moral philosophers believe the matter is not solved quite as easily as this, though they agree on the usefulness of Schlick's distinction when discussing the determinist's model.[26]

Are Actions Really "Caused"?

The more present day ethical theorists think about the matter, the more subtle and complex do they seem to find questions concerning human action that were considered simple and solvable a generation or two ago. For example, at one time it was thought that human actions—say, where freedom of choice was concerned—might be illumined by talking about the part played by intentions, motives, and wishes as "causes" of such actions. But now it is pretty generally held that the concept of causality, as traditionally used, is too crude to be helpful in clarifying problems like those of deliberation, decision, and action. The notion that a human action is "caused" by internal factors—that for every action there must have been some thinglike entity such as an intention, volition, or motive to "produce" it—has been pretty well abandoned by philosophers of the Anglo-American tradition of "philosophy of action."[27] They say it is a mistake to assume that the causal model used in the natural sciences, even in psychology, will cover ordinary explanations of actions in terms of intentions, motives, volitions, and so on.[28] Some moral philosophers even think it might be a good idea to set aside the concept of "cause" when discussing the internal ingredients of human action. Instead, human action would be taken as primary, as something not required to show causal credentials. "To do something meaning to do it," says Philippa Foot, "is to do it in a certain way, not to do it as the result of the operations of a causal law." If having a motive means being determined, then all actions are determined—since a motiveless action would not be a true act. But assigning a motive to an action, she says, is not to bring it under any law, causal or otherwise: "It is rather saying something about the kind of action it was, the direction in which it was tending."[29]

A Phenomenological View

Continental phenomenologists like Merleau-Ponty would say that the free will problem arises when the human is treated as a complex of parts and the human body is looked at from the outside as an *object*. The definition of an object implies that it is composed of parts and that consequently there exist between its parts, or between itself and other objects, only external and mechanical relationships, whether in the narrow sense of causality transmitted and effects received or in some other wider set of external relations. For certain practical purposes I may construe my body as a physical object existing among other physical objects—when I weigh myself, for example. But the human body is not an object like other objects. I cannot walk around my body. I am with it. I communicate to the world with it. My body is not a passive thing, but a process projected forward, colored and heated by *intention* like an iron glowing red in the fire:

The life of consciousness, cognitive life, the life of desire or perceptual life, is subtended by an intentional arc which projects round about us, our past, our future, our human setting, our physiological, ideological and moral setting. . . . It is the intentional arc which brings about the unity of the senses, of intelligence, of sensibility and motility.[30]

Determinism arises when I separate this intentional arc from human acts, when I regard myself as identical with my body and take this body to be a physical object among physical objects, externally related according to causal laws. But I do not *experience* myself or my acts in this way. Considered as a physiological system, looked at from the outside, the human body cannot be seen other than as a determined process. Taken as a lived life, experienced from the inside, it is impossible to deny it contact with freedom—even though material and external circumstances may sometimes limit that freedom to the point where it makes little difference to a man whether he possesses it or not.

Is the Problem Insoluble?
Unimpressed by recent claims that free will can be reconciled with strict determinism, some moral philosophers say that the problem of free will versus determinism is probably insoluble. If these philosophers are right, there is one reason for it, which should be clear from our discussion thus far. The champion of determinism and the defender of free will base their respective cases on two different premises. Since they have two different world-models before their eyes, the rivals pass quickly from moral dialectic to a standoff of two competing systems of metaphysics. So there is a sense in which there is no real argument at all on this issue. The determinist starts off with a universe-model that implies determinism, a useful diagram in which freedom has no logical place. The libertarian rests his case on the data of immediate personal experience and ·on the extension of this in universal social practice. Which set of premises is the right one? To answer, we should have to agree on which is the right way to begin philosophizing. Should we start with the external world or from the immediate data of consciousness? Do we begin with the belief that science is true and go on from there? Or do we take personal or social experience as our starting point and hold the scientific world-picture to be in need of correction if it is incompatible with that experience at any point? Should our images of ourselves in the world be drawn from the natural sciences or from the phenomenology of moral experience? Do we see through the eyes of Bertrand Russell or William James?

The free will versus determinism debate is a little like the controversy in early twentieth-century physics over the question of whether atoms should be described in terms of groups of particles or groups of waves, two concepts seemingly incompatible when used to describe the same entity, yet both needed to explain these basic physical events. The principle of *complementarity,* developed by the physicists Niels Bohr and Werner Heisenberg, was put forward to solve the problem of incompatibles by claiming (in effect) that if you are dealing with a problem in terms of one of these concepts, the choice will blur the other beyond possibility of useful measurement—and the other way around. But this did not invalidate either the concept of wave or of particle; both were needed in the physicists' investigations. Perhaps the free will versus determinism debate needs its own principle of complementarity—a principle that will enable us to talk coherently about human action as determined or free, depending on the context of our analysis and the practical ends of our inquiry. In any case, recent debate on the free will problem seems to have produced yet another impasse in the debates that have marked the long history of the problem. A. J. Ayer says:

The strength of the determinists lies in the fact that there seems to be no reason why the reign of law should break down at this point [human action] though this is an argument which seemed more convincing in the age of classical physics than it does today. The strength of the indeterminists lies in the fact that the specific theories which alone could vindicate or indeed give any substance to their opponents' case have not yet been more than sketched, though this is not to say that they never will be. Until such theories are properly elaborated and tested, I think there is little more about this topic that can usefully be said.[31]

VI

A Note on Responsibility and Punishment

Freedom, in the sense we have been discussing it, entails responsibility. Responsibility seems to be an indispensable social presupposition—at least in society as constituted at present. In human society the idea of personal responsibility is closely associated with the concepts of praise and blame, reward and punishment. This is not to say that these concepts have no meaning apart from the assumption of personal responsibility. They have. Animal trainers use techniques of reward and punishment to obtain desired behavior, yet they do not think of their charges as morally responsible persons. A strict behaviorist society of the future might well consider its citizens incapable of free choice, yet use praise and blame, reward and punishment, as part of the official conditioning or reinforcing technique. But normally, when it is a question of the social issue of rewards and punishment, we assume some kind of responsibility on the part of the person being rewarded or punished—if only to the extent of believing that he might have done other than he did. It is true that we cancel or mitigate punishment when we find the person in question mentally impaired or incompetent; in these circumstances he is said to not be responsible for his acts, at least not wholly responsible. From Aristotle to the M'Nagten rule,[32] the assumption has been that the agent must have known what he was doing if he is to be held responsible.

In the context of praise and blame, reward and punishment, there are (very roughly) two areas of responsibility—moral and legal. They are not identical, though we know they often overlap. For offenses against moral and legal order, society imposes sanctions. Suppose in a fit of temper I throw a baby into the water so that it drowns. I am brought to trial, found guilty, and sentenced to a prison term. That is my punishment under law. Now suppose that I was never inclined to throw a child in the water, but that one day I see a child drowning in a lake with no one nearby to help but myself. I refuse to go to the child's aid, even though I can easily do so with little risk to myself. This is not a legal offense, but a dereliction in the moral order only. For what I have done—or left undone—I could not be brought to trial and punished by a prison term. Yet the parents of the child would probably denounce me, the people on the beach would call me names and say that I am "morally responsible" for the death of the child. I might lose a friend or two, even find myself in a position of social ostracism. Perhaps late-blooming remorse might torment me for the rest of my life. All this is punishment, though I escape arrest and a prison term. As Mill says, we do not call an action *wrong* unless we mean to imply that a person ought to be punished in some way or other for doing it—"if not by law, by the opinion of his fellow creatures; if not by opinion, by the reproaches of his own conscience."[33]

There are many theories of punishment that try to answer the question of why we punish at all. In the usual writings on the legal aspect of the subject, the theories are grouped under two headings—the *retributive* and the *utilitarian.* Retributive theorists hold that one who has broken the law has contracted a sort of debt, which must be repaid. The simplest retributive concept is the law of retaliation (*lex talionis*), the biblical "eye for eye, tooth for tooth."[34] Kant comes close to approving that simple theory of punishment. He believed that the only conceivable penalty for murder was death.[35] An element common to most types of retributive theory is that the offender *deserves* the punishment. (If he were not morally responsible, he would not deserve it.) The utilitarian theory holds that punishment, if it is to be properly awarded, must have some beneficial effect—on the offender, on society, or on both. A common type of utilitarian theory is the view that punishment serves as a deterrent. But it is frequently claimed by opponents of capital punishment that the death penalty cannot be shown to have a deterrent effect. But a person who believes that the purpose of punishment is retribution may answer that this is irrelevant: what matters is that by imposing the death penalty for certain heinous crimes—the torture and killing of a child, say—society underlines its belief as to the *seriousness* of the crime. The torture-murderer of a child *deserves* death and society behaves with justice in executing the murderer. A variety of the utilitarian theory of punishment holds that punishment, such as imprisonment, is a first and necessary condition in the *reeducation* of the offender, a process necessary to his eventual rehabilitation. A contemporary euphemism for prison guard is "correction officer." But those with prison experience know that not much "reeducation" goes on there.

The debate between upholders of the two theories of punishment need not hold us up. One reason is that the concept of punishment, whether analyzed historically or systematically, is so complex that all the reasons for punishment just will not fit comfortably under the inclusive categories—retributive and utilitarian. Nietzsche gives an ironic summary of the multitudinous functions assigned to punishment at one time or another:

Punishment, as rendering the criminal harmless and incapable of further injury.—Punishment, as compensation for the injury sustained by the injured party. . . . Punishment, as an isolation of that which disturbs the equilibrium, so as to prevent the further spreading of that disturbance. —Punishment as a means of inspiring fear of those who determine and execute the punishment.—Punishment as a kind of compensation for advantages which the wrong-doer has up to that time enjoyed (for example, when he is utilized as a slave in the mines).—Punishment, as the elimination of an element of decay (sometimes of a whole branch, as according to the Chinese laws, consequently as a means to the purification of the race, or the preservation of a social type).—Punishment as a festival, as the violent oppression and humiliation of an enemy that has at least been subdued.—Punishment as a mnemonic, whether for him who suffers the punishment—the so-called "correction," or for the witnesses of its administration.—Punishment, as the payment of a fee stipulated for by the power which protects the evil-doer from the excesses of revenge.—Punishment, as a compromise with the natural phenomenon of revenge, in so far as revenge is still maintained and claimed as a privilege by the stronger races.—Punishment as a declaration and measure of war against an enemy of peace, of law, of order, of authority, who is fought by society with the weapons which war provides, as a spirit dangerous to the community as a breaker of the contract on which the community is based, as a rebel, a traitor, and a breaker of the peace.[36]

Debates on theories of punishment tend to be confused by the way associated images of dire penalties swim into the minds of some of the debaters. Dark shadows of hangings, electrocutions, firing squads, assorted floggings of children, and sundry mutilations take over the field and help win the day for antipunishment sentiment. Nietzsche himself asks us to beware those in whom the instict to punish is strong. But even the most socially restive of us will have to admit that the sanction of punishment extends far beyond scaffolds and whips. The threat of punishment *does* sometimes act with some efficacy as a deterrent. Forget capital punishment and think of Jeff Sawyer's income tax. Jeff is a moderately docile citizen who grudgingly files his return each spring. One of the motives behind his paying the tax is a very faint notion that he *owes* it. But another reason he pays up is that he honestly fears the stiff penalty the law provides for failing to cite sources and amounts of income. Or take Judy Baird's driving habits. She is inclined to exceed the speed limit. But after two successive tickets for going 55 miles per hour in a 35 miles-per-hour zone, she has now eased up on the gas pedal. Why? Because she knows that if she gets caught again her driver's license will be suspended.

The educative use of punishment is well known. This use is not confined to concentration camps that proclaim with brutal hypocrisy, "Reeducation through work!" Parents and psychologists alike are aware of the relevance of punishment to learning, to effecting desired changes in behavior. "That'll teach you!" rings as harshly on our ears today as "Spare the rod and spoil the child"—perhaps because we know such methods are used, with too little difference, on animals and children. Punishment in the learning process, behaviorist psychologists say, is "negative reinforcement"; other things being equal, negative reinforcement is less effective than the positive kind—rewards. But this is a question of efficiency rather than ethics. In its present state of evolution, and probably in any future state we can imagine, human society seems to require systems of rewards and punishments in order to hold together. This need holds for superstate or nuclear family, for schools or parliaments, for the internal judicial system of the Black Panthers or the Irish Republican Army. In ancient China, Confucius announced:

If proprieties and music do not flourish, punishments will not be properly awarded.

If punishments are not properly awarded, the people do not know how to move hand or foot.[37]

What the proprieties and music have to do with the proper award of punishment is not clear to us. But even in the new China, whose government condemns Confucianism as feudal and reactionary, punishments are still awarded. The judicial authorities of Peking make clear that these punishments are not awarded for the sake of revenge, however, but for individual and collective education. East and West, authorities like to give good reasons when justifying punishment.

We noted earlier that punishment is reduced or remitted in law in cases of defective responsibility. Absence of malicious intent, mental incompetence, immaturity of years, and coercion are just a few of the factors that work to cancel or diminish personal accountability. But until very recently little philosophical attention has been given to the question of defective responsibility by reason of social limitations—race, poverty, unemployment, lack of education. Ideally, the greater the personal independence of the agent (which is to say the more free he is from social and other forms of compulsion that may impede his autonomy as a moral being), the more strictly accountable should he be held in the matter of his personal deed. But in practice the situation is often the reverse. One of the reasons for the abolition of capital punishment is the heavy weight of evidence indicating that those executed have been, for the most part, people from the least privileged social class, people of low intelligence, uneducated, destitute, friendless, alone. It is true that the crime rate is highest among the urban and ghetto poor, true also that relatively affluent middle-class people tend to be relatively less troublesome in this respect. But that fact itself reinforces interest in the philosophical aspects of the question of social deprivation and its bearing on personal responsibility. Abstract discussions of free will rarely touch questions of diminished responsibility and freedom impeded by reason of social damage. The turbulence of social conditions of the present day may force reexamination of this, and new life may be given to an old problem.

NOTES: CHAPTER 9

1. Aristotle *Nichomachean Ethics* 1109b35.
2. Augustine, "The Free Choice of the Will," trans. Robert Russell, in *The Fathers of the Church* 60 vols. (Washington, D.C.: Catholic University Press, 1967), vol. 59, bk. 3, ch. 2.
3. François Mauriac, *Woman of the Pharisees* (New York: Farrar, Straus, & Giroux, 1946), p. 208.
4. Charles Dickens, *Martin Chuzzlewit* (1844; New York: Dodd, Mead, 1944), p. 564.
5. Thomas Hobbes, "The Questions Concerning Liberty, Necessity, and Chance," in *The English Works of Thomas Hobbes,* ed. Sir. William Molesworth, 11 vols. (London: John Bohn, 1841), vol. 5.
6. Benedict Spinoza, *Ethics,* pt. 1, propositions 16–17 (1677; New York: Dutton, 1910), p. 27.
7. Paul Henry Baron d'Holbach, *The System of Nature,* 1770.
8. Cited by A. J. P. Taylor, *Bismarck* (London: Hamish-Hamilton, 1955), p. 70.
9. John Hospers, "What Means This Freedom?" in *Determinism and Freedom in the Age of Modern Science,* ed. Sidney Hook (New York: Macmillan, 1961), pp. 126–127.
10. John B. Watson, *Behaviorism,* rev. ed. (New York: Norton, 1930), p. 104.
11. B. F. Skinner, *Beyond Freedom and Dignity* (New York: Knopf, 1971), p. 25.
12. Thomas Huxley, cited by Henri Bergson in *Creative Evolution* (New York: Holt, Rinehart & Winston, 1911), p. 38.
13. Bertrand Russell, "On the Notion of Cause," in *Our Knowledge of the External World,* rev. ed. (London: Allen & Son, 1949), p. 221.
14. William James, "The Dilemma of Determinism," in *The Will to Believe and Other Essays* (London: Longmans, 1908), p. 150.

15. John L. Austin, "Ifs and Cans," in *Free Will and Determinism,* ed. Bernard Berofsky (New York: Harper & Row, 1966), p. 321.

16. "He could have acted otherwise" is offered by P. H. Nowell Smith as a sort of minimum criterion of personal responsibility. His analysis of this concept led many to believe that determinism and libertarianism are not incompatible. *Ethics,* chap. 9 (Baltimore, Md.: Penguin, 1964).

17. Ibid., 201; Aristotle *Nichomachean Ethics* 1110a14.

18. In its simplest meaning, *dialectic* refers to any advance through opposites or contradictions. Hegel believed that the world process, including history, develops dialectically, that is, each stage of reality is one-sided and tends to be cancelled by its negation, or opposite. The contradictory elements are then taken up into a new and more advanced stage, which is itself in turn subject to dialectical development. Marx and Engels combined the dialectical method with their doctrine that reality is material or physical rather than mental or spiritual, and that in history we see the effects of material conditions on human societies.

19. V. P. Tugarinov, *O tsennostiakh zhizni i kul'tury* [On the Values of Life and Culture] (Leningrad, 1960), p. 133. Cited by Richard T. De George, *Soviet Ethics and Morality* (Ann Arbor, Mich.: University of Michigan Press, 1969), p. 70.

20. No visitor to the Soviet Union can fail to be impressed by some of the practical effects of that nation's collective responsibility. For example, the fare boxes at the center doors of many Moscow buses have no fare collector to supervise them. But the passengers keep an eye on the fare boxes, and whoever fails to deposit the proper fare is (as this writer was in Moscow, 1970) subject to immediate collectivist correction. The absence of defacement of public buildings in the USSR is due in large part to the strong sense of collective responsibility in Soviet citizens.

21. An example of the sense of collective responsibility was that shown by Japan when three anti-Israeli Japanese terrorists killed twenty-six people at Tel Aviv's airport in June 1972. High Japanese officials presented apologies, a large sum of money was offered by the Japanese government "for humanitarian purposes," and the father of the surviving terrorist requested that his son be speedily executed.

22. John L. Austin, "A Plea for Excuses," in *Philosophical Papers* (Oxford: Clarendon Press, 1970), p. 187.

23. Plato *Phaedo* 97–98.

24. Character determinism is one form of self-determinist doctrine through which some philosophers have tried to reconcile determinism with free will. Your character is your own, but your acts follow

necessarily from your character. Your particular generous act is determined by your character, for you are a generous person. We have some notion of what it means to "act in character"—but if character determinism is true, how can the act of a person who occasionally acts "out of character" be truly his own act? See note under Schopenhauer in Suggested Readings for this chapter.

25. Roderick Chisholm, "Freedom in Action," in *Freedom and Determinism,* ed. Keither Lehr (New York: Random House, 1966), p. 17.

26. Morris Schlick, *Problems of Ethics,* trans. David Rynin (Englewood Cliffs, N.J.: Prentice-Hall, 1939), pp. 143–156.

27. Philosophy of action refers to contemporary inquiry into various elements in human action such as purpose, intention, desire, wanting, and reason. English philosophers of action include Gilbert Ryle, G. E. M. Anscombe, J. L. Austin. Representative American philosophers are Richard Taylor, A. I. Melden, and Donald Davidson. Philosophical interest in theory of action arose in part from dissatisfaction with behaviorist views which interpret human action in terms of external factors, such as conditioning and reinforcement, with insufficient attention to the volitional and purposeful character of human action.

28. See, for example, A. I. Melden, *Free Action,* chaps. 5, 7, 14 (London: Routledge & Kegan Paul, 1961), pp. 43–55, 66, 199–215. Excerpted in Berofsky, ed., *Free Will and Determinism,* pp. 208–209. Melden and others have followed the lead of G. E. M. Anscombe, whose *Intention* opened new perspectives on philosophical analysis of human action. See note under Anscombe in Suggested Readings for this chapter.

29. Philippa Foot, "Free Will as Involving Determinism," *Philosophical Review* (October 1957) 66: 439–450.

30. Maurice Merleau-Ponty, *The Phenomenology of Perception,* trans. Colin Simth (New York: Humanities, 1962), p. 136.

31. Alfred J. Ayer, "Reasons and Causes," in *Readings in Ethical Theory,* ed. W. Wilfred Sellars and John Hospers (New York: Appleton, 1970), p. 684.

32. M'Nagten's Rule was formulated in 1843 by the House of Lords in London in answer to certain questions asked by the judges in the case of M'Nagten, a disturbed man who was tried for the murder of Sir Robert Peel's secretary. Their lordships said, "The Jury ought to be told in all cases that every man is presumed to be sane, and to possess a sufficient degree of reason to be responsible for his crimes, until the contrary be proved to their satisfaction; and that to establish a defense on the ground of insanity it must be clearly proved that, at the time of committing the act, the accused was

labouring under such a defect of reason, from disease of the mind, as not to know the nature and quality of the act he was doing, or, if he did know it, that he did not know he was doing what was wrong." Full text given in Kent, ed., *Law and Philosophy,* pp. 260–261.
33. John Stuart Mill, *Utilitarianism* (New York: Liberal Arts Press, 1949), p. 52.
34. Exod. 21:23–25.
35. Kant's theory of punishment may be found in his *The Metaphysical Elements of Justice*, trans. John Ladd (New York: Liberal Arts Press, 1965). Kant believed that if a civil society were to dissolve itself by common consent of all its members, every murderer left in prison must first be executed so that all would receive what they deserved.
36. Friedrich Nietzsche, *The Genealogy of Morals,* second essay, trans. Horace B. Samuel (New York: Modern Library, n.d.), pp. 71–72.
37. Confucius, *Analects,* bk. 13, chap. 3, in *Confucius: Confucian Analects, The Great Learning and The Doctrine of the Mean,* trans. James Legge (New York: Dover, 1971), p. 264.

PART THREE

Morals and Life

10

Morals and Love

The idea of punishment by law, by social disapproval, or by pangs of individual conscience has long been associated with a class of actions related to the sexual side of human nature. Men and women have always regarded sex activity with intense interest, joy, fear, guilt—and satisfaction. The basic human social unit is a socially approved mating arrangement, the sexual union of a man and a woman, together with such children as may come from the partnership. But interest in sex goes far beyond interest in the family as a stable social arrangement. Reasons for this interest in sex, often rising to obsession and even outright madness, are many and compelling. The pleasure of sex, its heightening effect on the feelings, its powerful physical and psychic involvements, its relation to love, its causal link to the making of new life, its involvement with kinship, its tie to religious rites, its relation to violence and death (e.g., the killing of the victim in rape and various types of infanticide)—all these relate to the fact that humans in every culture have surrounded the sexual aspect of things with elaborate controls, commandments, and laws. These range from complicated menstrual taboos to common-sense regulations prohibiting sexual molestation of young children. That sex is not only sweet but perilous, bringing not only love in its train but trouble as well, is proved by a mighty library of songs and stories from every age. Eve, Helen, Deirdre, Francesca, Isolde, Héloise, Juliet, Mélisande, and Kitty O'Shea are just a few of the countless women who have had to bear more than their share of responsibility for disasters that followed upon sexual involvement. (The male partner has usually been held less to blame in these matters.)

I

Sex and Morals

The close connection between sex and morality is shown by the fact that we often use the word *moral* as if it belonged only to the sexual sphere. We apply the word *immoral* to a person or action that transgresses sexual rules. "Moral turpitude" (a phrase now almost obsolete) refers to a record of sexual irregularity. For a man to be held on a "morals" charge usually means an alleged sexual offense against a minor of either gender. Writers on art and morality are often concerned with works of art having prominent sexual themes.

We are now living at a time when attitudes toward sexual matters are undergoing one of those periodic changes that have marked different eras in cultural history. The present change in attitude is especially visible in the educated middle classes of urbanized and industrialized societies. In the cultures of Western Europe and the United States, there had been a number of earlier shifts in social attitudes toward sexual behavior. The Puritan revolution in England was succeeded by the Restoration, an era of much sexual license among the governing classes. (The poor were thought to have no more restraint than animals in such matters.) The middle- and upper-class proprieties of the Victorian and Edwardian eras (which imperfectly concealed a number of horrendous scandals) were overturned by drastic changes in sexual manners following World War I. To the world between two wars, Jazz Age flappers and Scott Fitzgerald's golden girls brought awareness of sexual revolt. The generation born after World War II experienced further liberalization of sexual attitudes, rising to what some observers consider a revolutionary peak in the 1960s and 1970s. Part of the contemporary shift in attitude toward sexual matters is doubtless due to recent improvements in and increased availability of contraceptive techniques that have greatly diminished the fear of pregnancy after sexual intercourse. Part of the change is probably due to the lessening influence of religious sanctions as well as liberal trends within the churches themselves. Part comes from the refusal of young people to put up any longer with postponement of sexual activity for increasingly prolonged intervals separating sexual maturity and economic readiness for conventional marriage. The new awareness of the status of women may be either cause or effect—or both.

Sex and Law

Nowhere more than in the sexual sphere does Bergson's distinction between the "two sources of morality"—external and internal—show itself more clearly. From the outside, society imposes controls on sexual behavior; these controls usually take negative form, prohibitions that state, "Thou shalt not!" From sources within the individual person, the positive impulse of love—including the sexual but going beyond it—seems to tell us what is right and good.

Among societies earlier than ours sexual activity was strictly regulated by laws that were at the same time sacred and secular. This is particularly true of our own tradition. One of the Ten Commandments received by Moses from Jehovah specifically forbids adultery. The Book of Leviticus lists sexual prohibitions in careful detail, together with mandatory death penalties attached to major infractions of the law. Some of the intense concern over sex among people of Biblical times sprang from their anxiety over the disruptive potential of sexual irregularity upon societies that had to employ all possible means to ensure order and stability in order to survive. High infant mortality and dwindling populations increased this anxiety. The elaborate kinship structure in primitive societies was a relevant factor, as were those mysterious and powerful aspects of sex that seemed to link man directly to the supernatural.

There seem to have been few societies in which some aspect of sexuality was not taken seriously. The prohibition against incest is almost universal, and this includes our own society. Many societies have been very flexible in regard to the sexual liaisons of their young unmarried people, but even among these permissive societies there were customs and laws that regulated sexual activity once the family unit was established. In our own country, a large variety of sexual offenses not involving violence or injury are still proscribed by law with various degrees of penalty attached. Statutes forbidding many forms of sex behavior, from adultery to homosexual acts, remain on the books of most states, though in many cases these laws are not enforced. The tendency in contemporary society is to transfer the burden of responsibility in sexual matters from public to private conscience, except when violence or extreme youth is involved. Since World War II, there has been mounting pressure in Britain and in the United States to withdraw legal sanctions against certain sexual acts, so long as they are performed in private by "consenting adults." In 1957 the Wolfenden Committee in Britain recommended extending this tolerance to homosexual acts. The most common of these, however, is still referred to in some American statute books as "the unspeakable and abominable crime against nature."[1]

Many reasons are offered to explain the willingness of contemporary society to shift the burden of sexual offenses from the realm of public law to that of private morals. Some point out that the welfare and security of the modern state is not as directly affected by sexual irregularity as was the case with earlier societies, which were much smaller and close-knit and required the strictest social stability for their very existence. Others point to the decline of religious belief and the lessened power of the church to influence public behavior. Optimists say that people are just being more reasonable about sexual activity than they once were. Pessimists claim that the permissiveness is a symptom, not a cause, of what they see as the accelerating breakup of Western society.

The ways in which human beings can give sexual offense are many and various. People still have deep convictions and strong views that cover the whole range of sex acts—even though they are not always successful in making clear the reasons for their firmly held views. The outrage that certain sexual activities provoke and the deep sense of guilt so often found in participants contribute to a feeling experienced by many that *a law has been broken,* even though there may have been no applicable legal statute or even a very clear reason for social disapproval. This commonly felt sense of "breaking some law" is related to G. E. M. Anscombe's suggestion that concepts of "moral" and "immoral" are faded remnants of "contrary to Divine Law" or "forbidden by God."[2]

The whole business is difficult. We can take the easy way and turn the entire problem of sexual morality into popular psychology. We can say that something is morally wrong only when it becomes psychologically harmful. We can talk about the right and the good in terms of "healthy attitudes toward sex." But this carries with it the danger of reducing the moral realm to a province of psychological well-being. The matter is complicated by the fact that some questions of sexual ethics relate to morality as code, as external rule, as social guideline, while others have to do with an impulse that comes from the sense of a loving heart. The idea of sexual morality as an affair of inner loving impulse rather than adherence to external code is prominent in what today is called *situation ethics.* This is a new name for a notion long familiar to moralists: every moral situation is in some way unique and may require its own unique solution; it is foolish to focus moral judgment on an act or type of acts isolated from the whole person and the particular situation in which the person is acting.[3]

Ethics of Monogamy: Adultery

In James Joyce's novel *Finnegans Wake,* a striking theory of the origin of the human family and monogamous union is playfully linked to the thought of the Italian social philosopher Giambattista Vico. At the dawn of humanity, we see a beast-man copulating in the open with his random woman. Suddenly there is a great lightning flash and thunderclap.[4] The terrified creatures rush to the protective darkness of a cave, and sit there trembling, clinging to one another. In this way at the same moment was conceived the first family home and the first religious sentiment—the seed of domestic love and the fear of God. Though this charming theory of the origin of the monogamous family is a little wild, it is not so radical as the earlier hypothesis of Aristophanes in Plato's *Symposium* that among the original humans were double-sexed beings who were cut in two by Zeus and, ever since, these separate halves have been running about looking for one another. In this way love, and, presumably, monogamous marriage was born.[5] Nietzsche claims that the monogamous family is a late phenomenon, that early man had to pay a fine to the community for the arrogance of claiming one woman for himself.[6]

Today monogamy is the most usual marital arrangement among humans. In earlier patriarchal societies, polygamy was common. The material conditions in which pastoral peoples lived favored polygamy as a social arrangement. The usual form was *polygyny* (many women), though *polyandry* (many men) was not unknown. Polygamy survives in some parts of the world today. Conventional monogamy and the whole idea of the value of the family—particularly of the two-generation nuclear family—has been challenged by today's theorists of sexual revolution. But many of the current popular experiments in the new sexual arrangements are not so much alternatives to monogamy as they are modifications of the existing system, or attempts to make it more flexible. Arrangements in which a boy and girl (or man and

woman) live together enjoy a cautious degree of social acceptance that would have been unthinkable in the first half of this
century.[7] But many say these unions are not so much contradictions of monogamous marriage as they are new forms of
preparation for it. If the partners find that the informal arrangement does not work out, they may leave each other to form other
attachments. Some observers say that the successful unions
tend to lead to marriage. Practically, many of them do, though
there are cases of seemingly successful unions in which one of
the partners is abruptly forsaken and left with a bitter feeling
of having been exploited. But such failure is by no means peculiar to the recent informal boy-girl sexual union. In any case,
social observers agree that monogamous marriage will probably
survive for a while in some form or other.

In many early societies, such as those of Biblical times, the
penalty for adultery was death (it was usually the woman who
suffered it). In other cultures attitudes were more permissive—
though with specific limitations. Nomadic Eskimo groups did
not object to wife-sharing under certain conditions, but these
conditions were rather clearly understood. Among the Bantu,
adultery was not objected to so long as the affected husband
was complacent; if he did object, there might be violent reprisals.

The origin of laws forbidding adultery had much to do with
property rights. The woman was part of a man's possessions, like
his house and his domestic animals. The Tenth Commandment
makes this clear: "Thou shalt not covet thy neighbor's house,
thou shalt not covet thy neighbor's wife, nor his manservant, nor
his maidservant, nor his ox, nor his ass, nor anything that is thy
neighbor's." Property aspects of adultery were by no means
confined to early and primitive peoples. John Galsworthy's popular novel series *The Forsyte Saga* takes for its first theme the
reaction of an Edwardian man of property to his wife's falling
in love with another man. To Soames Forsyte, adultery was wife-
stealing, a flagrant offense against the right of property. Adultery
as property violation, with its discrimination against the wife
and the implied privilege of double standard for the husband,
reflects the larger issue of the traditional subordinate status of
women in human society. Even in a union in which the woman is
not thought of as the *property* of the man, adultery remains an
offense against the implied traditional right of *control* of women
by men. Recent feminists have offered persuasive arguments to
show that any question of sexual ethics ultimately goes back to
sexual politics.

There are a number of rational arguments to support the conclusion that adultery is wrong. Socially, adultery tends to be disruptive. In the system of monogamous marriage in which we live, family stability is advantageous. This is particularly true where children are concerned. The child who comes from a broken home is commonly regarded as suffering a disadvantage. People generally agree that a marriage attended by domestic harmony is better than one that is not. But adultery threatens domestic harmony and produces unpleasantness. It can bring an end to the marriage itself and can badly hurt the people involved. If we put the argument on the basis of an appeal to ethical rules and take as our maxim "Do not act in such a way as to hurt another human being," adultery is wrong because it tends to bring about hurt. Of course, one can challenge the "Don't hurt!" rule. It is not self-evidently valid. It is not the maxim of a warrior, conqueror, or revolutionary (imagine saying it to Napoleon or Lenin!), nor of a person who believes that in certain situations his self-fulfillment must take precedence over another's welfare even at the cost of hurt to someone. Then, too, there is always the pleasure of the situation to be considered, and the problem of balance between pleasure and pain arises. To the question, "Was it worth it?" one can imagine one adulterous pair saying yes, another no. What would Tristan and Isolde have answered?

Some find a different appeal to reason against adultery more persuasive. This argument applies more to an affair of some length and depth rather than to an isolated episode; it also assumes that one of the spouses is ignorant and not complacent. Adultery is wrong because of its essentially *deceptive* nature. Adultery is cheating, acting a lie, a serious breach of faith. The adulterous person accepts the trust of his spouse, knowing that he has broken that trust. That spouse is not an object, not a thing, but a human person like himself or herself. The adulterer is cheating and cheating is immoral. He knows that his spouse would not want to be cheated. He knows that he could not wish it to be a universal rule that, given the institution of marriage, all men and women would act the way he is acting.[8]

Henry James's *The Golden Bowl* portrays the moral effect of an adulterous deception in a way no textbook of moral philosophy, psychology, or spiritual guidance could possibly do. This subtle novel offers a *phenomenology* of adultery—a detailed, painstaking description of the way in which humans swindle each other and are corrupted in the process. Very late in the story the young wife Maggie, victim of an elaborate dissimulation on the part of her husband (the Prince) and Charlotte (who had passed as her best friend), speaks to her husband:

"It isn't a question of any beauty," said Maggie; "it's only a question of the quantity of truth."
"Oh the quantity of truth!" the Prince . . . murmured.
"That's a thing by itself, yes. But there are also such things all the same as questions of good faith."[9]

Just a moment before Maggie had thought of Charlotte, who must now part from her lover for good: "It's terrible," Maggie says, "I see it's *always* terrible for women." Her husband answers, "Everything's terrible, cara—in the heart of man."

Perhaps not every case of adultery has this corrupting moral effect. Maybe everything is *not* terrible in the heart of man. The decision to engage oneself in an act of love that "goes against the rules" may have, on occasion, an authority of its own. Tried and sound though they may be, the rules may not touch some special moment, some unique case. At least this is the claim of situation ethics, which tells us that every moral situation is unique, that some cases may not be resolved by an appeal to rules and principles. Kant would concede that in a certain sense every moral situation *is* unique. But he would quickly dismiss situation ethics as no more than a variation of the usual way people have of making exceptions of themselves when their duty is painful and breach of it is self-indulgence. The categorical imperative admits of no exceptions, situational or otherwise.

In any case, for all its injurious potential, adultery has shown a remarkable ability to coexist (within limits) with monogamous society. This does not necessarily mean that it is justified. It may simply show that monogamous social arrangements have proved tough, flexible, or both.

Love Between the Sexes

If adulterous love-making is morally wrong the fault has proved no bar to its celebration in song and story over the centuries. By contrast, poetic commemorations of chaste marriages are rather rare. Everyone knows the stories of David and Bathsheba, Lancelot and Guinevere, Anna Karenina and Vronsky. But poetry seems less drawn to married love. It may be that sin and evil are more interesting, dramatically speaking, than the right and the good. Milton's Satan easily steals the show from God in *Paradise Lost*.

In his *Love in the Western World,* Denis de Rougemont says that when it comes to a story, we all want to hear a high tale of love and death, not an edifying account of bourgeois wedded devotion.[10] That is why *Tristan and Isolde* has such an enduring, compelling appeal: it is the story of a *fatal* love, one doomed to shipwreck and foundering. (Hemingway's *Farewell to Arms* and Eric Segal's *Love Story* are variations on the theme.) Isolde as Frau Tristan, raising babies and cooking sausages, would leave us cold. We want to hear her voice, still aflame with passion, soaring over the dead body of her knightly lover. Our fascination with tales of love and fatality may date from the thirteenth century, when, according to a common scholarly opinion, romantic love was invented. In the High Middle Ages, the Virgin Mary was exalted to near-divine status. The cathedral of Chartres was built for her. In the songs of mortal passion sung by medieval troubadours, we sense the fervor of the cult of the Blessed Lady. Courtly love made Woman an object of devotion— but still, as Simone de Beauvoir reminds us, an object.[11]

The religious element in the medieval concept of love is part of a long tradition that links sexual love with the divine. According to Plato, the force that draws lovers together is Eros, a cosmic power bringing together the divine and the mortal. Lovers are mad, of course, but it is a divine madness that seizes them. Beauty is unique among the heavenly Forms; it is the only one visible to the senses. This explains why the lover adores his beloved, a mere mortal. Aristotle accounts for the creation of the world by assuming that the world moves toward God as toward an object of desire. Drawn to God, the world takes on form and character in the process. "The Final Cause, then, produces motion as being loved."[12] Seventeen centuries later, but in the same spirit, Dante said, "L'Amor che move il sole e l'altre stelle" —it is love that moves the sun and stars.[13]

Schopenhauer agrees—if love is understood without theological or religious illustration. In his book *The World as Will and Idea,* he works out a metaphysics of the love of the sexes. The world is not the product of a rational and benevolent God, but of an infinite Will that is mindless, instinctive, blind. The eternal striving of the World Will enters into each of its creatures, and they pass on this endless current through sexual reproduction. That is why we mortals bestow upon the beloved the transfigured features of divinity. Nature's illusion lasts until the World Will has accomplished its end in the birth of yet another creature to whom the torch of infinite longing is passed on. For us, the vision fades and love turns into its opposite, hatred, or into what is worse—ennui, boredom, disgust.[14]

The French novelist François Mauriac turns this Schopen-hauerian pessimism back to a traditional religious direction with his theme of *un seul amour* "one love alone." There is only one love, God. The complete commitment we so often make in human love is made to the wrong object, although we do not know this. After her attempted suicide, Maria Cross of Mauriac's *The Desert of Love* says:

I see everything so clearly now. The people we think we love, the loves that end so miserably . . . now at last I know the truth. It is not loves that we have, but one single love. It goes on inside us, and from a casual meeting, from the eyes and lips of some perfect stranger, we build up something we think corresponds to it . . . we choose the one path open to us, but it was never designed to lead us to our heart's desire.[15]

The complete giving of ourselves in love belongs to God alone. But the draw of sexual love is so strong that it is the one thing that makes us forget the object of our search. And for this mistaken application of the total giving of ourselves in human love, we pay dearly: "the desert" follows. Lucky for them that Tristan and Isolde met their deaths at the height of their passion. Had they lived, chained to each other, their desire would have curdled to disgust. "Death is the salt of love," Mauriac says, "it is life that brings corruption."

Besides its link of sexual love to the divine—with a resulting *disproportion* between what the lover sees in his beloved and what is really there—traditional philosophy of love has called attention to the *mixed* nature of the relation between man and woman. The love of the sexes is a mélange of selfishness and unselfishness, of the desire to possess for oneself and the desire to do good for the other. Plato contrasts the "uninitiated" lover who "is given over to pleasure, and like a brutish beast rushes on to enjoy and beget" with the "initiated" lover who has passed beyond possessiveness and thinks only of bringing good to the beloved—"for no feelings of envy or jealousy are entertained by them toward their beloved."[16] St. Paul detached the high form of love from sex altogether and thus laid the basis for the traditional contrast between *eros* (sexual love, essentially selfish) and *agapé* (unselfish love). It is of love of this second kind, love without self-interest, that he speaks when he says:

"Though I speak with the tongues of men and angels and have not love, I am become as sounding brass, or tinkling cymbal. . . . Love suffers long and is kind. It does not envy. It does not boast or puff itself up. . . . Love does not seek her own."[17] So with St. Paul begins the long history of the dualism of sacred and profane love—love of the spirit and of the flesh.

Today most writers on the subject of love between men and women recognize that both elements are usually present, in varying degrees, in sexual love. Such love contains within itself both eros and agapé, both the desire of pleasure for oneself and the will for the good of the beloved. The crudest sexual performance contains a faint trace of the spiritual, even if brutally suppressed, and in the fervor of spiritual love we should not be altogether surprised to find the sexual side of our nature remotely stirred.

With some men and women, when the erotic side of love diminishes or fades away altogether, the distinterested element fades too; interest in the other's happiness evaporates, all tender feeling is eroded, and the one desire is to get away. But in other cases, when sexual interest declines, the pleasure in the other's good remains and love endures. It is a commonplace of moral philosophy, as it touches sexual matters, that unselfish love is best. Bernard Gert says:

Unselfish love, i.e., delight in the pleasure of another regardless of who caused it, is the most satisfactory. Unlike selfish love, which delights only in the pleasure that one causes oneself, it cannot give rise to jealousy. Jealousy is displeasure caused by the pleasure of one you love when that pleasure is not caused by yourself. One who loves another selfishly may actually seek to deprive her of pleasure that was caused by someone else. But it is not only love between men and women that can be selfish. A parent may have a selfish love for his children. It is even possible for a man to love God selfishly.[18]

Both moral philosophers and popular psychologists like to remind us that the lover should remember that his partner in the sexual union is a person, a complete human being, not simply an object or instrument of pleasure. (Kant's categorical imperative requires that we treat others as ends in themselves, not simply as means.) Love does not coexist with the use or exploitation of another. The ancestry of this common doctrine in our religious and ethical traditions seems clear.

Some may find such moralizings about love between the sexes

reasonable enough, but may distrust them for having the air of truisms or received opinions. In a concrete existential situation, what would it really mean to two lovers, burning with passion, to know that "unselfish love is the most satisfactory kind"? Too often it is a sign, not of the beginning, but of the end, of the affair when the lover tells his partner that he "respects her as a person." Besides, there is an unsatisfactory dualism in the sharp cut between the selfish and unselfish elements of love. By what right does the moralist *segregate* love from desire? Passion can mean self-enrichment, but also self-forgetfulness.

So far as the earlier metaphysical theories of love are concerned, the most incisive criticism comes from the contemporary woman's movement, which rejects them out of hand as grotesque survivals of ideas that have come down to us from a past marked by absolute political and theological male control. Many feminists take all that talk about the divine or cosmic ingredient in human love as part of an age-old male stratagem, consciously or unconsciously present, to shut woman out from control of affairs by putting her on a pedestal, exalting her to the status of a semidivine being—her beauty reflecting that of another world, too "good" for the realities of this one.

II: VARIATIONS ON THE THEME

Masturbation

The sexual rigorist believes that *every* kind of sexual activity outside marriage and some within marriage are morally wrong. The sexual libertarian believes that *many* kinds of sexual activity outside and within marriage are *not* morally wrong and that some are morally commendable. (The word libertarian in this context refers to someone who favors the liberalizing of sex attitudes, not to one who believes in free will—as in the last chapter.) Consider masturbation.

Boys and girls of puberty age, subject to intensely active glandular secretions, tend to relieve their sexual tension in this way. Caught in the act, many have been nearly frightened to death by the moral outrage of their parents. As a schoolboy, André Gide was caught in the act and found himself suspended from school for three months. His parents took him to the family doctor:

"I know all about it my boy," he said, putting on a gruff voice, "and there's no need to examine or question you. But if your mother finds it necessary to bring you here again, that is, if you don't learn to behave, look behind you!" (and his voice became truly terrible). "Those are the instruments we should have to use—the instruments with which little boys like you have to be operated on!" And he rolled his eyes at me ferociously as he pointed out a panoply of Touareg spearheads hanging on the wall behind his chair.[19]

To this ferocious sexual rigorism, the libertarianism of Dr. Sol Gordon, director of the family planning center of Syracuse University's College for Human Development, provides permissive contrast. In his publication, *Ten Heavy Facts About Sex,* which is given to each incoming Syracuse University freshman of the class of 1975, the doctor offers this reassurance: "Masturbation is a normal expression of sex for both males and females. Enjoy it. There's no harm in masturbation no matter how often you do it. Masturbation is a sign that something is wrong only when it is compulsive."[20]

Somewhere between the extremes of rigorist and libertarian, a conservative might argue that masturbation can easily turn into an unlovely form of self-indulgence, while a liberal could conceivably object that the practice may be conducive to sexual sloth— the agent may become simply too lazy to get out and hunt up a partner. But both these objections apply more to adult addiction than to the adolescent form of what used to be called "solitary vice." Moral theologians of the Roman Catholic church have modified their once stern position on the matter of masturbation. Thomas Aquinas considered it a sin more grave than fornication. The church's ancient stricture against masturbation followed from a "natural law" premise that implied that any sexual activity separated from the intended channels of procreation is morally wrong. Today, even conservative theologians hold that masturbation is wrong only if it is indulged in deliberately, in clear knowledge, and with full consent of the will—conditions that are often difficult to achieve during adolescence.

Incest

Human societies tend to reserve their greatest songs and stories for graver faults than the one just considered. Masturbation has never inspired an epic. By contrast incest, regarded by nearly all societies as a most horrific sexual offense, is celebrated in a series of masterpieces that cross the ages from Sophocles's drama *Oedipus Rex* to Alberto Ginastera's contemporary opera

Beatrix Cenci. In modern Western culture, the ban against incest has usually applied only to members of the nuclear (two-generation) family, but earlier and primitive peoples extended the ban through many degrees of kinship. Unlike adultery, which was considered a private matter, incest constituted a grave public offense. With certain exceptions—for example, royal marriages among the Egyptians, Hawaiians, Incas, and the Azande of West Africa—every culture has regarded incest as a serious evil. The old Greeks had an absolute horror of it. So did the ancient Jews, Romans, medieval Arabs, and European Christians. So do the Peruvian Indians, Papuans, African pygmies, and Australian aborigines of our own day. It is often said that the strict moral ban on incest stems from the fact that it tends to create genetic defects.[21] But this reason seems not to have occurred to the multitudinous peoples of the world who forbade incest in the past. They were ignorant of genetics, and the genetic reason has a limited degree of truth, which is out of proportion to the horror universally inspired by incest. Every other conceivable reason has been given by one society or another to justify its intolerance of incest: it would offend the gods; it would cause crop failures, floods, famine, volcanic eruptions, barrenness, or earthquakes; it would interfere with the proper movement of the heavenly bodies.

Freudian psychology explains the incest on the ground that men *want* to marry their mothers and kill their fathers. The potentially disruptive effects of such an unconscious wish upon civilization is obvious. Hence the need to control the Oedipal drive forces itself into the consciousness of society in the form of strict legal and religious interdicts. Hence too the atmosphere of nameless horror that surrounds incest. Lévi-Strauss has an explanation of the incest ban in terms of social growth and the need to divide labor between the sexes. If incest were permitted, the roots of a single family would tend not to ramify beyond itself. The incest ban compels the human to go outside his or her family and to found another family.

The true explanation [of incest] should be looked for in a completely opposite direction, and what has been said concerning the sexual division of labor may help us to grasp it. This has been explained as a device to make the sexes mutually dependent on social and economic grounds, thus establishing clearly that marriage is better than celibacy. Now, exactly in the same way that the principle of sexual division of labor establishes a mutual dependency between the sexes, compelling them thereby to perpetuate themselves and to found a family, the prohibition of incest establishes a mutual dependency between families, compelling them, in order to perpetuate themselves, to give rise to new families.[22]

In his day, Thomas Aquinas advanced a similar argument.[23] The prohibition against incest causes people to look outside the family for their marriage partners. This is advantageous because the number of people with whom family members have good and friendly relations is now increased, and a social unity on a broader basis than that of blood relationship is developed. After reviewing the anthropological evidence, Margaret Mead draws the judicious if not wholly informative conclusion that the "universality of the occurrence of incest regulations . . . suggests that they are part of a very complex system with deep biological roots, a system that is both a condition and a consequence of human evolution."[24]

In practice, incest is probably more frequent than the stern interdictions of society would suggest. Reliable statistics on the frequency of incest in contemporary society are hard to come by. Such fragmentary data that we do have indicate that incest, while rare in comparison with other sexual offenses, nonetheless does exist. It is frequently found among socially deprived classes where crowded living conditions and sleeping arrangements provide the occasion. Father-daughter incestuous relations are not uncommon in rural or rural-origin families. There is a pathetic description of an incident of this type in Ralph Ellison's novel *The Invisible Man.* "But what you gon do after it happens?" screams the wife of a poor black sharecropper, "When yo black 'bomination is birthed to bawl yo wicked sin befo the eyes of God!" But her husband's fault seems to him less a blood sin than a dream sin.[25]

Some sexual libertarians hold that the middle classes themselves might benefit from a change in moral and social attitudes toward incest. If the genetic effect of this practice has been misunderstood and exaggerated, and if the need to proliferate families has today been satisfied, perhaps sexual life may be enriched by modification or abandonment of the old incest prohibition. A recent textbook says:

. . . we can expect people to begin to think of dispensing with taboos. If sexual relations can enhance the romantic love between man and wife, they may argue, perhaps sexual relations can enhance sibling love between brothers and sisters, Electra love between fathers and daughters, and Oedipal love between mothers and sons, and so on for grandfathers and grandsons. There may be many love-enhancing possibilities our society is suppressing, which, in the interest of closing the generation gap, it should encourage.[26]

Whether the nuclear family—already challenged by social critics of our day—could absorb the strain of complications suggested by the proposed new relationships is an interesting question. One benefit at least would be likely: the superabundance of material for family dramas by the new Strindbergs, O'Neills, and Albees of the twenty-first century.

Very often the word *taboo* comes up in discussions of "new morality." It is often used as a question-begging word: to beg the question is to assume as true what is to be proved. The word is loaded with every kind of negative connotation, including that of irrational primitive horror. No reasonable person would approve of perpetuating a taboo since he associates it with a senseless and superstitious practice. When we argue about a rule concerning sexual conduct, to refer to that rule as a taboo may blur in advance a necessary distinction between moral reasonableness and moral superstition. Some rules pertaining to sexual conduct are indeed no more than taboos in the most primitive sense of the word. But it is an open question as to whether all of them are. If morality has to do with right relations between humans, at least some questions of sex relations are of moral import. A question of how one treats another person, a human like oneself, is never without some ethical bearing. This is especially true of sexual love, in which so often someone is vulnerable to cruel or careless treatment.

Homosexuality
Homosexual behavior appears to be far more common than incest. Though aversion still marks public and familial reaction to sexual deviation from the "normal," in recent years increased understanding of the homosexual's situation has been achieved, as has a willingness to protest against some of the discriminations and civil liabilities to which he is subject. While there are no laws in this country against homosexuality as such (i.e., one may have homosexual feelings and desires with impunity), most states do retain statutes forbidding common kinds of overt homosexual behavior. In practice, homosexual acts between

"consenting adults" are rarely intruded upon by legal authorities if they are carried on in private. It is the public sex act, to which so many homosexuals are forced by circumstances and the nature of the particular need, that brings about arrest and prosecution. This does not include possible additional harassment by police, employers, or government agencies to which homosexuals may be subject.

Homosexuality was well known among early societies and primitive people. In a few such groups, homosexuals were accommodated in one way or another. The Chukchees of Siberia created a shamanlike role for the adult male homosexual. Nomadic Eskimos treated him with amused tolerance; he was odd, a little silly, a "character." Some tribesmen incorporated homosexual behavior in their ceremonials; the Keraki and Kiwei of New Guinea performed male homosexual acts in their puberty rites. In general, however, most primitive societies exerted specific social pressures against homosexuality. The ancient Jews considered it an abomination punishable by death.[27] The behavior that led the Lord to destroy Sodom and Gomorrah was traditionally believed to be homosexual. *Sodomy,* the legal name of a common homosexual act, derives from the first of these cities of the plain; its quaint synonym *buggery* derives from the name "Bogomil," a Manichaean sect of Bulgaria who allegedly practiced sodomy.

In our own society, the word "homosexual" covers a wide range of acts, attitudes, habits, and dispositions. According to surveys on the subject, a large number of adolescents have had homosexual experiences before settling into the usual heterosexual paths. Many men with wives and children find themselves compelled to seek homosexual satisfaction at varying intervals. According to the Kinsey report, thirty-seven percent of the male population of the United States has had overt homosexual experiences. A much lower, but still significant percentage of men adopt homosexuality as a way of life, defining their social lives in terms of "gay" bars and parties. Some homosexual men lead quiet and happy lives together. Some are forced to frequent public parks and toilets to find partners. Data on female homosexuality, or lesbianism, is not easy to obtain. As a rule, women homosexuals do not seek the stylized social life that so many committed male homosexuals seem to require, and hence are less visible as homosexuals than men. Women may also live together devotedly for years in a warm and loving relationship without ever having engaged in explicit homosexual acts. Although some male homosexuals live with one another for long periods of time, stable relations of that sort may be less common than the quick sexual contact. Reliable data on these matters is too thin to warrant secure general conclusions.

Homosexuality arouses curiosity and fear. People have heard that the phenomenon often attends talent, even genius, as in the case of Plato, Leonardo, Proust, Tchaikovsky, Wilde, Genet, and an assortment of major and minor greats. This produces wonder. But the predominant social reaction to homosexuality is fear and condemnation. Our society sets store by sharp division of the sexes. We exalt masculine and feminine ideals; consciously or unconsciously we apply powerful conditioning to children so that boys will be boys and girls, girls. Fathers are as fearful of their sons showing homosexual tendencies as mothers are lest their daughters not marry. Curiosity and concern about homosexuality demand causal explanations. People want to know why. Unfortunately there seems to be no clear answer to this question. Early observers thought homosexuality was a physical disease, perhaps something wrong in the glands. This was later changed to mental disease, then softened to "personality disorder" or "emotional disorientation." Ulrichs thought that homosexuality occurred when the soul of one sex inhabited the body of another. (The French novelist Proust followed this line in describing his homosexual characters.)[28] Freud traced the roots of male homosexuality to a parent-child relation in which the mother arouses her son's sexual interest and as a result makes him deeply anxious about incest. He cannot handle this anxiety, for he is afraid that his father will punish him. So his relations to women become inhibited through this powerful hidden fear of parental castration. Freud also believed that narcissism or obsessive self-love was an important element in male homosexuality.

Without necessarily agreeing with Freud's formulation, most observers today hold that the origin of homosexuality is psychogenic, a personality anomaly. It is a commonplace to account for the male variety by citing an excessively "mothering" mother and a father who is weak, detached, or absent. One difficulty with such causal theories is inadequacy of empirical verification. Many homosexuals do not have such parental backgrounds, and many of those who do have it are not homosexuals. Simone de Beauvoir sees homosexuality, not as an aberration, but as a choice made. For homosexual women particularly, it is

no more a perversion deliberately indulged in than it is a curse of fate. It is an attitude chosen in a certain situation—that is, at once motivated and freely adopted. . . . It is one way, among others, in which woman solves the problems imposed by her condition in general, by her erotic situation in particular.[29]

As for the morality of homosexuality, one variety of the libertarian position may be put this way: sexually immoral acts can indeed take place within a homosexual context just as they can in a heterosexual setting, but this does not mean that homosexual behavior, as such, is any more sinful than heterosexual behavior. Homosexuals, in the main, do not bother those not interested in deviate behavior; they pose no threat to the domestic stability of "straight" people. Occasionally, homosexuality may disrupt a hitherto settled married life, but this happens far less often than does the similar effect of heterosexual adultery. Exploitative relations between humans are wrong wherever they are found, but the moral burden should not be laid on the homosexual in view of the record of male-female exploitation, which is as long and heavy as history itself. The libertarian will urge that the blanket charge of immorality, whether in the sense of sin or of social destructiveness, should be lifted from homosexual behavior and that the homosexual no longer be considered an undesirable person. He urges too that laws against homosexual behavior now on the books be dropped or modified in such a way as to remove even the formal threat of legal prosecution from consenting adults participating in homosexual acts in private.

Some observers of homosexual life dismiss as irrelevant its alleged sinfulness or contrariety to "natural law," yet refuse to give that life their full endorsement. Whatever meaning may be left in that oldest ethical ideal, the Good Life, they say, we may be sure that the life of the homosexual male in today's society is usually not that life. Rarely if ever does he achieve even the small measure of happiness found in other ways of living. According to Dr. Martin Hoffman, a research psychiatrist who studied homosexuality in San Francisco, the gay world is a bad scene.[30] Although some couples may achieve a stable life together, the majority of overt male homosexuals are sexually promiscuous, their relationships transitory. Often the partners do not speak a word, says Hoffman, do not even know each other's names, never see each other again after a single contact. Constantine Cavafy, greatest of modern Greek poets and himself a homosexual, celebrates one of these transitory encounters that took place in his own city of Alexandria; the brief wordless experience may provide the stuff of some good verse the poet will make one day:

The fulfillment of their deviate, sensual delight
is done. They rose from the mattress,
And they dress hurriedly without speaking.
They leave the house separately, furtively; and as
they walk somewhat uneasily on the street, it seems
as if they suspect that something about them betrays
into what kind of bed they fell a little while back.
But how the life of the artist has gained.
Tomorrow, the next day, years later, the vigorous verses
will be composed that had their beginning here.[31]

Fine for the poet, comments W. H. Auden, himself a poet and homosexual. But maybe Cavafy does not appreciate his good luck in having the ability to transmute into valuable poetry experiences that, for those who do not have this power, may be trivial or even harmful. Fine for the poet, but what will be the future of the artist's companion?

A question for social ethics is whether society has a duty to help the homosexual overcome his outcast status—for he is still an outcast. Families reject him, employers fire him, government agencies persecute him. Psychoanalysts disagree among themselves as to whether they can "cure" him. But psychotherapists do say that one important way of helping to overcome the estrangement that separates the homosexual from the mainstream of society is to overcome the fear of homosexuality that so many of us carry with us. Freud taught that we all have homosexual as well as heterosexual tendencies but that, because of social pressure, we sternly suppress the former. This repression in turn produces the unreasonable fear and hate that so often mark the attitude of the heterosexual toward the homosexual. To expose the roots of this fear of homosexuals may help to lessen and even to dispel it. Some observers believe that a more general and practical way of overcoming the alienation of the homosexual lies in working for changing the rigid, two-valued sex orientation of our society. This way will include softening up the usual male (he-man) and female ("She's all girl!") stereotypes. Since the Beatles—already ancient history—such a road has been taken by many young people of our time. Sympathetic observers believe that this new way of life, the ready acceptance of male interest in colorful clothes, flowers, and long hair (but what about the beards?) has already helped to break down the dualism existing in our society between so-called masculine and feminine values, with consequent good effect on those who do not fit the older precut patterns of society.

Pornography and Obscenity

Philosophers like to distinguish between "first-order" and "second-order" matters. The first is the thing itself, the second the language about the thing. What we have been discussing up to now has been the morality of first-order sexual activity—sexual acts themselves. Now we can make a note on a second-order sexual affair—pornography and sexual obscenity. These are second order because in themselves they are not sexual; they are *about* sex. Since World War II, the tendency to withdraw sexual activity from the control of public law, if not of private morals, has been paralleled by rising permissiveness in the area of publications and entertainments on explicit sexual themes. The intense curiosity humans feel about sex is attested to by the flood of market material that attempts to satisfy that curiosity. Of course, for many using these commodities, more than curiosity is involved; reading about and seeing pictures of sex acts and/or naked bodies stimulates sexual desire and leads to sexual pleasure for them. This is particularly true of the male sex, which seems to respond to visual sex stimuli more than women do. The American sex-book trade is enormous and ranges from instruction manuals by respectable medical authors to cheap fiction and hard-core pornography of the sort sold in many bookstores that specialize in this commodity. In this country, recent constitutional uncertainty concerning the definition of obscenity have made it possible for much sex material, hitherto circulated privately or underground, to be bought and sold openly. The appeal of sex books, films, and entertainments seems to cross all social-class lines. On a downtown subway train, a workingman may be looking at a picture book displaying lesbian activity while uptown a bourgeois husband and wife pay fifty dollars to join a "club" so they can watch a couple perform actual, not simulated, sexual intercourse.

The classical argument for controls on explicitly sex-oriented and pornographic literature alleges that such material has a corrupting moral effect, that the young particularly should be protected from it, even at the risk of censorship. The difficulty with this argument lies in getting any agreement on what the metaphorical word *corrupt* means in this context and, having established minimal agreement on meaning, showing that the material objected to actually has this adverse effect on significant numbers of people. A synonym for *corrupting* sometimes heard in these discussions is *poisonous*. An argument by analogy may be put forward to this effect: just as we want strict controls on the availability of substances that can poison human beings physically, equally strict controls ought to be applied to those commodities that have morally poisonous effects. The analogy is shaky. Physical poisons are dangerous to all people, while obscene and pornographic material is harmful (if indeed it is harmful) only to some people and in some contexts. Furthermore, it is hard to produce reliable empirical evidence proving that harm is done by these things and just what that harm is. If it could be shown that a significant number of people were so stimulated by pornographic material to commit crimes of sex violence such as rape, we would then have good reason to demand strict social control. Some persons have confessed to investigators that they have been so stimulated, but the number does not appear to be large, nor is the trustworthiness of some of these confessions above question. There is no doubt that sex pictures are used by males, and of more than one age group, as a stimulus to masturbation. The material may range from nude photos in "girlie" magazines to brutal hard-core pornography. If to indulge in masturbation upon stimulus by such material is to be corrupted, then the argument condemning the material is sound. But, as we have seen, many social observers believe that masturbation is neither self-destructive nor socially destructive. Boys, they say, outgrow it, and their indulgence in it (as well as that of certain older men) may actually prevent crimes of sex violence by providing an outlet in which no unwilling and vulnerable partner is needed.

A more general version of the "corrupting" argument is that pornography debases humane values and leads to a degradation of moral outlook and to nihilism. In rejecting the 1970 report by the National Commission on Obscenity and Pornography, President Nixon advanced a version of this argument. The president argued that if, as the commission held, pornography has no lasting harmful effects, we must hold it to be false that fine literature and art have an elevating effect on the human spirit. But if great books and plays do indeed have an ennobling effect on us, how can we deny that books and plays that portray acts the majority of people believe to be morally wrong have a debasing effect on human spirit and culture? Even in a permissive democracy there must be a limit to radical attacks on civilized and humane values. That limit is reached and passed by certain forms of pornography and sexual obscenity. The notion that "everything is permitted" will destroy the quality of public life on which democratic government ultimately rests. The president was not impressed by the commission's recommendation that, while access to every kind of this material should be permitted to adults, access to it by children and young people should be controlled. "If the level of filth rises in the adult community," the president said, "the young people in our society cannot help but also be inundated by the flood."[32]

To the point about the ennobling effect of great art and literature and the consequent need to admit to the debasing effect of pornography, the libertarian may make this reply: no one has ever proved that any work of art ennobles, but even if this is true, the conservative argument neglects the contexts of these ennobling and debasing effects. It is only some people that a Beethoven symphony will affect at all. To play the Archduke Trio to the customers of the local bar on Saturday night may produce not ennoblement but violent rejection. Similarly, the availability of pornographic material will not result in its being snapped up by everybody. There are such things as taste, upbringing, and education. Pornography is used in special contexts by special people with special needs. Moreover, there is an enormous amount of bad literature and entertainment to which millions of people are greatly attracted, but which no one would think of subjecting to censorship. Most television programs would fall into this category, as would much material distributed by other media. Though these things undoubtedly cater to uncultivated tastes, no one would propose barring them on the strength of the argument that, since they are bad literature or entertainment, their dissemination will certainly debase taste and possibly morals as well. Who would want to censor soap opera?

The claim that obscene publications and pornographic litera- ture, plays, and films constitute a "radical attack on civilization" cannot be shown to be true. To lift bans on such material does not mean that "everything is permitted."[33] Availability of sex books and films does not mean that assault, robbery, and mur- der are permitted. Some claim, of course, that the spread of pornographic material will lead those who make use of it to violent sex crimes. But there appears to be no reliable evidence that this is true to any significant degree, any more than the showing of violence on home television screens can be proved to incite children to similar violent acts. On the contrary, many who have studied the matter believe that the availability of pornographic material may well function as a social safety valve and prevent many people from committing crimes of violence by allowing them to satisfy their curiosity or sexual desire in a way that harms (if it does harm) no one but themselves.

Some libertarians add that there is a bad *class* angle to any proposal to control pornographic material by governmental regu- lation. They say that the upper classes have always been able to get pornography, that even in proper Victorian times the rich had easy access to the most explicit sort of this material. According to this view, censorship regulation on the use of pornography by adults is a repressive means of control directed against the lower classes out of fear that, their base instincts stimulated, they will get out of hand. Thus censorship of pornography is seen as a social measure wielded by the class in power against the poor.[34]

The preceding arguments are some of the standard libertarian replies to proposals to regulate the distribution of sexually ob- scene or pornographic material. Now let us look at the matter for a moment from the other point of view. Those taking the op- posite position hold that they are not rigorist, but reasonable, that their arguments are not directed against *Ulysses* or *Lady Chatterley's Lover,* but against hard-core pornography. Whatever the reasons, there is little doubt that certain degrees of sexual obscenity and pornography are seriously disturbing to great numbers of people, very likely to the majority of the population of this country. There *is* something degrading and antihumane in writing, pictures, films, or stage displays that exploit "for kicks" sex organs, the human body, and the human sex acts that so many people associate with the deepest tenderness and love. Pornography is an inseparable part of the long history of the degradation of women. The availability of such material should be controlled in such a way that it does not (as it does at the present time in many areas and instances) offend public sensitivity or create a public nuisance. It is not illiberal for the police to arrest a sexual exhibitionist; while there is nothing obscene per se about any part of the human body, most people do not want certain parts of that body forced on their attention. People find such exhibitionism offensive and rightly demand that the offender be removed from the scene. The exhibition and sale of pornographic material is also offensive to a very large number of people, if not to the majority of them. It constitutes no infringement on the right of the minority to require that controls of pornographic material should be enforced in such a way that it does not become an offense to people who want nothing to do with it.

Critics of the libertarian position on obscenity and pornography add that belief in the social harmlessness of pornography is naïve. They point out that there is an industry back of pornography, big business that it is linked in many instances to organized crime; and criminals reap huge profits from the trade. An aura of criminality and violence hangs around the fringes of the sex-exploitation business, whether it be prostitution or hardcore pornography. Critics point out that frequently children and adolescents are exploited, their services even sold by their parents to manufacturers and purveyors of visual pornography, with resulting physical damage as well as mental harm to the children and young people so used. Libertarians who assert that pornography has no connection with social evil give the impression of having led sheltered lives and to have enjoyed a very imperfect acquaintance with the seamy side of the world.

During World War II, the Psychological Warfare branch of the British Foreign Office authorized a secret shortwave radio station to broadcast pornographic attacks on Nazi leadership. This radio pornography was designed not to corrupt the German people but to get their attention. The broadcasts proved successful to the extent that a considerable German public listened daily to obscenities against the leaders of their government. For months Sefton Delmer the program director devoted patient research to find ever fresh forms of sexual depravity to attribute to the high Nazis. He thus became one of our century's most accomplished pornographers, all in a good cause. Thirty years after his wartime efforts, Delmer looked at the mass-production pornography of Western Europe and America and asked himself whether he believed the contemporary "pornowave" to be the result of an international conspiracy to demoralize our society. He answered no to his own question, then added:

But I do think it [the pornowave] is a symptom of the moral deterioration of our western society just as the graffiti in the underground corridors of the Maginot Line were a symptom of the deterioration in the discipline and morale of the French army, a deterioration which led to its ultimate disintegration and defeat.[35]

A Conclusion that Follows from No Premises

Is there anything that can be said about the moral rightness or wrongness of sexual conduct without seeming either priggish or sentimentally fatuous? William James said that every desire has the right to be satisfied and if not, why not?[36] That is, the existence of the desire itself stands as prima facie evidence of the essential rightness of that action and the goodness of the end to which the desire impels us—unless, of course, there are good reasons why the desire should not be gratified, unless we can show why not. If we are so inclined, we can make up some questions based on ethical formulas now familiar to us:

1. Am I separating the act from the person?
2. Will it bring joy, increase pleasure, diminish loneliness and pain? Will the balance of pleasure be weighted in my favor only?
3. Will it help me become what I can be? Make me more rather than less a human? And the other person?
4. Am I using, exploiting, the other (or myself) as a thing, as an object, as an instrument only? Am I caressing the other or caressing myself upon the other?
5. Am I indulging myself, pressing my own claims only, forgetting the claims of others?
6. Will my action break down things on which I and others depend? Obligations accepted? Promises made?
7. If I am breaking faith, whose faith is broken?

Perhaps these questions are too close to the sort of thing Flaubert planned to put in his *Dictionary of Accepted Ideas,* a lexicon of "right ideas," a compendium of clichés. They are the questions we never ask, perhaps never can really ask, before the fact. But after the fact, when the time comes to construct reasons, justifications, and excuses, they may be of some convenience.

NOTES: CHAPTER 10

1. *The Wolfenden Report* (New York: Stein & Day, 1963).
2. G. E. M. Anscombe, "Modern Moral Philosophy," in *Ethics,* ed. Judith J. Thomson and Gerald Dworkin (New York: Harper & Row, 1968).
3. The term *situation ethics* derives from a 1966 book of that title by Dr. Joseph Fletcher of the Episcopal Theological School, Cambridge, Mass. (See Suggested Readings for this chapter.) Fletcher claims that there are three basic approaches in moral decision-making: the legalistic, the antinomian (anarchic), and the situational. He says that the unique character of the specific moral situation must be taken into account in questions of ethical decision, that the specific moral situation often generates its own rule. Many critics believe that Fletcher weakens his case for situation ethics by presenting the legalistic and antinomian positions in such a way that no one in his right mind would want to defend them, thus clearing the way for a thumping verdict in favor of situationism. As any reader of the Talmud knows, few of even the most conservative moral teachers hold that ethical rules should be applied without taking the character of the particular situation into account. It was taken for granted by ancient moralists, whether Jews or Greeks, Romans or Christians, that before we should correctly judge the agent in a moral situation we had to know his intentions, the situation in which he found himself, and the nature and result of his acts.
4. James Joyce, *Finnegans Wake* (New York: Viking, 1947), pp. 3, 44. Vico (1668–1744) was a philosopher of history whose best known work is his *Scienza Nuova* or "New Science," in English as *The New Science of Giambattista Vico,* trans. T. G. Bergin and M. H. Fisch (Ithaca, N.Y.: Cornell University Press, 1948). Both Vico and Joyce were morbidly afraid of thunder.
5. Plato, "Symposium," in *Five Dialogues of Plato,* trans. Michael Joyce (New York: Dutton, 1962).
6. Friedrich Nietzsche, *The Genealogy of Morals,* 3d essay, pt. 9.
7. Colonial Americans, including many Puritans, had more permissive attitudes toward sexual contacts among the young than did the United States of the nineteenth and the early twentieth centuries. It was assumed, of course, that such freedom was preliminary to marriage.
8. Bernard Gert, *The Moral Rules* (New York: Harper & Row, 1970), pp. 110–112.
9. Henry James, *The Golden Bowl,* 2 vols. (New York: Scribners, 1909), 2:349–350.

10. Denis de Rougemont, *Love in the Western World,* trans. Montgomery Belgion (New York: Pantheon, 1956), p. 15.
11. Simone de Beauvoir, *The Second Sex,* trans. H. M. Parshley (New York: Knopf, 1953), p. 398.
12. Aristotle *Metaphysics* 1072b5.
13. Dante, *The Divine Comedy,* Paradiso, canto 33, 1. 145.
14. Arthur Schopenhauer, *The World as Will and Idea,* 3 vols., trans. R. B. Haldane and J. Kemp (London: Routledge & Kegan Paul, 1957), vol. 3, pp. 345–349.
15. François Mauriac, *The Desert of Love,* trans. Gerard Hopkins (New York: Farrar, Straus & Giroux, 1951), pp. 172–173.
16. Plato *Phaedrus,* 251, 253.
17. 1 Cor. 13:1–113.
18. Gert, *Moral Rules,* p. 145.
19. André Gide, *If It Die* [Si le grain ne meurt] (New York: Modern Library, 1935), pp. 52–53.
20. Sol Gordon, *Ten Heavy Facts About Sex* (Syracuse, N.Y.: Syracuse University, 1971), p. 2. Published in comic book format.
21. A recent study made at the Institute of Child Development in Prague indicates that children whose parents are closely related may be ten times as likely to have birth defects as the offspring of parents not related by blood. *New York Post,* 13 September, 1972.
22. Claude Lévi-Strauss, "The Family," in *Anthropology,* ed. Samuel Rapport and Helen Wright (New York: New York University Press, 1967), pp. 160–161.
23. Thomas Aquinas *Summa Theologica,* 2a2ae, trans. the Dominican Fathers, 60 vols. (New York: McGraw-Hill, 1964), vol. 43, p. 239.
24. Margaret Mead, "Incest," in *International Encyclopedia of the Social Sciences,* ed. David I. Sills, 17 vols. (New York: Macmillan, 1968), 7:115–122.
25. Ralph Ellison, *The Invisible Man* (New York: Signet, 1952), pp. 50–65.
26. Arthur K. Bierman and James A. Gould, eds., *Philosophy for a New Generation* (New York: Macmillan, 1970), p. 122.
27. *Lev.* 18:22.
28. Marcel Proust, *Cities of the Plain,* trans. C. K. Scott Moncrieff, vol. 1 (New York: Modern Library, 1927), p. 20. Krafft-Ebing's, *Psychopathia Sexualis* (1886), which Proust read, takes a similar line.
29. Beauvoir, *Second Sex,* p. 424.
30. Martin Hoffman, *The Gay World* (New York: Basic Books, 1968), p. 180. Not all observers agree with Hoffman's pessimism in regard to the lot of homosexual men. John Schlesinger, director of the film *Sunday, Bloody Sunday,* says that the sobs and sorrows of *The Boys*

in the Band are about as up-to-date as the fox-trot. "This business of 'show me a happy homosexual and I'll show you a gay corpse' isn't the way it really is. That's the exception, not the rule. Lots of people manage to solve their emotional hang-ups; they make the adjustments that have to be made. Just as in Victorian times wives had to adjust to the fact that their husbands had mistresses." Quoted by Guy Flatley, *New York Times,* 3 October 1971, sec. D, p. 13.

31. Constantine Cavafy, *The Complete Poems of Cavafy,* trans. Rae Dalven, introduction by W. H. Auden (New York: Harcourt Brace Jovanovich, 1961), pp. ix, 109. Reprinted by permission of Harcourt Brace Jovanovich, Inc.

32. The text of President Richard M. Nixon's statement rejecting the report of the National Commission on Obscenity and Pornography is given in *The New York Times,* 25 October 1970, sec. 1, p. 71.

33. Not quite everything is permitted. According to standards established by two U.S. Supreme Court decisions (Roth v. U.S., 1957 and Memoirs v. Massachusetts, 1966), a publication or film may be ruled obscene if a jury finds that (1) to "the average person" the dominant theme appeals to a prurient interest in sex, (2) the material is "patently offensive" to the "common conscience of the community," going beyond "customary limits of candor," and (3) the publication or film is "utterly without redeeming social value." In June 1973, by a 5–4 decision, the U.S. Supreme Court tightened these requirements. The factor of "serious literary, artistic, political or scientific value" was deemed relevant in judging whether a work could be banned as offensive. Giving up attempts to set national criteria for defining obscenity, the Court returned to individual states and localities the right to judge and to forbid according to local community standards.

34. Comments on Irving Kristol's "Pornography, Obscenity, and the Case for Censorship," which appeared in *The New York Times Magazine,* 28 March 1971. Comments appear in 18 April 1971 issue of the magazine; see particularly those of J. L. Collier.

35. Sefton Delmer, "H. M. G.'s Secret Pornographer," *Times Literary Supplement* (London), 21 January 1972, p. 63.

36. William James, "The Moral Philosopher and the Moral Life," in *The Will to Believe and Other Essays* (New York: McKay, 1907), p. 195.

11

Morals of Death and War

In the last chapter we looked at some of the moral questions raised by certain forms of sexual conduct. We noted that many forms of sexual behavior are today still considered not only immoral but illegal, though their number is considerably less now than in the past. We also noted a growing permissiveness in public and private attitudes toward sexual morals, observing the tendency of contemporary society to allow the transfer of judgment of certain kinds of sexual behavior from the preserve of public law to that of private conscience. Now, if we shift our attention from those acts once interdicted by the Biblical commandment "Thou shalt not commit adultery" to those to which the imperative "Thou shalt not kill" applies, we may ask if the same tendency holds true. Does contemporary society show growing moral permissiveness toward the taking of human life? And if there is such a shift in public attitude, does it have any bearing on this question: are all forms of intentional taking of human life immoral?

The answer to the first question is easier than the second. Intentional taking of human life is still regarded in our society as a very grave matter legally as well as morally. Depending on what *kind* of intentional taking of life it is, there have been shifts both in the direction of permissiveness and in that of tightening up in regard to the rule "Don't kill." If abortion is regarded as the intentional taking of a human life (and many do not think that it is), current changes in private morals and public law with respect to abortion may be classified as permissive in that respect. At another part of the spectrum stand the attitudes of certain revolutionary groups toward the killing of public officials. Some militant radicals in the United States have defended the moral rightfulness of killing law officers in certain circumstances. Certain members of revolutionary organizations have denied that their killings were murder, insisting rather that they were "political acts." On the other hand, among the general public, there has been growing pressure toward strict interpretation of the "Don't kill" rule in two areas of public killing. The first and comparatively narrow field is that of capital punishment. The second, far more wide (and here the influence of youth has been strongly felt), is war itself. By contrast again, suicide or self-killing— once the object of public and general condemnation—has been allowed to drop quietly back into the realm of private morals.

Thousands of volumes have been written on the moral and legal aspects of these and other forms of man's intentional killing of his fellowman. Our inquiry can be little more than a summary glance at certain of the moral issues involved.

I

Killing in General

Generally speaking, in no culture has it ever been considered right for a man to kill another simply because he feels like it any more than it has ever been thought right for a man to have any woman anytime he wants her. But the exceptions to the "Don't kill" rule are so numerous and substantial that sometimes it seems that among humans killing is the rule rather than the exception. Convinced by the quantities of human blood copiously and regularly shed by humans, some moralists have regretfully concluded that man is *by nature* a killer; not only is he a born slayer of the living things that share the surface of his planet with him, but of humankind itself. The human record of killings in murder, robbery, rape, wars, revolutions, religious persecutions, and racial exterminations stands so horrendously visible that anguished observers have been led to proclaim that man is the only animal that kills its own kind. Strictly speaking, this is not so. Other animals sometimes destroy members of their own species; the fate of a strange rat dropped into a cage of rats who know each other is hair-raising to watch. But so overwhelming is the human killing-score that observers can be excused for overlooking the fact that nonhuman animals sometimes kill members of their own species.

Hobbes spoke of man in a state of Nature (that is, before any political arrangements were made) as part of a "war of all against all." In Africa the broken skull-tops of early humanoid remains have suggested to some anthropologists that man made his debut here on earth by devouring the brains of his fellows. Some social analysts postulate "aggression" as a specifically human way of behaving.[1] The president of the American Psychological Association recently called for the development of a drug to inhibit the aggressive drives of world leaders.[2] On the other hand, it is sometimes claimed that large-scale human killing has its functional side as a mechanism of nature to control excessive proliferation of the species. According to this view, civilization's development of moral standards and of a sense of the "sacredness of human life" may deprive the world of a possible solution to its overpopulation problem by inhibiting the tendency of men to exterminate each other. Avoiding claims of such sweep, we can look briefly at some arguments for or against certain forms of intentional taking of human or quasi-human life.

Infanticide

The killing of infant children can be a drastically functional way of dealing with surplus, defective, or unwanted births. It is not tolerated in modern society. But the Greeks and Romans had few moral scruples about killing newborn defective infants. The Spartans exposed such children on hillsides at birth. Plato recommended both abortion and infanticide for eugenic purposes.[3] For centuries in China infanticide by abandonment was a desperate measure families had to adopt to cut down the number of mouths to feed in a land where famine was endemic. Girl babies were the chief victims. In ancient Japan, the infanticidal practice of *mabiki* (literally, "thinning") was used to limit family size. Many primitive societies practiced infanticide for survival purposes. The killing of babies, particularly girls, was common until very recently on Tauu, an atoll in the southwest Pacific; the reason was limited food and the threat of overpopulation. At last report, the Yanomamö Indians of southern Venezuela were, in hard times, still killing unwanted babies of both sexes, though more girls than boys.[4]

Christian ethics proved powerless to prevent wars, but it contributed to the development of the presupposition that helpless human life is inviolable. Infanticide was outlawed in the West. In Goethe's drama *Faust,* Marguerite pays with her life for killing her illegitimate baby. Goethe himself, as privy councilor in Weimar, sustained the death sentence for a woman found guilty of the same offense.

Contraception and Abortion

In modern society the two most widely used means of limiting births are contraception and medical abortion. The first does not involve terminating life, but preventing it from starting— this is not killing. The second requires the destruction of the living embryo or fetus. Birth control by both artificial means and feticide have a long history in human culture. Only recently, however, have these methods of dealing with unwanted births achieved a level of moral and social approval, as well as safety and reliability, to a degree approaching general acceptance. Efficient human sterilization methods have been developed. Vasectomy in the case of the male and ligation of tubes for females have become standardized techniques in state programs of voluntary sterilization. In 1972 clinics receiving U.S. Federal funds reported sterilizations of 16,000 women and 8677 men. (One instance of involuntary sterilization of two minors was charged.)[5] India has encouraged voluntary sterilization among her still-expanding hungry masses; in some campaigns, free transistor radios have been offered to males who have vasectomies. But, for obvious reasons, voluntary sterilization has not yet come anywhere near the popularity of contraception and abortion as a means of birth limitation in contemporary society. Most men do not want vasectomies, and (apart from women's equal reluctance in the matter) tubal ligation is not a trivial operation.[6]

Moral and religious objections to birth control are as old as the Bible, wherein we are told that the Lord slew Onan, who "spilled his seed on the ground" so that his brother's wife should not conceive.[7] In the course of its long history, Jewish law has modified its ancient rigor in regard to birth control. But even today that law does not countenance interference with conception solely on grounds of comfort, convenience, or cosmetics; under Jewish law a wife is not justified in practicing contraception lest a pregnancy "mar her beauty." The Roman Catholic church has long opposed all forms of artificial birth control. Moral and philosophical grounds of the opposition can be tracked back to the fathers and doctors of the church, who condemned any and all means of frustrating the "natural end" of the procreative act. In modern times, the church's hostility to birth control by artificial means has been made explicit in a series of papal encyclicals up to and including Paul VI's *Humanae Vitae* of 1968.[8] Many observers, including some Catholic clergy, believe that the latest papal ban on contraception is a rearguard action only, that the church will have to come to terms with a practice engaged in by the majority of its married faithful. Catholic critics of the continuance of the ban claim that it rests on an obsolete "natural law" theory according to which the moral rightness or wrongness of an act can be judged by its fulfilling or frustrating a "natural end." This exaggerated teleology, they say, this too-purposive manner of viewing human sexuality (for marriage has a communicative as well as a procreative good) confines a deep and characteristically human activity within far too narrow limits. But church conservatives still maintain that the ban is justified on the ground that it is not licit to interpose an artificial block between the procreative act and its intended purpose. In its latest pronouncements on birth control, however, the church distinguishes between its ban on contraception—which it considers binding on members of its congregation—and its condemnation of abortion, which it holds morally wrong for all humans.

By abortion is meant the deliberate, not accidental, interference with the life of the embryo or fetus growing within the uterus. Abortion was well known in primitive society, though many groups were uneasy about its possible consequences— some thought the ghosts of the unborn children would return to haunt their parents.[9] Generally, however, primitive peoples did not think of abortion in any way comparable to slaying a tribesman. Such people, we have noted, countenanced infanticide as a means for survival where limited food sources existed. Many did not regard a child's life as sacred until he had been given a name and thus accepted as a member of the tribe. Ancient Jewish law forbade abortion, but regarded the act as less than ordinary homicide since the fetus did not become a "person" (*Adam nefesh*) until it was born and thus entitled to the full protection of the law. In general, the rabbinic tradition did not consider abortion a capital crime.[10] Today Jewish law is interpreted to permit abortion for serious reasons, including the physical and mental health of the mother. Canon law of the Roman Catholic church, on the other hand, strictly forbids abortion. The practice had always been considered a serious offense by church fathers, although they were by no means agreed that the fetus at an early stage was a human at all. They had some question as to just when the fetus became "ensouled." Some fathers, following Aristotelian embryology, said that ensoulment took place at forty days in males, eighty days in females. In 1211, Pope Innocent III distinguished between the viable and nonviable fetus, intimating that, while abortion must always be regarded as a serious sin, only the abortion of the formed (viable) fetus was to be construed as murder. But after the Council of Trent in the sixteenth century, it was generally agreed that abortion, at whatever stage of embryological development, was no different than murder. Even the progressive Vatican Council of 1965 (Vatician II) declared that abortion remained a "horrible crime."[11]

Prior to the 1960s, only cases of rape, incest, or direct threat to the mother's life constituted grounds for lawful therapeutic abortion in Britain and the United States. The 1967 Abortion Act in Britain extended types of lawful abortion to include those in which the well-being of the mother or of her existing children would be adversely affected. But this act also permitted account to be taken of the pregnant woman's social and economic environment. In the 1960s, sharp increases in the number of unwanted pregnancies, poverty factors, and the widespread use of illegal abortion (with its attendant danger to health and life as well as its social and economic inequities) led to increased public demand for a radical expansion of legalized abortion. The liberal abortion law of New York State, enacted in 1970, has been cited as a model for the rest of the nation. Medical complications and deaths resulting from abortions have markedly declined since the law took effect. About 168,000 legal abortions were performed in New York City alone in the first year of the law, more than half obtained by out of state patients. But the New York State law on abortion is not permissive in every respect; under the law, pregnancy must be terminated by the end of the twenty-fourth week. The recent U.S. Supreme Court decision on abortion prohibits abortion only during the last ten weeks of pregnancy.[12]

Is Abortion Murder?

What is murder? Most civil authorities today do not consider abortion murder for the simple reason that, subject to certain regulations, the law *permits* abortion, while it does not permit intentional homicide. Under law, murder is the most serious form of homicide, or human killing. For killing to be murder the act must be intentional and deliberate; it cannot be killing in defense of self, property, or country. With murder, there is no question of killing even by criminal negligence; the homicide must be performed "with malice aforethought." Legally, abortion is far from satisfying these conditions. It is not clear that in terminating the life of a human fetus, we are intentionally and with malice killing a human person. As noted, the fathers of the church were by no means in agreement that the fetus *was* a person. They distinguished between the degree of guilt attached to the killing of a viable and of a nonviable fetus. The Sacred Penitentiary (an ecclesiastical office) of the time of Pope Gregory XIII did not regard as homicide the killing of an embryo under forty days old. Thomas Aquinas rejected the notion that a mother should be allowed to perish so that the infant within her could be baptized: "Evils are not to be done that good may come from them, and therefore a man ought rather to let the infant perish than that he himself perish [spiritually] committing the original sin of homicide upon the mother."[13] True, we know that as the centuries rolled on toward modern times, the Catholic church tightened up its attitude toward abortion; to this day its teaching office continues to instruct the world that abortion is a grave sin. But secular law, the attitudes of other religions, and those of lay society generally do not agree with the church's strict stand. This does not mean, however, that other secular and religious authorities regard abortion as a light thing, that there is no moral problem involved.

Part of the trouble lies in the muddle created by trying to define a "person." There is no doubt that in abortion a living organism is destroyed. Whether the fetus is "human" or not has been endlessly debated, some sages taking refuge in the distinction between the fetus as "potentially" human as opposed to the infant that is "actually" human. The same difficulty arises in the argument against abortion from the premise that abortion violates the principle of the "sacredness of human life." At what point in the process of gestation does life become human? An obvious reply is that the question is badly put: it assumes that there *is* a point at which what was nonhuman becomes human. But there *are* no points in nature; points are abstract entities we superimpose on things in order to analyze them. In the question, "Would *you* like to have been aborted?" it is assumed as true what needs to (and probably never can be) proven: *was* there a "you," was there an "I" at that stage of fetal development?

Recently, many women's groups advocating liberalized abortion laws have indignantly criticized the way in which lawmaking assemblies (usually all male) sit in judgment, as they consider abortion, as to what is right or wrong for a woman to do with her body. Every woman has a right to her body, runs this argument, and no group of legislators, however well-intentioned, has the right to tell her what to do and not do with her own body. Well, there *are* laws that forbid certain kinds of self-mutilation on the part of either sex; but apart from that, the challenge raises a question as hard to deal with as the query as to just at what point the fetus becomes human: is the unborn child a separate entity or is it part of its mother? One can only answer by a distinction: the fetus is not part of the mother in the sense that her arms, heart, or uterus is part of her; but the fetus is part of her in the sense that during gestation it is entirely enclosed within her body and intimately attached to it as well as nourished by it. The Aristotelian distinction would say that the fetus is potentially but not actually an independent human life. Jewish law held that the fetus, at least in its earlier stages, is part of the mother; only when birth begins is it considered a separate body. The Protestant theologian Karl Barth says:

The unborn child is from the very first a child. It is still developing and has no independent life. But it is a man and not a thing, nor a mere part of the mother's body. . . . He who destroys germinating life kills a man and thus ventures the monstrous thing of decreeing concerning the life and death of a fellow-man whose life is given by God and therefore, like his own, belongs to Him.[14]

The contemporary anthropologist Ashley Montagu, who does not oppose abortion as such, claims that the fetus, despite its newness and (in its early stages) man-from-Mars appearance, is a living, striving human being from the very beginning of life—which starts at conception.[15] On the other hand, it is possible to think of the fetus, at least under some circumstances, as an unwanted guest foisted upon the mother without so much as a by-your-leave.[16]

Now where does all this leave the argument as to whether abortion is murder or not? So long as law and general social practice do not recognize the unborn fetus as a human person with the right to life and legal protection that pertains to that social status, it does not seem that abortion *is* murder in any legal sense of the term, although it can certainly be *called* that by parties who oppose it as immoral. To say abortion is murder is a little like saying war is murder. Which abortions? Which wars?

But many who dismiss the "abortion is murder" claim would not deny that good reason should be given to justify the destruction of nascent human life, particularly if development is advanced. To slip into the habit of terminating unborn life without reflection as to what one is doing may lead to moral callousness. The destruction of a fetus is never a pleasant thing at any stage of its development; in the case of a relatively advanced pregnancy, the effect of this destruction can be disturbing not only to the woman, but also to the man responsible for the pregnancy as well as to the conscience of the physician whose traditional duty is to preserve life, not to destroy it.

With the crisis of world population, it may be that a number of serious moral questions pertaining to abortion will prove no more than academic. Some observers believe that in the next century measures sterner than abortion will have to be taken to prevent the extermination of the human race by overcrowding. This pessimism may be excessive, an instance of what some call "the demographic fallacy." In any case, nearly all parties to the dispute on the morality of the question agree on one point: if there must be abortions, better to have them legally sanctioned and medically sound than to go back to the bad old ways when the affluent could obtain abortions safely, if illegally, while the poor were driven to butchery and despair.

Euthanasia

The question of abortion deals with the morality of terminating the life of a nascent human. At the opposite pole there is the moral question of inducing the death of old people who are helpless and incurably sick. Many, if not most, of those who have no ethical scruples about abortion hesitate to permit equal latitude here. *Euthanasia* is a graceful word (meaning "dying well" or "pleasant death"), but to many people it has sinister connotations. Why is this?

First, we should note that the term is applied widely to cover a number of different forms of supposedly justifiable homicides. Euthanasia can be voluntary or involuntary. In the first instance, it is assisted suicide; a patient, knowing that he is incurably ill, asks his family or his physician to put him out of his pain. Freud died this way. Involuntary euthanasia includes "mercy killing" which itself may take more than one form. One form is infanticide, as in the well-known case of the Belgian mother who in 1962 killed her eight-day-old child, who was born deformed as a result of the mother's having taken the drug thalidomide during pregnancy.[17] Then there is the termination of the life of a senile patient, his consent not having been obtained, or the killing of a cancerous wife, drugged during sleep by a husband who can no longer bear to see her suffer. On a quite different dimension, we have involuntary euthanasia by public authority, perhaps as part of a state eugenics program. Plato's blueprint for his ideal republic called for the killing of defective children where abortion did not succeed. In 1940 the Nazi German state was operating a systematic program of euthanasia for mental defectives and other "incurables"; the authorities were forced to discontinue or at least postpone the program because of loud protests by church leaders.[18]

Most euthanasia lobbyists in Britain and the United States want only *voluntary* euthanasia made legal. Their arguments may range from a simple defense of "the right to die with dignity" to proposals for a formal procedure in which the patient signs a document giving permission to end his life; the family gives consent; and a committee, including physicians, gives the sufferer a "final examination" to determine the hopelessness of the case. Support of the right to die with dignity need not involve the moral difficulties of euthanasia at all if it is only the abridgment of elaborate medical means used to prolong life in the hopelessly moribund.[19] There is nothing necessarily illegal or immoral in such a shortening of medical procedures, though physicians are understandably reluctant to give up a fight for the patient's life before every means of preserving it has been tried. Again, it is a question of the particular situation. If the patient is truly *in extremis,* why keep him gasping another twenty-four hours by chemical, electrical, or mechanical means? True, much may depend on whether the patient is young or of extreme age. Most religious authorities are permissive in these situations, particularly where the elderly are concerned. Even those most strict about questions of human life recognize that there are times when, ordinary means of sustaining life having failed, extraordinary means are not morally obligatory. The conservative Pius XII applied the ethical principle of the "double effect" to justify this position. If in some cases of hopelessly ebbing life, he said, "the actual administration of drugs brings about two distinct effects, the one the relief of pain, the other the shortening of life, the action is lawful."[20] Liberal or conservative, a careful moralist will recommend that the living, in these cases, scrutinize their motives with great care lest the phrase "the right to die with dignity" be used as no more than a fine-sounding cover for the survivors' inclination to be rid of the inconvenience of a patient's lingering illness. Phrases like "it's a blessing if he goes" and "she's really better off" come more easily to the lips of the healthy and the busy than to those who are struggling for life.

The termination of life by formal procedures involving permission of the sufferer is not so simple. This is true euthanasia and, as such, is not countenanced by most nations today. Recent efforts of British lobbyists, who have been pushing a euthanasia bill for thirty-five years, were defeated in the House of Lords in 1969. Euthanasia by consent is, after all, assisted suicide, and although in Britain suicide itself was in 1961 declared no longer illegal, *helping* a person to end his life is still very much against the law.

The uneasiness of contemporary moralists when even voluntary euthanasia is concerned is heightened by the inescapable association of euthanasia with certain terrible events in our century associated with Nazi Germany. The Nazi eugenics program began with the killing of mental defectives, then went on to encourage the mating of Aryan warriors with suitable German girls—even out of wedlock. It ended in the extermination camps, where millions of Jews and other "racially undesirables" were killed. Thus a eugenics program that began with euthanasia ended with *genocide*—a program that has for its conscious and intended end the destruction of an entire people.[21] This was an evil the contemporary world believed impossible.

Sanctity of Human Life?

That the world reacted in horror to revelations of the Nazi death camps seemed to many moralists a confirmation of the universal belief in the principle of the sanctity of human life. The reaction to the Nazi deeds, they say, constitutes at least part of the reason why programs involving modifying laws against even the mildest forms of euthanasia have run into stubborn resistance on the part of lawmakers nearly everywhere in the world. But, we may ask, what is meant by "the sanctity of human life"? The traditional religions had little trouble answering the question. Every human life, their teachers declared, is equally dear to God, who loves that life with an infinite love. Therefore no man has the right to interfere with the life of another, except for gravest cause. Of course, with history in mind, we know that people have lived devoutly within these religious traditions and have, nevertheless, dealt out death very vigorously. When human passions are aroused by war, revolution, crusades, or persecutions, the principle of the sanctity of human life is one of the first casualties. It is always disillusioning to observe what people *do* in contrast to what they *say* they *believe.* It is true that in modern times of peace, of political and religious stability, the principle of the sanctity of human life has been more or less generally respected. This respect seems actually to have increased in contemporary secular society, which has moved away from the religious beliefs of older days. Some inquirers, who still hold religious beliefs, ask this question: if the sanctity of human life does not derive from God's love (God being absent or dead), on what then does it rest?

John Dewey would reply that the sanctity of human life lies not in some source beyond nature, but in the human person itself. "Naturalism," Dewey says, "finds the values in question, the worth and dignity of men and women, residing in human nature itself."[22] But just what is there about human nature that makes that nature *in itself* worthy of this absolute respect? Perhaps the value of every human life resides in the potential or promise of that life for good. Or perhaps we talk about "the dignity and worth of each individual human" because we humans constitute an exclusive tribe or club and hence are sworn to protect each other as members against all that threatens us, living or not living. Or perhaps the highest social fulfillment requires that each individual person constituting society be valued as essential, his or her life inviolable. Or perhaps, as Kant would argue, each person has an inherent dignity or worth. If Kant is right, we have come a long way from the attitudes of early and primitive peoples, who would have been puzzled by the concept of the sanctity of individual human life because for them the good of the individual counted for far less than the good of the community. In any case, the fact that the concept of the sanctity of human life may have derived from religious beliefs is not cancelled out by the fact that so many today in the West reject those beliefs. Some say that the idea of the sacredness and inviolability of human life may have *entered* our thinking because of its religious origin, but it *remains* in our thinking because it is built into the house in which we live and could not be removed without bringing it down.[23]

Suicide

One obvious difference marks off suicide from other forms of intentional killing. It is the agent who dies, not another; the direct victim is oneself. If a person's life is his to dispose of as he sees fit, the moral issue involved is quite different from that of other forms of homicide. Certain cultures have regarded suicide as legitimate and at times meritorious. The Romans believed that a man's life was his own; he was free to end it when outward circumstances and his own will combined to make suicide appropriate. Roman history is ornamented by pageants of noble suicides: Cato falling heroically on his sword after Pompey's defeat, Petronius elegantly opening his veins in a bath (he was ordered to do so by Nero), Lucretia embracing death to repair her dishonor at the hands of Sextus Tarquinius. Slaves were not punished for attempted suicide because the Romans held that everyone, even a slave, had a right to his own life. Like Rome, classical Japan admired the warrior's code of life and death. To the Japanese, death was a traditional way of setting troubles right, hence suicide could be a sacrifice deserving of high moral esteem. There was *shiaju,* the suicide of unhappy lovers; *junshi,* suicide after one's lord died; and other even more ceremonial forms of self-destruction. Though many considered it a foolish and anachronistic act, the ritual self-disembowelment (*seppuku*) of the noted writer Yukio Mishima in Tokyo, 1970, profoundly moved the Japanese public, whom Mishima had wished to remind of the stern virtues of Japan's old order.[24]

A quite different attitude toward suicide gained ascendancy in the Christian West. But it was the pagan Plato who first expressed it. In the *Phaedo,* when Cebes asks Socrates, who is in prison awaiting execution, why he believes that a man ought not to take his own life, Socrates replies: "I believe that the gods are our guardians and that we men are a possession of theirs. . . . a man should wait, and not take his own life until God summons him, as he is now summoning me."[25] The Jews believed suicide was a crime against God, although they allowed for exceptions. An example is the death of Saul, who fell on his own sword to prevent his being mocked and tortured by the Philistines.[26] The church fathers taught that our life came from God, that its final disposition remains in his keeping, not ours. (Hamlet reflects traditional Christian belief when he cries, "O . . . that the Everlasting had not fix'd His canon 'gainst self-slaughter!'") Thomas Aquinas added that suicide is a serious breach in the charity one should have toward oneself, a notion not inconsistent with contemporary psychiatric belief that many people have such a poor idea of themselves that they are led to suicide.[27] Though it was never the universal teaching of the church, many theologians, like Augustine, believed that suicide was an "unforgivable sin." Because the agent had no opportunity to repent his act, suicide put one beyond God's mercy forever. Suicides were refused burial in consecrated ground. Such severe views strengthened the belief that suicide was a unique disgrace. To spare the living, as well as the memory of the dead, coroner's juries have been inclined to find that those who died by their own hand did so "while of unsound mind." But some contemporary students of suicide concede that no more than twenty to thirty percent of suicides have been insane. To this very day, physicians almost unanimously regard suicidal inclinations as a manifestation of psychic illness. They try to restrain the suicidal patient by every means at their command, including involuntary hospitalization.[28]

Suicide is well known among primitive people, and it seems to be a serious social problem among "advanced" societies today. More than once a minute in the United States someone either tries to or does kill himself with conscious intent. Among white males, suicide is the fourth leading cause of death; among college students, it is the second most common cause. Yet on a 1957 list ranking suicide frequencies by country, the United States was not the first but the fifteenth nation. West Berlin had the highest suicide rate of any city and Austria the highest of any nation, followed by Japan, Finland, and Denmark.[29] Alfred Alvarez gives national frequency charts of suicides by countries as follows: 1. Hungary; 2. Finland; 3. Austria; 4. Czechoslovakia.[30] Why some countries have markedly higher suicide rates than others has puzzled sociologists. Why should one Scandinavian country (Denmark) rank high and another (Norway) low on a suicide-frequency list? In his classic work on the subject, Emile Durkheim noted that Protestants have a higher suicide rate than Catholics; he was able to tally only a very few Jewish suicides.[31] Yet Durkheim found that in Bavaria Jews killed themselves twice as often as Catholics and confessed he did not know why. Stekel says that a deep and authentic religious faith tends to inhibit suicide, and observers tell us that suicide rates are generally lower in countries with a predominating Catholic rather than Protestant population.[32] But should we conclude from these premises that Catholic countries have more "deep and authentic religious faith" than Protestant countries? It would be a risky conclusion.

Sociologists and psychologists have found the concept of suicide to be full of ambiguities. Just what is a suicide? Some people intend to carry out a suicidal act, but fail to accomplish it. Others do not so intend, but end up dead and officially listed as suicides—victims of a suicidal *gesture* that has miscarried.[33] What about Russian roulette? A man may load a revolver with one bullet, spin the cylinder, and pull the trigger. Such a man may not want to kill himself at all; it may be that his vanished enjoyment of the visible world can be restored only by risking its loss. We speak of soldiers carrying out "suicidal" missions; they risk their lives, but do not intend their own deaths. The kamikaze pilot of World War II knew for certain he would die, but his illustrious end was only a consequence of the purpose of his mission. Goering's cheating the hangman at Nuremberg by swallowing smuggled poison is a rather different matter; different again was Rommel's suicide to escape trial by a Nazi "people's tribunal." Some people put themselves in the way of death, yet are never known to be suicides. How many automobile accidents, fatal to the driver, are caused by semi-intention on the part of that driver? How many "accidental" drownings are half-consciously arranged by the bather? Were the early Christian martyrs suicides? When Joan of Arc resumed dressing in men's clothing in prison after her trial, did she not *know* this would lead her to the stake? According to Scobie in Graham Greene's *The Heart of the Matter,* a novel that turns on the concept of a carefully planned self-inflicted death, Christ himself was a suicide; for if Christ was the son of God, he would have been crucified only if he had willed his own death.[34]

Social scientists have written volumes seeking causal explanations of suicide, identifying motives, isolating intentions. No easy pronouncement on the morality or immorality of suicide can be made by ignoring their patient work or that of the various moralists in or out of the religious traditions who have pondered the question. Consider the wider range of possibilities. Outright psychosis. Fear of disgrace. Wish to return to the womb. Loss of a loved one in death. An unhappy love affair. Insurance money for a dependent. To save the emperor embarrassment. Loss of a job that was one's lifework. Tired of having to live hooked up to a kidney machine. To protest a war. Sudden financial ruin. Catastrophic military defeat. The death instinct victorious over the life instinct. Made to feel worthless as a child. Despondency because of ill health. Despair at all the bad things one has done. A pervading sense of incompetence and failure. Desire to revenge oneself on one's family. Drugs. Depression. Old age. Loneliness. Most of these factors have actually been found to be present singly or in combination in cases of suicide that have been investigated—though it is hard to prove or disprove the presence of a death wish or desire to return to the womb. What puzzles students of suicide is that these very same factors can be found, sometimes in heightened degree, in people who do *not* kill themselves. Why are some driven to this extreme and others not? Why do there seem to be so many suicides among writers, as in recent years Hemingway, Woolf, Montherlant, Mishima, Berryman, Kawabata, Plath?

Some modern philosophers have pondered the case for suicide. Schopenhauer offered a metaphysical explanation. The World Will, the cause of all things, pulses through us in all its blind infinite might; we are its creatures, filled with desire and wanting out of all proportion to the possibility of their ever being satisfied. To end the suffering entailed by existing, some people kill themselves. But the suicide's act is really a kind of affirmation of the self, that individual self that he believes to be real. But the conviction of personal reality is illusion. The individual is but *idea,* a second-line phenomenal affair only. The individual thinks he can put an end to suffering with a bullet, but as the pistol drops to the floor nothing more occurs than would if a bubble on the surface of a cauldron of boiling water were to burst. The tiny droplet of water falls back into the whole of which it has always been a part; nothing has really been subtracted from the total turmoil of the World Will. Where we have suicide, metaphysically speaking, nothing really happens. The suicide does not put an end to desire; his lethal act proclaims the will to live.[35] Only the saint, by renouncing the will to live by a life of selflessness can detach himself from the wheel of endless wanting.

William James and Albert Camus treat suicide as a challenge. In his essay "Is Life Worth Living?" James reminds his readers,

"That life is *not* worth living the whole army of suicides declare —an army whose roll-call . . . follows the sun round the world and never terminates."[36] In his "The Myth of Sisyphus" Camus claims, "There is but one truly serious philosophical problem, and that is suicide."[37] Each writer asks, "Why *not* commit suicide?" and each in his way gives an answer. The American philosopher's reply is optimistic. We do not know the outcome of things; we do not own the key to the universe, if indeed there is a key. Perhaps we shall be crushed, annihilated, forgotten. Perhaps all our individual efforts, the mighty cultural and religious efforts of the human race will be rubbed out, leaving no trace on the dark spaces of the cosmos. Perhaps the balance of evil in life far outweighs the good. In that case, life would not be worth living. But we do not know this, nor can science prove it. Since we do not know it, we have an option, the choice to act as if in our life something *could* be done to tip the balance a little way toward the good. And from that choice, the worth of life may follow. "Do not be afraid of life," James tells his readers, "Believe that life *is* worth living and your belief will help create the fact."

The French moralist's answer is less confident, but he too is convinced that one has options, that a choice exists in the matter of making what one can out of life. For Camus, the universe has no meaning. We *are* going to be crushed, rubbed out, annihilated. The hunger within every human heart for that which transcends the human condition has no object. There is no God, no supernatural destiny. Life has only the meaning we choose to give it. Our fate is time and death. But there is something to be said for *knowing* that our situation in the world is absurd—"the absurd, born of this confrontation between the human need [of explanation] and the unreasonable silence of the world."[38] Why not suicide? Because there is something fine in a person knowing he is licked and fighting back anyway. "For a man without blinkers there is no finer spectacle than that of intelligence at grips with a reality that transcends him."[39] What is left to a brave man or woman is lucid, lonely, continuous effort, like that of Sisyphus, whom the gods, for punishment, condemned to push a stone to the top of a hill from which forever it is fated to roll back down again: "One must imagine Sisyphus happy."[40]

Camus's moralism may be cold comfort to one who has known the terrible depths of that mental depression an older day called *raptus melancholicus,* an abyss beyond right and wrong, beyond morality. There probably are many who kill themselves for trivial and selfish reasons, who use suicide (in Hesse's phrase) as "a shabby and illegitimate emergency exit." The garrulous notes left behind by some suicides do suggest vanity and narrow egotism. A man may use suicide to sneak out of life, leaving debts and disasters for others to cope with. Yet it would be a serious offense against charity to presume to know, let alone condemn, the motives of any individual soul drawn perhaps at the moment of decision to terrible lucidity. Wittgenstein asked if one can know, really know, that another is in pain.[41] If it is hard to really know another's physical suffering, what can we really know of the quality of another's mental anguish and despair? Or of the point at which an individual refuses to go on with a life that, because of his suffering, is no longer, in a sense, *his* life. All one can do is to fall back on the old maxim, "Judge not, lest you be judged," construing this to mean: let those judge who have themselves experienced the depths of suicidal anguish and have survived. For those of us who elect to remain among the living, whether or not we believe that life is worth living, Nietzsche has a word of consolation: "Suicide is a wonderful thing. The thought of it enables us to get through many a bad night."[42]

II

Death and the State

Under law, homicide is divided into criminal and noncriminal categories. Criminal homicide includes murder (in this country, of the first and second degree) and manslaughter, voluntary (nonnegligent) and involuntary (negligent). Noncriminal homicide includes killing in self-defense and killing by legal execution of a death sentence. Traditionally, killing in warfare is also noncriminal, provided that the killing is done without breach of the rules and practices of war recognized by the "law of nations" (international law). In considering what moral questions may be raised concerning capital punishment and war, we move from the area of private acts by individual persons to public acts wherein the primary agent is the state. In *revolutionary* killing, the state is not the agent taking the initiative, though the state may claim the right of self-defense in putting down armed revolt by killing. The revolutionary may claim that when he kills in a justified uprising against the state, it is a political act and should not be judged as murder. The state in turn may claim that armed revolt is treason and as such punishable by death. Cynics like to point to the pragmatic and relativistic factors here: armed uprising against the state may be a "glorious revolution" if it succeeds, but "foul crime" and "despicable treason" if it fails.

Capital Punishment

In recent years, capital punishment has fallen out of favor as an ordinary means of social control. At least this is true in circumstances of peace and social stability. But in the course and wake of armed revolt, the death penalty is still implemented frequently and with vigor. After the success of the Cuban revolution in 1956, the new Castro government executed more than one thousand of its enemies by firing squad. The Korean and Vietnam conflicts provided dismal spectacles of executions, formal and informal. After the failure of the small-scale Moroccan revolt of August 1972, 11 officers were shot. Later in the same year, large-scale measures were put into effect by Pakistanis against the revolting Bengalis, of whom nearly one million were put to death. In their turn, after the Pakistani defeat, the revengeful Bengalis staged some torture-executions of their own at a rally in Dacca; the preliminaries were internationally televised. But it is not these slaughters in hot blood that people have in mind when they debate the merits of capital punishment. They think, rather, of the usual peacetime civil executions carried out according to due process of law.

The history of capital punishment is well known. Until comparatively recently, executions were public affairs, drawing immense crowds in holiday mood. In 1825 near Slagelse, Denmark, Hans Christian Andersen was among the schoolboys who watched the beheading of a young girl and her lover, together with the farm servant who had helped them murder the girl's father. As Andersen remembers the scene:

The top form [senior class] was given permission to go down and see it . . . the girl was very pretty, but deathly pale . . . she lay in her lover's arms; he was pink and healthy to look at; the farm hand looked pale and yellow with long black hair that fell down over his face. A few other farm hands shouted out Goodbye to him: he took off his hat and nodded. . . . It was such a lovely morning; all of them sang a hymn and I could hear the girl's clear voice above all the others. . . . At the end she kissed her lover once again. Her head did not fall until the second blow.[43]

In the United States during the years 1930–1966 there were 3,857 executions, an average of a little more than one hundred per year.[44] Most of these were punishments for murder, though many states enforced the death penalty for rape—particularly against blacks in the South. A number of other capital offenses stand on the books of the several states, including kidnapping, train wrecking, arson, and bombing. The execution of Julius and Ethel Rosenberg, which shocked the world in 1953, was carried out under a federal espionage law.

In July 1972, by a five-to-four decision, the Supreme Court of the United States ruled that the death penalty *as currently administered by the states* was cruel and unusual punishment in violation of the eighth and fourteenth amendments to the Constitution.[45] Only two of the justices stated their belief that capital punishment was cruel and unusual *in itself.* Similar reluctance to enforce the death penalty is common in most of the developed nations of the world today. Where it is a question of enforcement in the cold blood of peace and political stability, the death penalty now seems barbarous and anachronistic. But some of the poorer developing countries have not yet been able to afford this attitude. In Nigeria, for example, in the two-year period from 1970 to 1972, 170 men convicted of armed robbery have been executed, most of them publicly.[46] And, as we have already noted, attitudes toward the death penalty quickly harden during wartime. Martial law takes over from ordinary civil law, and the usual citizens' rights are overborne by the exigencies of the moment. United States involvement in World War II had hardly begun when five German would-be saboteurs, captured shortly after beaching on Long Island, were hustled off to the electric chair in the nation's capital after summary trial by military court.

Liberal opinion argues that the death penalty is not a good thing, that it is a primitive and repulsive means of social control, that the sooner it is gotten rid of as an ordinary penal measure the better. Such a position does not necessarily deny that under certain extraordinary circumstances capital punishment may not be justified and appropriate. Just what these circumstances are may be hard to specify. Some would reserve the extreme penalty for certain offenses against law officers, such as killing a policeman while doing his duty. Others would allow the penalty to be invoked in the case of certain crimes against children, such as their killing by torture. Still others would call for the death penalty for those directly involved in crimes, such as genocide. Israel's hanging of Adolf Eichmann in 1962 is a case in point.

But even with the case of Eichmann the elusive question of the *purpose* of punishment will not fade. What *was* the end and purpose of hanging him? What good was served? Was it an act of vengeance, a paying back? But what did this one man's life count when thrown into the balance against those of the millions he helped kill? Was it to effect an emotional release, a collective catharsis in the psyches of all those who cried to heaven against the enormity of the Nazi crimes? Nearly the whole world agreed that Eichmann *deserved* hanging. But does this not mean that his punishment was simply retributive, thus bringing us back to "a life for a life"? Perhaps the hanging of Eichmann had, as Nietzsche would say, a *mnemonic* purpose, a solemn ritual whose end was to remind the world of certain crimes and to proclaim that all those now living should not forget and should see to it that they never happen again.

Many would classify Eichmann's offense as a "war" crime, and we must now look very briefly at the arguments of those who hold that war itself is the greatest of crimes, that war is by its very nature "immoral," that the killing required by the state of the soldier in war is nothing other than "legalized murder."

III

War: Kinds and Causes

War, in the sense of an armed and bloody struggle between organized groups, is as old as human history. Human beings have played every conceivable variation on this theme: tribal wars, wars of enslavement, wars among city-states, wars of religion (crusades, holy wars, Protestants versus Catholics), genocidal incursions like those of Tamerlane and Genghis Khan, wars of territorial conquest, civil wars, revolutionary wars, blood feuds, wars where the object is not to kill the enemy but to keep the armies intact (certain Chinese wars), grand-scale world wars, colonial wars, police actions, class-struggle wars, wars of national liberation—the categories overlap and the list is endless. The very gods needed war: the Olympians engaged in armed strife, and Teutonic warriors hewed each other to pieces in Valhalla to rise up whole in the morning, only to hew again. The angels in heaven, under St. Michael's command, fought Satan and his legions to the brink of Hell. Even the compassionate Indian sages were not immune to the human fascination with war. The Hindu epic *Ramayana* has its Book of War, and the sacred Hindu book, the *Bhagavad Gita,* ends with a signal

for battle. If gods and heroes must have war, it is hard for man
to remain at peace; small wonder that war is thought by so many
to be a universal and necessary part of the human condition.
"Homo homini lupus," runs the Latin tag, "Man is a wolf to man."
Hobbes thought that man in the prepolitical state of nature was
part of the "war of all against all."

The easiest explanation of war is to attribute it to the human's
"aggressive instinct."[47] But, so far as causal explanations are
concerned, this may be not much better than saying opium puts
people to sleep because it has a "dormative virtue." It _could_ be,
as some have suggested, that frail protoman was forced into
collective aggression for survival purposes and that our later
belligerence is rooted in this. Fragmentary evidence of primitive
skeletal remains have suggested that humans are natural preda-
tors, but wider evidence indicates that, while early humans did
adapt to predatory conditions, they also adapted to nonpredatory
agricultural environments. Traditional theology explained man's
incorrigible war-making as evidence of human nature's fallen
state: war, like crime and hatred, is a sign of some aboriginal
catastrophe that befell the human race, as a result of which man
found himself estranged from God and alienated from himself.
Some find in psychoanalytic doctrine an analogue of the old
teaching of original sin. Shortly after the outbreak of World War
I, Freud wrote to a Dutch psychopathologist:

Psychoanalysis has concluded . . . that the primitive, savage and evil
impulses of mankind have not vanished in an individual but continue their
existence, although in a repressed state—in the unconscious, as we
call it in our language—and that they wait for opportunities to display
their activity.

It has furthermore taught us that our intellect is a feeble and dependent
thing, a plaything and tool of our impulses and emotions; that all of us are
forced to behave cleverly or stupidly according as our attitude and inner
resistances ordain.

And now just look at what is happening in this wartime, at the cruelties
and injustices for which the most civilized nations are responsible, at the
different way in which they judge of their own lies, their own wrong-
doings, and those of their enemies, at the general loss of clear insight;
then you must confess that psychoanalysis has been right with both its
assertions.[48]

From ancient times to our own day, social reformers have
pointed to the prime causes of war as _economic._ Wars, said

Plato, are caused by love of money. Wars, said Marx, arise from the material conditions of history: civil wars leap from conflict between those classes that possess the means of production and those forced by these dominant classes to toil for them; wars among nations explode out of rivalry and competition for markets. An old notion about war is that conflict is essential to the life and well-being of race and culture. Some evolutionists have claimed that aggression promotes the preservation of the stronger species; war is a selective factor that ensures that the stronger survive and multiply their species. Warlike nations have glorified conflict as the great stimulus to life. German poets and philosophers have vied with field marshals in praising war as the necessary condition of a nation's greatness. Kant believed that war, provided it is conducted with order and a "sacred respect" for the rights of civilians, has something sublime about it, while a prolonged peace tends to favor the rule of a purely commercial spirit.[49] The Prussian military genius Helmuth von Moltke said that without war civilization would rot. Transvaluing the values, Nietzsche's Zarathustra exalts war: "You should love peace as a means to new wars. And the short peace more than the long. . . . You say it is the good cause that hallows even war? . . . I tell you: it is the good war that hallows every cause. War and courage have done more great things than charity."[50] Admirers of Nietzsche say that by "war" the philosopher did not mean literal blood-and-iron affairs like the Franco-Prussian war of 1870, but rather conflicts of a spiritual and cultural kind. That whole peoples, or most of them, may actually *want* war is something that liberals in the Anglo-American tradition have a hard time understanding.

Morality of War: Ethics and the State

The Greeks commonly regarded ethics as a subclass of *politics.* Ethics treats of the good of the individual person, while politics has for its object the good of the corporate entity of which the individual person is a member. Plato believed that the crucial question "What is justice?" could not be answered satisfactorily if the problem were restricted to the behavior of men taken individually. In his *Republic,* Plato expands the framework of the province of justice so that it includes the state, which Plato regarded as the individual person "in capital letters." Plato believed that the state had certain proper powers in its own right. These included the right to make war. Not only was this right justly exercised in self-defense—by analogy to the individual man who is justified in repelling an attacker by force—but the state was justified, on appropriate occasions, in taking aggressive action against other states to secure its own good. The early moderns, Machiavelli and Hobbes, agreed: war is essential to the state's existence. Grotius, father of international law, tried to humanize war; in an effort to reduce its brutality he appealed to the "law of nations" (grounded on "natural law"), to which even warring powers owed obedience and respect.[51] In addition, Grotius called attention to alternatives to war, including international congresses to search for peaceful solutions to conflicts among nations. Nevertheless, Grotius did not deny the right of a nation to make war, for just cause, thus reflecting a long tradition of Christian theological analysis of the concept of the "just war."

The reasoning shared by most traditional political philosophers is this: under natural law a state has the right in certain circumstances, to use force to secure its own good. The right to use force is part of the very essence of the state; the *right* use of force is the *proper good* of politics. If the state has the right, in certain circumstances, to secure its own good, it follows that a state has the right, under certain conditions, to use *war* to secure its own good. Many theologians and moral philosophers of our century *deny* that war can ever be a part of the proper task of the state. For example, the Protestant theologian Karl Barth:

What Christian ethics has to emphasize is that neither inwardly nor outwardly does the normal task of the state, which is at issue even in time of war, consist in a process of annihilating rather than maintaining and fostering life. . . . It is no part of the normal task of the state to wage war; its normal task is to fashion peace in such a way that life is served and war kept at bay. . . . It is when the state does not rightly pursue its normal task that sooner or later it is compelled to take up the abnormal one of war, and therefore to inflict this abnormal task on other states.[52]

To which some political and moral philosophers reply: while the politics of war may be abnormal and the politics of peace normal, it does not follow that war can never be a legitimate instrument of the political order. It was Barth's older compatriot Clausewitz who pointed out that war is the continuation of politics by other means.[53] This is not a cynical definition if it is taken to mean that there is no sharp and absolute separation between the politics of war and the politics of peace. In the modern system of nation-states—even when at least two of them are superstates— there is still no international authority that has the power to enforce peaceful settlement of all international disputes. Despite its accomplishments in the realm of international cooperation, the United Nations has been unable to prevent a number of serious international armed conflicts. Unless we deny any reality or value at all to the political order, the use of power by nations to secure their own good (which need not necessarily exclude the good of others) is indispensable to political action. In crucial circumstances, war or the threat of war *may* be the only way of bringing this power to bear. A professor of Christian ethics at Princeton reminds us that the criterion of *personal morality* will not provide an exact, one-to-one fit when applied to *political conduct.* No nation, including the United States, is *morally obliged* to do all of the "ought to be" (the world political good), but only that part of it that is congruent with its national good:

Therefore I say the use of power and possibly the use of armed force, is of the *esse* of politics and inseparably connected with those higher human goods which are the *bene esse* of politics in all the historical ages of mankind. This interpretation of political authority is held in common by the Augustinian tradition and its two main branches: the natural law theory of politics and the Lutheran analysis of the state as an "order of necessity."[54]

Traditional Conditions of a Just War
Throughout the centuries, scholars of the major Christian traditions have pondered the concept of the "just war." Both Catholic and Protestant moralists have agreed that war involves both great physical and moral evils. But they have nevertheless held to the principle that *some* wars, particularly defensive wars, are morally justifiable—that the evil produced by *some* wars is not so great as the evil of not fighting those wars would be. Typical of the traditional criteria for a just war are these:

    1. The war must be declared as a last resort, after all peaceful means of settling the dispute have been exhausted.

    2. The war must be declared by a lawful authority.

    3. The war must be declared for a just cause—for example, to repel serious injuries.

    4. The war should employ just means—for example, there should be no direct destruction of the innocent.

5. There must be a reasonable expectation of success of the war.

6. The principle of proportionality must be observed—that is, the violence must not produce a greater evil than that which it seeks to correct.

Marxist-Leninist analysts have evolved a somewhat different set of conditions of justified warfare. According to Soviet criteria, any war in which an oppressed class overthrows an oppressor class is justified. This would include class struggle, or civil wars of revolution in which workers or peasants seize the government and take over the means of production from feudal or capitalist overlords. Wars against fascist invasions are obviously justified. So too are anticolonial wars and wars of national liberation. According to the latest edition of the Soviet diplomatic dictionary:

War is the struggle between states or classes by means of armed force. From a social viewpoint war is the continuation of the policy these states or classes pursued before the war. Marxist-Leninist theory divides war into two types: just, that is liberation wars, and unjust, that is aggressive wars. Just wars are the wars of peoples defending their countries against aggression, national liberation wars, civil wars of the workers for their liberation. Unjust wars are waged by exploiting classes in order to seize and enslave other countries, other peoples, in order to extend and assert their domination.[55]

A good exercise for us all is to select a particular war of the past or present and check it against either of the lists above. Try Hitler's invasion of Poland in 1939 (an easy one!). Or Darius's punitive expedition against the Greek states in 492 B.C. Or Lumumba's armed revolt in the Congo. Or Franco's assault on the Spanish Republic in 1936. Or Frederick the Great's war against the Grand Coalition. Or our own War between the States. Or the United Nations' "police action" under United States leadership as the North Koreans crossed the 49th parallel in 1950. Or the American response to Pearl Harbor. Or Castro's revolt launched from Cuba's Sierra Madre. Or Israel's six-day war against the United Arab Republic. Or India's two-week war against Pakistan.

One response to the question as to whether there can be a just war is this: perhaps one cannot justify war as such, or even a particular war as such, but one may be able to justify one side or another taking up arms in defense against the party who started the war. That is, one justifies taking up arms on the ground of self-defense. True enough, but the question of who started it is not always easy to decide. The aggressor-defender dualism is loaded with ambiguities, as we shall see below.

A Just War No Longer Possible?

Many critics of war as an instrument of national policy believe that, given the conditions of late twentieth-century warfare, a just war is simply no longer possible. The efficiency of modern fire-power and the destructiveness of air bombing make even conventional warfare impossible to justify. How much the more so nuclear warfare, in which dozens of world cities would be instantly destroyed and tens or hundreds of millions of human lives lost. The late twentieth-century model of the conventional war is the Vietnam conflict. This war was limited in scope: it lacked the scale of either of the two world wars, and it was not fought with atomic or thermonuclear weapons. Yet the destruction and loss of life wrought in the Vietnam War, say the critics, was so terrible that any attempt to defend it in the light of the principle of *proportionality* alone simply fails. The other just war criteria are equally inapplicable or, at best, dubious. Such is the lethal effect of contemporary firepower that military commanders *know* that the noncombatants will suffer and that the suffering will be all out of proportion to the value of the military or political results achieved. Wars like the Vietnam conflict by their very nature produce—with their massive destruction of life, limb, property, and natural resources—far greater evil than whatever good (debatable as that is) they were intended to secure.

Now let us consider nuclear warfare, which certain nations of the world have the resources to wage, and ask whether *that* can be morally justified under any circumstances. In the closing weeks of World War II, the United States dropped a single primitive atomic bomb on each of two Japanese cities, Hiroshima and Nagasaki. In the first instance, more than eighty thousand were killed, in the second more than forty thousand. Most of the lives lost were civilians. The president of the United States and his advisers, both military and civilian, were aware of the probabilities that the death and injury toll among noncombatant Japanese would be very high. But in 1945 a shred of moral justification of the decision to bomb was available. This was the belief on the part of most American authorities that the atomic bombing would bring the war to an immediate close, thus preventing the great loss of life to all parties to the war that would inevitably occur if the United States was forced to invade a resisting Japan. The war did stop and no invasion of the Japanese homeland was required. But Pandora's box had been opened and the race was on among the victorious powers for a superbomb.

In the early 1950s, thermonuclear fusion was achieved; the hydrogen bomb had captured the power of the sun. The postwar superpowers—USA and USSR—began to stockpile nuclear weapons, while lesser powers joined the race to become members of the "nuclear club." The superpowers perfected nuclear-powered submarines equipped to launch rockets with nuclear warheads. Then came intercontinental ballistic missiles that could deliver single (later multiple) nuclear warheads in a few minutes to targets many thousands of miles away. An informed description of the superpowers' state of nuclear readiness in the early 1970s tells us that 100 American nuclear warheads delivered on target can inflict unacceptable damage to the Soviet Union; that the United States now has between 5,000 and 8,000 such warheads; that the Soviet Union has a comparable overkill capacity in its formidable array of giant SS-9 intercontinental ballistic missiles. The explosive force of 5 million tons of TNT were packed into the device tested underground at Amchitka, Alaska, in November, 1971—a charge destined to form the warhead of the new Spartan antiballistic missile. There is good reason to believe that the Soviet Union has equally heavy nuclear destructive capacity at its command.[56]

Antiwar critics ask if there is any possibility of moral justification of the use of that ghastly arsenal. What conceivable cause could legitimate a war that, if it did not immediately turn the world into the graveyard of humanity, would at least throw much of humanity back into the Stone Age? Pacifists hold that *all* war is bad. "Nuclear" pacifists, while allowing that some conventional wars may still possibly be justified, declare that any use of nuclear weapons is immoral. To support their claim, they point to the unacceptable evil represented by the lethal capacity of these weapons, the genocidal potential of which is indicated by the projected numbers of those who would be killed.

The nonpacifist reply to this argument is sometimes given in the following terms: it is true that nuclear weaponry, if actually used in warfare, can unleash unheard-of destruction. For this reason, it is probable that the balance of evil in such a war would far outweigh the good, whether we think of the good of the warring parties or that of humankind in general. But the existence of nuclear weapons and the capacities of certain nations to use them have not resulted in unmitigated evil. The possession of nuclear arsenals by the greatest world powers seems so far actually to have worked to prevent the rivalry between the superstates from deteriorating into all-out armed conflict. In fact, the nuclear stalemate has forced a significant degree of accommodation upon the superstates. World War III, which some predicted would occur twenty years after aggressive warfare had been outlawed at Nuremberg, seems now a more remote, though still not a negligible, possibility. Modest beginnings have actually been made in agreements between the United States and the Soviet Union to control the senseless proliferation of nuclear arms. Some observers are worried about China, for that great country (now a member of the United Nations) has had for some time the capacity to make nuclear bombs, though still perhaps on a modest scale. But it is hard to see how China's national interest could be served by her launching a nuclear assault on the West, even supposing she had the resources to do so. It is not necessarily true that the nation-state system, even under present conditions, must lead to world conflict. *Balance of power* brought a long peace to early nineteenth-century Europe after the Congress of Vienna. As the twentieth century moves toward its last quarter, a new balance of power appears to be emerging—the United States, the Soviet Union, China, Japan, and Western Europe are the weights in the scales.

The nuclear standoff among the great powers has permitted, indeed forced, the continuation of warfare by conventional means. But the deadly efficiency of conventional weapons has fearfully increased since the end of World War II. Are we therefore to say that all warfare, including nonnuclear conventional warfare, is immoral? If we take the Vietnam War as our single model, it is hard to avoid an affirmative answer. Just about everyone today agrees that the Vietnam War was a bad war. In the cynical words of Napoleon's lieutenant, when asked about the religious persecution under the Revolution, "It was worse than a crime, it was a mistake." It is hardly less cynical (but perhaps just a little true) to suggest that part of the badness of the Vietnam War from the American point of view resides in the fact that it was a failure. Had United States intervention met with quick military success, had Viet Cong and North Vietnamese resistance crumbled and surrendered, there might today be less than general agreement that the conflict was a bad war—though what good the long-range results of an American presence in Southeast Asia might have achieved are debatable. A crucial factor in the "badness" of the war in Vietnam was the obvious evil of the destruction wrought there over the years upon human life, property, and natural resources, a destruction clearly out of all proportion to whatever good might have been achieved (if indeed it would have been a good) in suppressing the Communist-oriented insurgence that threatened the government of South Vietnam in the early 1960s. No need to detail a sad story with which the world is all too familiar.

Nonpacifist critics, conceding that the Vietnam conflict was a bad war, may still ask if that war need be taken as the ethical paradigm of all wars, even those of the late twentieth century. It may be that there is no such thing as a "good" war today, but it is still conceivable that a war can be waged to prevent a greater evil, that is, a war in which the principle of proportionality does in fact hold. It would be useless to argue the case here for the moral justification of any particular war—the Korean police action, the Arab-Israeli six-day war, the Biafran or Bengali uprisings, and so on. The point is that it is one thing to denounce a given war as a hopeless evil and quite another to conclude from this that no war is morally justifiable today under any circumstances. Some analysts try to ease the moral problem involved by making a distinction between an *aggressive* war and a *defensive* war. They may point to the Nuremberg trials of 1945, in which leaders of Nazi Germany were condemned for planning and waging an aggressive war of conquest. Objectors will reply that the Nuremberg trials are dubious as precedents, since they were military trials of the vanquished by the victors in which defendants were found guilty of aggression under ex post facto laws, a proceeding contrary to international law.

But how can we today distinguish between aggressive and defensive wars? Suppose nation X moves its armed forces or weapons into a position to damage nation Y. Then Y initiates military action with a sharp ground and air attack, dispersing X's forces and destroying its weaponry. Which is the aggressor? Under terms of the aggressor-defender distinction a revolutionary war to throw off an oppressor government would raise the same question because the revolutionaries, by taking the initiative, would become, at least in a narrow sense, the aggressors.

To which the revolutionaries might reply that the oppressor state against which they are rising is really the aggressor. So the aggressor-defender distinction does not help much in providing a criterion of moral justification of war, though there may be circumstances in which the distinction is more clearly applicable. Many would say that the principle of the distinction patently applied to the war initiated by Germany against Poland in 1939 and to the German invasion of Russia in 1941, and that consequently the declaration and implementing of war against Germany by the Allied Powers was both politically and morally justifiable.

To various forms of pacifism, nuclear and otherwise, those nonpacifists who take the position that a resort to war, even in the late twentieth century, need not necessarily be immoral, may sum up their argument in the following terms: so long as humans live in a political order, the use of power, even of force, will on occasion be necessary and justifiable in order to achieve good or to avoid greater evil. Even if the nations of the world surrendered their sovereignty, and with it the prerogative of exerting power and force, to a world governing body, that "parliament of man" would have to reserve to itself the use of power and (on occasion) force to keep order and to achieve good. How much the more so will the political order of nation-states, under which we still live, necessitate the retention of power and the prerogative of use of force by individual nations? Force necessary for self-defense is a right recognized by the Charter of the United Nations on the part of its member states. Nothing in this argument should be construed as justification of the use of power or force for bad ends. An example of the use of power for bad ends would be the way in which Nazi Germany used force to secure her good. Her aggrandizement as a nation—an end not necessarily illegitimate in itself—was achieved by means so obviously repugnant both to the political and moral consensus of humanity as to render detailed analysis of those means unnecessary. This is not to say that the nations that crushed Nazi Germany were themselves guiltless.

But what many people of education and goodwill fail to see is that bringing to bear power, even force, for political purposes is not essentially evil so long as we live in a politically organized world. The availability of force in international relations need not necessarily mean bad use of force, nor need it mean war. Reference to force, through ordinary channels of diplomacy and negotiation, may and often does result in the avoidance of war—though routine diplomacy achieves success without coming anywhere near that critical point. Not all achievement of national good by force need be "blackmail" on the part of the power using it nor "appeasement" on the part of the power to which it is applied.

Conscientious Objection on Moral Grounds

A word in conclusion may be said about conscientious objection to participating in present-day wars. In an earlier chapter, we noted that there is a kind of consensus among contemporary Western peoples that no one should be forced to do anything against the command of his own conscience, provided that what his conscience dictates is not repugnant to public morals nor detrimental to individual or national safety. This agreement to acknowledge the authority of individual conscience is rooted in the great religious traditions, in their doctrines of the accountability to God of each individual soul. In modern times, Luther in the religious order and Kant in the secular realm reinforced social belief in the autonomy of conscience. The secular humanist tradition took up and carried forward the concept of the autonomy of conscience by declaring that the religions had no monopoly on the right of conscience, which can be upheld on purely rational and ethical grounds. The concept of "conscientious" objection to participation in war, that objection based on religious reasons, was recognized by most Western nations by the nineteenth century—though not all nations honored individual pleas to conscience as disqualification for war service.[57] The "conchies" of World War I in England and in this country did not have an easy time, though usually noncombatant work was provided for them—albeit grudgingly. Less objectionable, though far from perfect, means of handling conscientious objectors were worked out in this country during World War II. A significant number of these young men performed useful noncombatant service (often under dangerous conditions), as did some of their counterparts in the Korean and Vietnam conflicts.

Until very recently the conscientious objector to war service had to base his plea on (1) his sincere opposition to *all* war and (2) *religious* grounds. But with the Vietnam War, the lid of this arrangement rattled loudly as far as the United States was concerned. Hundreds of young men pleaded sincere conscientious objection to their draft boards not on the grounds that they believed *all* war was immoral, but that *this* war conspicuously was. They further pleaded that it was discriminatory to restrict grounds for conscientious objection to *religious* reasons because today so many people are *not* religious yet have, nonetheless, strong objections to war on moral and ethical grounds. These young men found that their reasons for objecting to military service did not constitute legal grounds for objecting to military service as conscientious objectors. In Chapter 6, we noted that the Supreme Court of the United States ruled in favor of purely ethical reasons as adequate grounds for conscientious objection. But the Court did not set aside the requirement that the objector must object to all wars, not just a particular war.

The arguments of these conscientious objectors have some force of logic. The contemporary Western world no longer abides by the presuppositions of religious faith. Unless a definition of conscience in terms other than religion is ruled out (and this would be arbitrary), there is no reason to believe an objection to war on ethical grounds reflects an obligation less deep or sincerely felt than one based on religious belief. As for the requirement that one must object to *all* wars rather than to one in particular, surely the Nuremberg judgments are relevant here. Those judgments made clear what was already the case under international law: the duty of a soldier to obey orders is not a principle so absolute as to blanket unlawful and criminal acts. The judges at Nuremberg declared that for the defendant charged with war crimes to plead that the act was committed under orders from his superior did not relieve him of responsibility. Not only does the soldier have the moral and legal right to refuse to obey criminal orders (such as shooting helpless civilians), but he also has the duty to refuse.[58] From these premises, the would-be conscientious objector argues that he has both the right and the duty to refuse induction into the military service if his country is waging a war he sincerely believes to be immoral and criminal.

In the context of the Vietnam War, the case for modifying conscientious objector status requirements were regarded by many potential inductees and their supporters as persuasive, even conclusive. But critics of the argument pointed out that if such widening of conscientious objector status were permitted, the whole problem of who is or who is not qualified as a bona fide conscientious objector becomes entirely unmanageable. In older days, when the external correlates of religious belief were more observable than they are today, the sincerity of a person's religious beliefs could be tested with a little more quasi-objectivity than they can be today. For example, the objector might have been a member of a special religious sect publicly known to be opposed to all war. Or the objector might bring biblical texts to support his beliefs, and members of his tribunal might know enough about Scripture to make an educated guess as to whether his argument was faked or not. Today, even that sketchy presupposition of common understanding in religious matters is gone. A person may disclaim all ties to traditional or organized religion and still claim to be as deeply religious as the pope or the archbishop of Canterbury. The case for widening the grounds for conscientious objection may be unassailable in the abstract, say the critics, but the concrete consequences of the proposed liberalizing of requirements would permit just about any candidate for military induction who did not *want* to serve in a particular war or in any war at all to refuse induction on the grounds of conscientious objection with little or no chance of disqualifying him. As far as the Nuremberg precedent is concerned, that tribunal held no ordinary soldier responsible for war crimes and made no judgment that would render a man who accepted military induction liable for such crimes.

Opponents of broadening qualifications for conscientious objectors, and even many of those who favor some modification of the present requirements, point out that under the present nation-state system the conscientious objector does not have the *right* to be accorded special treatment by the state. The state's granting him special status is a concession, a favor, a dispensation; it is not something that justice requires be *exacted* from the state. On the other hand, the principle that the state *has* the right to require military service of all able-bodied male citizens in time of need is still accepted by nation-states today in common consent. Some may regard this situation as one more reason to work for the abolition of the nation-state system. Others may argue that in a truly democratic society conscientious objection would be an individual and personal right, not a mere concession or act of grace granted to the individual by the state. Even a "united world" organization, whose primary peace-keeping forces would be composed of volunteers, would have to reserve the right to require military services of its citizens in case of extraordinary need. (A world civil war? An interplanetary invasion?) Such a world organization might indeed find it easier to recognize conscientious objection as an individual right than do the imperfect democracies and other forms of government of the present time.

NOTES: CHAPTER 11

1. For example, Konrad Lorenz and Ralph L. Holloway, Jr.. Alexander Alland, Jr., argues against their views on the importance of innate aggressiveness in man. See writings by these men in Suggested Readings.
2. Kenneth B. Clark, in his presidential address to the American Psychological Association, September 6, 1971; also in his "Leadership and Psychotechnology," *New York Times,* 9 November 1971, p. 47.
3. Plato *Republic,* 461.
4. Napoleon A. Chagnon, "Yanomamö Social Organization and Warfare," *War: the Anthropology of Armed Conflict and Aggression,* ed. Morton Fried, Marvin Harris, and Robert Murphy (New York: Natural History Press, 1968), p. 139.
5. "Sterilization in Alabama," *New York Times,* 12 July 1973, p. 38.
6. In the United States the popularity of sterilization seems to be increasing. In 1969, 212,000 vasectomies were performed; the 1973 expected total is 700,000. Tubal ligations were performed on 56,000 American women in 1969; the anticipated total for 1973 is expected to be in excess of 300,000. Sylvia Porter, "Sterilization Boom," *New York Times,* 9 May 1973, p. 46.
7. Gen. 38:9.
8. Paul VI, "Humanae Vitae," *New York Times,* 30 July 1968, pp. 20–21.
9. George Devereaux, *A Study of Abortion in Primitive Societies* (New York: Julian, 1955), p. 73.
10. David M. Feldman, *Birth Control in Jewish Law* (New York: New York University Press, 1968), p. 259.
11. John T. Noonan, Jr., "An Almost Absolute Value in History," in *The Morality of Abortion,* ed. J. T. Noonan (Cambridge, Mass.: Harvard University Press, 1970), pp. 45–46.
12. The Supreme Court decision of January 1973 allows patient and physician to determine that an abortion should take place any time during the first three months of pregnancy. Prior to the final ten weeks of pregnancy, states may regulate abortion only to protect the health of the mother. The Court's decision had the effect of repealing most anti-abortion laws in the states where they now exist.
13. Thomas Aquinas, *Commentary on the Sentences of Peter Lombard,* cited by Noonan, *Morality of Abortion,* p. 24.

14. Karl Barth, *Church Dogmatics,* 4 vols. (Edinburgh: T. & T. Clark, 1961), 3:415–416.
15. Ashley Montagu, *Life Before Birth* (New York: Signet, 1965), p. 12.
16. Judith Jarvis Thomson, "A Defense of Abortion," *Philosophy and Public Affairs* (Fall 1971), pp. 47–66.
17. The case is discussed in Norman St. John-Stevas, "Law and the Moral Consensus," in *Life or Death: Ethics and Options,* ed. D. H. Labby (Seattle: University of Washington Press, 1968), pp. 49–50.
18. Terence Prittie, *Germans against Hitler* (Boston: Atlantic, Little, Brown, 1964), pp. 83, 103.
19. Joseph Fletcher, "The Patient's Right to Die," in *Euthanasia and the Right to Death,* ed. A. B. Downing (New York: Humanities, 1970), pp. 63–64.
20. Papal statement of 1957, cited by Norman St. John-Stevas, *Life, Death and the Law* (London: Eyre and Spottiswoode, 1961), p. 276.
21. The United Nations Genocide Convention, which makes the systematic extermination of racial, religious, or cultural group a crime punishable under international law, has been ratified by sixty-nine nations, including Germany and Turkey. The Turkish action against the Armenian minority in World War I has been cited as early-twentieth-century genocide by Marjorie Housepian in "The Unremembered Genocide," *Commentary* (September 1966), pp. 55–61.
22. John Dewey, "Anti-Naturalism in Extremis," in *Naturalism and the Human Spirit,* ed. Yervant Krikorian (New York: Columbia University Press, 1944), pp. 8–9.
23. St. John-Stevas, Labby, ed., *Life or Death,* p. 45.
24. Yukio Mishima's ritual suicide is strikingly anticipated in his story "Patriotism," in *Death in Midsummer* (New York: New Directions, 1966), and in his late novel *Runaway Horses* (New York: Knopf, 1973).
25. Plato *Phaedo* 61–62.
26. 1. *Sam.* 31:4–5. In A.D. 27 several thousand Jews killed themselves after heroically resisting the Romans at Masada.
27. Thomas Aquinas, in *Summa Theologica,* 2a2ae, trans. The Dominican Fathers, 60 vols. (New York: McGraw-Hill, 1964), vol. 35, Q.64, art. 5.
28. This is according to Thomas S. Szasz, M.D., "The Ethics of Suicide," *Intellectual Digest* (October, 1971), pp. 53–55.
29. Figures cited in E. R. Ellis and G. N. Allen, *Traitor Within* (Garden City, N.Y.: Doubleday, 1961), pp. 40–41.
30. Alfred Alvarez, *The Savage God: A Study of Suicide* (London: Weidenfeld & Nicholason, 1971), pp. 85–86.
31. Emile Durkheim, *Suicide: A Study in Sociology,* trans. J. A. Spaulding and G. Simpson (New York: Free Press, 1951), p. 86.

32. W. Stekel, in *On Suicide,* ed. Paul Frieman (New York: International Universities, 1967), p. 90.

33. Jack D. Douglas, *The Social Meanings of Suicide* (Princeton, N.J.: Princeton University Press, 1967), p. 361.

34. Graham Greene, *The Heart of the Matter* (New York: Viking, 1948), p. 207. The question had been raised as early as the third century by Tertullian.

35. Arthur Schopenhauer, *The World as Will and Idea,* 3 vols., trans. R. B. Haldane and J. Kemp (London: Routledge & Kegan Paul, 1957), vol. 1, sec. 69, pp. 514–515.

36. William James, "Is Life Worth Living?" in *The Will to Believe and Other Essays* (New York: McKay, 1907), p. 62.

37. Albert Camus, *The Myth of Sisyphus and Other Essays,* trans. Justin O'Brien (New York: Knopf, 1955), p. 3.

38. Ibid., p. 28.

39. Ibid., p. 55.

40. Ibid., p. 123.

41. Ludwig Wittgenstein, *Philosophical Investigations,* trans. G. E. M. Anscombe (Oxford: Blackwell, 1953), sec. 302; also pp. 222–244.

42. Friedrich Nietzsche, *Beyond Good and Evil,* chap. 4, aphorism 157.

43. Quoted in P. V. Glob, *Danish Prehistoric Monuments,* trans. J. Bulman (London: Faber, 1970), pp. 197–198.

44. Hugo A. Bedau, ed. *The Death Penalty in America,* rev. ed. (Garden City, N.Y.: Doubleday, 1967), p. 35.

45. Text of the U.S. Supreme Court decision and opinions in *New York Times,* 30 June 1972, pp. 14–15.

46. *New York Times,* 27 July 1972, p. 3.

47. In his paper "Human Aggression," Ralph L. Holloway, Jr., is critical of the "aggression instinct" explanation of war given by Lorenz and others; in Fried et al., *War: Anthropology of Armed Conflict,* pp. 33–48.

48. Quoted in Ernest Jones, *The Life and Work of Sigmund Freud,* 2 vols. (New York: Basic Books, 1955), 2:74.

49. Immanuel Kant, *The Critique of Judgment,* trans. J. C. Meredith (Oxford: Clarendon Press, 1928), pp. 112–113. Kant was no philosophical war-monger; he envisioned the ideal of lasting world peace secured by a congress of nations. See Kant, *Perpetual Peace,* trans. Lewis W. Beck (New York: Liberal Arts, 1957).

50. Nietzsche, *Thus Spake Zarathustra,* trans. R. J. Hollingdale (Baltimore, Md.: Penguin, 1961), p. 74.

51. Huig De Groot (Grotius), a seventeenth-century Dutch lawyer and theologian, is the author of *The Rights of War and Peace,* trans. A. C. Campbell (London: M. W. Dunne, 1901). The concept of "natural law"

developed in the Middle Ages by Aquinas and other theologians, refers not to laws or statutes made by men, but to those supposedly universal principles of reason and humanity which underlie just man-made laws.

52. Karl Barth, *Church Dogmatics,* 4 vols., trans. G. T. Thomson (Edinburgh: Clark, 1957) 2: p. 456.
53. Karl von Clausewitz, *On War,* trans. O. J. Mattije Jolles (New York: Modern Library, 1943), p. 16.
54. Paul Ramsey, *The Just War* (New York: Scribner, 1968), p. 7.
55. A. A. Gromyko et al., eds., *Diplomaticheskii slovar',* 3 vols. (Moscow: Izd. politocheskoi literatury, 1971–   ), 1:332; passage translated by Prof. Peter Juviler.
56. From "Laird vs. Nixon," *New York Times,* 26 October 1971, p. 40.
57. Conscientious objection to military service is a relatively recent historical phenomenon, a result of mandatory universal military service that appeared late in the history of nation-states.
58. See Richard Wasserstrom, "The Relevance of Nuremberg," *Philosophy and Public Affairs* (Fall 1971), pp. 22–46.

12

The Extension of the Moral

In recent years many people have tended to widen the concept
of morality and to extend it into areas where, in the past, the
notions of "moral" and "immoral" were not so directly applied.
This extension of the moral idea has run parallel to the widening
of the concept of politics. In efforts to stimulate political awareness, the new pacificism has brought arguments against war that
are based on personal morality. Dissenters have defended civil
disobedience by declaring certain laws of the state to be immoral. Critics have weighed the socioeconomic arrangements
of our country in the balance of moral judgment and have found
them wanting. Charges against government agencies, from village
boards to the executive branch of the nation are commonly expressed in the language of morals. The *New York Times* worries
about "the moral climate" of our nation's capital.[1] From the Left
have come questions about the morality of industrial capitalism;
from the Right have come objections on moral grounds to government economic controls.[2] The question has been raised as to
whether it is not in fact immoral to submit oneself to *any* form of
government, including a representative democracy. The contemporary educational situation of children (for example de facto racial segregation) has been challenged on moral grounds. Organized religion has been judged severely for its incompatibility
with intuitions of individual moral consciences. Some critics have
widened the field of moral discourse to include application to
nature itself—our ecological responsibilities and our obligations
toward our natural environment have been widely discussed in
the idiom of moral concern.

I

Morality and the State

Some of the roots of today's expansion of moral categories to cover increasingly wider areas of human experience lie in deep dissatisfaction with the long-standing separation of the principles of personal morality from those thought to belong to the behavior of governments and states. In the context of twentieth-century wars, people have been shocked to discover anew the old gulf between the moral rectitude expected of them personally and the record of guilt, deception, cruelty, greed, and homicidal power so often deployed in the name of the good of the state. Today it is as if people had at last grown tired of the airless compartmentation between individual and political standards of conduct that has existed since the emergence of the nation-state system. Critics of political arrangements are now insisting that personal and political morality be brought closer together in the same focus.[3]

Many contemporary moralists would agree that current dissatisfaction with the old segregation of private morality from public policy is well-grounded. They would agree that it is needful to extend the limits of personal morality with a view to achieving closer integration between private and political good. Other moralists, however, caution us not to expect too much from the contemporary extension of morality into adjacent spheres. They argue that it is a mistake to believe that the standards of individual and personal morality can ever be applied without change to the conduct of any large social unit, particularly the state. Such a view is politically naïve, they say, for it implicitly claims that an organized society, such as the state, is no more than an aggregate or collection of the individuals that make it up.

A social organization is not wholly *other* than the individuals that make it up. But it is not on that account *identical* with the individuals composing it. The state, said Plato, is man "writ large"—but he did not mean by this that the state was no more than the arithmetical sum of its members.[4] New and quite real dimensions of social being—particularly the political—come into play when social unities are achieved and utilized. Humans are individual beings, but not just that alone. With rare exceptions, they cannot survive by themselves. Man is a political animal, said Aristotle, and he who would live outside a human community must be either above humanity or below it, a beast or a god.[5]

We may think of the state as a natural political arrangement that has always existed, in one form or other, as long as there have been creatures possessing a rational and social nature. Or we may think of the state as having come into being as the result of a social contract made by these creatures for their own protection and benefit. In any case, it seems that we must admit that the political order is not identical with the individual and personal order. Though political unity grows out of individual persons, these persons depend on the political unity. There would be no state without individuals, but the state is more than the collection of individuals composing it. Just as an individual person, morally speaking, has an important (Kant would say "absolute") degree of value in himself, so the political order has a relative but nonetheless real autonomy. So we must be careful, our politically minded critics would say, not to look for a one-to-one correspondence between personal morality and the actions of a state, however "just" the state may be.

But the fact that there is a real distinction between the individual person and the sociopolitical order of things does not justify a radical dualism between the respective moralities of the individual person and the state. The distinction between the individual and the political order does not mean that, while the individual person must treat other persons as inviolate, as ends in themselves, the state is justified in acting as a beast of prey, behaving as if the sole law were "might makes right." Yet neither does this in turn mean that the state is wicked if it does not follow Christ's counsels of perfection or Buddha's precepts of renunciation. We live in the world, and the city of man is not the city of God. On a planet that has not yet achieved a world government, people and countries must look after themselves if they are to survive as peoples and countries. No one else will do that for them.

Some critics have observed that the United States, almost alone among nations, is given to public examination of conscience and admission of national guilt. If this is a fault, it is not the worst kind; it may even be an asset. In any case, the habit surprises others. A recent visitor to our country was startled to find among intellectuals guilt feelings about past treatment of Indians, a sense of remorse usually associated with strict personal morality: "America still doesn't seem to understand that every great achievement in history—and America is one—comes out from a number of contractions. History shows it is impossible to build something great without stepping on someone's rights or without hurting another's susceptibilities."[6] Speaking generally, this type of argument proves too much. To claim that nothing great comes into being without "stepping on someone's right" leaves unanswered the crucial question as to just what kinds of duress stepping on somebody's rights is intended to cover. There is taking what belongs to another but with adequate compensation; there is taking with inadequate compensation; there is taking with no compensation; and there is taking with no compensation but with massacre, murder, and rapine. Nietzsche had no hesitation in comparing "the strong" to birds of prey:

There is nothing very odd about lambs disliking birds of prey that they carry off lambs. And when the lambs whisper among themselves, "These birds of prey are evil, and does not this give us a right to say that whatever is the opposite of a bird of prey must be good?" there is nothing intrinsically wrong with such an argument. . . .[7]

By "the strong" Nietzsche did not mean the state—he hated states. He meant individuals. A passionate individualist, he despised every form of political arrangement, even the negative form of anarchism. But Nietzsche's argument, using the same type of metaphor, can be turned to support what Plato himself called the worst form of the state—tyranny. Hitler did not hesitate to use the argument to justify the aggression of the Nazi state: "The whole work of Nature is a mighty struggle between strength and weakness—an eternal victory of the strong over the weak. There would be nothing but decay in the whole of Nature if this were not so. States which offend against this elementary law fall into decay."[8]

Out of this dialectic we may tentatively extract the following conclusion: it is a mistake to apply the standards of personal morality to the political order without allowance for change between orders. Reason: the personal and political order are two different levels; their dynamics are not the same. But it is also a mistake, and a graver one, to conclude from the premise, there is a real difference between the personal and the political order that must modify the way we apply ethical and legal categories to them, that the political order *has no connection* with the moral order, that the two realms are eternally cut off from one another.

As long as we do not have a world government and must live

in a system of nation-states or superstates, we can expect that nations or supernations will act so as to give their self-interest highest priority. Each will put his welfare and security first. However, the result *need* not be a Hobbesian war of all against all with no holds barred. States have repeatedly discovered that their welfare is bound up with the welfare of other states. And, looking at the situation historically, certain ameliorating factors have developed from the welter of political conflict. International law has been able to exercise *some* restraining effect, international congresses and associations (the United Nations is one) have been able to keep *some* tempers below the boiling point of destructiveness. As early as the eighteenth century, nations were aware of the need to justify their conduct before the bar of world opinion. In our own century, world opinion—in which humane morality is an important though not the sole factor —has been brought to bear at one time or another against Britain, Germany, Turkey, Japan, the Soviet Union, South Africa, India, and the United States, with various degrees of positive effect.

Whoever believes that standards of personal morality can and should be simply extended to cover political affairs may not sufficiently appreciate the relative but nonetheless concrete autonomy of the political order. Such a person, the politically minded critic would say, is *unpolitical,* and this is a defect in him. On the other hand, whoever believes that the political order is wholly cut off from the moral order may not appreciate the reason and authority of individual conscience, nor the continuity between individual virtue (as Plato would say) and the sovereign virtue of the state, which is *justice.* Justice—the rendering to each his due, fairly and impartially—is secured by *law.* Long after he finished his treatise *The Republic,* Plato wrote an even longer political document, *The Laws.* There cannot be an earthly state, he said, without laws and a constitution. In modern idiom, morality comes into politics, even world politics, by way of the mediating concept of law. We know that personal morality and law are far from being identical. But strong threads connect them—the need for social cooperation and for reason and order in human affairs if life is not to be, in Hobbes's phrase, nasty, brutish, and short.

In fact, the argument for a real difference between personal and political morality could be used logically to defend the view that states should be *more,* not less, moral than individual persons. We know that in order to act ethically one must have alternatives to choose from. The spectrum of alternatives available to a modern nation with developed resources is greater than that available to many, if not most, of its individual citizens. Moreover, the state has the resources and means to create knowledge and awareness on many issues far surpassing that available to an individual person. Hobbes's social contract theory teaches that the state was constructed by humans in order to prevent or diminish the injuries men would do to each other, out of their own self-seeking instincts, in the state of nature. In other words, that political entity we call the state was created in order to be more moral than its individual members.

Law and the State: Democracy

According to classical social contract theory, the state comes into being when men, realizing that their own greed and violence in the state of nature would destroy them, agreed to hand over ("alienate") some of their individual powers and rights to an agency that would in return protect them from one another's aggression. This entity, the state, controls its members by law and provides sanctions, including punishment, to enforce these laws. In the Anglo-American tradition of political theory, the best government is usually held to be one that most efficiently and fairly secures the common safety and welfare with a minimum of individual coercion. John Stuart Mill's principle in his essay "On Liberty" is often cited:

That principle is, that the sole end for which mankind are warranted, individually or collectively, in interfering with the liberty of action of any of their number, is self-protection. That the only purpose for which power can be rightfully exercised over any member of a civilized community, against his will, is to prevent harm to others. His own good, either physical or moral, is not a sufficient warrant. He cannot rightfully be compelled to do or forbear because it will be better for him to do so, because it will make him happier, because, in the opinions of others, to do so would be wise, or even right. . . .[9]

In common with most political theorists, however, Mill believed that the individual has certain *obligations* to the state. These include an obligation to obey just laws. The state may legitimately *exact* from the individual duties that the individual may be quite averse to performing such as paying taxes. Conformity to law, Mill thought, is the mother-idea of justice.

In our political tradition, representative *democracy* is usually considered to be that form of government that best combines efficiency and fairness, respect for the individual and the common welfare, respect for law and justice. (At this point the reader may wish to refer to our earlier discussion of the views of Mill and Rawls on general happiness and justice as fairness. See Chapter 3, pp. 74–77.) Indeed, some political theorists hold that democracy is not just one among many alternative forms of government, but the only true *political* form. There are other ways of governing people—absolute monarchies, dictatorships, military juntas, and the rest—but these are not truly political; they are *nonpolitical* ways of ruling over people. The democracy of the ancient Greek city-states was relatively *direct*. Slaves and foreigners were not admitted to citizenship, but each citizen participated directly in the government of his city-state. Plato reasoned that democracy was a pretty poor form of government, since the level of "the many" could not logically be that of "the best." Democracy, to Plato, meant amateurs meddling in government. He felt that governing is a task requiring the highest degree of specialized training. Left to itself a democracy would degenerate into anarchy, a political condition so disastrous that the people would welcome a tyrant if only he would bring order out of chaos. Aristotle believed that a democracy with a constitution (he calls it a "polity") was a good practical government for a state in which the middle class formed the largest group.[10] The founding fathers of the American Republic were familiar with classical political theory as well as with English political philosophy, particularly that of Locke, who advocated broad principles of tolerance in civil government. Our founders, however, were suspicious of *direct* democracy. In the *Federalist Papers,* James Madison wrote that the main cause of strife in the state is *factions.*[11] By factions, he had in mind the poor versus the rich. To avoid possible tyranny of the poorer citizens (who were in the majority) over the wealthier ones (who were fewer), Madison advocated *representative* government. Majority rule would be safeguarded, but the representatives elected by that majority would be above the factional strife that a direct confrontation of rich and poor would engender.

Anarchism

Representative democracy based on the rule of the majority and amalgamated with socialist ingredients to meet the problems of the welfare state satisfies the conditions laid down by many political theorists for a theoretically sound and practically workable form of government. But the *anarchist* is not satisfied. He believes that *all* government is inherently bad, including majoritarian democracy (i.e., a government in which issues are decided by majority vote). Proudhon pointed out that the laws of the traditional commonwealth protect property, and he claimed that "property is theft."[12] While some governmental arrangement between capital and labor would survive for a time, eventually humans would progress to a stage where government would no longer be necessary. Of course, restraint is necessary if humans are to live together. But anarchy is a system in which all restraint comes from within a person, not from fear of external law. Thus Proudhon. Mikhail Bakunin offered headier wine. "The tempest and life," he said, "that is what we need. A new world, without laws, and consequently free."[13] Under his ideological leadership, anarchism took to the streets in czarist Russia. Alexander II died at the hands of terrorists who believed that despotism can be overthrown by violence. In our own country, President McKinley was shot by a disturbed man inspired by the fiery speeches of anarchist leaders. Sacco and Vanzetti were anarchists, and their celebrated case still provokes arguments as to whether they were executed for murder in the course of armed robbery or for their radical political beliefs.[14]

Because of its association with other problems raised by widespread social disturbances of the 1960s, anarchism—at least of a theoretical sort—has attracted the interest of some contemporary moral philosophers. In his essay "In Defense of Anarchism," Robert Paul Wolff argues that the fundamental problem of political philosophy is the question of "how the moral autonomy of the individual can be made compatible with the legitimate authority of the state."[15] Wolff reasons from Kantian premises. Kant taught that the individual person is truly autonomous; insofar as he is a person, he cannot be subject to the will of another. Personal autonomy means that I submit only to laws I have made for myself. If I am a person, hence autonomous, I may obey another person's command, not because he commands me, but because I freely choose to do so. Inherent in the very meaning of the state, Wolff argues, is its authority, its power over persons. One cannot live as a member of a state without surrendering a portion of one's autonomy. The only exception to this rule is a person who is a member of a *direct* democracy, in which every person votes on every issue and all votes must be unanimous if a measure is to be approved. But a direct democracy is out of the question in contemporary industrial and technological society. Hence the only moral alternative to the forfeiture of autonomy required even by a majoritarian democracy is *anarchy,* a social arrangement in which each individual will is sovereign, free of any compulsion exerted through the laws of the state. Wolff does not advocate that we should all do our best to put anarchy into immediate practice. He does argue that we should understand that there is no *moral* reason why people should forfeit their autonomy to the state, even when the state is, like our own, a majoritarian democracy.[16] The autonomy and sovereignty of the state are incompatible with the autonomy and sovereignty of the individual person. But the latter has priority. Therefore, the former must, in *moral* principle, give way.

This argument in favor of anarchy has weight provided that we admit its premise—the absolute moral autonomy of the individual person. The argument seems to draw confirming strength from the traditional teaching—defended by Aquinas, Luther, and Kant—that neither the state nor highest religious authority can command the individual conscience. This teaching says that when religious or political commands conflict with my reasoned conviction concerning right or wrong for me *in a particular situation,* it is my conscience that renders final judgment. But it does not follow from this doctrine that the individual person's moral autonomy is absolute in every respect. The belief in absolute personal autonomy appears rather late in human history, and even today it is not shared by all. For millennia, Indian sages have maintained that any form of absolute personal reality is *maya,* illusion. In our own culture and day, the behaviorist tradition in psychology, represented by B. F. Skinner, claims that the idea of absolute personal autonomy ("dignity," "the absolute worth of the individual person") was valuable for human progress in a certain historical context; but the idea has now outlived its usefulness and threatens to become an obstacle in the way of solution of urgent social problems. The danger in such positions is the fallacy of contraries: if not all, then none; if not black, then white. Without going to either Indian or behaviorist extreme, a critic might argue that absolute personal autonomy can neither be demonstrated in theory nor confirmed in practice. If the individual person were completely autonomous he could not be a social being, as Aristotle was the first to point out. If each of us were absolutely autonomous human society would not *be* a society, but only an aggregate of individual persons, like marbles in a box.

In his wartime writings, such as *Being and Nothingness,* Sartre pushed personal moral absolutism about as far as it would go. Thereafter he modified his radical individualism in the direction of "humane" Marxism. As for Kant himself, for all his emphasis on the moral autonomy of the individual person, he did not believe autonomy to be absolute in every respect. He did not think that morality was compromised by one's duties as a citizen. Nor did Luther or Aquinas believe that one's personhood was compromised by obedience to the legitimate laws of the state. The founder of the Christian religion, who preached a new and radical moral autonomy in religious terms, said "Render to Caesar the things that are Caesar's."[17] That legendary star might not have shone over Bethlehem had not his parents made a journey in obedience to a Roman statute.

Critics of theoretical anarchy of the kind which appeals to the Kantian principle of personal autonomy may argue this way. Let us grant the principle of the moral autonomy of individual conscience where a particular moral decision is concerned. But it does not follow that we can extend this to the far wider principle that a person cannot surrender to a government any part of his autonomy without moral compromise. As Durkheim pointed out, it is both logically and empirically impossible to conceive of a society without laws. Since most men do not have the capacity to act according to law *within* themselves without treading on the autonomy of other men, external laws and a state with the power to enforce them are necessary.

The Ethics of Revolution and Violence: Marcuse

In our own day we have seen and felt the dynamic of armed revolution against established governments in many parts of the world. The success of violent uprisings against colonial and postcolonial governments and the failure of "big power" counterinsurgent techniques to wipe out guerilla warfare and national liberations movements quickly brought attention to the idea of the justification of violent revolt, with particular emphasis on its political and moral correlates. In our country, the black ghetto disturbances of the 1960s and 1970s plus the emergence of militant revolutionary organizations such as the Black Panthers raised the specter of rebellion by force against constituted authority. The problem was pulled into sharp focus by the student uprisings of the same decades. Berkeley, Columbia, Cornell, and other scenes of campus unrest dramatized the claim that violent disobedience to authority actually *can* bring about positive changes and improvements to the social situation. Universities temporarily ceased to be institutions ruled by "reason and civility," but when the dust settled few, even among the conservatives of faculties and student bodies, were willing to go back to the old ways when the nod of a dean and the fiat of trustees were absolute.

Many will say that those disturbances were revolts, not revolutions. But these days it is not always easy to draw a clear line between the two—the word *revolution* is often applied even to minor shifts in social attitude. In any case, we may ask: do the predicates of ethics and morals apply to revolutions, big or little? The French Revolution of 1789 might well have succeeded without the Terror, though it is doubtful that it could have without violence. Was that revolution immoral? Or moral? The concepts do not seem to fit. If by "moral" in this connection we mean "justified" or even "we're rather glad now that it happened rather than not," few of us would deny the morality of the Glorious Revolution of 1688 that put an end to Stuart absolutism; of the American Revolution; of the French Revolution; of the Russian Revolution; and even of the Chinese Communist Revolution that pushed Chiang Kai-shek out of mainland Asia and, in time, brought the new China to the United Nations.

The subject of revolution, justifiable or not, is a thorny one; it takes for its province vast areas of politics and history. Herbert Marcuse says that *some* revolutions and their attendant violence can be justified ethically. Marcuse is the philosophical father of the student revolts of the 1960s. He holds that the world is dominated by a global "corporate capitalism," a huge economic, social, and military complex that *uses* democratic institutions for its own purposes. Even the "socialist" countries (like the USSR) are kept at bay by the mighty productive forces of corporate capitalism and are forced into defensive postures requiring rigid bureaucracies and competitive coexistence measures in order to survive. One does not look today to the Kremlin for revolution. In his "Essay on Liberation," Marcuse declares that although ghetto populations may provide the first "mass basis" of revolt, they are not capable of revolution. At present, neither the masses of the ghettos nor the activist students have anything like the material power they would need to stand up to the tremendous productive might and hold of corporate capitalism. But Marcuse finds it encouraging to note that student opposition is spreading in the old socialist as well as in capitalist countries. The "great refusal" takes many forms.[18]

Though his attitude toward the Western socioeconomic system is uncompromisingly hostile, Marcuse's analysis of the conditions justifying revolution and violence seems as formalistic and judicious as that of any traditional professor of political philosophy. In his essay "Ethics and Revolution," Marcuse asks whether a revolution can be justified as right and good, not just in political, but in ethical and moral, terms.[19] By "revolution" Marcuse means "the overthrow of a legally established government and constitution by a social class or movement with the aim of altering the social as well as the political structure."[20] By "right" and "good" Marcuse means that which would serve "to establish, to promote, or to extend human freedom and happiness in a commonwealth, regardless of the form of government."[21] To claim ethical and moral justification, he says, a revolution must be able to point out *rational grounds* to those to whom it appeals; these grounds must set forth real possibilities for freedom and happiness, as well as the adequacy of the means proposed by the revolutionaries to attain them.

To succeed in accomplishing such a shift in the social center of gravity, Marcuse says, revolution will almost always imply violence. Historical experience shows that violence has been necessary to sweep away unjust and oppressive social conditions, to replace the worse by the better. Modern society could not have emerged without the civil wars in 17th century England, the American and French revolutions—and all of them entailed violence. So did the Russian revolution. Terror is never justified as an end in itself, but it may be required as counterviolence. Liberation will always involve a certain amount of coercion as well as a degree of relative unfreedom. For one thing, the liberty of the oppressing classes will certainly be interfered with; their rights will be abrogated and their privileges taken away.

But how to decide whether the revolution is morally justified? Marcuse proposes a set of criteria, "historical calculus," by which the claims for or against moral justification of a revolution can be weighed. Rational grounds for justifying revolution must take into account how much evil, injustice, oppression, and victimization there is in the older society; how much sacrifice, injury, and death in war it demands of its adherents. One must consider the material and cultural resources of the older society, ponder to what degree they are being used to bring about a peaceful and happy existence to its members under the status quo. On the other side, the calculus must weigh the chances of the revolution for success, for making the worse better, for substantially improving the condition of the society as currently constituted. If such a calculus seems to be cold-blooded and inhumane, Marcuse suggests that critics think of the coldness of history. History itself is inhumane.

But the inhumanity of history cannot be used as a base from which to justify every form of violence and suppression in the name of revolution. Marcuse agrees. There are forms of violence and fear *no* revolutionary situation can morally justify. Arbitrary violence, indiscriminate cruelty, and terror for terror's sake contradict the end and purpose for which revolution is a means. Violence cut off from reason cannot be defended from *any* ethical point of view.

Accepted moral standards are closely connected, if not identical, with the values of established society. For this reason, Marcuse says, revolution will always seem to that society immoral by definition. Revolution proposes to crush the rights of the existing state, to allow and even to require deceit, robbery, destruction of property, and the taking of human life. The ethical justification of the revolution must be objective, that is, in terms of good results to those formerly deprived and oppressed. If the proposed revolution is to be in line with the objective tendency of the outstanding revolutions of modern times, its projected results must include the broadening of the entire spectrum of liberty, the bringing of a better life to greater numbers of people, and the lifting of the burden of oppression from the victims of a society whose arbiters of power ignore the quality of human life.

Many readers of Marcuse have been made uncomfortable by his stern indictment of "corporate capitalism." They have been frightened by his call for the end of capitalist societies, committed to "oppression" through their "mania for production and power." But so far as Marcuse's criteria for a justified revolution are concerned, they do not seem inconsistent with the rational tradition of Bentham and Mill as well as the whole tradition of

Anglo-American liberal political theory. Marcuse's historical calculus for discriminating between ethically justifiable and unjustifiable revolutions turns on the postulate of maximizing happiness —the traditional moral axiom of the utilitarians. The Marcusean view of the ethically justified revolution as one that "increases individual freedom and happiness" is almost self-evidently true in utilitarian terms, and perhaps it is this abstract quality that critics of Marcuse's criteria find unsatisfactory. Marcuse's criteria may be useful for judging the moral quality of revolutions after the fact—when they have become history, like the American, French, and Russian revolutions. But what rational grounds do the criteria provide in the gathering storm, before the fact? A revolution ethically justified before the fact is an impossible ideal, according to Albert Camus: "Rebellion sets us on the path of calculated culpability. Its sole but invincible hope is incarnated in innocent murderers."[22]

Civil Disobedience

The social unrest of recent years has focused new attention on the concept of civil disobedience. Thoreau's refusal to pay his poll tax stemmed from his opposition to the United States' war against Mexico. In our day, the civil rights conflict and the Vietnam War provided the context for a massive wave of civil disobedience. Demonstrations in violation of local law, sit-downs to obstruct normal business or teaching routines, refusal to pay taxes, occupation of administrative offices, public violation of federal law by burning draft cards, and so on have called into question anew the obligation of the citizen to obey all laws and to the circumstances, if any, under which he or she may be justified in disobeying them.

Civil disobedience is an old or new idea depending on the understanding we have of the term. It was a commonplace of medieval thought that a person has the right, under special circumstances, to disobey an unjust law. Scholars such as Aquinas and Maimonides were alert to the possibility of conflict between civil and religious commands. Hence they taught that, when the sovereign requires something against the moral law, the subject owes first duty to his conscience. The line from this doctrine descends (with some wriggles) to the U.S. Supreme Court's declaration that the "Bill of Rights recognizes that in the domain of conscience there is a moral power higher than the State."[23]

But Aquinas and his colleagues believed the authority of the state was derived from God and advocated putting up with unjust laws of a legitimate sovereign so long as these laws did not raise ultimate questions of conscience. These would occur if a ruler commanded his subjects to do something in clear violation of Divine Law. Centuries earlier, Plato's Socrates took a conservative stand on obedience to government even though he himself was regarded by his city-state as a public nuisance and a threat to legitimate authority. When Socrates was in prison he was asked by his friends why he did not try to escape—it would have been easy, and the Athenian government would have looked the other way. He replied that by the very act of living as a citizen of a state one accepts a contract with that state to obey its laws, even those he considers unjust.[24] Some years after Socrates' death, Aristotle observed that our duty to the state is not absolute; a good citizen, he said, can be a bad man. This is particularly likely if his state is a bad state.[25]

Contemporary moral philosophers tend to take a rather liberal attitude toward civil disobedience. They point out that it should not be confused with revolution. The civil disobedient wishes only by his action to protest against an unjust law with the purpose of calling attention to its injustice and thereby getting it changed. He does not want to overthrow the government or to replace the social system with an entirely new one. Unlike the revolutionary, the civil disobedient willingly submits to arrest and prosecution and accepts the penalty for his violation of the law. Thus understood, civil disobedience does not mean contempt for law. Martin Luther King said: "I submit that an individual who breaks a law that conscience tells him is unjust and willingly accepts the penalty by staying in jail to arouse the conscience of the community over its injustice, is in reality expressing the very highest respect for law."[26]

Just what is the definition of civil disobedience and what are the conditions under which it may be justified? According to John Rawls, an act of civil disobedience is a political act, that is, an act justified by moral principles that underlie a right conception of civil society and the public good. Such an act is a public nonviolent and conscientious act contrary to law, usually done with the intent of bringing about a change in the policies or laws of the government. Rawls does not say that the existence of every unjust law requires that one must disobey it. His position is not that of Augustine, who said, "That which is not just seems to be no law at all," or of Thoreau, who could hardly wait to transgress an unjust law. Professor Rawls holds that citizens of a majoritarian democracy stand under a social contract to obey the decision of that majority:

In agreeing to a democratic constitution . . . one accepts at the same time the principle of majority rule. Assuming that the constitution is just and that we have accepted and plan to continue to accept its benefits, we then have both an obligation and a natural duty . . . to comply with what the majority enacts even though it may be unjust. . . .[27]

But is the unjust law to be put up with in all circumstances? When is enough enough? Rawls lays down three conditions warranting civil disobedience: it is justified

1. when one is subject to injustice more or less deliberate over an extended period of time in the face of normal political protests,
2. when the injustice is a clear violation of the liberties of citizenship, and
3. provided that the general disposition to protest in a similar manner in similar cases would have acceptable consequences.

Rex Martin lists six conditions of "justified" civil disobedience.

1. The citizen does not violate the law on the ground that he opposes the governmental authority behind the law. That is, he does not wish to destroy the government or its rule of law.
2. The citizen admits that the law against which he protests, however unjust it may be, was derived democratically as part of the "law of the land."
3. The citizen does not intend that his action cause the replacement of democratic political procedures with nondemocratic ones.
4. The citizen is acting not merely out of self-interest, but in the interest of the public good, justice, social utility, human rights.
5. In disobeying the law, the citizen wishes to act nonviolently. He does not intend harm to person or property.
6. The citizen should disobey the law publicly and on the condition that he is willing to take the consequences as regards punishment.[28]

A radical critic would probably find the criteria for civil disobedience justification rather abstract and formalistic. Under such conditions, he would say, civil disobedience is reduced to a pretty tame affair, with little dynamic for real social change—barely distinguishable from Uncle Tomism. Civil disobedience under conditions so circumspect, so careful, so deliberately *non*revolutionary, can accomplish little lasting good in the face of injustice and oppression. Gandhi's program of civil disobedience forbade violence, but at least it *was* revolutionary. Without that ingredient of revolution his program would not have led to a new social order, to the independence of India and its emergence as a great modern state. Moreover, civil disobedience that begins as nonrevolutionary may escalate to revolutionary proportions. The civil disobedience that began our American Revolution soon led to measures that were revolutionary *and* violent. Ten years before the "shot heard 'round the world" at Concord, the Sons of Liberty burned the records of the vice-admiralty court at Boston, ransacked the home of the comptroller of finance, and looted the house and library of Chief Justice Hutchinson—all in "civil protest" against the Stamp Act. Civil disobedience without violence, yes, but is it possible? Civil disobedience itself may be a *form* of violence.

In his turn, the conservative critic may complain that the seriousness with which many intellectuals today take the concept of civil disobedience is just another example of the current mode of dragging in the claims of individual conscience and personal morality to cover every conceivable social and political issue. In stretching the moral territory this way, this critic says, we are led to *devalue* the legal realm. In our eyes, then, the law becomes something *opposed* to morality. So it seemed to Yale Chaplain William Sloane Coffin, Jr., when he characterized the murder trial of the Black Panthers at New Haven as "legally right but morally wrong."[29] The conservative critic might cite Justice Benjamin Cardozo: "The constant insistence that morality and justice are not law, has tended to breed distrust and contempt of law as something to which morality and justice are not merely alien, but hostile."[30] The self-justifying civil dissenter, the conservative critic would conclude, does not have any monopoly on morality. The law too has its share.

Nearly all parties to the argument over the moral value of civil disobedience (except the anarchist) would concede that we have a prima facie obligation to obey the law. That is, the fact that a law exists is an indication that we should obey it—if not, show why not. The burden of proof is on the person advocating civil disobedience. He must show that there is grave reason for *not* obeying the law. It is one thing to say that there may be cases of law in which serious conscientious objection may be brought forward. It is another to conclude from this that one's obedience to every law should be a matter of conscience, to be judged in each instance in terms of personal morality.

Morality and Law
Law and morality are not identical, but there are areas of overlap between the two realms. For example, it is generally held by both jurists and laymen that murder, stealing, and certain other crimes are both morally and legally wrong. But an important difference between morality and law is that law focuses its concern on the general good of the community, while morality goes beyond this in its concern with individual good. Law takes little account of motives, while morality gives motive much weight. Law imposes physical sanctions, such as fine or imprisonment, while moral sanctions do not go beyond the reproach of individual conscience or the disapproval of other people—though the latter may extend, in extreme cases, to social ostracism.

The *purposes* of law are usually said to be concerned with providing that order and security without which humans could not live together and survive. But undue stress on the order and security aspect of law may lead to thinking of law only as a negative restraining force, a rigid system of controls superimposed on human lives. But law has the positive end of securing *justice*—"rendering to each his due," as Plato says, seeing to it that what is required of one citizen for the good of the whole is fairly and impartially required of another. Legality and justice act by known rule, open to public scrutiny. This is not the case in a tyranny. A legal system presupposes that we know or can know the laws we are supposed to obey. It assumes some uniformity of procedure that such like cases will be given like treatment. There is no need to think of law only as a rigid structure designed to preserve the status quo and to inhibit all positive change. Law itself can be an instrument of social change. This has certainly been true in the United States, where social change has often been given impetus from decisions of the courts. The trade union movement, monopoly control, suffrage reform, and social welfare are just a few areas in which the decisions of the courts have implemented programs of social change. The Supreme Court decision in the case of *Brown* v. *Board of Education* in 1954 ushered in the contemporary era of civil rights reform.

The women's rights movement of recent years was given powerful support when the High Court in 1971 struck down as unconstitutional job-hiring practices that discriminated against women.

Jurists still dispute how much, if any, of the foundation of law is morality. The "natural law" theorists (deriving from Aquinas and late medieval thought) hold that the basis of law and morals alike is "right reason" applied to problems raised by our relations one to another, to nature, and to God. Natural law theory distinguishes between natural law and positive law. Positive law is man-made. Though it depends on natural law, it need not itself have any direct foundation in the natural order. Critics of natural law theory say it is hard to see just how promise-keeping, which is indeed a social virtue, has any foundation in the natural order. In nature there are neither promises nor keeping of promises. In any case, say the critics, theory of law is best served by keeping the ethical out of it as much as possible. Hans Kelsen says, "The concept of law has no moral connotation whatever."[31]

In the Anglo-American tradition, law is thought to be concerned only incidentally with goodness or morality. What is relevant is the guilt or innocence of the accused. Political and civil liberties, say defenders of this tradition, depend on this distinction between morality and guilt. A person's rights are far better protected if he can be prosecuted only for having broken a particular law, not for being immoral. Oliver Wendell Holmes's explanation of this concept of law is classic:

What constitutes the law? You will find some text writers telling you that it is something different from what is decided by the courts of Massachusetts or England, that it is a system of reason, that it is a deduction from principles of ethics or admitted axioms or what not, which may or may not coincide with the decisions. But if we take the view of our friend the bad man we shall find that he does not care two straws for the axioms or deductions, but that he does want to know what the Massachusetts or English courts are likely to do in fact. I am much of his mind. The prophecies of what the courts will do in fact, and nothing more pretentious, are what I mean by the law.[32]

To Holmes's observation, the defender of the connection between morality and law may reply that we need not take the point of view of the "bad man" in this inquiry. *His* interest is to avoid running into trouble with the law, and to that end it behooves him to have a pretty good idea of what the courts will in fact do. *Our* inquiry has to do with whether or not there is at the foundation of law some irreducible moral element. Lord Patrick Devlin seems to think so. The criminal law of England, says this conservative jurist, has from the very first concerned itself with moral principles. As proof, he cites the fact that under law a crime has been committed even though the victim has consented to being injured. A man who kills or maims another who asks him to do so stands guilty under the law. Lord Devlin believes that the criminal law as we know it is based on moral principles, and that in the case of many crimes the function of that law is to enforce a moral principle:

There are certain standards of behavior or moral principles which society requires to be observed; and the breach of them is an offense not merely against the person who is injured but against society as a whole. . . . Every moral judgment, unless it claims a divine source, is simply a feeling that no right minded man could behave in any other way without admitting that he was doing wrong. It is the power of common sense and not the power of reason that is behind the judgments of society.[33]

Lord Devlin believes that a common moral sense, a faculty more akin to *feeling* than to *reason,* backs criminal laws against certain kinds of conduct. This viewpoint was sharply challenged in the debate that erupted in England after the Wolfenden Commission (1957) recommended that criminal laws against certain sexual practices—for example, homosexual conduct between consenting adults—be dropped on the ground that it is not the business of law to enforce what should be a matter of private morals. Following the line laid down by John Stuart Mill in his essay "On Liberty," H. L. A. Hart and others claim that it is not the business of law to enforce morality unless the breach of morality entails injury to others.[34] Lord Devlin's appeal to the moral sense of the average, decent, right-thinking citizen runs straight into the problem of how we distinguish moral sense from social prejudice. This is true in the case of homosexual acts, one of two classes of offenses the Wolfenden Commission recommended be removed from the judgment of public law to that of private morality, provided the acts in question were performed by consenting adults. Lord Devlin has stated that all decent people hold homosexual behavior in abhorrence, and that the outraged feelings of such citizens provide a sufficient basis for society's passing moral judgment on the matter and for society's enforcing that judgment by means of law. His critics have pointed out that it is hard to show that the term "the right-minded man" means any more than "the man who feels as Lord Devlin feels about homosexuality." Lord Devlin's position in this case seems no stronger than that of the man or woman who judges homosexuality to be immoral on the ground that "it makes me sick." The weakness of this type of position in moral matters was dramatized in the 1970 motion picture *Joe,* which took for its theme the conflict between American hard hats and the hippies, whose appearance and life-style disgusted the hard hats.

II

Science and Morality

Science and technology have been made to bear their share of blame for the "moral vacuum" and "dehumanization" many sensitive people feel in our highly organized society. Critics like Marcuse, Ellul, Roszak, and Reich have found our late-twentieth-century "corporate state" to be technologized to the point of moral paralysis.[35] There are those who believe that industrialized economy and runaway technology have so proliferated as to have irremediably spoiled the quality of human life. Scientists have been accused of "immorality" for lending their research talents to the state for military purposes. Scientists themselves had a "crisis of conscience" when the atom bomb was developed during World War II. The crisis extended into the postwar years, with deepening concern over the destructive potential of the hydrogen bomb. The sensitivity of American intellectuals to the use and abuse of scientific research by government has persisted to the present day. The academic community's moral rejection of the Vietnam War extended to its scientific apparatus and led to heightened uneasiness about the relation of science and technology to the moral life. Many American scientists today are critical of "the system." Some take this to be the military-industrial complex to which science and technology are necessary instruments; some go further and condemn the whole technological apparatus of today's society as inhumane.

Discoveries in science and technology have always been closely related to the needs of the societies of which they are a part and have had, as we know, enormous social consequences. No need here to recap the massive social changes that followed the discovery of steam power in the West. The chronicle of the Industrial Revolution is too well known; so too is the tale of the transformation of the United States from an agricultural-rural to an industrial-urban state within a decade or two of the Civil War.

The story of the exploitation of science and technology for military purposes is quite old.[36] The ancient world possessed crude assault chemicals like "Greek fire," as well as ballistic machines such as those the Roman army used for siege purposes. Gunpowder was known in the Middle Ages, having been brought to the West from China, where it was used in fireworks and primitive handguns. It was Europe that first exploited gunpowder for the use of cannon; there was no turning back from that road. The notebooks and drawings of Leonardo da Vinci show how much thought this great artist and inventor gave to machines designed for military purposes—though none of his inventions seem to have had much practical effect on warfare. World War I initiated the development and use of poison gas, a technological development hastily foresworn by the major powers at the war's end. (The balance of power in lethal chemicals anticipated the later nuclear standoff among the superpowers in the decades following World War II.) Far more important than its chlorine or mustard gas was the powerful shove World War I gave to the development and mass production of automobiles and aircraft. World War II opened a new and larger Pandora's box from which an astonishing line of scientific and technological "gifts" emerged, the two most outstanding being radar and atomic power.[37]

So far as the question of science and morality was concerned, the early-twentieth-century scientist tended to reflect the Continental European (particularly, the German) image of the scientist as one whose dedication to reason and objective truth set him apart from the rest of the world and from concern with its mundane social and moral bickerings. In the early 1930s in England, a few scientists, such as J. D. Bernals and his school of "scientific humanists," repudiated this allegedly ivory-tower isolation. Concerned over the economic and social conditions of the world during the Great Depression, the scientific humanists blamed capitalist society and the profit motive for many social ills and looked with hope to the socialist experiment in the Soviet Union. In England the scientific humanists were opposed by anti-Marxist scientists, such as Michael Polanyi, J. R. Baker, and their Society for Freedom in Science. But the big shock to the "ivory tower" position of European scientists came with the rise to power of war-oriented Germany under Hitler's leadership. Top European scientists fled from Germany and other countries to England and the United States to put their talents at the services of their host countries. In 1938 the German physicists Otto Hahn and Fritz Strassmann published a paper showing that nuclear fission was possible. Refugee scientists Lise Meitner, Leo Szilard, and Albert Einstein sounded the warning to the Western democracies concerning the terrible weapon that could be produced on the basis of nuclear fission research. President Roosevelt initiated the Manhattan Project, and a crash program for the atom bomb was on. Led by Robert Oppenheimer, a team of scientists working in the United States was successful and in due course solemnly watched the test shot of the new weapon at Alamogordo, New Mexico. The bomb would shortly be dropped on the Japanese cities of Hiroshima and Nagasaki, and World War II would come to an end. "The physicists have known sin," said Oppenheimer, "and this is a knowledge which they cannot lose."[38]

Postwar tensions marked the development of the hydrogen bomb—a weapon far more powerful than that which wiped out Hiroshima. Oppenheimer was reluctant to give the go-ahead signal on the new weapon—we will probably never know how much his moral distaste for the H-bomb led him to argue that its development was impracticable. But the new weapon *was* developed, and not only in the United States; the Soviet Union soon added the hydrogen bomb to its postwar arsenal. The nuclear standoff between the two superpowers became a tense reality. Oppenheimer likened Russia and America to two scorpions in a bottle, each capable of killing the other, but only at the risk of his own life. The years after Stalin's death brought a partial détente between the two superpowers.

Although today the lion's share of nuclear material still goes into atomic weapons deliverable by intercontinental ballistic missiles and by submarines themselves powered by nuclear energy, hope still exists that the use of atomic energy for benefit of mankind will one day outweigh its potential for the destruction of humanity. Some political analysts believe that this day will never arrive so long as our small planet is organized along the divisions of nation-states or superstates. Only a world government, these observers say, a new political arrangement in which national or ideological interests are subordinated to the common welfare of the planet, can remove the threat of nuclear holocaust and world graveyard.

Those who are puzzled by the charge of science's "threat" to moral values point out that scientists cannot be held responsible for the consequences of their researches. If a scientific discovery yields immediate beneficial application, but proves harmful in the long range, the only thing to do is to get rid of it and not blame the scientists. Thalidomide is a case in point, but not DDT nor atomic power because it is yet by no means clear that their long-range effects will prove inimical rather than beneficial to mankind. Those who talk about the corruption and dehumanization of science do not usually choose medical examples to illustrate their point. The removal of the terrors of diphtheria and poliomyelitis from children are instances that show that science is no cold metal-and-glass abstraction but has concrete existential effect on the "lived life" of humans, and that this effect is in the direction of the better rather than the worse. Intellectuals who adopt a position of antagonism to science do not seem to have any idea of what life was like before the development of experimental science; they appear incapable of imagining existence under the Black Death. Of course, the question of the part played by medical advance in the dangerous worldwide population expansion quickly comes up, but the difficulties of dealing with that serious problem do not require that we return to the days of Jean-Jacques Rousseau, when two out of every four children in France died. Today's analysts of population control recommend that ways be found—political, social, as well as scientific—to see that two rather than four children are born and that these two children stay alive to enjoy a decent life.

A common answer to the question whether science has ethical implications is that science is morally neutral. What is moral or immoral is the use to which science is put. John Dewey refused to accept that convenient answer. Ends do not lie wholly outside means, he said. Science contains great moral potential within itself. Dewey was thinking of more than the values of the scientific attitude usually cited—rationality, devotion to objective truth, extension of knowledge, universal sharing of results of research, etcetera.[39] He believed that science's moral potential resides in its power to transform the worse into the better. Dewey argued that it has been demonstrated that science already has improved the human condition, and science has the power to permanently improve the condition of life. Scientific method is concerned with the control and improvement of our material environment; methods in morals help us deal with those problems that arise from our relation to other humans. But the two methodologies, the scientific and the moral, are not cut off from each other. Rather, they interpenetrate. Science has enormous moral possibilities, for it has almost unlimited power to better the human condition. Moral problems can yield to the application of scientific method, for a moral problem is a situation of blocked action calling for reflection, hypothesis, intelligent choice, and confirmation in experience. Like other ends, moral ends are instruments by which we remove obstacles to practical action, that is, they are ends that are at the same time means. Ethics and morals are not compartmented off from science and technology. "Moral insight," Dewey says, "and therefore moral theory consist simply in the every-day workings of the same ordinary intelligence that measures dry-goods, drives nails, sells wheat, and invents the telephone."[40]

Complaints about the dehumanizing effects of a "mechanized" society have been heard since industrialization began in the western world. The problem was horribly acute in Engels's day, and his book *Conditions of the Working Classes in 1845* was a powerful force in exposing the enslavement of human beings to machines owned by their masters.[41] Those who find positive moral value in science and technology point out that it is a little late for moralistic critics of the 1970s to get worked up about the problem of machine versus man. Poets and film makers of the 1920s and 1930s played nearly every variation on that theme. Chaplin's movie *Modern Times* exposed the problem of man against machine as effectively as Reich's *Greening of America*—and it was much funnier. Like sex and the family car, science and technology are here to stay. "For society to quarrel with technology," says Edward de Bono, "is like a man quarreling with his legs."[42] We live in a world that cannot be detechnologized save by a nuclear disaster, the threat of which is still real, which could in one stroke put us back into a preindustrial age—at least for a time. Paul Goodman asks, "Can technology be humane?"[43] Perhaps the query resolves itself into a different question: Can society be humane? Or does this question assume the essential moral neutrality of science and technology, which Dewey denies? In any case, the fact that so many American scientists conscientiously objected to the way in which their government was putting science and technology to use in Vietnam (e.g., napalm and chemical defoliants) is evidence that scientists are at least as concerned as other people when humane values are threatened. If science is indifferent to morals (and this is arguable), scientists are not.

III

Moral Obligation to Nature?
Large numbers of young people who have rejected "the system," with its six or eight approved careers for youths and its stress on gain, competition, and getting ahead, have turned to the beauty of the earth, the reality of our natural environment to defend it from spoilage and pollution by the further encroachment of a feverishly expanding industrial society. In so doing, the young people have moved a step toward the classical position of the East toward nature—nature is an object of interest, not because it is something to be controlled or because of what we can get out of her, but because of the moral insight that it brings.

Of course, progressive youth has no monopoly on ecological concern over the pollution of our natural environment; the wastage of resources; the destruction of wildlife; the invasion of wilderness land for timber, minerals, real estate, and industrial development. The conservationist movement in this country goes back to the 19th century when the first lumber companies stripped the land of trees, leaving behind them eroded earth that could not hold the rainwaters. It took decades to bring the lumber and mining companies to book for their worst practices. But the protests of conscientious citizens who loved the land had their effect in governmental regulation against the more outrageous acts of thoughtless go-getters.

The conservation movement in this country is not very old if we consider its beginnings to be in the middle 1880s. At the century's turn, Gifford Pinchot, then chief of the Forestry Division of the Department of Agriculture, won Theodore Roosevelt's interest in the conservation cause. Their alliance, when Roosevelt became president, did much to save the nation's forests and other natural resources from destruction. Conservationist principles were soon extended to water resources, farmland, cattle ranges, minerals, and wildlife. The lumber and mining companies fought hard at first, but at length submitted to government regulation. Grudgingly or willingly, they began to develop their own conservation programs—just as nearly every industry has been forced to do today. While the early conservationists appreciated the value of forests and land as things of beauty in themselves, their primary justification of conserving resources was expressed frankly in terms of national utility and enlightened self-interest. Americans would need these precious natural resources in the future; it would be something like treason to waste them. Franklin D. Roosevelt carried on the conservation interests of his cousin in presidential office. His Civilian Conservation Corps gave work to thousands of young men in tending the land and forests, until the coming of World War II put an end to unemployment and directed priorities elsewhere.[44]

After World War II, a new breed of conservationists appeared. They were less concerned with governmental regulation of forest and mineral land than with protecting humans from the impact of air pollution, pesticides, and superexpanding junk yards. Rachel Carson's book *The Sea Around Us* (1951) brought to its readers a new "whole earth" sense of the beauty and reality of their natural environment. Her *Silent Spring* (1962) launched an attack on chemical insecticides, particularly DDT, and prompted the federal government to take action against air and water pollution. Horrified by what hamburger stands, pizza joints, and auto junk yards had done to American highways, Mrs. Lyndon Johnson threw her own personal talent as well as her weight as wife of the president of the United States into the antipollution fight. The Wilderness Bill of 1964 transferred nine million acres of national forest land into the wilderness preservation system. In the "new consciousness" atmosphere of the 1960s, activist young people gave the conservationist cause a dynamism and urgency that some found wanting in older private groups such as the Audubon Society and the Sierra Club. High school classes cleaned up roadsides and vacant lots, fought against detergent use, and supported the recycling of aluminum cans. Antipollution literature poured from libraries, bookstores, and newsstands. Radio, television, and motion pictures took up the cause. The 1970 film *Five Easy Pieces* conveyed a sense of the beauty of forests, cold mists, and arms of the sea, and also made some satirical observations on naïve ecological fanaticism. Whether the intensity of the current popular ecological enthusiasm has any relation to how long that enthusiasm will last remains to be seen.

By its very nature, industry tends to affect natural beauty adversely. A poor agricultural region may be more pleasing to the eye than a rich industrial one. Today a visitor to Oxford University in England cannot help being saddened by the press of its industrial surroundings. As early as 1879, the poet Gerard Manley Hopkins had noted it, in addressing his beloved Oxford:

Thou hast a base and brickish skirt there, sours
That neighbour-nature thy grey beauty is grounded
Best in; graceless growth, thou has confounded
Rural rural keeping—folk, flocks, and flowers.[45]

But industrial capitalism cannot be blamed exclusively for ecological catastrophe. Environmental pollution occurs in the socialist and in the emerging countries as well as in Western capitalist nations. As Americans were waking up to the fact that their Great Lakes were threatened by ecological death, Soviet citizens learned that their magnificent Lake Baikal had been seriously polluted by industrial wastes. In Tanzania, small rivers began to fill up with dead fish because of wastes discharged from fiber factories and coffee-processing plants. By free will or compulsion, industry has tried to do something to reform older bad practices; in the United States alone, industrial corporations spend hundreds of millions of dollars annually on conservation programs. A hopeful sign for the future is the use of atomic energy for power. Though there are problems of size reduction and radioactive waste disposal, atomic energy is achieved without the usual smoke and other air pollutants associated with the burning of coal and petroleum products.

Government and industry, however, are not the sole villains in the environmental drama. The real problem is the rapidly expanding world population. Where there is less room, there is more trampling on things. In his book *The Population Explosion,* Paul Ehrlich says: "Too many cars, too many factories, too much detergent, too much pesticide, multiplying contrails, inadequate sewage treatment plants, too little water, too much carbon dioxide—all can be traced easily to too many people."[46] There were 3.5 billion persons on the planet in 1970. Demographers project a population of 7 billion in the year 2000 and 14 billion in 2015 *if* the population growth rate of 2 percent continues and *if* there are no global catastrophes such as plague or thermonuclear war. The alleged geometrical rate of increase of global population itself raises some interesting moral questions.

Does the reader of this book or his or her children, present or to come, have a moral obligation to reproduce at zero rate of increase? It is almost an academic question so far as the American middle class is concerned, since this class appears to reproduce itself at a rate just a fraction above that. The more prolific sections of world population understandably resent being instructed by affluent whites to cut their birthrate. The caution is too easily interpreted in terms of racial control. The idea of genocide comes easily to the minds of minority ethnic groups and people of underdeveloped countries who are urged not to increase and multiply beyond demographic parameters. Some experts are not wholly pessimistic. So far as the United States is concerned, they point out that the birthrate has been declining since 1958. New methods of birth control plus liberalization of abortion procedures will further reduce the birthrate to livable proportions. By the early 1970s, the United States birthrate had declined sharply. Many elementary schools, maternity and pediatric hospital wards have been closed down for lack of customers. Fine for North America, for Western Europe, or even for Japan, goes the usual rebuttal—but what about the rest of the world? Increasing birthrates in Asia, Africa, and Latin America will catastrophically widen the gap between the starving poor of the larger part of the globe and the affluent whites holed up in their technological-industrial citadels. Some critics believe that this is just one of the problems, like war, insoluble as long as the people of the world cling to the political system of nation-states and superstates. They believe that prolongation of that system into the future is inconsistent with the good life.

As for the aesthetic argument, the concrete situation of many poor people in the world makes it hard for them to appreciate ecological arguments for unspoiled natural beauty. It makes little impression on a Cape Breton small farmer, who can no longer make ends meet, to tell him that selling his land for a trailer park will adversely affect the unspoiled loveliness of the Bras d'Or waters. He needs the money, and, besides, the vacationers themselves, whose camping trucks and trailers will park on the land he has sold, have come to enjoy the natural beauties they are charged with spoiling. A protein-hungry African tribesman, his blowpipe aimed at a feeding giraffe, will not be dissuaded by someone telling him what a beautiful animal the giraffe is and how few of them are left. "When a population is at bare subsistence level," says David Coyle, "the basic necessities of course take priority. The hungry citizen naturally cares more about eating than bird-watching."[47] The problem is not just one for poor countries. Many of the world's affluent nations, including the United States, are facing an energy crisis. The rapid rate of increase of demand for fuel to run machines and to supply power is rising well beyond the ready availability of natural fuel sources. The United States can no longer produce all of the oil it needs for petroleum products such as gasoline and fuel oil, and we are importing a large part of the oil we consume. This creates major balance-of-payments and national security problems. Nuclear energy, although increasingly available, is still very expensive. In the near future, some hard choices must be made. Certain North American natural fuel reserves can be tapped, but at the probable cost of some ecological damage. New automobiles equipped with pollution-control devices reduce mileage and increase fuel consumption. American oil companies are asking consumers to cut fuel consumption, join car pools, and to strike a balance in their environmental demands.

Faced with global questions like those of the dimensions of world pollution and possible world death, William James used to recommend deglobalizing them as the first step to solution. The problem of Evil with a capital *E* will advance a long way toward solution if each person would only try to take care of the evil in his own backyard: "The submission which you demand of yourself to the general fact of evil in the world, our apparent acquiescence in it, is here nothing but the conviction that evil at large is *none of your business* until your business with your private and particular evils is liquidated and settled up."[48] The state in which table and floor of the cafeteria or student union are left when undergraduates depart, after discussing ways and means of implementing ecological ideals, is a case in point. If we are to follow the humble precept, "Let each sweep his own doorstep," the whole problem might not be solved, but a beginning may have been made. At least so say William James and the legends on the New York City litter baskets.

Whether we have moral obligations with respect to nature is a question that requires at least one distinction before an answer can be tried. The obligation to treat our natural environment in a nonexploitive way can be taken simply as a corollary of the obligation to respect the claims of other humans. The traditional ethic of woodsmen, hikers, and campers includes the rule to clean up, to tidy the fire area, and to leave some fresh wood

—all in consideration for the next person who comes along. So the most obvious justification of the ecological ethic is the reasonableness of treating nature in such a way as to share its enjoyment and continued use with those who come after us. To gut the environment for our own selfish purposes is to deprive others of those fruits of the earth to which they have as much right as we.

A harder question is whether, apart from human benefit, we have any moral obligation toward nature in itself. One answer is that the kingdom of beauty is as sovereign as the moral realm and that we have an obligation, aesthetic as well as moral, to treat the beauty of nature as an end in itself. In his graduation speech at Harvard, young Thoreau said, "This curious world which we inhabit is more wonderful than it is convenient: more beautiful than it is useful: it is more to be admired than to be used." Some may take this rule to imply that there is a value in *variety,* that we have an obligation to preserve, not to destroy, the plenitude of nature's forms, organic or inorganic. The destruction of a rare species (whales, tropical birds, tigers) or the elimination of a beautiful waterfall removes irretrievably an aspect of nature's variety.

A related argument is that man is not discontinuous with nature, but rather is part of it, and that therefore we have a certain moral obligation to respect nature's autonomy as an extension of our own. Albert Schweitzer extended the ethical postulate of respect for *human* life to respect for *all* life. He seized his key idea of "reverence for life" a moment after he had seen a herd of hippopotamuses break the surface of an African river.[49] As a young scholar, Schweitzer had been disturbed by the fact that all moral philosophers wrote as if "man's ethics end with men, that man's concern is centered on man, and that man's unselfishness ends with men."[50] Schweitzer declared that human ethics must go beyond the human, that we have a moral obligation to extend our loyalty and concern to all living things.

These arguments are attractive, even plausible, but they seem compromised by the fact that humans, like other living things, must exploit, indeed destroy and feed upon nature in order to live. Do we have a moral obligation to nonhuman animals? We do not act as if we had. The fact that we kill and eat them shows that we treat them as means, not ends, and do not feel a need to excuse ourselves for so doing. Slaughterhouses and meat-packing plants are not pleasant places to visit, but they are there all the same, and most of us do not often give a second thought to our use of their products. Nature herself seems to follow the axiom, "Eat or be eaten." Classical philosophers tried to put a good face on it: we are justified in our slaughter and enslavement of animals, they wrote, because the order of nature—with its levels of being arranged from lower to higher, each in turn dependent on the other—not only permits, but requires such use. Traditional moral theology taught that brute beasts are put here by God for human use.

The idea that wanton cruelty to animals is morally wrong no doubt represents a rather advanced stage in human ethical evolution. It is certainly a notion strange to other peoples and other times. Bertrand Russell was shocked to find that people in the Far East were often amused by the sufferings of animals.[51] (Russell himself was a relentless opponent of bullfighting.) Richard Brandt found that the Hopi shared all the ethical values to which he was accustomed, except that they were indifferent to animal misery and pain.[52] By what rational argument can one defend the position that cruelty to animals is wrong? One consideration is similar to that by which we judge indifference to human suffering to be wrong. "He is a man like me," we say, or "They are human beings too." Although nonhuman animals are not persons, they are living things. The argument against cruelty to them may take the form, "They too are living things like us. They too feel pain." One trouble is that many well-fed people who proclaim this principle tend to restrict their concern to animals of the cute furry kind, like rabbits, cats, or baby seals, forgetting the possible sensibilities of the less attractive amphibians or fish. ("They don't really *feel* anything!") Moral concern for nonhuman animals can be turned into a luxury of the affluent and is easily corrupted by sentimentality and displaced love. "I like a dog," said G. K. Chesterton, "so long as you don't spell his name backwards." Bashō, Japanese master of the *haikku,* wrote:

The ancient poet
Who pitied monkeys for their cries,
What would he say, if he saw
This child crying in the autumn wind?

Unless we all choose to become vegetarians—and some people think we would all be better off if we did—we cannot avoid killing and eating animals for food. We also recognize that, although we can make do with a virtuous cloth coat, some people in the world must still kill animals for their skins in order to clothe themselves. While we cultivate our fields with tractors, others must still use yoked oxen for this purpose. We should acknowledge as well that a certain amount of controlled experimentation on animals is necessary for advances in medical sciences, assuming that we are interested in controlling or eradicating certain terrible diseases that kill humans or other animals. (Thousands of monkeys were necessary for production of the Salk vaccine.) But most of us have come around to the conclusion that there is something wrong with killing animals for the fun of it. From the angle of expediency, we may argue that thoughtless killing may upset the balance of nature and bring on ecological injury in which we humans will be involved to our detriment. But more than that, we are coming to recognize the existence of a postulate—at least in part ethical—that every living thing has a prima facie claim on life and that if we override that claim in a particular instance we should be able to justify our action by sound reasons. That is why William James says:

The sentiment of honor is a very penetrating thing. When you and I, for instance, realize how many innocent beasts have had to suffer in cattle-cars and slaughter-pens and lay down their lives that we might grow up, all fattened and clad, to sit together here in comfort and carry on this discourse, it does, indeed, put our relation to the universe in a more solemn light.[53]

Schweitzer's ethical man acts as if he were illumined by that "solemn light":

He tears no leaf from a tree, he plucks no flower, and takes care to crush no insect. . . . If he walks on the road after a shower, and sees an earthworm which has strayed onto it, he bethinks himself that it must get dried in the sun, if it does not return soon enough to ground into which it can burrow, and so he lifts it from the deadly stone surface and puts it on the grass. If he comes across an insect which has fallen into a puddle, he stops a moment in order to hold out a leaf or a stalk on which it can save itself.[54]

IV

Personal Morality and Religion

Many today have tried to extend personal morality to the areas left vacant by the traditional organized religions, with which they have become dissatisfied. There is no question that formal religion no longer plays the part in people's lives that it once did. Even the most conservative of the surviving religious traditions have "reformed" themselves in keeping with the personalist and detheologizing trend of our day. Insofar as we see the traditional churches as part of the "establishment" or "the system," we tend to reject their claim to authority. Seeing pretense and hypocrisy as inseparable from ecclesiastical hierarchy, we demand the same "honesty" on the part of the church that we exalt as the leading virtue of personal life. Yet many people in our secular society find themselves still drawn to something they feel lies back of the formal doctrine and ritual of the religion they reject. University undergraduates continue to be interested in religion. At least, they take courses in it, compare Eastern and Western traditions, explore the spiritual and physical sources of mysticism. That they tend quickly to lose interest and to go on to something else should not be held against them. (Perhaps their teachers are at fault, or perhaps the standards of the time are inconsistent with serious study that does not yield quick rewards, or perhaps they try to find in ideas and concepts something that must first be deed and act.) The person and message of Jesus are the objects of a new round of popularity, even devotion. "Jesus people" take to the streets to preach their simplified gospel. An undergraduate does not have to be one of them to see Jesus as an "outsider," the sort older persons would condemn as a hippie type, complete with long hair, beard, and sandals, given to the company of disreputable people, preaching peace and love. Some observers have seen hard-cash confirmation of the Jesus idea in the success of the musicals *Godspell* and *Jesus Christ Superstar;* the latter enjoyed one of the longest runs for a musical in Broadway history. Leonard Bernstein's relatively formalistic *Mass,* though semi-pop in style, could not compete with *JCS* in popularity.

Whether there could be any religion at all that is not in some way "organized" is a tough question. While religion has always had its personal and inner aspect, it has never appeared without its external social side. In this, religion reflects the double aspect of the moral teaching that is part of it: morality as inner individual impulse—sympathy and love—and morality as social rule —survival and welfare of the group. When in the history of a particular religion a tendency supervenes to judge the worth of a human act exclusively in terms of its conformity to law, the claims of the inner impulse to love (agape, caritas) tend to be overlooked and the religious attitude becomes arid and formal. But when law, rule, Scripture, teaching, tradition—all that holds the religious body together as a social group—are waved aside in favor of a purely personal morality, that religious tradition runs like water into the sand and disappears.

One of the remarkable things about Jesus—insofar as we know him and his teachings from the documents that have come down to us—is the way in which his life and teaching dramatize the conflict between the claims of the inner impulse to love and the need to conform to external law. Jesus appears to have been a good Jew who taught reverence and respect for the law. But he insisted that conformity to the law, though necessary, was not sufficient if one were to achieve one's being at a time in history the culmination and end of which was thought to be not far off. He saw too that defining one's own personal worth solely in terms of conformity to the law led to the vice of hypocrisy, a failing for which the rabbi and wonder-worker from Nazareth had little patience. To him the authorities, secure in their virtue, are "whited sepulchres," "generation of vipers."[55]

What seems to have been particularly irritating to the authorities in Jesus's case was his apparent insistence that the highest virtue, the best lived life, meant going to extremes, going all out, trying to be *perfect* with little interest in what we would call the bourgeois virtues of moderation, reasonableness, and circumspection. He seems to have shown scant respect for the claims of the traditional institutions of family and property. He was rude to his mother ("Lady, what business is it of yours?"),[56] put the claims of his teaching above those of filial piety ("Let the dead bury their dead"),[57] and made quite plain that those people who followed his counsels of perfection would have to abandon conventional social arrangements.[58] His idea of love and peace apparently did not mean sweetness and light; he did not forbid unpeaceful means to realize love and peace. He said that his mission was not to bring peace, but a sword, to set sons against their fathers and daughters against their mothers.[59] This kind of talk could not possibly have sounded well in the ears of hard-pressed authorities who, at that particular place and moment in history, were terrified at the thought of a violent worsening of a social order already badly deteriorated.

The ethical teaching at the heart of the doctrine of the man called Christ (an honorific title meaning "the Anointed One," as

"Buddha" means "the Enlightened One") seems to be one common in some way to all the great religions of the world. This is the teaching that the highest personal good does not consist in aggrandizing the self, gathering for it, achieving, cutting a figure in the world, gaining and holding power over men—but rather in giving up the self. In surrender of self, one achieves it; in losing it, one finds it. "He that saveth his life, shall lose it: and he that loseth his life for my sake, shall find it."[60] Power over men and things is vain. Power appears to be a reality, all seek it, but in the end it turns to dust and ashes in one's hand. This moral teaching is at the heart of Judaism. Throughout its thousands of years, that great tradition has reminded men and women of the vanity of power. The Jews, says Lion Feuchtwanger,

. . . . knew that to exercise power and to endure power is not the real, the important thing. The colossi of force, did they not all go to rack and ruin one after another? But they, the powerless, had set their seal upon the world. And this lesson of the vanity and triviality of power was known by the great and small alike among the Jews, the free and the burdened, the distant and the near, not in definite words, not with exact comprehension, but in their blood and their feelings.[61]

Pascal, scientist and fervent Christian of the seventeenth century, thought much about the vanity of power, the illusion of action, the poverty of self. What does it mean, he asks, to be a powerful minister of state, a chancellor or university president but to have people crowding into your office every fifteen minutes, leaving you without one hour of the day when you can be alone and think about yourself. And yet to be made to sit in a room alone, with no books, no papers, no companions, no diversion, is torture; the self will do anything rather than abandon its feverish quest for something other than itself. It wants constantly to be with other people, to manage and manipulate them. It is afraid to look at itself. For the self is hateful, says Pascal: "The ego is hateful . . . it is essentially wrong since it makes itself the centre of everything; it is a nuisance to others because it tries to enslave them, for each 'ego' is the enemy and wants to be tyrant of all the rest."[62] The drag of self makes it hard to do good for purely natural motives; religious motives help us to do the good our natural self has little inclination to do.

If we turn to the Scriptures of the East we find the same lesson taught in the doctrine of *maya,* the Indian scriptures' teaching of the highly illusory nature of the world and of the individual self.

That the individual self is the absolute point of reference, that its nourishment, fattening, flourishing is the highest good constitutes the great error, the grand illusion, the sharpest arrow of suffering. No human, no living thing is separated from another like an isolated stronghold or autonomous citadel. Rather, we are part of everything that is. *Tat twam asi*—"This thou art." It is hard to give up the self, but there is sweetness in renunciation. Bsodnams Rgyamtso, third Gyalway Rimpoche of Tibet, says:

To others give the victory and the spoils; the loss and defeat take upon oneself.

All the efforts of wisdom must aim for our liberation from *samsara,* from all illusory hopes.[63] Some critics of the ideal of self-renunciation see in it little more than masochism, a delight in being made to suffer. Others find in it an ideology historically used by the ruling classes against social unrest, a means to get the ruled to lie down and get kicked. To these critics, the principle of renunciation is neither a good nor a moral one.

Other critics, more sympathetic to the notion of renunciation, giving up the world, dying to self, find it a beautiful moral ideal and a consolation in adversity. Like Nietzsche on suicide, the thought of it enables one to get through many a bad night. But even those sympathetic with the ideal of renunciation may remind us that the world is not an illusion, at least not an absolute one. We are part of the world and must live in it. The self too is part of that world, the self has a relative but nonetheless real autonomy, just as there is a real social and political order with which the self interacts. Just as one must come to terms with political realities without fear of defiling one's fingertips, so one must learn to deal with the self and otherselves, "hateful" though they may be. Action itself, it is true, may contain the seeds of corruption. Action may be a form of sleep or an insult to God. But, like the dear self, it is part of all we have. Buddhism and Judeo-Christianity alike call attention to the vanity of self and achievement, but both award an important degree of reality to practical action. Buddha asked his followers not to speculate on where the arrow of suffering comes from or what its construction is—the first thing is to think of ways of getting it out. Christ gave the world and its social and political order its due ("Render to Caesar the things that are Caesars") and even found something to admire in a swindling steward because he acted shrewdly according to the narrow principle of self-interest which was all the ethics he had.[64] Of course, one can always refrain from action, embrace illusion and nothingness. One can, when caught half-frozen in a mountain blizzard, lie down in the snow, lay back one's head, and sleep. This may be very sweet to do, but there is the question of not waking up again, in this world at least.

There are various ways, including certain drugs, of embracing illusions, putting pain to sleep, letting one's soul expand to what seems to be the limits of the cosmos, high above the urgency and venom of the world, far above the anxiety, suffering, the nagging realities that drag us down. But sometimes a price must be paid for this artificial paradise, particularly if longing for it pushes one to certain extremes. Kurt Vonnegut wrote a novel, *Slaughterhouse Five,* about the bombing of Dresden; one page is given to the state where "Everything was beautiful, and nothing hurt." But it is only a legend on a tombstone.[65]

Last Word
Moral conduct seems to require both handed-down principles and individual decisions in applying them. A society that relies too heavily on handed-down principles may find itself handicapped by moral rigidity. In his *Two Sources of Religion and Morality,* Bergson describes such a society as thinking of moral behavior solely in terms of compliance to the external rule of law. On the other hand, a people that pays little or no attention to moral principles, focusing exclusively on the worth of individual decision, personal sincerity or authenticity, or the promptings of the heart alone, may lack moral discipline and stability. Reflection on the age-old oscillation between reliance on tried-and-true principles and the instinctive seeking for the freedom of new and individual decisions may clarify for us today the actions of those who have chosen to revolt and those who have chosen accommodation. Rightfully will the rebels cry from the housetops, as the English moralist R. M. Hare says, that some or all of the old moral principles are worthless:

. . . some of these rebels will advocate new principles of their own; some will have nothing to offer. Though they increase the confusion, these rebels perform the useful function of making people decide between their rival principles; and if they not only advocate new principles, but sincerely try to live by them, they are conducting a moral experiment which may be of the utmost value to man (in which case they go down in history as great moral teachers), or may, on the other hand, prove disastrous both to them and to their disciples. . . . Morality regains its vigor when ordinary people have learnt afresh to decide for themselves what principles to live by, and more especially what principles to teach their children.[66]

So—since one must stop somewhere—perhaps the last word in moral theory is best left to the Anglo-American tradition of practical action and common sense. Those who still hold religious beliefs may think there may be more to it than that. When at the battle of Midway, the Japanese admiral Kusaka saw an American pilot just miss crashing his plane onto the bridge of the *Akagi,* cartwheeling instead into the sea he murmured a prayer for the pilot's soul. Then he turned back to defend his carriers. Prayer and battle. Today we may tend to think of these as just two polarized forms of folly. Or as an outmoded dualism, like the opposition of contemplation and action. It may be so.

The ancient Indian book, the *Bhagavad Gita,* tells of a young lord Arjuna, facing an enemy army. He hesitates to act, holds back the signal for battle. He ponders the death of so many on both sides that such an action will entail. Some of his kinsmen are in the opposing forces. He lowers his bow. But a higher wisdom (Krishna) counsels him to break of his hesitation. The world is what it is, though it is not the whole of reality. One must live in the world and act in it, if one is a part of it. There are many duties, certain social obligations that may be repugnant to our individual moral sense. This understandable repugnance should not paralyze our carrying out our obligation to the community of which we are a part. In the end, Arjuna gives the signal for battle.[67]

Prayer and battle, action and contemplation, what is and what ought to be—each has its own degree of reality, is the lesson of the ancient Hindu scripture. It may be that something of the same doubleness still holds in the realm of ethics and morals. There is the demand of external law, the need of discipline and order, the pressure of the social group that must have its way if the group is to survive. But then there is also the impulse of the individual loving or dissenting heart. Both have their claims, and these claims do not rest on illusion but on the double nature of things—on the way things are and on the way things should be.

NOTES: CHAPTER 12

1. For example, see "The Moral Climate," *New York Times* on The Watergate Affair, Sun 29 April 1963, see 4. p. 1. Elliot L. Richardson, who resigned as Secretary of Defense to accept from President Nixon the office of Attorney General, stated that he felt "betrayed by the shoddy standards of morals of those Administration officials who were involved in the Watergate Affair." *New York Times,* 11 May 1973, p. 1.

2. Prof. Milton Friedman found the U.S. wage and price controls of 1971 "deeply and inherently immoral"; *New York Times,* 12 November 1971, p. 47. H. B. Acton, a professor of moral philosophy at the University of Edinburgh, holds that competition and the market are, for all their limitations, a "more moral" form of social organization than any alternative we have; *The Morals of Markets* (Harlow, Essex, England: Longmans, 1971).

3. Prof. Henry Steele Commager sees the recent extension of morality as "a tendency to avoid specific moral questions, and to fall back on general declarations of immorality and guilt, as we find today with reference to the war, to the atrocities, to the race issues." *New York Times,* p. 70.

4. Plato *Republic* 2. 368.

5. Aristotle *Politics* 1. 1253a2–5, 1253b25–29.

6. Alberto R. Oliva, "The American Sense of Guilt," *New York Times,* 6 October 1971, p. 47.

7. Friedrich Nietzsche, *The Genealogy of Morals,* 1st essay, trans. Francis Golffing (New York: Doubleday), sec. 13, p. 178. A similar distinction between the morality of nature and that of convention had been made by Callicles in Plato's dialogue Gorgias, 482–483.

8. Alan Bullock, *Hitler: A Study in Tyranny* (New York: Harper & Row, 1952), pp. 398–399.

9. John Stuart Mill, *"On Liberty, Representative Government, The Subjection of Women.* (1859; London: Oxford University Press, 1960), pp. 14–15.

10. Plato *Republic* 8. 561–564; *Aristotle* Politics 4. 1295b35.

11. James Madison, "The Federalist No. 10," in Alexander Hamilton, John Jay, and James Madison, *The Federalist* (New York: Modern Library, 1938). Madison's argument that the poor and the rich will form factions is close to Aristotle's, *Politics,* 4. 1296a8.

12. Pierre Joseph Proudhon, *What Is Property?* trans. Benjamin R. Tucker (1840; New York: Howard Fertig, 1966), pp. 11-12.

13. Cited by Albert Camus, *The Rebel,* trans. Anthony Bower (New York: Knopf, 1956), p. 158.

14. See note in Suggested Readings under Francis Russell.
15. Robert Paul Wolff, *In Defense of Anarchism* (New York: Harper & Row, 1970), p. 18.
16. Ibid., p. 57.
17. Luke 20:25.
18. Herbert Marcuse, *An Essay on Liberation* (Boston: Beacon, 1969), p. viii.
19. Herbert Marcuse, "Ethics and Revolution," *Ethics and Society,* ed. Richard T. De George (Garden City, N.Y.: Doubleday, 1966), p. 133.
20. Ibid., p. 134.
21. Ibid., p. 133.
22. Camus, *Rebel,* p. 297.
23. *Girouard* v. *United States,* 326 U.S. 68 (1946). Cited by Robert T. Hall in "Legal Toleration of Civil Disobedience," *Ethics* 81, no. 2 (January 1971).
24. Plato *Crito* 51, in *Dialogues of Plato,* 2 vol., trans. Benjamin Jowett New York: Random House, 1937). But see *Apology,* 29 for an exception.
25. Aristotle *Politics* 4. 1267b33–35.
26. Martin Luther King, Jr., "Letter from Birmingham City Jail," in *Civil Disobedience,* ed. Hugo A. Bedau (New York: Pegasus, 1969), pp. 78–79.
27. John Rawls, "The Justification of Civil Disobedience," in *Law and Philosophy,* ed. Edward A. Kent (New York: Appleton, 1970), pp. 343–354.
28. Rex Martin, "Civil Disobedience," *Ethics* 80, no. 2 (January 1970) pp. 123–139.
29. Reported in *Time Magazine,* 4 May 1970, p. 59. Explaining his motives in the Watergate break-in to the Senate investigating committee in 1973, Jeb Stuart Magruder cited Coffin's course in ethics he (Magruder) took at Williams College in 1958, and Coffin's later indictment for civil disobedience activities during the Vietnam war. Coffin commented that Magruder's activities showed that he had failed the ethics course, adding that Magruder had not learned to distinguish between civil disobedience and violations of the Constitution by the Administration. He emphasized the difference between the open and public character of the civil disobedience of Martin Luther King and Dr. Benjamin Spock, and the secrecy in which the Watergate participants tried to hide their illegal activities. *New York Times,* 15 June 1973, p. 19; 19 June 1973, p. 39.
30. Cited by Beryl Levy, *Cardozo and the Frontiers of Legal Thinking,* rev. ed. (Cleveland: Press of Case Western Reserve University, 1969), p. 134.
31. Hans Kelsen, *General Theory of Law and State* (Cambridge, Mass.:

Harvard University Press, 1946), p. 5. Kelsen (1881–), formerly head of The School of Law of Vienna University is one of the most influential our century's legal theorists.

32. Oliver Wendell Holmes, "The Path of Law," *An Introduction to Law* (1897; Cambridge, Mass. Harvard Law Review Association, 1957), pp. 460–461.

33. Lord Patrick Devlin, "Morals and the Criminal Law," in *Morality and the Law,* ed. Richard A. Wasserstrom (Belmont, Calif.: Wadsworth, 1971), pp. 30, 40.

34. H. L. A. Hart, "Immorality and Treason," and Richard Dworkin, "Lord Devlin and the Enforcement of Morals," in Wasserstrom, ed. *Morality and Law.*

35. See items under these names in Suggested Readings.

36. See John U. Nef, "The Birth of Modern Science," *War and Human Progress* (Cambridge, Mass.: Harvard University Press, 1950); Lewis Mumford, "The Premonitions of Leonardo da Vinci," *New York Review of Books,* 29 December 1966; and J. D. Bernal, "Science and War," *The Social Function of Science* (1939; reprint ed., Cambridge, Mass.: Massachusetts Institute of Technology Press, 1967).

37. Historians of science may object to this lumping together of "science" and "technology," and they will be right. The two fields were rather separate until the middle of the nineteenth century. The Industrial Revolution in England (1770–1830) drew heavily upon technology but hardly at all on science. The first clear case of industry's drawing heavily on science was that of the German dye and chemical industry in the 1860s.

38. Peter Michelmore, *The Swift Years: the Oppenheimer Story* (New York: Dodd Mead, 1969), p. 16.

39. For example, see reference to values of rationality, objectivity, and so on, cited by Bernard Barber in his *Science and the Social Order,* chap. 4 (New York: Free Press, 1952).

40. John Dewey, *The Philosophy of John Dewey,* ed. Joseph Ratner (New York: Holt, Rinehart & Winston, 1928), p. 154.

41. Friedrich Engels, *Conditions of the Working Class in 1845.*

42. Edward De Bono, *Technology Today* (New York: Macmillan, 1971), preface.

43. Paul Goodman, "Can Technology Be Humane" in Martin Brown, ed., *The Social Responsibility of the Scientist* (New York: Free Press, 1971), pp. 247–265.

44. For the history of the movement in the United States, see Frank Graham, Jr., *Man's Dominion: the Story of American Conservation* (New York: Evans, 1971).

45. Gerard Manley Hopkins, "Duns Scotus's Oxford," *The Poems of*

Gerard Manley Hopkins, 4th ed., ed. W. H. Gardner and N. H. Mac-Kenzie (1879; New York: Oxford University Press, 1967), p. 79. Lines quoted with permission of the publisher.

46. Paul H. Ehrlich, *The Population Bomb,* cited in "The Population Explosion," *Congressional Quarterly* (Washington, D.C.: August 1970), p. 9.

47. David C. Coyle, *Conservation* (New Brunswick, N.J.: Rutgers University Press, 1957), p. 230.

48. William James, "Is Life Worth Living?" in *The Will to Believe and Other Essays* (New York: McKay, 1910), p. 50.

49. Albert Schweitzer, *Out of My Life and Thought* (New York: Holt, Rinehart & Winston, 1949), pp. 156–158.

50. George Marshall and David Poling, *Schweitzer: A Biography* (Garden City, N.Y.: Doubleday, 1971), p. 5.

51. Bertrand Russell, "The Chinese Character," in *Selected Papers of Bertrand Russell* (New York: Modern Library, 1927).

52. Richard Brandt, *Hopi Ethics* (Chicago: University of Chicago Press, 1954), p. 245.

53. James, *Will to Believe,* p. 50.

54. Albert Schweitzer, *Civilization and Ethics* (New York: Macmillan, 1960), pp. 310–311.

55. Matthew 23:27, 33.

56. John 2:4.

57. Luke 9:60.

58. John 2:4, and Luke 9:60.

59. Matt. 11:34.

60. Matt. 11:39; Mark 8:35; Luke 17:33; John 12:25.

61. Lion Feuchtwanger, *Power* (Jew Süss), (New York: Viking, 1948), p. 165.

62. Blaise Pascal, *Pensées,* trans. H. F. Stewart (New York: Pantheon, 1950), pp. 64, 79.

63. Fosco Maraini, *Secret Tibet* (New York: Viking, 1952), p. 75.

64. Luke 16:1–11.

65. Kurt Vonnegut, Jr., *Slaughterhouse Five* (New York: Dell, 1969), p. 122.

66. R. M. Hare *The Language of Morals* (New York: Oxford University Press, 1964), p. 73.

67. The *Bhagavad Gita* ("Song of the Lord") is a religious poem, the most sacred text in Hinduism. Written in Sanskrit, the *Gita* was the work of many hands and minds, who worked on it from the fifth century B.C. to the second century B.C. See Suggested Readings: Chapter 11.

SUGGESTED READINGS: INTRODUCTION AND CHAPTER 1

American Bar Association. *Code of Professional Responsibility and Canons of Judicial Ethics.* Chicago: 1969.

Anscombe, G. E. M. "On Brute Facts. *Analysis* 18 (1958): 69–72. Reprinted in Thomson and Dworkin, *Ethics.*

Austin, John L. *How to Do Things with Words.* Cambridge, Mass.: Harvard University Press, 1962.

Ayer, Alfred J. *Language, Truth and Logic.* rev. ed. London: Gollancz, 1948. Chapter 6 argues for an emotive theory of ethical statements.

Bennion, Francis. *Professional Ethics.* London: Knight, 1972.

Edwards, Paul, ed. *The Encyclopedia of Philosophy.* vol. 3. New York: Macmillan, 1967. There are useful essays in bibliographies under various headings of "Ethics."

Foot, Philippa, ed. *Theories of Ethics.* New York: Oxford University Press, 1967. A small collection of papers on contemporary ethical theory.

Hare, R. M. *The Language of Morals.* New York: Oxford University Press, 1952.

Hume, David. *An Enquiry Concerning the Principles of Morals* (1777). LaSalle, Ill.: Open Court, 1938.

———. "Of Morals." In bk. III, vol. 2 of *Treatise on Human Nature,* 2 vols. New York: Dutton, 1911.

Moore, G. E. *Ethics.* London: Cambridge University Press, 1951.

———. *Principia Ethica.* 1903. Reprint. London: Cambridge University Press, 1959. A classic of twentieth-century ethical theory.

Nowell-Smith, P. H. *Ethics.* Baltimore, Md.: Penguin, 1964.

Searle, John R. "How to Derive 'Ought' from 'Is.' " *Philosophical Reivew* 73 (1964): 43–58. Reprinted in *Theories of Ethics,* edited by P. Foot.

Sellars, Wilfred, and Hospers, John, ed. *Readings in Ethical Theory.* New York: Appleton, 1970. A large and useful collection of papers on contemporary ethical theory.

Stevenson, Charles L. "Moore's Arguments against Certain Forms of Ethical Naturalism." In *The Philosophy of G. E. Moore,* edited by P. A. Schilpp. Evanston, Ill.: Northwestern University Press, 1942. Reprinted in Foot, ed., *Theories of Ethics.*

———. *Ethics and Language.* New Haven, Conn.: Yale University Press, 1944.

Thomson, James, and Thomson, Judith Jarvis. "How Not to Derive 'Ought' from 'Is.' " *Philosophical Review* 73 (1964):73–76. Reprinted in Sellars and Hospers, eds., *Readings in Ethical Theory.*

Thomson, Judith Jarvis, and Dworkin, Gerald, eds. *Ethics.* New York: Harper & Row, 1968. Short book of readings in contemporary ethical theory.

Wittgenstein, Ludwig. *Philosophical Investigations.* New York: Macmillan, 1953. Twentieth-century classic in the philosophy of language.

SUGGESTED READINGS: CHAPTER 2

Barnsley, John H. *The Social Reality of Ethics.* London: Routledge & Kegan Paul, 1972.

Benedict, Ruth. *Patterns of Culture.* Boston: Houghton Mifflin, 1934.

Bergson, Henri. *The Two Sources of Religion and Morality.* Translated by R. A. Audra and C. B. Brereton. New York: Holt, Rinehart & Winston, 1935. Chap. 1.

Brandt, Richard B. *Hopi Ethics.* Chicago: University of Chicago Press, 1954.

————. *Ethical Theory.* Englewood Cliffs, N.J.: Prentice-Hall, 1959.

Brown, Ina C. *Understanding Others Cultures.* Englewood Cliffs, N.J.: Prentice-Hall, 1963. Contains useful bibliography for readings in anthropology.

Castaneda, Carlos. *The Teachings of Don Juan: A Yaqui Way of Knowledge.* Berkeley, Calif.: University of California Press, 1968. Young anthropologist tells story of his introduction to the Mexican Indian drug culture.

Fox, Robin. *Kinship and Marriage.* Baltimore, Md.: Penguin, 1967.

Frazer, Sir James F. *The Golden Bough.* New York: Macmillan, 1930. Early classic of ethnography and primitive mythology.

Freud, Sigmund. *Totem and Taboo.* Translated by A. A. Brill. New York: Moffat, Yard & Co., 1918. Freud uses data from late-nineteenth- and early-twentieth-century ethnographers.

Hallpike, C. R. *The Kenso of Ethiopia.* Oxford: Clarendon, 1972.

Lazari-Pawlowska, Ija. "On Cultural Relativism." *Journal of Philosophy* 76 (1970): 577–584.

Lévi-Strauss, Claude, "The Family" in *Anthropology,* edited by S. Rapport and H. Wright. New York: New York University Press, 1967.

————. From *Honey to Ashes. Introduction to a Science of Mythology.* Translated by John and Doreen Weyhtman. New York: Harper & Row, 1973. This is vol. 2 of *Mythologique,* 4 vols. Vol. 1 is *The Raw and the Cooked.* Translated by John and Doreen Weightman. New York: Harper & Row, 1969.

————. *The Savage Mind.* Chicago: University of Chicago Press, 1966.

————. "Today's Crisis in Anthropology." *Anthropology,* edited by S. Rapport and H. Wright, New York: New York University Press, 1967.

Malinowski, Bronislaw. *The Sexual Life of Savages in Northwestern Melanesia.* New York: Liveright, 1929.

Mead, Margaret. *Cultural Patterns and Technical Change.* Paris: UNESCO, 1953.

Ossowska, Maria. *Social Determinants of Moral Ideas.* London: Routledge & Kegan Paul, 1972.

Pryde, Duncan. *Nunaga: Ten Years of Eskimo Life.* New York: Walker, 1972. Culture shock in the Arctic, including wife-lending.

Rapport, S., and Wright, H., eds. *Anthropology.* New York: New York University Press, 1967. A book of readings.

Redfield, Robert. *Human Nature and the Study of Society.* Chicago: University of Chicago Press, 1962.

Sumner, Charles G. *Folkways.* Boston: Ginn, 1906.

Turnbull. Colin M. *The Mountain People.* New York: Simon & Schuster, 1972. Portrait of the disagreeable Ik people of northern Uganda.

Westermarck, Edward A. *The Origin and Development of Moral Ideas,* 2 vols. New York: Macmillan, 1906–1908.

———. *Ethical Relativity.* New York: Harcourt, 1932. A further development of Westermarck's preceding book.

Willoughby, W. C. *The Soul of the Bantu.* New York: Doubleday, 1928.

SUGGESTED READINGS: CHAPTER 3

Bergson, Henri. *The Two Sources of Religion and Morality.* Translated by R. A. Audra and C. B. Brereton. New York: Holt, Rinehart & Winston, 1935. Chap. 2.

Bentham, Jeremy. *The Principles of Morals and Legislation* (1789). New York: Hafner, 1948.

Hefner, Hugh M. *The Playboy Philosophy.* 4 pts. Chicago: HMH Publishing, 1962–1965.

Hume, David. *An Enquiry Concerning the Principles of Morals* (1777). LaSalle, Ill.: Open Court, 1938.

Huysmans, Joris-Karl. *Against the Grain.* New York: Illustrated Editions, 1931. Original title *A Rebours,* Paris, 1884. Translated by Robert Baldick as *Against Nature.* Baltimore, Md.: Penguin, 1966.

Lucretius (Titus Lucretius Carus). *On the Nature of Things* [De Rerum Natura]. Translated by William Ellery Leonard. New York: Dutton, 1957. Classical philosophical poem in Latin on the materialist-atomist cosmology of Epicurus, supporting an ethics that removes fear of death and exalts pure pleasure (tranquility, the peace of the blessed gods) as the highest good.

Marcuse, Herbert. *An Essay on Liberation.* Boston: Beacon, 1969.

Mill, John Stuart. *Utilitarianism* (1863). New York: Liberal Arts Press, 1949. Classic short treatise on utilitarianism.

Moore, G. E. *Principia Ethica* (1903). Hedonism, chap. 3; The Ideal, chap. 6. Reprint. London: Cambridge University Press, 1959.

Pater, Walter. *Marius the Epicurean.* London: Macmillan, 1903. A recreation of the Epicurean ideal.

Petronius Arbiter. *The Satyricon.* Translated by William Arrowsmith. Ann Arbor, Mich.: University of Michigan Press, 1959. A classic picture of sensual hedonism in ancient Rome, which inspired Fellini's film of the same title.

Plato. *Philebus.* In vol. 2 of *The Dialogues of Plato.* Translated by Benjamin Jowett. 2 vols. New York: Random House, 1937. A late dialogue of Plato in which Socrates compares pleasure and wisdom.

Rawls, John. *A Theory of Justice.* Cambridge, Mass.: Harvard University Press, Belknap, 1972. Rawls's alternative to utilitarianism as a social ethics in terms of a new social contract theory.

Sidgwick, Henry. *The Methods of Ethics.* 7th ed. London: Macmillan, 1901. The most durable of modern textbooks on ethics, which carefully considers the claims of an enlightened hedonism.

SUGGESTED READINGS: CHAPTER 4

Anscombe, G. E. M. *Intention.* Oxford: Blackwell, 1957. A subtle and difficult treatise of ninety pages that stimulated a generation of younger philosophers to examine the complexities involved in the concept of human action.

Ayer, A. J. *The Concept of a Person; and Other Essays.* New York: St. Martins, 1963.

Beauvoir, Simone de. *The Second Sex.* New York: Knopf, 1953. The classic French feminist treatise of our time.

Buber, Martin. *I and Thou.* 2d ed. Translated by R. G. Smith. New York: Scribner, 1958.

Confucius. *Confucius: Confucian Analects, The Great Learning, and The Doctrine of the Mean.* Translated by James Legge. 1893. Reprint. New York: Dover, 1971.

Dostoyevsky, Fyodor. "Notes from the Underground." In *The Short Novels of Dostoyevsky,* translated by Constance Garnet. New York: Dial, 1945.

Downie, R. S., and Telfer, Elizabeth. *Respect for Persons.* New York: Schocken Books, 1970.

Frankfort, H. G. "Freedom of the Will and the Concept of a Person." *The Journal of Philosophy* 68 (1971): 5–20.

Haezrahi, Pepita. "The Concept of Man as an End-in-Himself." In *Kant: A Collection of Critical Essays,* edited by Robert Paul Wolff. London: Macmillan, 1968.

Hare, Richard M. *Freedom and Reason.* Oxford: Clarendon, 1963.

Kant, Immanuel. *Foundations of the Metaphysics of Morals* (1785). Translated by L. W. Beck. New York: Liberal Arts Press, 1959. Kant's most widely known and used treatise on ethics.

Lyons, David. *Forms and Limits of Utilitarianism.* Oxford: Clarendon, 1965.

Maimonides. "The Ladder of Tzedakah." New York. Ktav Publishing, 1964. An illustrated chart showing the various kinds of charity according to their moral worth.

Millett, Kate. *Sexual Politics.* Garden City, N.Y.: Doubleday, 1970. How men treat women as objects, not persons, with copious and explicit literary illustrations from D. H. Lawrence, Henry Miller, Norman Mailer, Genet, and others.

Nietzsche, Friedrich. *Human. All-Too-Human; a Book for Free Spirits,* vol. 2. Translated by Paul V. Cohn. 2 vols. London: Allen and Unwin, 1910, 1924.

Paton, Herbert James. *The Categorical Imperative.* London: Hutchinson, 1948.

Singer, Marcus G. *Generalization in Ethics.* New York: Knopf, 1961.

Skinner, Burrhus Frederic. *Beyond Freedom and Dignity.* New York: Knopf, 1971. The famous behaviorist psychologist argues that we can no longer afford exaggerated ideas of personal worth and liberty.

Strawson, P. F. *Individuals.* London, Methuen, 1959. Not for beginners.

Weil, Simone. "Human Personality." In *Selected Essays,* translated by Michael Rees. New York: Oxford University Press, 1962. A strong and beautiful mind analyzes the concept of personhood.

Wolff, Robert Paul, ed. *Kant.* London: Macmillan, 1968.

SUGGESTED READINGS: CHAPTER 5

Aristotle. *Nichomachean Ethics.* Translated by W. D. Ross. In *The Basic Works of Aristotle,* edited by Richard McKeon. New York: Random House, 1941.

———. *Politics.* Translated by Ernest Barker as *The Politics of Aristotle.* Oxford: Clarendon, 1961.

Confucius, "The Doctrine of the Mean." In *Confucius: Confucian Analects, The Great Learning, and The Doctrine of the Mean.* Translated by James Legge. 1893. Reprint. New York: Dover, 1971.

Dewey, John. *The Philosophy of John Dewey.* Edited by Joseph Ratner. New York: Holt, Rinehart & Winston, 1928. A large volume of selections from Dewey's work.

———. *Human Nature and Conduct.* New York: Modern Library, 1930.

———. *Reconstruction in Philosophy.* 1920. Reprint. New York: The American Library, 1950.

———. *Dewey on Education.* Edited by Martin S. Dworkin. New York:

Teachers College, 1959. This small book contains a number of Dewey's important early papers on education, including "The School and Society" (1899) and "The Child and the Curriculum" (1902).

Locke, John. *Some Thoughts Concerning Education.* In *John Locke on Education,* edited by Peter Gay. New York: Bureau of Publications, Teachers College, Columbia University, 1964.

Monan, J. Donald. *Moral Knowledge and its Methodology in Aristotle.* Oxford: Clarendon, 1968.

Mure, G. R. G. *Aristotle.* New York: Oxford University Press, 1964.

Nietzsche, Friedrich. *The Birth of Tragedy* (1872). Translated by W. A. Haussman. New York: Macmillan, 1924. More recently translated by Francis Golffing in *The Birth of Tragedy and The Genealogy of Morals.* Garden City, N.Y.: Doubleday, 1956.

Plato. *Phaedrus.* In vol. 1 of *The Dialogues of Plato.* Translated by Benjamin Jowett. 2 vols. New York: Random House, 1937. Here Plato presents his allegory of human nature in terms of a charioteer driving two horses, one light and one dark; in three elements corresponding to intelligence, vital energy (spirit), and instinctive drives (desire).

Walsh, James J. *Aristotle's Conception of Moral Weakness.* New York: Columbia University Press, 1963.

SUGGESTED READINGS: CHAPTER 6

Aristotle. *Nichomachean Ethics.* Translated by W. D. Ross. In *The Basic Works of Aristotle,* edited by Richard McKeon. New York: Random House, 1941. Book 6 discusses the "intellectual virtues."

Bergson, Henri. *The Two Sources of Religion and Morality.* New York: Holt, Rinehart & Winston, 1935. Chap. 3.

Breasted, James Henry. *The Dawn of Conscience.* New York: Scribner, 1934. Old-style, but still fascinating survey of early human beliefs.

Curatorium of the C. J. Jung Institute, Zurich. *Conscience.* Evanston, Ill.: Northwestern University Press, 1970. Essays on conscience from various psychological and religious standpoints.

Dewey, John. *Human Nature and Conduct.* New York: Modern Library, 1930. Chapter 8 discusses the relation of intelligence to desire and impulse.

Freud, Sigmund. *Civilization and its Discontents.* Translated by James Strachey. New York: Norton, 1961. Freud contrasts the power of instinct contrasted with the flickering spark of intelligence; he accounts for civilization's mastery of the individual's natural aggressiveness by the creation of the super-ego or conscience.

Gide, André. *Lafcadio's Adventures (Les Caves du Vatican)* (1914). Translated by Dorothy Bussy. New York: Random House, 1953. Classic story of a gratuitous act that happens to be a crime.

Gunther, Bernard and Fusco, Paul. *Sense Relaxation.* New York: Collier Macmillan, 1968. Stories and pictures of neglected delights of body and senses.

Hare, R. M. *Freedom and Reason.* Oxford: Clarendon, 1963. Chapter 11 illustrates the role of reason in ethics by example of intelligent analysis of the moral problem or race prejudice.

Johnson, C. A. *The Moral Life.* London: Allen and Unwin, 1970. A short book arguing for the essential place of reason in ethical judgments.

Langer, Susanne K. *Mind: an Essay on Human Feeling.* 2 vols. Baltimore, Md.: Johns Hopkins Press, 1967. Title explains thesis of this large-scale attempt to synthesize art, science, and philosophy in support of unity of mind and feeling.

May, Rollo. *Love and Will.* New York: Norton, 1969. Popular psychotherapist's views on sex and civilization.

Mercer, Philip C. *Sympathy and Ethics.* London: Oxford University Press, 1971.

Rousseau, Jean-Jacques. *Emile.* Translated by Barbara Foxley. New York: Dutton, 1911. Book 4, pp. 181–188. Rousseau argues for the origin of moral sentiment in natural sympathy.

Santayana, George. *The Life of Reason.* 2 vols. New York: Scribner, 1922. Magnum opus of a twentieth-century admirer of the Greek ideal of reason and harmony.

Spinoza, Benedict. *Ethics* (1677). New York: Dutton, 1938. Part 3 deals with the origin and nature of emotions; part 4, with its famous title "Of Human Bondage," tells of the strength of the passions and how to overcome them.

SUGGESTED READINGS: CHAPTER 7

Emerson, Ralph Waldo. "Self-Reliance." In *The Writing of Ralph Waldo Emerson,* edited by Brooks Atkinson. New York: Modern Library, 1940. This essay, a classic of Yankee individualism, appeared in Emerson's *Essays: First Series* in 1841.

Erikson, Erik. *Childhood and Society.* 2d ed. New York: Norton, 1963.

——. *Identity: Youth and Crisis.* New York: Norton, 1968. By the formulator of the "identity crisis" concept fashionable during the 1960s.

Gide, André. *Fruits of the Earth* (1897). Translated by Dorothy Bussy. London: Secker & Warburg, 1949. Gide's influential testament of individualism in the form of a fictional diary.

——. *The Immoralist* (1902). Translated by Dorothy Bussy. New York: Knopf, 1951. Famous short novel in which Gide pushes the idea of the value of self-actualization and sincerity to see how far it will go. There is a more recent translation by Richard Howard. New York: Knopf, 1970.

Hesse, Hermann. *Steppenwolf.* Translated by Basil Creighton. New York: Holt, Rinehart & Winston, 1929. Psychodrama with occult and drug props. A man turned just fifty learns not to take his unique self quite so seriously.

————. *Demian.* Translated by N. H. Priday. New York: Holt, Rinehart & Winston, 1948. There is a more recent translation by Michael Roloff and Michael Lebeck: *Demian.* New York: Harper & Row, 1965.

Horney, Karen, *Neurosis and Human Growth: the Struggle Toward Self-Realization.* New York: Norton, 1950.

James, William. *Letters of William James.* 2 vols. Edited by his son Henry James. Boston: Atlantic Monthly, 1920.

————. *Psychology: the Briefer Course* (1892) Edited by Gordon Allport. New York: Harper & Row,1961. Chapter 11 contains James's famous concept of the "stream of consciousness."

Jung, Carl G. *Modern Man in Search of a Soul.* New York: Harcourt, 1933. The Swiss psychoanalyst urges self-forgiveness and self-acceptance, an idea basic to twentieth-century psychotherapy.

Kierkegaard, Sören. *The Sickness Unto Death.* (1849). Translated by Walter Lowrie. Princeton, N.J.: Princeton University Press, 1941.

Lukes, Steven. *Individualism.* Oxford: Blackwell, 1973.

Maslow, Abraham H. "The Good Life of the Self-Actualizing Person." In Maslow, *Moral Problems in Contemporary Society.* Englewood Cliffs, N.J.: Prentice-Hall, 1969. Old wine of self-realization poured into attractive mid-century psychotherapeutic bottle.

May, Rollo. *Love and Will.* New York: Norton, 1969.

————. *Toward a Psychology of Being.* 2d ed. Princeton, N.J.: Van Nostrand Reinhold, 1968. Popular psychological counsel.

Mill, John Stuart. *On Liberty* (1859). London: Oxford University Press, 1960. In *On Liberty, Representative Government, The Subjection of Women.* Classical defense of individual liberty in the British tradition.

Mills, Gordon, ed. *Innocence and Power: Individualism in Twentieth Century America.* Austin, Tex.: University of Texas Press, 1965. Published results of symposium on individualism.

Nietzsche, Friedrich. *Schopenhauer as Educator.* Translated by J. W. Hillesheim and M. R. Simpson. Chicago: Regnery, 1965. Originally one of three essays making up Nietzsche's book *Thoughts Out of Season* (1874). First section of essay is classic defense of personal individualism.

Plato. *Symposium.* In vol. 1 of *The Dialogues of Plato.* 2 vols. Translated by Benjamin Jowett. New York: Random House, 1937. Portrait of Socrates with individual quirks and human virtues. There is a more recent translation by Michael Joyce in Joyce. *Five Dialogues of Plato.* New York: Dutton, 1952.

Rousseau, Jean-Jacques. *Confessions.* New York: Dutton, 1931. Appearing in late eighteenth century, Rousseau's autobiography is a classic of individualism.

Solzhenitsyn, Aleksandr. I. *The Cancer Ward.* Translated by R. Frank. New York: Dial, 1968. Themes of personal and political individualism unite in this novel by the Soviet Union's foremost literary nonconformist.

Thoreau, Henry David. *Walden and Civil Disobedience.* Edited by Owen Thomas. New York: Norton, 1966.

Tocqueville, Alexis de. *Democracy in America* (1848). Translated by George Lawrence. Garden City, N.Y.: Doubleday, 1969. Part 2, Chapter 1, "On Individualism in Democracies," is especially pertinent.

Trilling, Lionel. *Sincerity and Authenticity.* Cambridge, Mass.: Harvard University Press, 1972. A distinguished critic traces modern literary history of ideas of sincerity.

Whitman, Walt. "Song of Myself." In *Leaves of Grass (1855). A good* edition is Emory Holloway, ed., *Walt Whitman: Complete Poetry and Selected Prose and Letters.* London: Nonesuch Press, 1967.

Zweig, Arnold. *The Case of Sergeant Grischa.* Translated by Eric Sutton. New York: Viking, 1929. Unforgettable novel of a World War I prisoner of war done to death by a military bureaucracy that cares nothing for the value of an individual human life.

SUGGESTED READINGS: CHAPTER 8

Barnes, Hazel. *An Existentialist Ethics.* New York: Knopf, 1967.

Beauvoir, Simone de. *The Prime of Life.* Translated by Peter Green. Cleveland: World, 1962. Best of the autobiographical volumes of this famous French feminist and friend of Sartre.

Camus, Albert. *The Myth of Sisyphus.* Translated by Justin O'Brien. New York: Knopf, 1955. This famous essay, half literary and half philosophical, was published in occupied France in 1942, close to the appearance of Camus's famous tale *The Stranger.*

———. *The Rebel.* Translated by Anthony Bower. New York : Knopf, 1956. An essay on the rebel as artist and revolutionary.

———. *The Stranger.* Translated by Justin O'Brien. New York: Knopf 1946. Camus's famous short novel of a man who refused to fake emotions he did not feel.

Heidegger, Martin. *Existence and Being.* Chicago: Regnery, 1949. Shorter and much easier going than *Being and Time.*

———. *Being and Time.* Translated by John Macquarrie and Edward

Robinson. New York: Harper & Row, 1962. The German metaphysician's unfinished magnum opus. It is not easy to translate "Heideggerdeutsch" into English.

Husserl, Edmund. *Cartesian Meditations.* Translated by Dorion Cairns. Nijhoff: The Hague, 1964. Late treatise by the master of phenomenology, who died in 1938.

Kierkegaard, Sören. *A Kierkegaard Anthology.* Edited by Robert Bretall. New York: Modern Library, n.d.

Koestler, Arthur. *Darkness at Noon.* New York: Macmillan, 1941. A novel based on the Moscow trials of 1936–38.

Marx, Karl, and Engels, Friedrich. *The Marx-Engels Reader,* ed. Robert C. Tucker. New York: Norton, 1972.

Merleau-Ponty, Maurice. *Phenomenology of Perception.* Translated by Colin Smith. New York: Humanities, 1962. Major application of phenomenological method to psychology by Sartre's most brilliant pupil.

Murdoch, Iris. *Sartre: Romantic Rationalist.* Cambridge, England: Bowes & Bowes, 1955.

Nietzsche, Friedrich. "The Joyful Wisdom" (1881). Vol. 10. Translated by T. Common. Edited by Oscar Levy. *The Complete Works of Friedrich Nietzsche.* 12 vols. New York: Russell & Russell, 1964. The section on "the Madman" contains the long "death of God" passage.

———. *Thus Spake Zarathustra.* 1886. Vol. 11 of Nietzsche, *Complete Works.* There are two more recent editions, translated by Marianne Cowan. Chicago: Regnery, 1957, and by R. J. Hollingdale. Baltimore: Penguin, 1968.

Pascal, Blaise. *Pensées.* Translated by W. F. Trotter. New York: Dutton, 1948. Also, a bilingual edition, translated by H. F. Stewart. New York: Pantheon, 1950.

Sanborn, Patricia F. *Existentialism.* New York: Pegasus, 1968. A short, easily readable exposition.

Sartre, Jean-Paul. *Being and Nothingness.* Translated by Hazel Barnes. 1943. New York: Philosophical Library, 1956. Sartre's big wartime philosophical book.

———. "Existentialism Is a Humanism" (1946). Translated by Philip Mairet. In *Existentialism from Dostoyevsky to Sartre,* edited by Walter Kaufman. Cleveland, Ohio: World Publishing, 1956. Sartre's popular lecture on existentialism in terms he no longer defends.

———. *Search for a Method.* Translated by Hazel Barnes. New York: Knopf, 1963. This prefatory essay of Sartre's big *Critique of Dialectical Reason* (1960) is the best introduction to Sartre's "postexistentialist" philosophy.

————. *Nausea* (1938). Translated by Lloyd Alexander. New York: New Directions, 1964. Sartre's early novel about a man who is nearly driven mad by a vision of bare existence.

Warnock, Mary. *Existentialist Ethics.* New York: St. Martin, 1967.

SUGGESTED READINGS: CHAPTER 9

Anscombe, G. E. M. *Intention.* Oxford: Blackwell, 1957. Subtle and difficult short treatise on a crucial element in human action. Already a classic in the field of philosophy of action.

Aristotle. *Nichomachean Ethics,* bk. 3. Translated by W. D. Ross. In *The Basic Works of Aristotle,* edited by Richard McKeon. New York: Random House, 1941. Chapters 1–5 discuss the part of free choice in human action.

Augustine. "The Free Choice of the Will" [De Libero Arbitrio]. Vol. 59 translated by Robert Russell. In *The Fathers of the Church,* 60 vols. Washington, D.C.: Catholic University Press, 1967. Excerpted in Dewey and Gould as "Free Will and God's Foreknowledge."

Austin, John L. "Ifs and Cans." In *Philosophical Papers.* London: Oxford University Press, 1961. Reprinted in Berofsky.

————. "A Plea for Excuses." In *Philosophical Papers.* Oxford: Clarendon Press, 1970.

Berofsky, Bernard, ed. *Free Will and Determinism.* New York: Harper & Row, 1966. A book of readings on the problem.

Brand, Myles, ed. *The Nature of Human Action.* Glenview, Ill.: Scott, Foresman, 1970. Readings on the philosophy of action.

Darwin, Charles. *The Origin of Species.* New York: D. Appleton, 1900.

Davidson, Donald. "Actions, Reasons, and Causes." *Journal of Philosophy* 60. (1963): 685–700. Reprinted in both Brand, ed., *Human Action,* and Berofsky, ed., *Free Will.*

De George, Richard T. *Soviet Ethics and Morality.* Ann Arbor, Mich.: University of Michigan Press, 1969.

Dewey, Robert E. and Gould, James A. *Freedom: its History, Nature, and Varieties.* New York: Macmillan, 1970. Selected readings.

Engels, Friedrich. *Ludwig Feuerbach* (1888). New York, International Publishers, 1941. Chapter 4 touches the problem of historical determinism versus individual choice.

Foot, Philippa. "Free Will as Involving Determinism." *Philosophical Review* October 1957, vol. LXVI.

Gerber, Rudolph J. and McAnany, Patrick D. *Contemporary Punishment.* South Bend, Ind.: University of Notre Dame Press, 1972. A good selection of papers on crime and punishment.

Heisenberg, Werner. *Physics and Philosophy; the Revolution in Modern Science.* New York: Harper & Row, 1958. Formulator of the "Uncertainty principle" discusses relation between science and philosophy.

Hobbes, Thomas. "The Questions Concerning Liberty, Necessity, and Chance." In vol. 5 of *The English Works of Thomas Hobbes.* 11 vols. Edited by Sir William Molesworth. London: John Bohn, 1841. Reprinted in Morgenbesser and Walsh.

Holbach, Paul Henry, Thiry, Baron d'. *The System of Nature.* (1770) Classic eighteenth-century mechanistic determinism. Excerpted as "Determinism" in Dewey and Gould, *Freedom.*

Hook, Sidney, ed. *Determinism and Freedom in the Age of Modern Science.* New York: Macmillan-Collier, 1961. Conference papers on free will and determinism.

Huxley, Aldous. *Brave New World.* New York: Harper and Row, 1932.

Kant, Immanuel. *The Metaphysical Elements of Justice.* Translated by John Ladd. New York: Liberal Arts Press, 1965. Contains Kant's theory of punishment.

Kent, Edward A., ed. *Law and Philosophy: Readings in Legal Philosophy.* New York: Appleton, 1970. A useful book of readings on the philosophy of law.

Lamont, Corliss. "On Free Will," in *Freedom of Choice Affirmed.* New York: Horizon Press, 1967.

Laplace, Pierre Simon Marquis de. *Celestial Mechanics.* 4 vols. New York: Chelsea Publication Co., 1966. A reprint of Nathaniel Bowditch's translation of 1829–1839.

Lucas, J. R. *The Freedom of the Will.* New York: Oxford, 1970.

Melden A. I. *Free Action.* London: Routledge & Kegan Paul, 1961.

Monod, Jacques. *Chance and Necessity: An Essay on the Natural Philosophy of Modern Biology.* Translated by Austryn Wainhouse. New York: Knopf, 1971. Nobel prize-winning biochemist argues that every living organism, including man, is a self-constructing machine.

Morgenbesser, Sidney and Walsh, James, eds. *Free Will.* Englewood Cliffs, N.J.: Prentice-Hall, 1962.

Nowell-Smith, P. H. *Ethics.* Baltimore: Penguin, 1964. Freedom and responsibility are discussed in Chapters 19 and 20.

Orwell, George. *Nineteen Eighty Four.* New York: Harcourt, Brace and Jovanovich, 1949.

Ryle, Gilbert. *The Concept of Mind.* London: Hutchinson, 1949. A classic in philosophy of action.

Schlick, Morris. *Problems of Ethics.* Translated by D. Rynin. Englewood Cliffs, N.J.: Prentice-Hall, 1939.

Schopenhauer, Arthur. *The World as Will and Idea.* 3 vols. Translated by

R. B. Haldane and J. Kemp. London: Routledge & Kegan Paul, 1967. Volume 1, Book 4, in freedom of the will; section 55 discusses character determinism.

Schrödinger, Erwin. *What Is Life?* New York: Macmillan, 1945. A famous physicist's mechanistic explanation of organic life, contains a mystical appendix on free will.

Skinner, B. F. *Beyond Freedom and Dignity.* New York: Knopf, 1971. Behaviorist arguments against classical free will position.

————. *Science and Human Behavior.* New York: Macmillan, 1953.

————. *Walden II.* New York: Macmillan, 1948.

Snow, C. P. *The Sleep of Reason.* New York: Scribner, 1968. Novel about a murder trial involving idea of diminished responsibility.

Spinoza, Benedict. *Ethics* (1677). New York: Dutton, 1910.

Watson, John B. *Behaviorism.* rev. ed. New York: Norton, 1930. A crude but stimulating analysis of human behavior in terms of conditioned reflexes.

SUGGESTED READINGS: CHAPTER 10

Altman, Dennis. *Homosexual; Oppression and Liberation.* New York: Dutton, 1968.

Anscombe, G. E. M. "Modern Moral Philosophy." *Philosophy* 33 (1958): 1–19. In Judith Jarvis Thomson and Gerald Dworkin, eds., *Ethics.* New York: Harper & Row, 1968.

Beauvoir, Simone de. *The Second Sex.* Translated by H. M. Parshley, New York: Knopf, 1953.

Cunningham, R. L., ed. *Situationism and the New Morality.* New York: Appleton, 1970. Readings in situational ethics.

D'Arcy, Martin. *The Mind and Heart of Love: a Study in Eros and Agape.* rev. ed. New York: Meridian, 1958. A theology of love.

Durkheim, Emile. *Incest: the Nature and Origin of the Taboo.* Translated by Edward Sagarin. New York: Lyle Stuart, 1963.

Fletcher, Joseph. *Situation Ethics: the New Morality.* Philadelphia: Westminister, 1966.

Fox, Robin. *Kinship and Marriage.* Baltimore, Md.: Penguin, 1967.

Galsworthy, John. *The Forsyte Saga.* New York: Scribner, 1933. Book I is "The Man of Property."

Greene, Graham. *The End of the Affair.* New York: Viking, 1951. A novel of an adulterous lover trying to escape divine love.

Hoffman, Martin. *The Gay World.* New York: Basic Books, 1968. A study of homosexuality as a life-style by a San Francisco physician.

James, Henry. *The Golden Bowl.* 2 vols. New York: Scribner, 1909. James's subtle novel of the corruption of trust by way of adultery.

James, William. "The Moral Philosopher and the Moral Life." In *The Will to Believe and Other Essays.* New York: McKay, 1907.

Kinsey, Alfred C., Pomeroy, Wardell B., and Martin, Clyde E. *Sexual Behavior in the Human Male.* Philadelphia: W. B. Saunders Co., 1948.

Kristol, Irving. "Pornography, Obscenity and the Case for Censorship." *New York Times Magazine,* 28 March, 1971, pp. 24–25, 112–114. Letters and comments in issue of 18 April 1971.

Lévi-Strauss, Claude. "The Family." In *Anthropology,* edited by Samuel Rapport and Helen Wright. New York: New York University Press, 1967.

Mauriac, François. *The Desert of Love.* Translated by Gerard Hopkins. New York: Farrar, Strauss & Giroux, 1961. Mauriac's novel of mortal love diverted from its true object, the divine.

Outka, Gene. *Agape.* New Haven: Yale University Press, 1972. The author examines both Catholic and Protestant writings on agape including those of Barth, Ramsey and Tillich.

Paul. 1 Corinthians 13. St. Paul's letter to the Christian community of Corinth proclaims the necessity of love.

Plato. *Symposium.* In *Five Dialogues of Plato,* translated by Michael Joyce. New York: Dutton, 1952. Plato's metaphysics of love delightfully recited by Socrates to a supporting cast at a banquet in ancient Athens.

Plato. *Phaedrus.* In vol. 1 of *The Dialogues of Plato.* 2 vols. Translated by Benjamin Jowett. New York: Random House, 1937.

Proust, Marcel. *Cities of the Plain* (Sodom and Gommorha I.) Translated by C. K. Scott Moncrieff. New York: Modern Library, 1927. The fourth volume of Proust's great novel *Remembrance of Things Past* [A la Recherche du temps perdu], in which homosexuals take center stage.

Rougemont, Denis de. *Love in the Western World* [L'Amour et l'occident]. Translated by Montgomery Belgion. New York: Pantheon, 1956. History of development of theme of love, with particular attention to Tristan and Isolde.

Schopenhauer, Arthur, "The Metaphysics of the Love of the Sexes." In vol. 30 *The World as Will and Idea.* 3 vols. Translated by R. B. Haldane and J. Kemp. London: Routledge & Kegan Paul, 1957, chap. 44, pp. 336–375.

Tolstoy, Leo. *Anna Karenina.* Translated by Constance Garnett. New York: Random House, 1939. Tolstoy's classic novel of adulterous love and its disastrous consequences.

Weinberg, Martin S., and Bell, Alan P., eds. *Homosexuality; an Annotated Bibliography.* New York: Harper & Row, 1972.

The Wolfenden Report. New York: Stein & Day, 1963. Originally published as *Report: the Wolfenden Commission.* Cmnd. 247. London: Her Majesty's Stationery Office, 1957.

SUGGESTED READINGS: CHAPTER 11

Alland, Alexander, Jr. *The Human Imperative.* New York: Columbia University Press, 1972. An anthropologist argues against alleged overstatement of the case for innate aggression in humans by Lorenz and others.

Alvarez, Alfred. *The Savage God: A Study of Suicide.* London: Weidenfeld & Nicholson, 1971. Includes an introductory essay on the poet Sylvia Plath, who died a suicide, as well as an epilogue on the author's own suicide attempt.

Anscombe, G. E. M. "Is War Murder?" In *Moral Problems.* Edited by James Rachels. New York: Harper & Row, 1971.

Aron, Raymond. *On War.* Translated by Kilmartin. Garden City, N.Y.: Doubleday, 1959.

Barth, Karl, *Church Dogmatics: a Selection.* Trans. G. W. Bromley. New York: Harper & Row, 1962.

Bedau, Hugo Adam, ed. *The Death Penalty in America.* rev ed. Garden City: Doubleday, 1967. A book of readings about capital punishment in the United States.

Bhagavad Gita, The. There are a number of translations of this Indian classic that debates the values of action versus renunciation in this world. Among them are Franklin Edgerton, trans. *The Bhagavad Gita.* New York: Harper & Row, 1964; and Eliot Deutsch, trans. *Bhagavad Gita* [Song of the Lord]. New York: Holt, Rinehart & Winston, 1968. Both editions include notes and comments.

Bohannan, P., ed. *Law and Warfare: Studies in the Anthropology of Conflict.* New York: Natural History Press, 1967.

Callahan, Daniel. *Abortion: Law, Choice and Morality.* New York: Macmillan, 1970.

Camus, Albert. *The Myth of Sisyphus and Other Essays.* Translated by Justin O'Brien. New York: Knopf, 1965. Camus claims the suicide is the most important philosophical problem, as does William James in his "Is Life Worth Living?" (See under James.)

Clausewitz, Karl von. *On War.* Translated by O. J. Mattijs Jolles. New York: Modern Library, 1943.

Devereaux, George. *A Study of Abortion in Primitive Societies.* New York: Julian, 1955.

Douglas, Jack D. *The Social Meanings of Suicide.* Princeton, N.J.: Princeton University Press, 1967.

Downing, A. B., ed. *Euthanasia and the Right to Death.* New York: Humanities, 1970. A book of readings.

Durkheim, Emile. *Suicide: A Study in Sociology.* Translated by John A.

Spaulding and George Simpson. New York: Free Press, 1951. Durkheim's classic study sees suicide, not as a supremely individual act, but as inseparable from the individual's relation to his social context.

Ellis, Edward R., and Allen George N. *The Traitor Within.* Garden City, N.Y.: Doubleday, 1961.

Engels, Friedrich. *The Condition of the Working Class in England.* Translated by W. O. Henderson and W. H. Chaloner. New York: Macmillan, 1958.

Feldman, David M. *Birth Control in Jewish Law.* New York: New York University Press, 1968.

Fletcher, Joseph. "The Patient's Right to Die," in Downing.

Freud, Sigmund. *Civilization and its Discontents* (1930). Translated by James Strachey. New York: Norton, 1962. Freud claims that the tendency to aggression is an innate, instinctive disposition in man, that this aggressive instinct is the most powerful obstacle to culture.

Frieman, Paul, ed. *On Suicide.* New York: International Universities, 1967. Selected essays.

Ginsberg, Robert, ed. *The Critique of War: Contemporary Philosophical Explorations.* Chicago: Regnery, 1969. A book of readings.

Goodman, Paul, ed. *The Social Responsibility of the Scientist.* New York: Free Press, 1971.

Greene, Graham. *The Heart of the Matter.* New York: Viking, 1948. Memorable novel about a British police commissioner in wartime West Africa who offers his suicide as a sacrifice to God. With a new chapter added in 1971, in *The Portable Graham Greene.* New York: Viking, 1973.

Grotius (Huig De Groot). *The Rights of War and Peace,* including the Law of Nature and the Law of Nations. Translated by A. C. Campbell. London: M. W. Dunne, 1901.

Holloway, Ralph L. Jr. "Human Aggression." In *War: The Anthropology of Armed Conflict and Aggressor,* edited by M. Freud, M. Harris, and R. Murphy. New York. The Natural History Press, 1968.

James William. "Is Life Worth Living?" In *The Will to Believe and Other Essays.* New York: McKay, 1907. James anticipates Camus's "Myth of Sisyphus" by assigning philosophical priority to the problem of suicide.

Kant, Immanuel. *Perpetual Peace.* Translated by Lewis W. Beck. New York: Liberal Arts Press, 1957.

Labby, D. H., ed. *Life or Death: Ethics and Options.* Seattle, Wash.: University of Washington Press, 1968. A book of readings.

Lorenz, Konrad. *Aggression.* New York: Harcourt, Brace, Jovanovich, 1966.

Montagu, Ashley. *Life Before Birth.* New York: Signet, 1965.

Mothersill, Mary. "Death." In *Moral Problems,* edited by James Rachels. New York: Harper & Row, 1971.

Murray, John Courtney, S. J. "We Hold These Truths." In *Law and Philosophy,* edited by Edward A. Kent. Pp. 23–32. An explanation and defense of natural law theory.

Noonan, John Thomas, Jr., ed. *The Morality of Abortion.* Cambridge, Mass.: Harvard University Press, 1970. Selected readings.

Paul VI. "Humanae Vitae." U.S. Catholic Conference, Washington, D.C., 25 July, 1968.

Plato. *Republic.* In vol. 1, Book 5 of *The Dialogues of Plato.* 2 vols. Translated by Benjamin Jowett. New York: Random House, 1937. Includes Plato's suggestions for marriage reform, eugenics, and birth control in his ideal city-state.

Ramsey, Paul. *The Just War.* New York: Scribner, 1968.

St. John-Stevas, Norman. *Life, Death and the Law.* London: Eyre and Spottiswoode, 1961.

Shannon, William H. *The Lively Debate: Response to Humanae Vitae.* New York: Sheed and Ward, 1970. Recent history and discussions of papal encyclicals on birth control leading up to Paul VI "Humanae Vitae," reaffirming the Roman Catholic Church's traditional stand on birth control.

Schopenhauer, Arthur. "On Death and its Relation to the Indestructibility of Our True Nature." Vol. 3. In *The World as Will and Idea.* Translated by R. B. Haldane and J. Kemp. 3 vols. London: Routledge & Kegan Paul, 1957. See also Volume 1, Section 69, where the philosopher argues that suicide affirms rather than denies the will to live.

Thomson, Judith Jarvis. "A Defense of Abortion." *Philosophy and Public Affairs* 1 (1971): 47–66.

Toynbee, Arnold J. *War and Civilization.* In *A Study of History,* edited by A. V. Fowler. New York; Oxford University Press, 1950.

Wasserstrom, Richard, "The Relevance of Nuremberg," *Philosophy and Public Affairs,* Fall 1971, pp. 22–46.

Wells, Donald A. *The War Myth.* New York: Pegasus, 1967.

SUGGESTED READINGS: CHAPTER 12

Aristotle, *Politics.* Translated by Ernest Barker. New York: Oxford University Press, 1958. The Greek philosopher's classic political treatise in which he argues that by nature man is a political animal.

Barber, Bernard. *Science and the Social Order.* New York: Free Press, 1952. Chapter 4 discusses the moral values of science.

Bedau, Hugo Adam, ed. *Civil Disobedience.* New York: Pegasus, 1969.

Bernal, John D. *The Social Function of Science* (1939). Cambridge, Mass.: Massachusetts Institute of Technology Press, 1967.

Bhagavad Gita, The. See entry under this title in Suggested Readings for Chapter 11.

Brown, Martin, ed. *The Social Responsibility of the Scientist.* New York: Free Press, 1971.

Camus, Albert. *The Rebel* [L'Homme Revolté]. Translated by Anthony Bower. New York: Knopf, 1956. Camus compares the political rebellion of the revolutionary with the metaphysical revolt of the artist.

Carson, Rachel. *The Sea Around Us.* Rev. ed. New York: Oxford University Press, 1961.

————. *Silent Spring.* Boston: Houghton Mifflin, 1962. Rachel Carson's two books are poetic-ecological classics.

Commoner, Barry. *The Closing Circle: Nature, Man and Technology.* New York: Knopf, 1971.

Coyle, David Cushman. *Conservation.* New Brunswick, N.J.: Rutgers University Press, 1957.

De Bono, E., ed. *Technology Today.* New York: Macmillan, 1971.

Devlin, Lord Patrick. "Morals and the Criminal Law." In *Morality and the Law,* edited by Richard A. Wasserstrom. Belmont, Calif.: Wadsworth, 1971.

Dewey, John. *Reconstruction in Philosophy* (1920). Boston: Beacon, 1948. Chapter 7 discusses science and morals.

Dworkin, Richard. "Lord Devlin and the Enforcement of Morals." In *Morality and the Law,* edited by Richard A. Wasserstrom.

Ellul, Jacques. *The Technological Society.* New York: Knopf, 1964.

Ehrlich, Paul H. *The Population Bomb.* New York: Ballantine, 1970.

Feuchtwanger, Lion. *Power* [Jew Süss]. New York: Viking, 1948. The theme of this historical novel, based on the rise and fall of the financial adviser to a German duke, is the vanity of power.

Graham, Frank, Jr. *Man's Dominion: the Story of American Conservation.* New York: Evans, 1971.

Hall, Robert T. *The Morality of Civil Disobedience.* New York: Harper & Row, 1971.

Hart, H. L. A. "Immorality and Treason." In *Morality and Law,* edited by Richard A. Wasserstrom. Belmont, Calif.: Wadsworth, 1971.

Holmes, Oliver Wendell. "The Path of the Law." In *An Introduction to Law,* edited by Arthur A. Sullivan. Cambridge, Mass.: Harvard Law Review Association, 1957.

Kelsen, Hans. *General Theory of Law and State.* Cambridge, Mass.: Harvard University Press, 1946.

Kent, Edward A., ed. *Law and Philosophy: Readings in Legal Philosophy.*

New York: Appleton, 1970. See note in Suggested Readings, Chapter 9.

Levy, Beryl. *Cardozo and the Frontiers of Legal Thinking.* Rev. ed. Cleveland: Press of Case Western Reserve University, 1969.

Lord, Walter. *Incredible Victory.* New York: Harper & Row, 1967. The story of the battle of Midway, June, 1942.

Maddox, John. *The Doomsday Syndrome.* New York: McGraw-Hill, 1973. Arguments against prophets of doom by overpopulation.

Madison, James. "The Federalist No. 10." In Alexander Hamilton, John Jay, and James Madison. *The Federalist.* New York: Modern Library, 1938.

Marcuse, Herbert. "Ethics and Revolution." In *Ethics and Society,* edited by Richard T. De George. Garden City, N.Y.: Doubleday, 1966.

————. *An Essay on Liberation.* Boston: Beacon, 1969.

Martin, Rex. "Civil Disobedience." *Ethics* 80 (1960): 123–139.

Mill, John Stuart. "On Liberty." In *On Liberty, Representative Government, The Subjection of Women* (1859). London: Oxford University Press, 1960.

Mumford, Lewis. "The Premonitions of Leonardo da Vinci." *New York Review of Books,* 29 December 1966, pp. 3–4. An artist-scientist's experimental designs of war machines.

Nef, John U. "Birth of Modern Science," chap. 3. In *War and Human Progress.* Cambridge, Mass.: Harvard University Press, 1950.

New Testament: The Gospels according to Mark, Luke, Matthew, and John. A reading or rereading is always in order before any discussion of what the Christian ethic is or is not.

Nietzsche, Friedrich. First Essay in *The Genealogy of Morals.* 1887. Translated by Horace B. Samuel. New York: Modern Library, n.d. There is a more recent translation by Francis Golffing in Nietzsche, *The Birth of Tragedy and The Genealogy of Morals.* Garden City, N.Y.: Doubleday, 1956. Nietzsche claims that "good" originally meant "that which the noble (lord, ruler, master) wants."

Plato. *Gorgias.* In vol. 1 of *The Dialogues of Plato.* 2 vols. Translated by Benjamin Jowett. New York: Random House, 1937. Socrates almost loses his temper arguing with Sophists, who seem to him to claim that might makes right.

————. *The Republic.* Translated by Frances Cornford. Oxford: Clarendon Press, 1941. Also *The Republic of Plato.* Translated by Allan Bloom. New York: Basic Books, 1968.

Proudhon, Pierre Joseph. *What Is Property?* (1840). Translated by Benjamin R. Tucker. New York: Howard Fertig, 1966. The first chapter contains Proudhon's claim that property is theft.

Rawls, John. "The Justification of Civil Disobedience." In *Law and*

Philosophy, edited by Edward A. Kent. This essay (with additions) corresponds to Rawls's *A Theory of Justice.* Cambridge, Mass.: Harvard University Press, Belknap, 1971. Chapter 6, 57, pp. 371–377.

Reich, Charles A. *The Greening of America.* New York: Random House, 1970. Arguments in popular style for a new social consciousness (Consciousness III) including ecological awareness.

Roszak, Theodore. *The Making of the Counterculture.* Garden City, N.Y.: Doubleday, 1969.

Russell, Francis. *Tragedy in Dedham: the Story of the Sacco and Vanzetti Case.* New York: McGraw-Hill, 1962. Fascinating and objective account of famous trial and execution of two anarchists in Massachusetts in the 1920s.

Schweitzer, Albert. *Out of My Life and Thought.* New York: Holt, Rinehart & Winston, 1949.

———. *Civilization and Ethics.* New York: Macmillan, 1960.

Stumpf, Samuel A. *Morality and the Law.* Nashville, Tenn.: Vanderbilt University Press, 1966.

Thoreau, Henry David. "Civil Disobedience." In Thoreau, *Walden and Civil Disobedience.* Edited by Owen Thomas. New York: Norton, 1966. "Civil Disobedience" is reprinted in Bedau, ed., *Civil Disobedience.*

Wolff, Robert Paul. *In Defense of Anarchism.* New York: Harper & Row, 1970.

Index